THE ENGAGED INTELLECT

John McDowell

The Engaged Intellect

Philosophical Essays

HARVARD UNIVERSITY PRESS

Cambridge, Massachusetts, and London, England

First Harvard University Press paperback edition, 2013

Library of Congress Cataloging-in-Publication Data

McDowell, John Henry.
  The engaged intellect : philosophical essays / John McDowell.
      p. cm.
  Includes bibliographical references (p.   ) and index.
  ISBN 978-0-674-03164-7 (cloth: alk. paper)
  ISBN 978-0-674-72579-9 (pbk.)
  1. Philosophy. I. Title.
  BD21.M225 2009
  190—dc22   2008013845

Contents

Preface   *vii*

I Ancient Philosophy

1 Falsehood and Not-Being in Plato's *Sophist*   *3*

2 Eudaimonism and Realism in Aristotle's Ethics   *23*

3 Deliberation and Moral Development in
Aristotle's Ethics   *41*

4 Incontinence and Practical Wisdom in Aristotle   *59*

II Issues in Wittgenstein

5 Are Meaning, Understanding, etc., Definite States?   *79*

6 How Not to Read *Philosophical Investigations:*
Brandom's Wittgenstein   *96*

III Issues in Davidson

7 Scheme-Content Dualism and Empiricism   *115*

8 Gadamer and Davidson on Understanding
and Relativism   *134*

9 *Subjective, Intersubjective, Objective*   *152*

IV   Reference, Objectivity, and Knowledge

10   Evans's Frege   *163*

11   Referring to Oneself   *186*

12   Towards Rehabilitating Objectivity   *204*

13   The Disjunctive Conception of Experience as Material for a Transcendental Argument   *225*

V   Themes from *Mind and World* Revisited

14   Experiencing the World   *243*

15   Naturalism in the Philosophy of Mind   *257*

VI   Responses to Brandom and Dreyfus

16   Knowledge and the Internal Revisited   *279*

17   Motivating Inferentialism: Comments on Chapter 2 of *Making It Explicit*   *288*

18   What Myth?   *308*

19   Response to Dreyfus   *324*

Bibliography   *331*
Credits   *339*
Index   *341*

Preface

The title of this volume works in two ways.

An intellect—a writer's or a reader's—may be engaged in a certain task, the thinking that goes into writing or reading philosophy. Taken like this, the title fits, in a general way, the activity of philosophizing, whatever the particular topic, and it can embrace all the essays in this somewhat miscellaneous collection.

But I also intend the title to capture a theme that runs through some of the essays. In them I resist a rationalistic conception of the intellect, in this sense: a conception that disengages reason, which is special to rational animals, from aspects of their make-up that they share with other animals. The engaged intellect, on this interpretation, is the intellect conceived as integrally bound up with the animal nature of the rational animal. In the case of the practical intellect, the disengagement to be opposed is a disengagement from motivational propensities associated with feelings, and also from animal capacities for physical intervention in the world. Resisting this disengagement ensures that we do not fall into philosophical difficulties that reflect a distancing of the intentional agent from its bodily nature. In the case of the theoretical intellect, the disengagement to be opposed is a disengagement from what figures in Kant as sensibility, sensory responsiveness to features of the environment. Resisting this disengagement ensures that we are not vulnerable to familiar supposed problems about the possibility of empirical knowledge.

Essays 2, 3, and 4 belong, in part, in the second category. They elaborate various aspects and implications of a non-rationalistic reading of Aristotle on the excellence of the practical intellect that, as he sees things, is, or is a central element in, ethical virtue. Essay 1 fits with these essays only in that its topic is also ancient; in this essay I build on and modify G. E. L. Owen's reading of Plato's *Sophist* as a document from the dawn (at least so far as the Western philosophical tradition is concerned) of what we now call "philosophy of language".

Essay 5 centres on a sketch for a reading of the concluding sections in Part I of Wittgenstein's *Philosophical Investigations*. In my view that material often exerts insufficient pressure on how commentators understand Wittgenstein's conception of meaning and understanding, and—in association with them—such states as intention and expectation. In Essay 6, which obviously might just as well have been placed in the final part, I use Robert Brandom's interpretation of Wittgenstein's discussion of rule-following as a foil, to bring out by contrast how I think those passages ought to be understood.

I have put the third group of essays together because Donald Davidson is prominent in them. But the division of these essays from those in the fifth group is not sharp. Davidson is prominently present in Essay 14 too, and a central topic there, as in Essays 7 and 9, is the opposition I expressed in *Mind and World* against a rationalistic conception of theoretical reason, in its guise as governing intellectual activity directed towards empirical knowledge. On the view I oppose, which Davidson takes to be the only possible view, reason is at most triggered into operation by episodes of sensibility; whereas on the view I recommend, reason enters into the very constitution of episodes of sensibility as they are enjoyed by rational animals. In Essay 8 I make a comparison between Davidson and Gadamer, in partial response to the objection that the view I recommend has unpalatably idealistic consequences.

In Essay 10 I suggest, among other things, that the interest of Evans's reading of Frege lies in its allowing us to see Frege's treatment of singular reference as a contribution to opposing the disengagement of the intellect— to insisting that the rationality of understanding must not be separated from animal situatedness in the world. Essay 11 urges, among other things, that a central element in self-consciousness is self-awareness in intentional bodily action. In Essay 12, I argue that Richard Rorty goes too far when he takes it that just any philosophical concern with objectivity falls into what he rightly sees as the misguided obsessions of modern philosophy. Essay 13 discusses an epistemological exploitation of the roughly Sellarsian conception of perceptual experience I have been recommending since *Mind and World*.

Essay 14 constitutes a kind of introduction to the themes of *Mind and World*. And in Essay 15 I elaborate the treatment of the idea of the natural that I sketched there, and draw out its implications for the philosophy of mind.

Essays 16 and 17 take issue with Brandom's motivation for inferentialism, the thesis that we should understand the significance of linguistic performances and the content of intentional states in terms of the location of linguistic performances in a complex of inferential proprieties, and with his application of inferentialism in his reading of my essay "Knowledge and the Internal". In Essays 18 and 19, which are my side of an exchange with Hubert Dreyfus, the theme of the engaged intellect is central. Dreyfus finds an objectionable intellectualism in the way I describe the perceptual experience of rational animals, and their intentional action. I respond that things seem that way to Dreyfus only because he reads my conceptions in terms of the idea that the intellect is disengaged from anything shared between rational animals and other animals. And much of the point of the conceptions he objects to lies precisely in opposition to such a picture.

I have cited works by author's name and title, leaving details of publication to the Bibliography at the end of the volume.

Many people helped with these essays, and I am sorry the specific acknowledgments that figure in some of them are so sparse and inadequate. Here I would like to express special gratitude to James Conant for his help with the selection and arrangement.

THE ENGAGED INTELLECT

PART I

Ancient Philosophy

Falsehood and Not-Being
in Plato's *Sophist*[1]

1. For me, G. E. L. Owen's "Plato on Not-Being" radically improved the prospects for a confident overall view of its topic. Hitherto, passage after passage had generated reasonable disagreement over Plato's intentions, and the disputes were not subject to control by a satisfying picture of his large-scale strategy; so that the general impression, as one read the *Sophist*, was one of diffuseness and unclarity of purpose. By focusing discussion on the distinction between otherness and contrariety (257b1–c4), Owen showed how, at a stroke, a mass of confusing exegetical alternatives could be swept away, and the dialogue's treatment of not-being revealed as a sustained and tightly organized assault on a single error. In what follows, I take Owen's focusing of the issue for granted, and I accept many of his detailed conclusions. Where I diverge from Owen—in particular over the nature of the difficulty about falsehood that Plato tackles in the *Sophist* (§§5 and 6 below)—it is mainly to press further in the direction he indicated, in the interest of a conviction that the focus can and should be made even sharper.

2. By 256e5–6 the Eleatic Stranger (ES) can say "In the case of each of the forms, then, what is is multiple and what is not is indefinite in number". Yet it is only at 258b6–7 that Theaetetus is allowed to announce the availability, at last, of the application for "what is not" that was needed in order to flush the sophist from his refuge. Why was it not available already at 256e5–6? What is the relation between the application for "what is not" vindicated in the earlier passage and the application vindicated in the later passage?

We can make the question more pressing. What was needed in order to capture the sophist was a non-paradoxical characterization of the sort of

---

1. This essay was written for a Festschrift for G. E. L. Owen.

unreality a semblance has, and of falsehood (236d9–237a9, 239c9–240c6, 240c7–241b3). Ultimately the first task is merged into the second (264c10–d5).[2] Now when the ES tackles the second task, the backward reference (263b11–12) with which he seeks to justify his use of the expression "what is not" is to 256e5–6: the *earlier* of our two passages, not the one in which Theaetetus notes the participants' acquisition of the equipment necessary for their project of pinning down the sophist. But if the project required the ES to go beyond 256e5–6, how can the reference back to the earlier passage be appropriate in its execution?[3]

I shall deal with this composite difficulty by dividing it. First (§3 below) I shall consider the relation between the passages in which 256e5–6 and 258b6–7 are embedded, in abstraction from the question how either is related to the final characterization of falsehood. Then (§4 below) I shall return to the latter question.

3. 256e5–6 expresses a generalization of the results of 255e8–256d10. So its employment of "what is not" must be warranted by the fact that each form or kind *is not* indefinitely many others, as change is not rest (255e14), the same (256a5), other (256c8), being (256d8); that is, that it is other than—nonidentical with—each of them. If, then, we were to consider the expression "(is) not beautiful" within the framework constructed in this passage, we would find ourselves understanding it so as to be true of anything other than the form or kind *beautiful*; no less true, then, of Helen or Aphrodite than of the snub-nosed Socrates, and hardly a plausible reading for day-to-day uses of the expression (cf. 257d10). So it would be unsurprising to find the ES moving beyond 255e8–257a7—where we are supposed to have been made comfortable with the use of "is not" in statements of non-identity—in the direction of making room for the use of "is not" in statements of negative predication. And I believe that is indeed what we are meant to find in the passage that starts at 257b1.[4]

---

2. See Owen, "Plato on Not-Being", pp. 250, 259.

3. See Edward N. Lee, "Plato on Negation and Not-Being in the *Sophist*", at p. 299, n. 53. (The difficulty is more serious than Lee allows: the treatment of falsehood is not just "one of [Plato's] major 'analytic' problems", but the very problem alluded to at 258b6–7.) James P. Kostman, "False Logos and Not-Being in Plato's *Sophist*", acknowledges that he cannot explain the reference to 256e5–6 (pp. 197, 210, n. 11).

4. A *caveat*: when I write, as I shall, of the "is not" of non-identity and the "is not" of negative predication, I do not mean to imply that Plato aims to distinguish *senses* of "is not" (and correspondingly of "is"). See Owen, "Plato on Not-Being", pp. 257–8.

Not that the enterprise of 257b1 ff. is to be conceived as disconnected from that of 255e8–257a7. Together the two passages constitute a careful step-wise response to Eleatic doubts about "is not". The first does not merely assume that "is not" is acceptable in statements of non-identity, but painstakingly works for that conclusion. And the second, in arguing that "is not" is acceptable in statements of negative predication, employs a strategy essentially involving the materials that have proved useful in the first.

(1) It has been accepted that the nature of *the other* is all-pervasive (254d4–e7). The ES begins the first passage with particular exemplifications of that conclusion: not (brazenly) statements like "Change is-not rest", but (cautiously) statements like "Change is not-rest" (the negative particle is ostentatiously annexed, by word order, whose effect I have tried to capture by hyphenating, to the name of the kind than which change is being said to be other, not to the verb). We may be hard pressed to see a real distinction here. But it was the negating of the verb "to be" in particular, not negation in general, that Parmenides found unintelligible. The ES is starting with something that should be uncontentious: something against which, as it stands, no Parmenidean strictures apply. The upshot, indeed, will be that the puzzling distinction marks no real difference; but in the dialectical circumstances this needs to be argued, not assumed.

The ES proceeds innocently through a series of examples of the form presumed uncontentious: "Change is not-rest" (255e14), "Change is not-the-same" (256a5), "Change is not-other" (256c8). Then he unsheathes his knife. Being was one of the five kinds of which it was agreed, at 254d4–255e2, that each is other than all the others; so anyone who has allowed the first three examples to pass, as true in virtue of the fact that change is other than rest, the same, and other, has no ground for protest when, in virtue of the structurally indistinguishable fact that change is other than being, we insist on what is in fact another example of the same form: "Change is not-being" (256d8). Moreover, the same can be said of any other kind (other than being itself) (256d11–e2). It is clear now that we must abandon any hope of accepting the negative statements that constitute the natural expression for the pervasiveness of otherness, while divesting them of counter-Eleatic significance by insisting that being is not what is negated; and the ES now takes himself to be entitled to relocate the "not" in statements of non-identity like the first three examples— statements other than those in which one term is being itself. The puzzling distinction vanishes, shown up as empty; and, on the strength of 255e3–7, the ES can conclude that each kind or form is-not all of the indefinitely many others.[5]

(2) The second passage also attacks (on a less restricted front) a Parmenidean refusal to make sense of "is not". The ES diagnoses the refusal as based on a mistake about negation: that of supposing that the addition of "not" yields an expression for the contrary of what was meant by the original expression (257b1–c4).[6] In the case of, say, "not beautiful", the mistake does not have the effect of depriving the negative expression of meaning altogether. The meaning of "ugly" is a perfectly good meaning, even though it is wrong to assign it to "not beautiful". But in the case of "is not", the mistake is destructive. An expression that meant the contrary of what "is" means would mean, if it meant anything, the same as what would be meant, if anything could be, by "in no way is"; and this is an expression for which no use (as distinct from mention) can be found, even in attempts to formulate in the material mode the thought that it has no application (237b7–239c8, on "in no way being"; recalled, in terms of "contrary of being", at 258e1–259a5).[7]

The ES works up to the destructive form of the mistake from a consideration of the non-destructive form. What makes it possible to say significantly of something that it is not-beautiful—what ensures that the expression "not beautiful" is not condemned, whenever uttered, to fly out vainly into a void, so much empty chatter—is not (as the erroneous view might have it) that, should the statement be true, the negative expression would strike home against the subject's being *ugly* (for such statements can be true even though their subjects are not ugly); but rather that the negative expression, if uttered in a true statement, would strike home against some attribute *other* than *beautiful*, possessed by the subject (257d10–11). (It is not that the

---

5. Cf. Owen, "Plato on Not-Being", pp. 233–4, n. 21. The "both . . . and . . ." construction is strained, on Owen's construal of 256c11–12; and the strain is unnecessary, given the evident intelligibility of the line of thought I have set out.

6. See Owen, "Plato on Not-Being", passim: e.g., pp. 231–2. (It seems perverse to take 257b1–c4 as anything but an introduction, no doubt partly promissory, to what follows. Cf. Lee, "Plato on Negation and Not-Being", pp. 268–9; and, differently, Frank A. Lewis, "Plato on 'Not' ", at pp. 111–12, n. 19.)

7. The mistake would undermine statements of non-identity too; (1) has dealt piecemeal with that application. Note that it would not help to protest that we should be considering not "is not", but "is not . . .". If to negate being is to deny all being to one's subject, thereby defeating one's attempt to speak of it, then it cannot make any difference if one writes (say) "beautiful" after the incoherent "is not".

erroneous view, applied to "not beautiful", generates a worry about idle chatter; that it does not is precisely what is meant by describing this application of the view as non-destructive. But an adherent of the view would be saddled thereby with an account of why admittedly "safe" examples of negative expressions are safe, as "not beautiful" is, which could not but make "is not" problematic.)

I intend the phrase "strike home against" as a counterpart, coloured in the interest of conveying a feeling for what I take to be the ES's point, for drabber terms that Plato uses: "indicate" (relating expressions and things, 257b10) and "utter . . . of" (relating utterers, expressions, and things, 257d10). We should not, I believe, commit Plato to the view that the relation in question, between negative expressions and things (specifically, something like attributes) other than those meant by the words negated, is in any strict sense a semantic or meaning-determining relation.[8] Compare the tolerance of phrases like "true in virtue of". Sometimes we would decline to fill the gap, in " 'Socrates is not beautiful' is true in virtue of . . .", with anything that would not count as displaying the sense of the quoted sentence. But this does not mean that we necessarily reject, for all purposes, such claims as this: " 'Socrates is not beautiful' is true in virtue of Socrates' being snub-nosed"; and it is at least not wrong to say that the form or kind, *snub-nosed*, is other than the form or kind, *beautiful*. Of course such remarks do not begin to look like a determination of the sense of "not beautiful".

It can be tempting to elaborate them into such a determination—either reconstruing "other than" as "incompatible with", and analysing "Socrates is not beautiful" as "Socrates has some attribute incompatible with being beautiful", or leaving "other than" meaning what it does in 255e8–257a12, and using a universal quantifier: "All Socrates' attributes are non-identical with being beautiful." Commentators have not been reluctant to succumb to these temptations on Plato's behalf. But an interest in either sort of elaboration is, to say the least, not obviously present in the text.[9] (Incompatibility figures in accounts of the *Sophist* only because its proponents cannot see how Plato can achieve his purpose without it; and I think the same goes for the universal quantifier imported by those who rightly jib at an unannounced shift in the sense of "other than", but take the same view of the purpose.) This unconcern with analysis need not seem a defect, if we see the ES's project as what it

---

8. For this crucial point, see Lewis, "Plato on 'Not' ", p. 112, n. 27.

9. See Lewis, "Plato on 'Not' ", pp. 105–6; 113, n. 40.

is: not to give an account of the sense of phrases like "not beautiful", but rather to scotch a mistake about what entitles us to our confidence that they are not idle chatter, that they do indeed have the precise sense that we take them to have. (No need, in executing this project, to produce any substantive theory about what that sense is.)[10] The mistake is worth scotching here, not for its own sake, but because if it is allowed to pass in this case it can be carried over to undermine our confidence in the intelligibility of "is not".

We might put the ES's point about "not beautiful" thus: "not beautiful" is to be understood, not in terms of the contrary of *beautiful*, but in terms of that part of the nature of otherness that is set over against it. My suggestion is that "understood in terms of" (at least in the affirmative component of this thesis) is best not taken as promising an analysis. "Not beautiful" means exactly what it does, namely, *not beautiful*; the role of the notion of otherness is in an explanation, at a sub-semantical level, of why we do not need to fear that such a semantical remark is condemned to vacuity.[11]

10. An attribute can be other than *beautiful* without being (ever) appropriately mentionable as that in virtue of which something is not beautiful. In order to *guarantee* that what is true in virtue of some fact expressible in terms of otherness is that something is *not* beautiful, Plato would need the commentators' extra apparatus. But he does not need extra apparatus for his different purpose. His point is this: what the attributes that *can* be cited in the role in question have in common is that they are *other* than *beautiful*. (See Lewis, "Plato on 'Not'", p. 104.) This suffices without further ado to correct the error about contrariety, which is what threatens the intelligibility of "is not". (It is not to the point to object that someone who is, e.g., long-haired has an attribute other than *beautiful*, but is not necessarily not-beautiful on that account. This contradicts no thesis of Plato's. Cf. David Wiggins, "Sentence Meaning, Negation, and Plato's Problem of Non-Being", at pp. 291, 294.)

11. Here I diverge from Lee's thesis that otherness plays a novel, "constitutive" role at 257c5 ff. What seems correct is this: 255e8–257a12 yields nothing that could be called "the nature of the not beautiful" (in the sense which that passage could countenance, the not beautiful—e.g., the attribute *snub-nosed*—is rightly so called, not by virtue of its own nature, but by virtue of partaking in the form of otherness: cf. 255e4–6); whereas 257c5 ff. is concerned with something of which it can be said that its nature is being not beautiful (258b8–c4). But Lee's "constitutive" role for otherness seems problematic. He explains it in remarks like this: "The determinate sense of 'x is not tall' . . . lies precisely, but lies entirely, in saying that tall is what x is not" ("Plato on Negation and Not-Being", p. 295); but this would scarcely cut any ice with Parmenides. It seems preferable to relocate Lee's distinction: 255e8–257a12 equips us to understand a supervenient role, and 255c5 ff. a constitutive role, for the notion of *being not beautiful*; the notion of otherness plays a semantical role in the former passage and a sub-semantical role in the latter. (The only semantical thesis suggested by the second passage is to the effect that "not beautiful" means *not beautiful*; I believe this captures in semantical terms the point of the implicit thesis that the nature of the not beautiful is not being beautiful.)

The ES proceeds to the case of negating being by generalizing his point about "not beautiful" (258a1–2, 4–5, 7–9), and then representing the case of "is not" as a further instance of the generalization (258a11–b3). But the inference by instantiation can be understood also as a matter of reformulating the generalization:[12] 258a11–b3 introduces the idea, not of a part of the nature of otherness contrasted with being as such (whatever that might mean), but of a part of the nature of otherness contrasted with being . . . (e.g. with being beautiful). We can capture the movement of thought as follows. The thesis from which the ES generalizes—that *not beautiful* is to be "understood in terms of" (see above) otherness than *beautiful*—could be written thus: (*being*) not beautiful is to be "understood in terms of" otherness than (*being*) *beautiful*. When the ES instantiates the generalization with respect to being, what happens is, in effect, that "not" shifts back to the hitherto implicit verb, and the complement recedes out of focus. The point becomes this: *not being* (e.g. *beautiful*) is to be "understood in terms of" otherness than *being* (*beautiful*—to stay with the same example).[13] Only the mistake about contrariety—which has been adequately refuted by the discussion of the case, presumed uncontentious, in which "not" does not go with the verb "to be"—could make it seem that the change in the placing of "not" makes a difference.

4. If I am right, the not-being welcomed at 258b6–7, as what was needed in order to pin down the sophist, is the not-being that figures in *negative* predications like "Socrates is not beautiful". (That statement attributes not-being to Socrates in that it says that he is not—beautiful.) When the sophist's escape is blocked (cf. 264b9–d9) by the production of a non-paradoxical characterization of falsehood, the point, in the example chosen, is evidently that a false *affirmative* predication attributes what is not to its subject (263b9). Part of our composite problem (§2 above) was to explain why pinning down the sophist requires the materials of 258b6–7, not just those of

---

12. See Lee, "Plato on 'Not'", p. 282, n. 21.

13. Owen ("Plato on Not-Being", p. 239, n. 33) objects to supplying "part of" with "the nature of being" at 258b1, on the ground that it implies the reductive thesis (i.e., insistence on detaching "not" from the verb "to be": Owen, pp. 236–41). But if the notion of a part of the nature of being were established, as applying to such items as *being beautiful*, the reading Owen objects to could make the point in my text, precisely without implying the reductive thesis. A better reason against "part of" is that the notion of parts of the nature of being has not been established (see Lee, "Plato on Negation and Not-Being", pp. 283–4).

256e5–6. So we need to explain how the ES's description of a false affirmative predication, in 263b, can be seen as an application of the conceptual equipment established in the discussion of negative predication.

This component of the problem is easily solved if we understand the "is not" of 263b as arrived at by a "converse" reformulation of the "is not" of 258b6–7. The earlier passage signals vindication of the legitimacy of "is not" in statements like "Socrates is not beautiful"; that statement can be reformulated as claiming that *beautiful* is not in relation to Socrates, and now we have the terminology of 263b (capturing the falsity of "Socrates is beautiful").[14] This answers the question why we have to wait until 258b6–7 before being told we have what is needed for pinning down the sophist: what 263b requires is (a "converse" version of) the "is not" of negative predication, which is not yet available at 256e5–6.[15]

The other component of our composite problem was to explain why it is appropriate for the treatment of falsehood to refer back to 256e5–6, even though the conceptual equipment it needs was not yet established in that passage. We can now see at least the outline of a solution to this problem too. The ES's vindication of the "is not" of negative predication builds essentially on the fact that, whatever attribute one takes, there are plenty of attributes other than it—the negative part of what was said at 256e5–6. If the use of "is not" at 263b is nothing but a transformational derivative of the "is not" of negative predication, the ES's entitlement to the former must be justified by precisely what justifies his entitlement to the latter. So it is exactly to the point for 263b11–12 to hark back, past the treatment of negative predication, to the foundation on which that treatment builds.[16]

There is a complication, resulting from the usual way of understanding 263b11–12 and 256e5–6. What we find at 263b11–12 is this: "For we said that in the case of each (thing) there are many (things) that are and many that are not." On the usual view, this relates to its context as follows.

14. On the "converse" idiom, see Michael Frede, *Prädikation und Existenzaussage*, pp. 52–5, 80, 94–5; Owen, "Plato on Not-Being", e.g., pp. 237–8. As will emerge, I think there is less of this idiom in the *Sophist* than is commonly thought.

15. No doubt the equipment of 256e5–6 would serve for an account of falsity in identity statements. But it would not be generalizable to cover false predications, whereas the account of false predications could be applied to identity statements ("*The same as Socrates* is not about Theaetetus").

16. In fact, as we shall see, 256e5–6 is more straightforwardly relevant to the "converse" use of "is not" than this outline explanation suggests: not just obliquely relevant through its bearing on the non-"converse" basis of the transformation.

Universal instantiation of its negative part, with respect to Theaetetus, is supposed to yield, as something the ES could address to Theaetetus, "There are many (things) that are not in relation to (in the case of) you". Then "*In flight* is not in relation to you" (263b9, with "in relation to you" supplied from 263b4–5, 11: the ES's account of the falsity of "Theaetetus is in flight") is an exemplification: it cites one of the many such things that the instantiation assures us there are. On this view, then, 263b11–12 is taken to contain "converse" uses of "is" and "is not", with the universal quantifier "each (thing)" binding what would be in the subject place in a more straightforward formulation. The force is: in the case of everything (including Theaetetus), there are many things that it is (e.g., seated) and many that it is not (e.g., in flight). Since 263b11–12 purports simply to re-peat 256e5–6 ("we said", 263b12), the standard view imposes a structural parallel in the interpretation of 256e5–6: again, "converse" uses of "is" and "is not", with the universal quantifier binding what would be in the subject place in a more straightforward formulation. Here, then, the force is: in the case of each form, there are many things that it is and an indefi-nite number that it is not (that is—this is all that 255e8 ff. has licensed—an indefinite number with which it is non-identical).[17]

These interpretations evidently raise a difficulty about "we said", at 263b12. On this reading, 263b11–12 does not simply restate what was said at 256e5–6; it makes two tacit modifications—modifications that, in view of its bland claim to be a repetition, we would be constrained to regard as sur-reptitious. First, the range of the universal quantifier is extended, from forms to everything (including Theaetetus). Second, the negative part of the generalization is extended from denials of identity to cover negative predi-cations as well.

Can these modifications be incorporated into an overall interpretation that solves our problem: that is, one that gives 257b1 ff. the sort of impor-tance in the final characterization of falsehood that 258b6–7 would lead us to expect, and accounts for the fact that 263b11–12 refers back to 256e5–6? It could be claimed, plausibly enough, that the modifications are licensed by 257b1 ff., given that that passage extends the scope for acceptable uses of "is not" precisely from statements of non-identity between kinds or forms to statements like "Socrates is not beautiful" (§3 above). But the surreptitious-ness is still a mystery. It constitutes, in effect, a pretence that nothing of

<hr />

17. See, e.g., Owen, "Plato on Not-Being", p. 235.

importance for the project of 263b has happened since 256e5–6. Thus, even if *we* can see 257b1 ff. playing the role we have been led to expect, we find *Plato* unaccountably refusing to acknowledge it.[18]

Is it possible, then, to eliminate the tacit modifications: to understand 263b11–12 as nothing but a repetition of 256e5–6?

This requires us to suppose that "in the case of each (thing)" at 263b12 can be glossed, from 256e5, as "in the case of each of the forms", and that the negative part of 263b11–12 involves nothing but statements of non-identity. It would follow that the relation between "There are many (things) that are not about (in the case of) each (thing)"—the negative part of 263b11–12—

---

18. Owen ("Plato on Not-Being", p. 260) conspicuously fails to appeal to 257b1 ff. in explaining the tacit modifications. What Owen explains is not the extension in the later passage, but the restriction to non-identity in the earlier. The idea seems to be as follows: Plato wants to be able to say, of *any* attribute, that it is not (in relation to some subjects) (p. 259); this desideratum can be met for pervasive forms like being, identity, and difference only if the "is not" is understood as that of non-identity; hence that is what figures in 256e5–6. But: (1) Why the putative desideratum? Not for 263b: Plato would hardly be at pains to secure that "*In flight* is not about Theaetetus" should seem an example of a general kind of truth (examples of which hold about all forms, including the pervasive ones), when the move needed to construct the general kind of truth (understanding the "is not" as that of non-identity) actually renders problematic the status of the "exemplification" (in which the "is not" is precisely not to be so understood). (2) The putative desideratum is not enunciated by 256e5–6 as Owen interprets it; he takes 256e5–6 to say, not that any attribute is not in relation to something, but that an indefinite number of attributes are not in relation to every form. Of course the indefinite number, in any case, will be all the attributes other than the topic form itself, including the pervasive ones. But we have no reason to suppose Plato wants to be able to say "an indefinite number" because he *anyway* wants to be able to say "all" (to include the pervasive forms) and *consequently* has to understand "is not" in terms of non-identity, rather than that he finds himself able to say "an indefinite number" (or "all", if he had felt like it) because he is *anyway* understanding "is not", at this stage, in terms of non-identity. (3) It is not the restriction to non-identity in 256e5–6 that needs explaining. If we do not believe that Plato unpardonably helps himself in mid-argument to a new construal of "other" (as we should not: Owen, "Plato on Not-Being", p. 232, n. 19), we must regard non-identity as fundamental in his anti-Eleatic strategy. What more natural, then, than that he should begin on "is not" by making room for its use in statements of non-identity? As for what does need explaining: against Parmenides, it takes more than the mere observation that *beautiful, in flight*, etc., are non-pervasive kinds to justify going beyond 256e5–6 so as to allow oneself the use of "is not" in negative predications (or "converse" counterparts thereof). Owen's suggestion that the observation is enough to explain the "tacit extension" leaves no room for 257b1 ff., understood as a careful defence of the use of "is not" in negative predications.

and *"In flight* is not about (in relation to) Theaetetus"—the ES's account of the falsity of "Theaetetus is in flight"—cannot be one of exemplification. However, so long as "about each (thing)", in the generalization, is understood as supplementing "converse" uses of "is" and "is not", it seems impossible to see what else the relation could be, and the tacit modifications seem unavoidable. The key to an alternative reading is the possibility that the "about" phrases function differently. As before, "about Theaetetus" supplements a "converse" use of "is not", in *"In flight* is not about Theaetetus"; but we can take "about each (thing)", at 263b12, to constitute a simple quantifier phrase (like "concerning everything" in, at least, logician's English), binding what the subjects of *non-"converse"* uses of "is" and "is not" are said to be and not to be; and similarly with "about each of the forms" at 256e5.[19]

The force of 256e5–6, on this alternative reading, will be as follows: in the case of each of the forms, what is (it) is multiple and what is not (it) is indefinite in number. There is no problem about understanding this as a conclusion from what precedes it, so long as we see that the generalization ("each . . . (it) . . . (it)") picks up, not the role of change in the preceding demonstrations, but the role of, for instance, *the same.* In the case of the form, *the same,* change both is it (256a7–8) and is not it (256a5 "is not-it", convertible to "is-not it" after 256d8–9: §3 above).[20] Just so, in the case of every form, there are many things (or at any rate many forms; forms are all that the ES's variables have so far ranged over) that are it and an indefinite number that are not it.[21]

19. The preposition *"peri"* governs different cases in 263b11 and 263b12, and the same case in 263b12 and 256e5.

20. We are likely to suppose that "is" functions differently in its two occurrences; but Plato seems to suggest, rather, that the difference of function is in what replaces "it" (256a10–12). See Owen, "Plato on Not-Being", p. 258, n. 63. (Cf. n. 4 above.)

21. R. S. Bluck, *Plato's Sophist*, p. 158, considers taking 256e5–6 this way round, but rejects it on the ground that on this interpretation the passage does not have the right inferential relation to 256d11–e3. But as regards the negative part, whatever we can say to explain the inferential relation which, taken one way round, it bears to 256d11–e3 (or, better, 255e8–256e4)—and Bluck says something (pp. 158–9)—will serve equally well for the inverted reading; and the positive part, on either view, needs generalizing beyond anything said in 256d11–e3 (my view makes it a perfectly intelligible extension of the results of 255e8–d10). Two further possible objections: (1) If 256e5–6 said (as Owen implies: "Plato on Not-Being", pp. 235, 254) that about each form what is not is more numerous than what is, it would be an objection that, taking the passage my way, this would be false of pervasive forms: all the forms that are not *the same* are *the same*—in the relevant senses—and there is one more form that is *the same,* viz. the same itself. But "many" does

The meat of the remark, in the context of Plato's anti-Eleatic project, lies in its negative component; and of course I do not pretend that it makes any doctrinal difference whether we suppose the ES to say that in the case of each form it is not an indefinite number of others, or that in the case of each form an indefinite number of others are not it. The point of the second reading is not that the substance is different, but that it permits us to extract an appropriate sense from the text without understanding "in the case of each of the forms" as supplementing "converse" uses of "is" and "is not". This way we can take 263b11–12 to say, as it purports to, the very same thing, without threatening the intelligibility of its relation to the claim that *in flight* is not in relation to Theaetetus.

The claim that the form, *in flight*, is not in relation to Theaetetus is a claim on whose availability, to capture the falsity of "Theaetetus is in flight", the ES insists. He needs to defend the claim against an Eleatic objection to the effect that its use of "is not" makes it undermine itself, offering, so to speak, to deprive itself of a topic. Not at all, says the ES. That which is not, in the relevant sense, is not that which utterly is not (long since dismissed), but that which *is* other[22] (than that which is in relation to

---

not exclude "indefinite in number", and the text leaves it open that in some cases the many may be *more* than the indefinite number. The distinction is adequately explained by the fact that with non-pervasive forms there are fewer exemplifications of the "is . . ." component. (In the case of each form, what is it is—at least—multiple, and what is not it is indefinite in number.) (2) On my view, 257a4–6, where being is the subject to "is . . ." and "is not . . .", cannot be (as is often said: see, e.g., Lee, "Plato on Negation", p. 282, n. 21) an instantiation of the generalization of 256e5–6, where the quantifier binds what follows "is . . ." and "is not . . .". But the affirmative part of 257a4–6 ("being is its single self") never looked, on any view, like an instantiation of 256e5–6. (And, given the reversibility of statements of non-identity, the negative part follows by instantiation from 256e5–6 taken either way round.)

22. "*Onta hetera*" ("things that are other"), 263b11. Cf. Wiggins, "Sentence Meaning, Negation, and Plato's Problem of Non-Being", p. 295: he renders the relevant sentence thus: "[i.e. it says] things which are[2], but different things which are[2] from the things which are[1] respecting Theaetetus"; and he takes "are[2]" as synonymous with "are[1]"—"In *Theaetetus is flying* the kind Flies is[1] because it applies to *something* even if it does not apply to Theaetetus." It must be on this foundation that Wiggins bases the idea that Plato "persists in seeing Socrates' being able to purport that 'Flying is respecting Theaetetus' as explained by there being such a *genos* as Flying (rather than vice versa)" (p. 298); there being such a *genos* being for Plato, Wiggins thinks, a matter of its having an extension (cf. also p. 287). But where Wiggins has Plato (deplorably) insisting that the meaningfulness of "Theaetetus is in flight" requires that *in flight* be *instantiated*, what Plato in fact insists is that *in flight* is *other* (than what is in relation to Theaetetus); this is not Wiggins's dubious condition for the statement to be *meaningful*, but a perfectly correct condition for it to be *false*.

the subject).[23] And the "is" I have stressed, which emphasizes that the claim does not deprive itself of a topic, cannot now be queried; for it has been accepted, at 256e5–6, that for every form there *are* plenty of forms that are not (because they *are* other than) it. This fills out our outline answer to the second component of our composite question; it shows how it can be that, although 263b uses "is not" in a way that is established only in the course of 257b1 ff., it is nevertheless entirely appropriate for it to justify its doing so by a restatement (just that, not a surreptitious improvement) of 256e5–6.[24]

5. It may seem back to front to broach only now the question what puzzle about falsehood the sophist is supposed to hide behind. But this way we can let our interpretation of the problem be influenced by the desirability of finding Plato saying something to the point in response to it.

Many commentators suppose that the puzzle about falsehood is on these lines: the falsity of a false belief or statement would have to consist in the fact that the *situation* or *state of affairs* it represents is an utter nonentity, something totally devoid of being; but there is no coherent way to express such a "fact" (237b7–239c8), so no coherent way to formulate a characterization of falsehood made inescapable by a correct understanding of what falsehood would be (if there were any such thing).[25] However, when the ES comes to use the dangerous phrase "what is not" in the characterization of falsehood, his point, as we have seen, seems to be that the falsity of "Theaetetus is in flight" consists in its attributing what is not to its subject, in that *in flight* is not in relation to Theaetetus. And if the puzzle was the one about situations or states of affairs outlined above, this response (on its own

23. This would translate *"ontōn . . . peri sou"* at 263b11. But *"ontōn"* is very dubious: in favour of the manuscripts' *"ontōs"*, see Frede, *Prädikation und Existenzaussage*, pp. 57–8. Even so, it is natural to supply *"tōn ontōn"* ("than the things that are") between *"hetera"* and *"peri sou"*.

24. Owen ("Plato on Not-Being", p. 260) gives a clear statement of the relevance of non-identity between attributes to the justification of the "is not" of "converse" negative predication, but does not see that this removes the need to interpret 263b11–12 as modifying 256e5–6.

25. See especially Wiggins, "Sentence Meaning, Negation, and Plato's Problem of Non-Being". For a variant, Owen, "Plato on Not-Being", p. 245: he uses the word "situation", but what he has in mind, as missing from reality when the statement "Theaetetus is in flight" is false, is the flight of which the statement accuses Theaetetus. (This is in an account of *Theaetetus* 188c9–189b9. But the difference on which Owen insists (p. 243) between that passage and the *Sophist*'s puzzle lies not in the content of the puzzle but rather in Plato's attitude to its materials.)

at least) seems irrelevant. The sophist might reasonably object: "Attributes, like *in flight*, are not the sort of thing that I thought a description of falsehood in beliefs and statements would have to represent as not being. And it was not in the sense you exploit—not being in relation to something—but in precisely the sense you agree is problematic—not being anything at all—that I thought a description of falsehood would have to represent my different items, situations or states of affairs, as not being. You have not shown that the description of falsehood I found problematic is not compulsory, dictated by the nature of the concept of falsehood; and you have certainly not shown that it is not problematic."

Some commentators are sensitive to the vulnerability of 263b, considered as a response to the puzzle about situations; and they shift attention to the passage (261c6–262e2) that leads up to the explicit discussion of truth and falsity in statements. There the ES distinguishes (in effect) between a kind of sentence-constituent whose function is to make clear what is being talked about and a kind of sentence-constituent whose function is to make clear what is being said about it. The commentators draw the obvious moral: a sentence (one of the simple kind Plato considers, at any rate) gets its purchase on reality through its possession of a sentence-constituent of the first kind. And they suggest that any inclination to protest against 263b, on the lines envisaged above, would stem from a failure to grasp this point. Worrying about the apparently total absence from reality of states of affairs answering to false statements, or of what would be components of such states of affairs, answering to the predicates of false statements, would manifest a lack of enlightenment about the localization, within sentences, of the relation that gives them their bearing on the world.[26]

But the puzzle about situations is a deeper puzzle, and the objection to 263b, considered as a response to it, is a better objection, than Plato's strategy, on this view of it, gives them credit for being. The puzzle turns on the thought that the falsity of "Theaetetus is in flight" should consist in the fact that the state of affairs that the sentence offers to represent, or perhaps the flight in which an utterer of the sentence would accuse Theaetetus of being engaged, is nothing at all. And that thought, properly understood, is absolutely *correct*; it needs no support from a half-baked conception of how speech has its bearing on reality, such as would be undermined by the distinction drawn at 261c6–262e2. In conjunction with 237b7–239c8, the

---

26. See Owen, "Plato on Not-Being", pp. 263–5.

thought threatens to undermine the possibility of falsehood; what we would need in order to neutralize this destructive effect is, not the considerations of 261c6–262e2 (which are powerless for this purpose), but something to show us why a description such as "dealing, in thought or speech, with what is in fact nothing at all" (which might figure in a characterization of falsehood on the lines of what this puzzle represents as problematic) does not incoherently represent the thought or speech it applies to as (genuine thought or speech, but) possessing no subject matter. And the *Sophist* contains no trace of the necessary distinction.[27] Of course it is possible that Plato simply fails to deal adequately with the difficulty he tackles—fails to see its full depth; but charity recommends that we credit him, if possible, with better success at a different project.

261c6–262e2 does indeed, obliquely and inexplicitly, undermine a paradoxical argument for the impossibility of falsehood. But it is an argument distinct both from the commentators' puzzle about situations and from the difficulty about falsehood that is the *Sophist*'s main concern.

What the passage's differentiation of functions would correct is a position indifferent to, or ignorant of, the distinction between mentioning something and saying something; and such a position does make appearances elsewhere. The idea might be expressed on these lines: the unit move in the language-game of informative discourse (occupying a position analogous to that which we might ascribe to statements; but that term carries a burden of logical theory that includes at least the missing distinction) is the putting into words of some thing. A dim perception that the minimal informative performance must have some complexity (the point of which 261c6–262e2 evinces a clear, if partial, perception) can, in the absence of the distinction, yield only the requirement that the thing put into words must be consti-

---

27. For the distinction, see Wiggins, "Sentence Meaning, Negation, and Plato's Problem of Non-Being", pp. 274–5. Owen suggests ("Plato on Not-Being", p. 246) that in the *Sophist* Plato does not want to deny that "we can speak of mythical centaurs or chimerical flights" (such items are not wholly devoid of being, since we can say what they are). But on Owen's own account (p. 229) the dialogue contains no direct evidence of hospitality to the chimerical. And there is nothing in the *Sophist* (or in *Parmenides* 160b6–161a5, also cited by Owen) to show how the acceptability of reference to the chimerical, on the ground that its target is not devoid of being, might be reconciled with the thought—surely acceptable on some construal—that such "items" as the flight of which Theaetetus is falsely accused are in fact nothing at all. So long as this thought is not disarmed, it must remain unclear how 237b7–239c8 can fail to have its full destructive effect.

tuted of parts, so that the putting of it into words can be a complex performance by virtue of consisting in the successive mentioning of the parts.[28]
This position would undermine the possibility of contradicting another
person's remark: the best one could hope to achieve would be a change of
subject.[29] Equally, it would undermine the possibility of speaking falsely.
Failure to put a certain thing into words cannot constitute false speech: for
either one will have put a different thing into words, and so spoken truly
(though with a different topic); or else one will have failed to put anything
into words, which is the nearest we can come, in the terminology I have
adopted to express the position that lacks the crucial distinction, to the conclusion that one will not have said anything at all.[30]

This crude position makes no explicit appearance in the *Sophist*.[31] But
261c6–262e2 says exactly what is needed to correct it. And it seems plausible that some terminological apparatus, introduced at 262e5 and used at
263a5, a9–10, c5, c7, is meant to signal Plato's awareness of the bearing of
261c6–262e2 on the crude position. The crude position lends itself to a
slogan on these lines: "A thing can be put into words only by its own form
of words."[32] This slogan encapsulates the destructive effect of inability, or
refusal, to distinguish mentioning and saying: any attempt to formulate the
notion of a form of words that is erroneous succeeds in describing only idle
chatter, or else a flawless capturing in words of some other thing. Having
drawn the necessary distinction, Plato continues to use the possessive to express the "about" relation, now safely localized, between (what we can now
without risk of misleading describe as) statements and things (263a5,
a9–10; "about me" and "mine" are interchangeable). The terminology irre-
sistibly suggests an echo of the old slogan, verbally almost unaltered, but

28. See *Theaetetus* 201d8–202c5; cf. Aristotle, *Metaphysics* 1024b26–1025a1.

29. Cf. *Euthydemus* 285d7–286b6.

30. Cf. *Euthydemus* 283e7–284c6.

31. *Pace*, apparently, Owen, "Plato on Not-Being", p. 241, claiming that "237b7–e7 is a
version of the familiar paradox". In fact (as Owen immediately concedes) that passage
does not purport to undermine the notion of falsehood. There is no reason to take it as addressing anything except the *Sophist*'s question: how is it possible to mention or speak of
(not "say") what is not?

32. See *Theaetetus* 202a6–8; cf. *Metaphysics* 1024b32–3. ("Form of words" here represents "*logos*", the noun cognate with "*legein*". Ordinarily these might be translated "statement" and "say"; but as "*legein*" here expresses the notion, straddling those of mentioning
and saying, that I am rendering by "put into words", I use a term similarly free of un-
wanted theoretical connotations for "*logos*".)

now rendered quite innocuous: "A thing can be talked about only by a statement of its own."

The puzzle about falsehood thus obliquely disarmed by 261c6–262e2 is perceptibly less sophisticated than the difficulty about situations or states of affairs outlined above. The notion of a state of affairs is the notion of something with a complexity of a different kind from that of a mere composite thing; it is the notion of a chunk of reality with a structure such as to mirror that of the proposition or statement it would render true. Anyone who could genuinely be credited with this notion would already have advanced beyond a stage at which he could be instructed by 261c6–262e2. And, as I urged above, this would not immunize him against a worry, should he conceive it, about the utter absence from reality of the states of affairs represented by false statements or beliefs. Something similar holds for the notion of a component of a state of affairs answering to the predicate of a statement (the crude position precisely lacks the equipment to effect any such singling out); and for a worry about the total absence of such an item from reality when a statement or belief is false.

Although the difficulty about falsehood generated by the crude position (unlike the puzzle involving situations or states of affairs) is cogently answered in the course of the *Sophist*, the crude position cannot easily be read into the passage in which the dialogue's official problem about falsehood is set out in detail (240c7–241b3). Not-being figures in the crude position's difficulty in that one of the candidate descriptions of falsehood it suggests and portrays as problematic (the other being, irrelevantly for present purposes, in terms of change of subject) is: a form of words such that what it puts into words is not (is nothing at all). The problem about this is that in the attempt to characterize the form of words as false we undermine its bearing on reality. Now the *Sophist*'s paradox is directed against both of two distinguished kinds of falsehood: both falsehoods that represent what is not as being (240e1–4, understanding *"doxazein"* at e3), and falsehoods that represent what is as not being (240e5–9). The threat to the former of these, if this were all that we had to consider, might perhaps be assimilated to the problem posed by the crude position. But this will hardly do for the latter, where the fact that what is represented (as not being) is *what is* ensures that whatever difficulty there is about the falsehood's purchase on reality does not arise in a comparable way. No doubt the fact that what is is represented *as not being* generates a difficulty that could be expressed as one about the falsehood's hold on reality. It remains the case, however, that the *Sophist*'s

problem evidently arises in rather different ways for affirmative and negative falsehoods; there is a complexity here for which the crude position has
no counterpart.[33]

6. What, then, is the *Sophist's* difficulty?

Bearing in mind the desirability of finding something to the point in
263b, we should understand the disjunctive characterization of falsehood at
240c7–241b3 in terms of attributes. Thus an example of the kind of falsehood that represents what is as not being might be "Theaetetus is not
seated", uttered when Theaetetus is seated. This represents *seated*, which is,
as not being; that description correctly captures the statement's falsity if
we take "is" and "not being" as "converse" uses and supply "in relation to
Theaetetus". The other kind of falsehood is illustrated by the example actually discussed in 263b, "Theaetetus is in flight". This represents *in flight*, which
is not, as being; again, that description correctly captures the statement's falsity if we take "is not" and "being" as "converse" uses and supply "in relation
to Theaetetus".

Why should the sophist find these characterizations of falsehood problematic, so that their putative incoherence affords him a hiding place? Because
he makes the mistake we have seen that the ES devotes himself to correcting: he cannot see how "is not" could be anything but a synonym for
"has the contrary of being" or "utterly is not" (note how these latter expressions figure in the problem-setting passage: 240d6, e2, e5), and he can find
no coherent significance for it under that interpretation (237b7–239c8). So it
seems to him that when we try to capture the falsity of "Theaetetus is in
flight" by saying that it represents *in flight*, which *is not* (in relation to

---

33. Owen's remark ("Plato on Not-Being", p. 265), "Falsehood had appeared an
abortive attempt to mention something", appears to miss this complexity. I am taking it
that 236d9–237a9 announces, without precise detail, the difficulties about images and
falsehood spelled out in 239c9–240c6 and 240c7–241b3. (237a3–4 might be taken to
imply a simpler paradox, turning on the idea that a falsehood itself—sc. the content of a
false belief—is not. But all that the lines say is that we are committed to the being of what
is not when we claim that falsehood occurs: a commitment we can understand
240c7–241b3 as explaining.) Cf., e.g., Wiggins, "Sentence Meaning, Negation, and Plato's
Problem of Non-Being", who extracts a puzzle to which Owen's remark would be appropriate from the earlier passage together with 237b7–e7 (cf. n. 31 above), ignoring the
complexity of the later passage (pp. 268–71); and I. M. Crombie, *An Examination of Plato's
Doctrines*, volume 2, who suggests (pp. 505–7) that the later passage introduces a new (and
spurious) difficulty.

Theaetetus; given the mistake, the addition does not help),[34] as being, we must be talking nonsense; and when we try to capture the falsity of "Theaetetus is not seated" by saying that it represents *seated*, which is (in relation to Theaetetus), as *not being*, we describe the statement as talking nonsense, and hence contradict ourselves if we also describe it as significant.

This paradox is utterly disarmed by the ES's painstaking demolition of the Eleatic mistake about negation. Once the mistake has been corrected, it suffices simply to restate the characterization of falsehood that had seemed problematic; this time carefully avoiding the erroneous equation between "not being", on the one hand, and "opposite of being" or "in no way being", on the other.[35]

If we understand the *Sophist*'s problem about falsehood on these lines, we can see Plato's response to it as an unqualified success. (Contrast the interpretation in terms of situations or states of affairs: §5 above.) What makes this possible is that—to stick to the less complicated case of affirmative falsehoods—we regard the sheer unavailability of anything answering to the words "in flight", in the false statement "Theaetetus is in flight", not as a *premise* in an argument purporting to show that a description that captures the statement's falsity is incoherent (an independently obvious reformulation, that is, of the claim that the statement is false); but rather as an *inference* from the claim (which does, in fact innocuously, capture the statement's falsity) that what answers to the words is not (in relation to Theaetetus). The former problematic unavailability (the unavailability of the flight of which the statement accuses Theaetetus) is indeed a concomitant of the statement's falsity; and it is not something Plato shows us how to cope with. (See §5 above.) The latter unavailability (the unavailability of the attribute or kind, *in flight*) is simply a mistake, and one that Plato definitively corrects.

It may seem a cost of this reading that it separates Plato's concern in the *Sophist* from the deep philosophical difficulty raised by Wittgenstein when he writes: "How can one think what is not the case? If I think that King's College is on fire when it is not, the fact of its being on fire does not exist. Then how can I think it?"[36] But it is surely not a cost but a gain that we find in the *Sophist*, not an unconvincing attempt on that interesting difficulty, but a wholly successful solution to a different one.

34. See n. 7 above.

35. This is actually done only for the affirmative kind of falsehood; once the diagnostic point is clear, the other kind can be left as an exercise for the reader.

36. *The Blue and Brown Books*, p. 31.

It is true that we cannot easily find the different difficulty pressing. Indeed, there may be an inclination to protest: how could anyone suppose that the claim "*In flight* is not in relation to Theaetetus", by trying to describe its subject as not being, incoherently represents itself as lacking a subject altogether? Is it not obvious that not being . . . (for instance not being in relation to Theaetetus) is not the same as utterly not being? But the fact is that it was not obvious to Parmenides, if Plato's diagnosis is correct. According to Plato's suggestion, it was precisely by equating "not being" with "being in no way" that Parmenides excluded plurality, qualitative diversity, and change from what can sensibly be affirmed to be the case. The *Sophist*'s puzzle, on the present interpretation, applies the same method in order to cast doubt on the concept of falsehood: an intriguing employment of Parmenides' destructive elenchus at a metalinguistic level, which would impose limitations (for instance) on the strictures available to Parmenides himself against failures to take his point. But what the puzzle elicits from Plato is a move which, by destroying the foundation, has the effect of dismantling the entire Eleatic position.

Eudaimonism and Realism
in Aristotle's Ethics

1. Aristotle evidently holds that all, or nearly all, mature human beings (at least those who are proper subjects for ethical assessment) organize their lives in the light of a conception of *eudaimonia* (*Nicomachean Ethics* 1102a2–3).[1] A conception of *eudaimonia* is a conception of *eu prattein*, doing well (1095a18–20). The relevant idea of acting with a view to *eudaimonia* is the idea of acting in a certain way because that is what doing well comes to.[2] That occurrence of "well" signals a distinctive sort of point, or worthwhileness, that one takes oneself to see in acting like that; I think Aristotle aims to explain what this distinctive sort of perceived worthwhileness is when he in effect glosses the "well" in "doing well" as "in accordance with virtue" (1098a16–18).

Now it is clear that Aristotle thinks some such perceptions are correct and others not. That is, his attitude towards the question whether some action has that kind of worthwhileness is realistic in some sense. (At least to begin with we can leave it open whether the sense is one that implies anything seriously metaphysical.) Aristotle's thought is that there is a right answer,

---

1. *Eudemian Ethics* 1214b6–12 may leave room for some who do not ("a mark of much folly", Aristotle says); that is why I put "or nearly all". (Unattributed citations henceforth will be from the *NE*.) My parenthesis is meant to register Aristotle's well-known views about women, slaves, and so forth. Having mentioned the point once, I shall ignore it from here on; this embarrassing feature of Aristotle's thinking is irrelevant to the philosophical issues that I want to consider.

2. No doubt one can act for the sake of doing well without conceiving what one does as itself constituting doing well. One's purpose in acting for the sake of doing well may be instrumental: to get oneself into a position in which one can act in the sort of way one sees as doing well. But this sort of action is not revelatory of character in the same direct way as action undertaken because it is seen as exemplifying doing well, as opposed to conducive to it. I think it is the latter that is Aristotle's concern.

and wrong answers, to the question what doing well consists in. And his usual remark about rightness on this kind of question is that the right view is the view of the person of excellence (the *spoudaios*), or the person of practical wisdom (the *phronimos*).[3]

It is often thought that this Aristotelian realism points to an extra-ethical basis for reflection about what *eudaimonia* consists in. The idea is that, in Aristotle's view, it is possible to certify that a virtuous person's conception of *eudaimonia* is genuinely correct—that the actions it singles out are really worth undertaking in the way it represents them as being—by showing that a life organized in the light of that conception would be recognizably worth living anyway; that is, worth living by standards that are prior to the distinctive values acquired in what Aristotle conceives as a proper upbringing. These prior standards would be standards for worthwhileness or choiceworthiness that any human being, just as such, could accept, independently of any acquired values and the motivational dispositions that are associated with them. So the idea is this: Aristotle thinks he can authenticate the distinctive values that are imparted by what he conceives as a proper upbringing, and establish that that is indeed how people ought to be brought up, on the basis of the thought that a life that puts those values into practice is one that is worth going in for anyway, for a human being just as such.[4] On this view, when Aristotle says that it is the excellent person who gets things right, the ethical assessment expressed by "excellent" is not a stopping-point for his thinking about getting things right. That the relevant kind of person is really excellent, and that he is really right about what is worth going in for, are together grounded on an extra-ethical basis.

I do not believe there is any sign of this supposed external validation in Aristotle's text. On the contrary, trying to read it into him disrupts our understanding of things he actually says. The external validation is an invention on the part of modern readers. I shall spend some time trying to make this plausible, and then offer some reflections on what underlies the invention: on what makes modern readers tend to suppose that Aristotle needs

3. See for instance, in a different context, 1176a15–16. Continent and incontinent people also have (in some sense) the correct conception of *eudaimonia*. But this just reflects the fact that they are, so to speak, imperfect instances of what excellent people are perfect instances of; we do not need to consider them separately, or as a counter-example to the thesis that Aristotle comes at rightness in the conception through the character of its possessor.

4. This talk of values is no doubt anachronistic, but I think harmlessly.

external validation to sustain his realism. I hope this will suggest some general conclusions about the prospects for ethical realism, independently of issues in the exegesis of Aristotle.

2. The supposed external validation involves a particular interpretation of the claim that the good life is the life that is really worth living for human beings: the assessment expressed in "really worth living" has to be prior to anything specifically ethical. People who take Aristotle to think like this credit him with an idea of the choiceworthy life that is related in some suitable way to the idea of an optimal combination of component goods. I shall distinguish some options for interpreting "related in some suitable way" in a moment, but first I want to put into place the appropriate idea of an optimal combination of component goods.

For the purposes of readings of this sort, the goodness of the component goods has to be established without presupposing the distinctive conception of worthwhileness in action that is supposed to be validated, the conception of worthwhileness in action that is inculcated when someone is brought up into the virtues. Only so could an external validation be forthcoming. In readings of this sort, the requirement is supposed to be met like this: the goodness of the component goods is revealed by the fact that they appeal to motivational forces—needs or aspirations—that are built into the human organism as such. The goodness implicit in the idea of optimality, as characterizing the combination of component goods, has to be handled similarly. We need not go into detail about what the component goods, or the specific values involved in assessing combinations of them, might be in a specific view of this kind; the point I want to make is about the shape of the position.

The simplest version of the kind of reading I am considering takes it that for Aristotle the good life, the life of *eudaimonia, consists in* such an optimal combination of component goods, independently certified as such. (This can be encouraged if we translate "*eudaimonia*" with "happiness", as we almost have to if we translate it at all; alternatives like "flourishing" make no difference on this point.) But in this form, it is very hard to make the reading cohere with a central Aristotelian claim about *eudaimonia*: that what it consists in is activity in accordance with virtue. (See 1098a16–18, a passage I have already cited. The explicit claim there is that the good for man is activity in accordance with virtue, but the claim is offered in the course of spelling out further an equation between the good for man and *eudaimonia*: 1097b22–4.)

Of course it is not impossible to make sense of a conception of the good life as made up of component goods, shown to be good by the fact that they appeal to motivations built into the human organism as such. But the idea of components has to work rather differently if we conceive the good life in the way the central claim indicates, as made up of actions. It might be natural to suppose that an optimal combination of goods is, if all goes well, *brought about by* the actions that, in this different sense, make up the life. But then if we say that the optimal combination of component goods is what *eudaimonia* is, we cannot also respect the central claim, and say that *eudaimonia is* the actions that, if all goes well, bring about the optimal combination of goods.

Consider also a remark that Aristotle makes in the course of a discussion of how the intellect is involved in choice (*proairesis*): ". . . what is made is not an end without qualification (but only in relation to something and of something), but what is done (*to prakton*) is; for doing well (*eupraxia*) is an end, and the desire (sc. the desire that is *proairesis*) is for that" (1139b2–4). When one acts with a view to doing well (here *eupraxia*: the abstract noun is obviously equivalent to the verbal phrase *"eu prattein"*, which we are told is equivalent to *"eudaimonein"* by common agreement, 1095a18–20), what one does (*to prakton*) is itself the end with a view to which one acts. Doing well does not figure here as something brought about by the actions undertaken for the sake of it; it figures simply as what those actions are.[5]

This recommends a more sophisticated version of the reading. In this version, we are to respect Aristotle's equation of *eudaimonein* with *eu prattein*, doing well (1095a18–20); we are to take "doing" there to mean *doing*, and we are to respect the central claim's interpretation of the "well" in "doing well" as "in accordance with virtue". So *eudaimonia consists in* virtuous actions undertaken for their own sake; it is not something brought about by such actions if all goes well. An optimal combination of independent goods cannot now be what *eudaimonia* is. But in this reading, the notion of an optimal combination of independent goods still figures in an extra-ethical certification of the correctness of one rather than another conception of *eudaimonia*—that is, in this context, of one rather than another conception

---

5. Compare T. H. Irwin, "Some Rational Aspects of Incontinence". At p. 65 Irwin represents "decision" (his rendering of *proairesis*) as involving thought about what *promotes* the agent's "happiness" (*eudaimonia*). That fits this first version of the kind of reading I am considering. If we take doing well to figure in a *proairesis* as what is *promoted* by the action it fixes on, we lose our grip on how doing well can be what the action is.

of which states of character are virtues. The idea is this: by appealing to the idea of an optimal combination of independent goods, we can show that the states of character that Aristotle identifies as virtues, and thus alludes to when he says that *eudaimonia* is activity in accordance with them, are worth cultivating anyway, independently of the distinctive habits of valuation of modes of conduct that one acquires when one has the virtues instilled into one. Virtuous activity for its own sake is what *eudaimonia* is, not some supposed optimal result of filling one's life with such activity. But it is worth becoming the sort of person who lives like that because such a life is likeliest to be satisfactory by independent standards—likeliest to secure an optimal combination of component goods whose goodness is independently established.[6]

This version of the reading does not flatly ignore the central claim. But it still has difficulty in giving what Aristotle says there, together with his claim that the action that manifests virtue is undertaken for its own sake (1105a31–2), full weight. Aristotle evidently wants the point of a bit of virtuous behaviour to be intrinsic to it, and it is hard to make this cohere with the idea that the worthwhileness that a virtuous agent sees in such behaviour is to be authenticated in this external way: that is, by arguing that it is a good plan to cultivate the states of character that such behaviour would manifest, on the ground that acting out those states of character is likely to secure a life that would come out best by standards that are independent of a specific ethical outlook.

We can make the difficulty vivid by considering cases of virtuous behaviour that seriously threaten the agent's prospects of achieving an optimal combination of independent goods, on any plausible interpretation of that idea. Take a case of courageous behaviour as Aristotle conceives it, for instance standing one's ground in the face of the dangers of battle. Suppose the result is, as is surely not unlikely, that one is maimed, or cut off before one's life has had a chance to exemplify to the full the combination of independent goods, whatever they are, that this reading takes to underlie the choiceworthiness of a life of virtuous activity. Surely that should not even seem to reveal that the point a courageous person thought he saw in the action was illusory. But how can we prevent it from seeming to have that effect, if we conceive the point of cultivating virtue as derivative from the

---

6. For this version of the reading, see John M. Cooper, *Reason and Human Good in Aristotle*, pp. 124–5.

attractiveness of a life conceived in terms of its procuring those independent goods? That is a kind of life that any courageous action is likely to deprive one of the chance to live, and that this particular courageous action *ex hypothesi* makes unattainable. This would be a case where acting out a virtue undermines the supposed point of having it in the first place. How can that not have the effect of making the action's value at least open to question?

On this reading Aristotle surely ought to have a problem about the value of this kind of action. But he shows no sign of disquiet anywhere in the vicinity of this issue. The closest he comes is when he says that if things go badly enough, in respect of "external goods", that can spoil blessedness (1099b2–6). But what he is getting at there need be no more than the sensible concession that in such cases the distinctive point of doing well, that is, of acting in accordance with virtue, can intelligibly lose its motivational pull. There is no suggestion that the distinctive point of doing well is rationally derivative from the motivational pull of goods that are independently recognizable as such.

3. If Aristotle thought he could establish, from first principles, that a possessor of the virtues as he conceives them is thereby equipped to get things right on the question which actions really have the distinctive kind of choiceworthiness signalled by the concept of *eudaimonia*, we would surely expect him to make much of it. But any such argument is surely conspicuous by its absence from the ethical texts.

Early in the *Nicomachean Ethics* he notes that he is addressing only people who have been properly brought up (1095b4–6). I believe this implicitly excludes from discussion issues, raised from outside, about whether their perceptions of choiceworthiness in action are correct. Substantive ethical questions are not under discussion in the *Ethics*. This is borne out by a feature of Aristotle's practice that I have already had occasion to mention. Where the topic of right and wrong views about this or that comes up, one might expect an allusion to an external validation of the right view if he thought he had one at his disposal, but he always disappoints any such expectation. As I remarked at the beginning, his standard move is simply to say that the correct view is that of the virtuous person or the practically wise person. (See, for instance, 1107a1–2, 1139a29–31, 1144a34.)

When Aristotle makes his identification of the good life for human beings with a life of activity in accordance with virtue (1098a16–18), he bases it on a train of thought that connects what doing well is, for a thing of a given kind, with the *ergon* or "function" of things of that kind (1097b24–1098a15). It is sometimes thought that in thus invoking the idea that human beings have an *ergon*, Aristotle is pointing to a special view of human nature, as something that would enable us to locate human beings in a teleologically organized account of nature at large. Then the details of this teleological view of human nature would be available for validating Aristotle's specific conception of the good life without presupposing the habits of evaluation and motivation that he assumes his audience shares with him. The idea would be that acquiring just these dispositions of conduct and feeling, the ones that correspond to the virtues as Aristotle conceives them, sets a human being on a pattern of life that would conform to some "inner nisus" built into human nature; so that it comes naturally to a human being to live a life of activity in accordance with just these dispositions of character, in something analogous to the sense in which falling comes naturally to a heavy body.[7]

However, even if we believe that Aristotle's talk of the *ergon* of a human being points in this sort of direction, the passage does very little towards bringing the supposed external validation back into the ethical texts. The most we could suppose is that the passage directs us elsewhere, for a validation for the conception of the good life that Aristotle assumes to be correct. (Elsewhere: where exactly?) If we take Aristotle to believe he can justify the specifics of his picture of the good life from first principles, it should still seem surprising that he should be so unforthcoming about the details of the justification in the ethical works themselves. (And is he less unforthcoming anywhere else?)

In any case, there is no warrant for taking talk of the *ergon* of a human being as an allusion to a general teleology. The notion of the *ergon* of an X is just the notion of what it befits an X to do. Exploiting the thought that X's have a place in a grand teleological scheme might be one way to cash out the notion of what it befits an X to do. But the mere word "*ergon*" is no indication that that is what Aristotle has in mind here. If he were asked to tell

---

7. I take the phrase "inner nisus" from Bernard Williams, *Ethics and the Limits of Philosophy*, p. 44: "in Aristotle's teleological universe, every human being (or at least every nondefective male who is not a natural slave) has a kind of inner nisus towards a life of at least civic virtue . . . ." The suggestion is only that there is an analogy. There is room for a disanalogy as well: that in this case it takes habituation to get an individual on a path of behaviour on which—according to this interpretation of Aristotle's thinking—it follows its natural bent. So this reading cannot be quickly dismissed, on the ground of the distinction Aristotle draws between human beings and stones at *NE* 1103a18–23.

us what it is that it befits a human being to do, there is no reason to suppose he would offer anything except the sort of thing he offers on similar questions elsewhere, always disappointing those who think he promises to validate his ethical outlook from first principles: he would say that these things are the way a virtuous person, or a possessor of practical wisdom, takes them to be.[8]

What Aristotle achieves by invoking the *ergon* of a human being is only this: he enables himself to represent his thesis that the good *for man* is activity in accordance with human virtue as a specific case of a general connection between good and virtue, or excellence. What he exploits is a conceptual link between an X's being such as to act as it befits an X to act and its having the excellence that is proper to X's. The conceptual link is truistic, and it leaves entirely open what sort of evaluative or normative background fixes a substance for applications of the notions of *ergon* and excellence, in any particular exemplification of the general connection.

4. I am objecting to the view that Aristotle thinks he has an external validation for a conception of worthwhileness in action that he takes for granted in his audience, the conception characteristic of someone who possesses the virtues. The view I am objecting to belongs with a reading of "eudaimonism" that casts it as a general theory of reasons for action. In such a context, the thesis that *eudaimonia* consists in acting in accordance with a certain specific set of character dispositions would have to be read as saying that the conception of reasons for acting, of choiceworthiness in action, that is characteristic of a possessor of those character dispositions is correct, because it matches up to the deliverances of a correct general account of which actions are choiceworthy. Just because it was general, this envisaged account would give no special position to distinctively ethical reasons for acting. Indeed, eudaimonism on this understanding would hold out a prospect that often tempts ethical theorists: that distinctively ethical reasons for acting might be authenticated by representing them as derivative from perhaps less contentious rational considerations. The envisaged external validation that I have been considering would be an instance of this kind of thing.

I think this is a misconception of eudaimonism as a context for ethical reflection. The idea of eudaimonism is indeed the idea that a life of virtuous

8. On the appeal to the *ergon* of a human being, see my essay "The role of *Eudaimonia* in Aristotle's Ethics".

activity is a life worth living, a choiceworthy life. But the relevant application of the notion of choiceworthiness need not be given its substance independently of the distinctive values that are instilled into someone who acquires the virtues.

From Aristotle's detailed discussion of the virtues, it emerges that we can summarily capture those values under the concept of the noble (see, for instance, 1120a23–4). In acquiring the virtues of character, a person is taught to admire and delight in actions as exemplifying the value of nobility. Coming to value the noble integrally includes an alteration in one's motivational make-up, in what one finds attractive: it shapes one's conception of what is worth going in for. It is true that eudaimonism attributes choiceworthiness to a life of virtuous activity. But the relevant choiceworthiness can be a choiceworthiness that such a life is rightly seen as having when, and because, it is seen as made up of actions that exemplify the value of nobility. It is not that "It would be noble to act thus and so" is certified as giving a genuine reason for acting on the ground that a life of such actions would meet independent standards for being worth going in for. The choiceworthiness of a noble action is simply a reflection of the action's being rightly seen to exemplify the value of nobility. It is because the value is authentic that the choiceworthiness is genuine, not the other way around.

The concept of *eudaimonia* is indeed the concept of a kind of choiceworthiness, but it is not choiceworthiness in general, something present wherever there is a reason for acting of whatever sort. There are many dimensions on which we can assess choiceworthiness in general. The concept of *eudaimonia*, as Aristotle uses it, marks out just one of the dimensions: one that he tries to delineate for us, in a general way, when he connects the idea of *eudaimonia* with the idea of how it befits a human being to act and the idea of human excellence (in I.7). It is obvious that not just any reason for acting can be sensibly glossed in those terms.

This may seem hard to reconcile with the passage (1097b6–20) in which Aristotle says that *eudaimonia* is self-sufficient. He explains the self-sufficient (1097b14–15) as "that which on its own makes life pursuit-worthy and lacking in nothing". And he goes on to say (1097b16–17) that *eudaimonia* is "most pursuit-worthy if not counted in with other things; if it were so counted, clearly it would be more pursuit-worthy with the addition of the smallest of goods". This can seem to support the idea that eudaimonism is a general theory of reasons for acting, since it is easy to suppose that, according to this passage, *eudaimonia* embraces anything whose presence would in any way make a life more desirable.

But I do not believe Aristotle means the scope of *eudaimonia* to include just any contribution to the desirability of a life. There are places where he seems to be trying to insist that *eudaimonia* is an agent's own achievement rather than a gift of chance.[9] Not that mere effort (or good willing on some roughly Kantian construal) is by itself enough to ensure *eudaimonia*. Factors outside an agent's control can make it impossible to live the life of a virtuous person (even if they leave isolated bits of virtuous behaviour still feasible), as perhaps in cases like that of Priam (1100a5–9).[10] But chance goods can surely make a life more desirable, in some obvious sense, otherwise than through their effect on what it is possible for the agent to achieve by his own efforts, and the ranking of lives as more or less desirable that is operative here ought not to be relevant to their assessment in terms of *eudaimonia*. On these lines we are required to discount at least some sorts of desirability when we try to understand what Aristotle means by saying that *eudaimonia* is self-sufficient. On a suitable restricted reading, what the passage says is that *eudaimonia* is self-sufficient precisely on the dimension of desirability that is connected with the idea of human excellence and how it befits a human being to live. *Eudaimonia* is self-sufficient with respect to the kind of desirability that Aristotle thinks is correctly captured by rightly applying the concept of the noble.

The point of saying that *eudaimonia* is revealed as "most pursuit-worthy if not counted in with other things" is, I think, the same as the point of its being *the* good with which *eudaimonia* is equated. This latter claim does not say that *eudaimonia* embraces all possible reasons for acting (all goods, in one obvious sense; see 1094a1–3). The point is that the relevant dimension of desirability is not just one dimension among others. Choiceworthiness along the relevant dimension—the choiceworthiness that actions are rightly seen as having when they are seen as noble, in the trained perception of a

9. See Cooper, *Reason and Human Good*, pp. 123–4; he cites *Politics* 1323b24–9, *EE* 1215a12–19, *NE* 1099b18–25.

10. There are difficult issues in this area about what it is for something to be a person's achievement. But Aristotle resists or is immune to the temptation, familiar in modern philosophy, to discount anything for which there are conditions that are not themselves within the person's control, with the result that one's achievement is restricted to something like the disposition of one's will (everything else being at the disposal of stepmotherly nature).

virtuous person—is choiceworthiness *par excellence*. If a consideration of the relevant type bears on an agent's practical predicament, someone who has learned to appreciate such considerations will rightly take it that nothing else matters for the question what shape his life should take here and now, even if the result of choosing the noble is, as it surely may be, a life that is less desirable along other dimensions than it might have been. If the result is a life that is more desirable along other dimensions, that is in the nature of a bonus. It is irrelevant to the point Aristotle is making when he says that *eudaimonia* is self-sufficient.

At one point (1102a2–3) Aristotle says "it is for the sake of this [*eudaimonia*] that we all do everything else that we do". Taken at face value, this may seem to make *eudaimonia* embrace all reasons for action, of whatever kind. But we know anyway that Aristotle does not think all human behaviour is aimed at *eudaimonia*; for instance, incontinent behaviour is precisely not aimed at *eudaimonia*. We could discount this remark as merely casual. Alternatively, we can read it so as to be consistent with what Aristotle says elsewhere, by taking it to employ a special, quasi-technical concept of "doing" (*prattein* in the remark; also *praxis*), to be understood precisely so that doings, in the relevant sense, are bits of behaviour undertaken as falling under a conception of *eudaimonia*, of doing well.[11] This way, the passage does not undermine my thesis that the concept of *eudaimonia* marks out a special category of reasons for acting.

5. Aristotle's habit of citing the judgment of the virtuous person as the standard of correctness, together with his insistence that only people who have been properly brought up are a suitable audience for his ethical lectures, may make it seem that on the substantive questions of ethics his stance is one of smugly accepting the outlook of a particular social group. Presumably he would say that what determines whether someone has been properly brought up is the judgment of the virtuous person. It is easy to want to complain that his thinking moves in a tight circle.

No doubt there is something right about this accusation of dogmatism. But we should not forget that when he puts his restriction on his audience, Aristotle says (1095b4–9): ". . . those who are going to be adequate listeners about what is noble and just, and in general about political matters, must have been nobly brought up in respect of their habits. For the starting-point

11. I elaborate such a reading in "The Role of *Eudaimonia* in Aristotle's Ethics".

is the *that*, and if that is sufficiently clear, there will be no need in addition for the *because*. . . ." In the immediate context, the point is that there is no need to have the *because* if one is to be a suitable member of Aristotle's audience. But it is also true, I think, that one does not need the *because* in order to shape one's life as one should; if one's grasp on the *that* is correct, and one acts on it, one will be living in accordance with virtue. However, Aristotle here registers at least the possibility of graduating from having only the *that* to having the *because* as well. He leaves room for a transition to a comprehending acceptance of a scheme of values, and thus connects himself to a tradition that stands precisely in opposition to dogmatism, a tradition that includes Socrates' commendation of the examined life.

What shape would the transition to having the *because* take? Obviously one possible answer takes us back to the style of interpretation I have been considering. The *that* is a piecemeal correctness, occasion by occasion, about what actions are worth undertaking in the distinctive way that the concept of *eudaimonia* signals, or perhaps about what features of situations require, in that way, what sorts of actions. The *because*, on this reading, is the story I have been considering, which could easily be cast as a story about *why* the actions that someone who possesses the *that* sees as choiceworthy are indeed choiceworthy: the idea is that acting in the light of such perceptions of choiceworthiness makes up a life that is desirable anyway, for a human being as such.

But that is not the only possible interpretation for the idea of a transition to the *because*. On a different reading, a comprehending acceptance of a scheme of values would not differ from an uncomprehending acceptance of it like that, with the comprehending view setting the accepted values on a foundation, so that the *because* would not only explain the *that* but also validate it from outside. Rather, in acquiring the *because* one would not be adding new material to what one acquired when one took possession of the *that*, but coming to comprehend the *that*, by appreciating how one's hitherto separate perceptions of what situations call for hang together, so that acting on them can be seen as putting into practice a coherent scheme for a life.[12]

We can picture the intellectual activity that would be involved in moving to the *because*, on this view, in terms of a version of Neurath's image of the

12. See M. F. Burnyeat, "Aristotle on Learning to be Good", especially p. 81. (But I think it is quite implausible that Aristotle conceives the *Nicomachean Ethics* itself as "setting out 'the because' of virtuous actions", as Burnyeat there suggests.)

sailor who has to keep his boat in good order while at sea. In this version of the image, the fact that the boat cannot be put ashore for overhaul stands for the fact that when one reflectively moves from mere possession of the *that* to possession of the *because* as well, one has no material to exploit except the initially unreflective perceptions of the *that* from which the reflection starts. One reflects on one's inherited scheme of values, or the perceptions of choiceworthiness in action in which that scheme of values expresses itself, from inside the ethical way of thinking that one finds oneself with, not by contemplating it from the external standpoint of a theory about motivations built into human beings as such.

Not everything in this Neurathian conception fits Aristotle's own approach. A feature of the Neurathian image that does not correspond to anything in Aristotle is this: reflection on a collection of putative perceptions of the *that* from within, directed at seeing how they hang together, runs a risk of recommending the conclusion that they do not hang together at all, or at least that they do not hang together very well. If that happens, it should put the perceptions in question. Neurath's sailor may need to tinker with the boat. Reflection aimed at the *because* puts what has hitherto passed as the *that* at risk, and there is no sign that Aristotle recognizes this. It is partly for this reason that I did not simply dismiss the charge that he is dogmatic in his confidence about the particular ethical views he embraces.

In one way it makes an enormous difference to Aristotle's ethical outlook if we require it to open itself to the risk of revision, as a result of Neurathian reflection. But in another way the reform is quite easy. In particular, it does not disrupt Aristotle's realism. On the contrary, it suggests a shape for a defence of an Aristotelian realism, without either dogmatism or an appeal to an external validation. Reflection aimed at the *because* makes a collection of putative perceptions of the *that* vulnerable to being unmasked as illusory, on the ground that they do not hang together so as to be recognizable as expressing a coherent scheme for a life. In that case, if a collection of putative perceptions of the *that* has run that risk and passed muster, that is surely some reason to suppose that the perceptions are veridical. Indeed, wherever the Neurathian image is the right image for reflection (which might be argued to be everywhere), that is the only kind of reason there can be for supposing that some putative sense of how things are is correct.

So on this kind of reading as well as on the kind of reading that I have been opposing, reflection towards the *because* can after all be seen as yielding a validation of the conception of the *that* from which it starts. The difference is that on this reading the validation is not from outside. It belongs with that difference that in this case we cannot aspire to a validation that is better than provisional.

Possession of the *that* is what is imparted by the moulding of ethical character that Aristotle describes in Book II of the *Nicomachean Ethics*. Full-blown possession of the *because* would presumably be the intellectual virtue, practical wisdom, that he discusses more particularly in Book VI. There is a tendency for commentators to overplay this distinction. The idea is that Book II is about the acquisition of motivational propensities that relate to reason only by way of obedience to its dictates (compare 1102b30–1); they prepare the agent to act in a way that conforms to prescriptions issued by the intellectual excellence, practical wisdom, which is going to come into view only later in Aristotle's text.[13] But Book II itself contains the claim that actions that manifest virtue of character must be chosen (1105a31–2). And Aristotle links the idea of choice to the idea of deliberation (1112a15–16, 1113a9–12), and thereby to the excellences of the intellect.[14] So it is already implicit in Book II that the virtue of character that is dealt with there, represented as the product of habituation, includes an intellectual excellence. A state of a person from which choices issue is itself a source of prescriptions, not just a motivational preparedness to obey prescriptions whose source is elsewhere.

In undergoing the moulding of character that is the topic of Book II, a person acquires a way of bringing behaviour under concepts, the conceptual scheme that we can summarily capture in terms of the idea of the noble and the disgraceful. A possessor of the *that* is already beyond uncomprehending habit; he is already some distance into the realm of the intellectual excellences. He has acquired apparatus for thinking and rea-

13. See John M. Cooper, "Some Remarks on Aristotle's Moral Psychology".

14. Aristotle clearly envisages actions that manifest virtue of character but do not issue from deliberation (for instance, at 1117a17–22). In conjunction with the link between choice and deliberation, this might seem to threaten the claim that all actions that manifest virtue of character are chosen. I think what has to give here is the connection between choice and (actual) deliberation. Note that 1117a21–2 is most naturally read as saying that an agent *chooses* spur-of-the-moment, and so not deliberated, courageous actions. This need not conflict with 1111b9–10, where the point need be no more than that actions whose occasions are sprung on one are not *in general* chosen. The point of the link between choice and deliberation is not that choice results from deliberation but that it reveals a shape to the way the agent is minded, a kind of shape that becomes explicit in actual courses of deliberation.

soning, and he is thereby equipped for reflection; he has the material for a transition to a full-fledged possession of the *because*. Aristotle's own presentation is defective in that it fails to register the possibility that reflection may undermine its starting-points. But that is no reason to hold Aristotle to a clear-cut separation of having the *because* from having the *that*, which would be congenial to the idea that a transition to the *because* requires a shift of viewpoint. On the contrary, Book II indicates that a possessor of the *that* is already not devoid of the *because*. He can say "Because it is noble". Moving to a more complete possession of the *because*, one sufficient to amount to full-blown possession of the relevant intellectual virtue, needs no more than internal reflection from the midst of what one already has.

6. I have been urging a Neurathian picture of reflection on an ethical outlook. One benefit of this is that it points to a way of understanding why it is so tempting for modern readers to credit Aristotle with a different picture of the sort of validation an ethical outlook needs: a picture in which, to modify the image, the boat is put ashore for a certification of its seaworthiness. Aristotle seems happy to assume that his outlook is simply correct. The tempting thought is that we cannot make sense of that in terms of no more than the prospect that his outlook would pass muster in Neurathian reflection, a prospect that, on the view I am suggesting, he assumes without even noticing that he is doing so. Neurathian reflection about an ethical outlook would be undertaken from within it. The tempting thought is that one could not achieve a justified conviction that a set of views about anything is objectively correct, by reflecting from within something as historically contingent as an inherited way of thinking; except perhaps by sheer accident, objective correctness would require breaking out of a specific cultural inheritance into an undistorted contact with the real.

   Intelligible though it is, I believe this line of thought is foreign to Aristotle. Here I do not mean merely to repeat what I have been urging, that he expresses his "realism" quite casually—he gives no sign that he thinks he needs to license it even by anticipating a favourable outcome for Neurathian reflection on his ethical outlook, let alone by making a grand metaphysical gesture. I mean something more than that. Making historical contingency and cultural specificity into a metaphysical issue is distinctively modern. It is anachronistic to read into Aristotle, as an underpinning for his casual "realism", a line of thought that makes sense only as a response to a kind of anxiety to which he is immune.[15]

That might leave it looking as if we do Aristotle a favour if we equip him with a response to that kind of anxiety—even if he is too philosophically primitive to feel the anxiety himself. But that presupposes that susceptibility to this kind of anxiety marks an intellectual advance over Aristotle's immunity to it, and that is open to dispute. On the contrary, we might say: organizing our metaphysics around the idea of transcending historicity is profoundly suspect. Its true effect is to undermine the very idea of getting things right. We can conceal that from ourselves only if we think we can make sense of the idea of a mode of inquiry that transcends historicity. In our modern culture, natural science tends, quite intelligibly, to be cast in that role, but any such conception of science is an illusion.

Inquiry is an intellectual activity in which we aim to make our thinking, about whatever subject matter, responsive to reasons for thinking one thing rather than another. The anxiety I am considering is one possible reaction to a thought that we can put like this: we have only our own lights to go on, in trying to ensure that the considerations that we are responsive to are really reasons for thinking one thing rather than another. But that thought is simply correct. It is no less correct about scientific inquiry than about any other kind of inquiry. That the concepts employed in laying out a scientific picture of the world are not anthropocentric—that they are in that sense "absolute", to use Bernard Williams's term—makes no difference to this point.[16] It is still true that how the concepts are taken to hang together

15. What about the theme of *nomos* and *physis* in ancient thought? (Robert Heinaman raised this question.) That is a large topic; obviously I cannot deal with it properly here. I think it is revealing that the theme surfaces in the *NE* only in connection with "justice" (V.7), and is there discussed in such a way that it is reasonable to connect *nomos* with the English "conventional". There is no sign of the general metaphysical anxiety that I am alluding to. More general ethical scepticism is of course a Greek phenomenon (even if not much in evidence in Aristotle). But, as represented, for instance, in Plato's *Gorgias*, it does not take this general metaphysical form. The Calliclean attack on ordinary ethical views does not scruple to exploit evaluative concepts, for instance the concept of the slavish, whose persuasive force ought itself to be open to question if the point were to express a metaphysical anxiety about what is culturally specific or historically contingent.

16. On "absolute", see Williams, *Ethics*, p. 139. For Williams's use of this notion in the reading of Aristotle, see p. 52: "Aristotle saw a certain kind of ethical, cultural, and indeed political life as a harmonious culmination of human potentialities, recoverable from an absolute understanding of nature."

rationally—what considerations are taken to be reasons for what conclusions of inquiry—is the product of the historical evolution of a particular human institution.

This is not to cast doubt on the idea that science is progressively revealing reality as it is. The moral is, rather, that we should learn not to see a threat in this thought: we have only our own lights to go on, and they are formed by our particular position in the history of inquiry. That should not seem to put in question our prospects for getting things right. The prospects are live in scientific inquiry (indeed, we have more than just prospects there), not because scientific inquiry transcends historical determination of its lights, but because its lights stand up to reflective scrutiny. Our conception of how to conduct scientific inquiry, or, more exactly, the conception that is acted on by practitioners of scientific inquiry, is continually self-correcting. But if that is how we should neutralize the potentially disquieting effect of attending to our historicity in the case of science, our paradigm of inquiry directed at an "absolute" conception of how things are, the same thought can work directly for inquiries that do not aim at "absolute" results. A "realistic" attitude to such inquiries does not need a different kind of warrant, with any conviction that we are getting things right needing to be grounded in a relation to the result of an "absolute" inquiry.

We can express the role of habituation into virtue of character in Aristotle's thinking by saying that possession of the *that*, the propensity to admire and delight in actions as noble, is second nature to those who have been properly habituated. And I have suggested that someone who possesses the *that* is not devoid of the *because*; full-blown possession of the *because*, the intellectual virtue of practical wisdom, is no more than possession of the *that* in a reflectively adjusted form. Now something that we can appropriately conceive as second nature surely cannot be in all respects autonomous with respect to first nature, so to speak: that is, the sort of thing that might be the topic of an investigation whose questions are framed in "absolute" or at any rate extra-ethical terms. If there are motivational tendencies that are built into human beings as such, they must put limits on what is possible in the way of habituation into an ethical outlook. So I am not ruling out explanatory connections between an ethical outlook and a pre-ethical account of human nature. But this is quite distinct from the idea that the perceptions that are characteristic of a specific second nature can count as correct only if they can be displayed as rationally derivative from truths about first nature.

I think that is exactly how *not* to be an ethical realist. Understanding the philosophical temptation to read such a position into Aristotle, and seeing through the post-Aristotelian philosophical ideas that underlie the temptation, is a good way of coming to appreciate the advantages of the different— less metaphysical—approach to ethical realism that Aristotle's thinking actually exemplifies.

Deliberation and Moral Development in Aristotle's Ethics

1. In this essay, I shall try to set out an understanding of a distinctively ethical application that Aristotle evidently wants to make of the notion of deliberation (*bouleusis*). The main obstacle in the path of the reading I want to recommend is the temptation to give an overly "intellectualistic" cast to the idea of a correct conception of doing well—the conception that is put into practice in actions that, in manifesting excellences of character in the strict sense, manifest the intellectual excellence of practical wisdom. I think Aristotle's view is that it is the moral development effected by upbringing that puts us in a position to undertake ethical deliberation. His account of the habituation that sets up states of character already contains enough to display states of character as having the intellectual aspect that he insists on. If the content of a correct conception of doing well is fixed by proper upbringing, that renders it superfluous to credit that role to an autonomous operation of the practical intellect, or to look to the intellect for a foundation for the claim that this rather than that conception of doing well is correct. I think those ideas figure in interpretations of Aristotle only because he is read in a modern, and hence alien, framework. Ironically enough, if we clear those ideas away, and equip ourselves with a different understanding of the sense in which practical wisdom is an intellectual excellence, we make it possible to see a certain convergence, in a context of undeniable divergence, between Aristotle and Kant.

2. *Nicomachean Ethics* III.3 discusses deliberation in general. The topic is thinking that starts from a proposed end and, when successful, arrives at something the agent can simply do with a view to that end—a project that he can put into effect without further thought. The idea is that it is only across a gap that the end, as proposed, casts a favourable light on doing

something in particular, and it takes an exercise of the intellect to bridge the gap.

This schema fits most straightforwardly where the thinking needed to bridge the gap between end and action is instrumental or technical. In this kind of case, there is no problem about what it would be for the end to have been achieved: say, for the agent to possess a winter covering. But proposing an end to oneself in such terms does not by itself single out an immediately practicable course of action. So a task is set for the intellect: to arrive at a course of action such that undertaking it will, if all goes well, result in achieving the end proposed. Perhaps there are several such actions; in that case comparisons in terms of efficacy, and perhaps other dimensions of desirability, come into play, to select between the competing options.[1]

Now Aristotle uses the concept of deliberation when he characterizes an intellectual excellence that is specifically ethical. He says excellence in deliberation with a view to living well in general is characteristic of the person who possesses practical wisdom (the *phronimos*): 1140a25–8. Practical wisdom is operative in actions that display the excellences of character—courage, temperance, and so forth. It is the involvement of practical wisdom that distinguishes the excellences of character, strictly so called, from mindless behavioural propensities that might (perhaps only roughly) correspond with them in behavioural output (VI.13).

Here we have a different sort of gap between an end and action undertaken with a view to it. The end is living well or doing well, which Aristotle tells us is the same as *eudaimonein* (1095a18–20). Here we cannot say it is clear, in a particular practical predicament, what it would be for the end to have been achieved. In fact it seems plausible that that is exactly the problem for thought directed at bridging this kind of gap between end and action. The agent has to determine which (perhaps we should add "if any"), from among the actions that he can directly set about performing, would here and now, in these circumstances, *amount to* doing well.

What might an exercise of the intellect, directed at this other kind of practical question, look like? And what is the content of the idea of deliberating excellently in this kind of case? Reflecting on technical or instrumental deliberation does not help with these questions. Where the problem is technical or instrumental, we can understand deliberation as

---

1. At 1112b17 "*kallista*" seems to indicate a ranking by something other than efficacy. (All references will be to the *Nicomachean Ethics*.)

working towards something immediately practicable, if necessary through intermediate means, with what figures at each stage singled out by the intellect as *conducive* to what figures at the preceding stage. And for these cases, we can begin to explain the idea that one person deliberates better than another by saying that good deliberation is such as to be *effective*: acting on its deliverances tends to achieve the proposed end.[2] But in the kind of deliberation that displays practical wisdom, the problem is precisely that it is not clear what it would be to have achieved the proposed end. We cannot exploit the idea of effectiveness to explain excellence in deliberation of this kind.

Some commentators have supposed Aristotle hoped to use technical deliberation to cast light on this other kind of deliberation, at least when he wrote Book III.[3] I have been urging that this idea is unpromising. And there is really no reason to saddle Aristotle with it. When he talks about deliberation in general, he is not addressing the question what it is for exercises of the practical intellect to be correct. It is an indication of this that, even when his discussion suggests a focus on the technical case, he shows no special concern with efficacy, as opposed to other sorts of desirability in action. What the general account of deliberation is supposed to give us is just the idea of using the intellect to bridge a gap between proposed end and action. It is true that technical problems provide the easiest illustrations of this idea. But that by itself leaves Aristotle's options open, when he comes to consider cases where the gap between end and action is of a different kind.[4]

3. In the kind of deliberation excellence at which is characteristic of practical wisdom, the question addressed is "What action here and now would

2. This is not the whole of an explanation. "Such as to" and "tends to" accommodate the fact that good technical deliberation may fail, and bad deliberation succeed, by luck. But we would still need to complicate the story in order to take account of the other dimensions of desirability in solutions, over and above efficacy. (See n. 1.)

3. For a version of this suggestion (coupled with the idea that Book VI introduces a new doctrine, in which correctness in non-technical deliberation is a matter of bringing cases under rules), see the essays by D. J. Allan, "Aristotle's Account of the Origin of Moral Principles" and "The Practical Syllogism". See the discussion by David Wiggins, "Deliberation and Practical Reason".

4. In chapter 4 of *Ethics with Aristotle*, Sarah Broadie seems to me to make more fuss than is warranted about dangers posed, she thinks, for Aristotle's conception of ethical deliberation by the role of crafts in his thinking about deliberation in general.

be doing well?"[5] The end proposed—doing well—is, logically speaking, a universal, and the problem is to arrive at an instance. That can suggest that deliberation of this sort requires arriving at, or otherwise availing oneself of, a blueprint, in universal terms, for doing well, and applying it to the circumstances at hand. This has perhaps been the main alternative, in modern readings of Aristotle, to the idea that he hopes to illuminate this kind of deliberation somehow by exploiting a technical model.[6]

But it is increasingly familiar that this picture does not fit Aristotle. He repeatedly denies that ethical truth can be stated in universal terms. (See, for instance, 1094b11–27, 1109b12–23, among many similar passages.) And there is a connected point about how he conceives bringing the universal end, doing well, to bear on the details of a situation. If one had a blueprint for doing well, applying it should be straightforward, perhaps even mechanical. The blueprint would suit actions to types of situation, and applying it would require scanning the circumstances to see if they bring the situation under one of the specified types. That might be laborious, but it would not call for anything special in the way of an excellence of the *practical* intellect. On this picture, having one's practical intellect in good order, in the relevant respect, would be a matter of having the right blueprint; applying the blueprint would require only general capacities for gathering information, and the capacity for logical inference. But this is difficult to square with a strong suggestion, in various passages, that practical wisdom, excellence at the relevant kind of deliberation, at least includes, and perhaps is even to be identified with, a proper responsiveness to the details of situations—something Aristotle is willing to conceive as like, and even as a kind of, perception. (See especially 1142a23–30, 1143a5–b5.)

The idea of the "blueprint" picture is that the content of a conception of the universal, doing well, is in principle available, and assessible for correctness, in abstraction from the judgments or actions, in particular circumstances, that we want to see as applications of it. We could make the universal explicit in context-independent words; they would pin down its content, in a way that should in principle be intelligible from outside the

---

5. No doubt the end of doing well can also figure in practical problems of a broadly technical kind. It may be that an action is undertaken, not as an instance of doing well, but as required in order to put the agent in a position to engage in other actions that will be instances of doing well. See G. E. M. Anscombe, "Thought and Action in Aristotle".

6. See, e.g., Allan, "The Practical Syllogism".

actualizations, in particular circumstances, of a propensity to make just such judgments or engage in just such actions (a propensity that would be possessed only by someone who had the corresponding end as his own). Whether some particular judgment or action was a correct application of the universal would be a question of what followed from the universal's content together with the facts of the situation. So the question whether some conception of doing well was correctly applied in some particular case would be separable from the question whether doing well so conceived was the right end to pursue. Correctness of application would be recognizable, in principle, from a stance that was neutral with respect to the corresponding end. And for a deliberator to be getting things right, arriving at what really is an instance of doing well, both conception and application would need to be correct.

But when Aristotle stresses discernment of the specifics of a situation, he seems to be pointing to a different way of keeping in place the notion of getting things right. A discerning view of a situation is one that reads the significance of the situation's features correctly. If we can get correctness into the picture on these lines, that might leave the idea that we must conceive application in terms of deduction, and must see questions about the correctness of applications as presupposing a separately established correctness in the universal conception of the end that is applied, looking like a mere prejudice— we might call it "rationalistic"—about the nature of this kind of exercise of rationality, perhaps reflecting a prejudice about rationality as such.

4. We are considering deliberation with a view to doing well. Early in the *Nicomachean Ethics*, Aristotle explains that "well", in that specification of an end, is to be understood as "in accordance with excellence" (1098a16–18). That is the pretext for the discussion of excellence and the particular excellences that starts at the end of Book I (1102a5–6). Aristotle deals with the excellences of character mostly by giving character sketches of their possessors, and one thing he achieves thereby is to put into place in his lectures a somewhat determinate picture of the content of the end that is constituted by doing well in general, as correctly conceived (by his lights, of course).[7] Doing well is acting in the sort of way that is characteristic of people such as

---

7. I shall ignore the exercise of the excellence of the theoretical intellect, which turns out in Book X to be (in some sense) the highest kind of doing well; I am concerned with the kind of doing well in which *practical* wisdom is operative.

he describes. This indirection is just what we ought to expect, if he thinks the content of a correct conception of doing well cannot be captured in a deductively applicable blueprint for a life.

Aristotle evidently does not mean it to be possibly contentious, as between him and his audience, that the excellences are just the states of character that he lists, or that the possessors of the particular excellences are just the sorts of people he describes in his character sketches. The ethical substance, the content of the conception of doing well that he puts into place by going through the particular excellences, is meant to be already shared between him and the audience, because they have been properly brought up (1095b4–6). They have been habituated into a propensity to admire and delight in the actions that are characteristic of the excellences. They see those actions as fine or noble (*kalon*); the concept of the noble organizes the evaluative outlook of a possessor of excellence. (See, for instance, 1120a23–4.)

This picture of habituation, in which it institutes a conceptual capacity—possession of the concept of the noble—in the course of shaping motivations, is helpful in bringing out how arriving at what really are instances of doing well need not be understood as applying a blueprint. There is nothing wrong with saying that a possessor of excellence grasps the content of the universal, doing well. But we need not conceive that grasp as separable, even in principle, from the state, one aspect of which is a motivational propensity, that results from having been properly brought up. Someone who has been properly brought up has been habituated into seeing the appropriate actions as worth going in for in the specific way that is expressed by bringing them under the concept of the noble. According to the "blueprint" picture, the content of the correct conception of doing well can be abstracted away from this psychological state, the result of habituating evaluative and motivational propensities into shape. The idea is that the content of practical wisdom's universal end could in principle be grasped in an act of pure intellect. But if we juxtapose Aristotle's stress on discernment with his picture of how the correct conception of doing well is acquired, we have the essentials of a contrasting picture, in which the content of the end cannot be pinned down in abstraction from the ability to put it into practice in recognizing specific occasions for action. In this contrasting picture, there is nothing for grasp of the content of the universal end to be except a capacity to read the details of situations in the light of a way of valuing actions into which proper upbringing has habituated one.

5. Even commentators who see that the "blueprint" picture is not Aristotle's can be influenced by the idea that applying a practical universal would have to conform to a deductive model. There is an instructive example of this in Sarah Broadie's reading of Aristotle's ethics.

Rightly, in my view, Broadie rejects the "blueprint" picture, which she calls "the Grand End theory", as a reading of Aristotle.[8] But she concludes that deliberation that displays practical wisdom cannot, in Aristotle's view, be thinking directed at bridging a version of the gap between end and action that figures in the account of deliberation in general, with doing well as the end. In her reading, deliberation that displays practical wisdom must be directed not towards doing well in general as its end, but towards this or that particular end, for instance the safety of one's *polis* or the well-being of one's friends. This is because she cannot find anything but the "blueprint" picture in the idea of doing well as an end needing to be brought to bear on action in a way that would fit Aristotle's general picture of deliberation.

Some commentators try to register Aristotle's hostility to the leading idea of the "Grand End theory", the idea that the shape of the good life can be specified in universal terms, while retaining the idea that the deliberation characteristic of practical wisdom is deliberation with a view to doing well. Broadie hears this combination as keeping the Grand End in play, and merely denying that it is, and perhaps that it could be, explicit in the minds of agents.[9] As she understands this combination, just because there is supposed to be deliberation towards the end of doing well, that end must have the logical character envisaged in the "blueprint" picture. It is just that the universal that is applied in this kind of deliberation, which involves movements of thought that could be made explicit in deductions, is only implicit in the mind of the deliberator.

I think this reflects a deductivistic prejudice about the very idea of applying a universal. Broadie does not see the possibility I have been urging: that grasp of the universal that forms the content of a correct conception of doing well need not be isolable, even in principle, as a component in the propensity to put that end into practice in specific situations, so that exercises of the propensity could be reconstructed as deductive steps from an autonomous object of the practical intellect, whether explicitly or only implicitly in view. We can suppose that grasp of the universal is not thus

---

8. *Ethics with Aristotle*, chapter 5.
9. *Ethics with Aristotle*, p. 236.

isolable, and still have grasp of the universal in our picture. We can still conceive exercises of the propensity as applications of a universal, and we can still conceive the resulting actions as products of deliberation with a view to doing well. That need not be bound up with the idea of a Grand End.

Broadie is surely not wrong to insist that on particular occasions on which practical wisdom is operative, the agent will be pursuing ends that are narrower than doing well in general—ends such as the well-being of a friend or the safety of one's *polis*. But we would not have a satisfactory picture of practical wisdom if we left it at that, without providing for any conception of how these pursuings of narrower ends hang together. Action directed at the well-being of a friend may display practical wisdom on an occasion, but there may be other occasions on which the well-being of a friend could be pursued (the situation affords that opportunity), but that is not what a possessor of practical wisdom would do; the right reading of the situation would focus on an opportunity it presents to pursue a different particular end. Why would that different reading of the situation be the right one? There must be room for an answer on these lines: "Because a correct conception of doing well, as brought to bear on this situation, dictates acting with a view to the different particular end. Although actions of the type, acting with a view to the well-being of a friend, can amount to doing well, and although an action of that type is available as an option in these circumstances, that is not what doing well would amount to here and now." Right readings of situations are not isolated from one another. They are such that the actions that result from them are all indeed instances of a universal, doing well.

It can be tempting to suppose we cannot have a thought like that, consistently with the multiplicity of the more specific ends that may be pursued in acting on right readings of situations, unless we take the content of the universal to embody principles that rank the various particular ends that might be pursued on the relevant occasions; perhaps the rankings would be relative to different sorts of situation.[10] This is just a version of the "blueprint" picture, and I think Broadie is right to set her face against that. But when we discard the "blueprint" picture, we do not discard all

---

10. See John M. Cooper, *Reason and Human Good in Aristotle*, pp. 94–6. For the idea that a conception of *eudaimonia* must embody a decision procedure, on pain of leaving out the unity in the succession of actions that constitute acting it out, see T. H. Irwin, *Plato's Moral Theory*, pp. 264–5.

forms of the thought that we can find a unity in actions that involve a multiplicity of particular ends, by seeing them as all undertaken with a view to doing well. It is just that the unity would not be discernible, any more than the rightness of a particular action is, apart from the specifics of particular situations.

Of course it would be implausible to suppose that a person of practical wisdom arrives at immediately practicable intentions by proposing a general end, doing well, and looking around for an action that might constitute doing that. But this is not damaging. It is anyway questionable to what extent Aristotle thinks the actions that manifest excellence—even excellence in the strict sense, which requires practical wisdom—issue from actual courses of thinking, the sort of thing one might call "deliberation". He remarks that appropriate actions are better indicators of courage if they are produced in emergencies, when there is no time to work out what to do (1117a17–22).[11] The point surely generalizes: actions that manifest excellence, and so display practical wisdom in operation, need not result from actual courses of deliberative thought. However, even when a possessor of excellence does not work out what to do, starting from an explicitly proposed end of doing well, his choice and action reveal a correct reading of the situation, one that centres on its being an opportunity for this action rather than any of the other actions for which it might be taken to present an occasion. My suggestion has been that there is nothing for a correct conception of doing well to be apart from this capacity to read situations correctly. We might gloss "reading situations correctly" as: seeing them in the light of the correct conception of doing well. The conceptual apparatus of universal end and application to the circumstances at hand still fits, even in the absence of any course of thinking that constitutes arriving at the application. So the structure of deliberation as Aristotle conceives it—thought that bridges a gap between end and action—can get a purchase in our understanding of an action, even if there is no train of thinking that actually moves from universal end to application. Actions can reveal the shape of a

11. This passage is most naturally read as saying that when an occasion for a courageous action is sprung on him, a courageous person *chooses* the courageous action in accordance with his character, rather than as a result of calculation. This need not conflict with 1111b9–10; there the point is only that acts whose occasions are sprung on one are not *in general* chosen. Choice (*proairesis*) is the main point of contact between Aristotle's discussions of the excellences of character and practical wisdom, the associated intellectual excellence; see 1105a31–2, 1139b4–5.

way of seeing situations in the light of the end. It is precisely by doing that that they display the character of their agent.

6. I have been urging that we should not try to see having the right conception of the end as separable from a capacity to read predicaments correctly— the intelligible upshot of being habituated into delighting in the sorts of actions that exemplify the excellences of character.

There may seem to be a problem for this reading in Aristotle's distinction between excellences of character and intellectual excellences. When he embarks on the topic of excellence and the excellences, he singles out the excellences of character as the results of habituation, and postpones the intellectual excellences for later treatment. Practical wisdom is an intellectual excellence. It may seem that in linking its ethical content, the universal end it pursues, so closely to the intelligible upshot of habituation, I am not separating it sharply enough from the excellences of character.

This objection fits a picture in which the ethical content of practical wisdom is established, independently of habituation, by an autonomous exercise of the practical intellect. On this view, habituation yields only non-rational motivational propensities. Habituation sees to it that the non-rational elements in the perfected ethical agent are obediently receptive to independent prescriptions issued by his practical intellect. A consequence that makes the shape of the picture vivid is that a reflective ethical agent has a double motivation for an action that displays an excellence of character: one motivation issuing from a non-rational motivational propensity, a result of habituation, and another motivation independently generated by an exercise of the intellect.[12]

But must the intellectual excellences in general be so sharply separated from the excellences of character? I do not think this is required by the way Aristotle organizes his treatment of the excellences.

He introduces the distinction between intellectual excellences and excellences of character in terms of a partitioning of the soul. The main division is into a rational part, the seat of the intellectual excellences, and a desiderative part, the *orektikon*. We are given to understand that the *orektikon* is the

12. For a clear formulation of a picture of this kind, see John M. Cooper, "Some Remarks on Aristotle's Moral Psychology". T. H. Irwin suggests a similar view in "Some Rational Aspects of Incontinence". See especially p. 83, where he concludes: "Non-cognitive training is necessary . . . because we need some non-cognitive preparation if we are to be able to listen carefully and without distortion or distraction to what practical reason tells us."

seat of the excellences of character, and Aristotle says that it is not rational in the sense of being capable of issuing directives, but it is not utterly non-rational, in that it is capable of being persuaded (see 1102b31–4). Now this seems quite consistent with supposing, as I have urged, that the directively rational excellence, practical wisdom, is not separable from the product of habituating the *orektikon*—that the content of that intellectual state is formed by moulding the *orektikon*.

Aristotle says that the desiderative element is not directively rational. Well, of course the desiderative element, as such, is not directively rational; if it were, then, for instance, mere animal appetites would be directively rational. But this leaves it open that some region, as it were, of the desiderative element is nevertheless the seat of directive rationality.

The claim that the desiderative element is capable of being persuaded might seem to suggest the picture I am questioning, in which excellence of character is a state of the desiderative element, by virtue of which the agent's non-rational inclinations are obedient to the autonomously generated prescriptions of his practical intellect. But when Aristotle talks of persuasion, he need not be alluding to the structure of a *formed* state of character and intellect. The persuasion he is talking about can be what takes place, not in the generation of action that displays a certain formed state of character, with an independently shaped practical intellect persuading the agent's non-rational inclinations, but in the *formation* of states of character. Here is an alternative gloss on the claim that the *orektikon* is open to persuasion: a directive-issuing state can be constituted (by "persuasion") out of psychic materials that, prior to the formation of character, are not a source of rational prescriptions.

Aristotle is strikingly casual about the precise significance of the partitioning of the soul that structures his treatment of the excellences (see 1102a28–32). The division into excellences of character and intellectual excellences looks like a mere expository convenience. There is no reason not to suppose he means a more complex picture of the relation between character and intellect to emerge as his account takes shape. By the time practical wisdom is prominently on the scene, it is clear that the excellences of character, in a strict sense that can now be made explicit, involve the intellectual state that is practical wisdom, not a mere non-rational desiderative propensity (see VI.13). And we need not take the intellectual and desiderative aspects of excellence of character, in the strict sense, to be even notionally separable components of a composite state, as they are in the picture I am disputing. Already in Books II–IV, where the division of excellences of character from intellectual excellences is as much in force as it ever is, and discussion of the intellectual excellences is still officially postponed to a later point in the exposition, it is clear that the habituation that produces excellences of character is not supposed to produce motivational propensities that are merely obedient to an extraneous exercise of reason, like those of a trained animal. The relevant habituation includes the imparting of conceptual apparatus, centrally the concept of the noble. That concept crystallizes the pleasure that an agent has learned to take in certain actions into the form of a reason for undertaking them. The ability to see actions as noble is already a perhaps primitive form of the prescriptive intellectual excellence, practical wisdom, with its content intelligibly put in place by habituation.

7. Talk of responsiveness to the specifics of situations, in the reading of Aristotle that I am urging, functions instead of a certain kind of generality that modern commentators tend to hanker after, in an account of how deliberation with a view to doing well might work: perhaps something modelled on the role of effectiveness in a general account of instrumental deliberation, or something on the lines of the "blueprint" picture. I think it is a strength of Aristotle's thought on these matters that he says so little in general terms about the workings of deliberation with a view to doing well. It shows his immunity to the temptation to suppose there ought to be something on the lines of a *method* for arriving at right answers to deliberative questions of the interesting kind.

Not that more could not be said, in a quite Aristotelian spirit. The concept of the noble comes into play when deliberation of the interesting kind has reached its goal, but other concepts must be operative *en route* to the goal, in capturing the potential significance of features of situations for what to do, and so bringing those features into view for the exercise of discernment. Some of the concepts that figure in Aristotle's character sketches of possessors of the particular excellences can be seen as playing this role, and this would be the place for some of those more explicitly ethical concepts that have figured in recent discussion under the head of "thick" ethical concepts.[13] Elaborating a battery of concepts of this kind could surely illuminate the general shape of an ethical outlook, a conception of doing well.

13. See Bernard Williams, *Ethics and the Limits of Philosophy*.

This elaboration might include registering an ethical direction in which such a concept generally points, by saying such things as this: "Other things being equal, an unpaid debt (say) should be paid." What that says is that if a situation has no other potentially significant feature, the presence of an unpaid debt is decisive for deliberation. I think it is harmless to acknowledge the availability of truths with that shape, so long as we are clear that the acknowledgment is no concession to the idea of a method—since (obviously enough) whether other things are equal will always depend on whether there are other potentially significant features, and, if there are, what importance they should be accorded in the case at hand.

8. In the "blueprint" picture, there is nothing in the way one arrives at instances of the universal, doing well, that looks as if it might be special to the *practical* intellect. So if we want something interesting for the practical intellect to do in this area, it is natural to credit it, rather than proper upbringing, with establishing the content of the universal. This is another basis, deeper than Aristotle's expository division of intellectual excellences from excellences of character, for the idea that, in his view, good upbringing merely institutes a propensity to obey prescriptions that originate in reason, conceived as external to a well-shaped character.

A closely related thought is that if it is habituation that determines the content of a correct conception of doing well (by Aristotle's lights), that leaves it mysterious how the notion of correctness can be in place at all—since other modes of upbringing would presumably issue in different conceptions of doing well. This can suggest that the intellect must play a grounding role. The idea is that the intellect must be able to stand outside the ethical outlook Aristotle takes for granted in his audience, the result of their having been well brought up (by his lights), and produce a justification of the outlook. (That would justify the claim that being brought up into that outlook is being well brought up.)

How is this to be done? Many commentators credit Aristotle with the idea that a justification of his ethical outlook can be based on goods whose status as such is indisputable even while the ethical outlook is in suspense. The justification would validate the outlook's distinctive conception of doing well, on the ground that it amounts to a plan for a life that would be optimal by the lights of such independent goods.[14] Presumably the idea is that the

14. For a version of this idea, see Cooper, *Reason and Human Good in Aristotle*, pp. 124–5.

justificatory argument can be given in a general way, in abstraction from particular circumstances to which one applies the conception of doing well that it justifies. So the envisaged target of the justificatory argument would be a blueprint for doing well, in something like the sense I have been considering.

Now it is striking that Aristotle seems to be immune to the sort of anxiety that might be alleviated by this kind of external validation. He simply assumes that in being brought up into the ethical outlook that he sketches by giving his inventory of excellences of character, the members of his audience have been brought up as they should be. There is no sign that he thinks this conviction of correctness stands in need of grounding from outside.

And it would be wrong to suggest that this leaves the conviction of correctness looking merely mysterious, unless an external grounding is available. As I insisted, Aristotle does not see the product of habituation into the excellences of character as a collection of mindless behavioural tendencies. The result of habituation is a motivational tendency, but one with a conceptual and hence rational aspect. People with a properly formed character have learned to see certain actions as worth undertaking on the ground that they are noble; they have acquired that reason-giving concept, in a way that is inextricably bound up with acquiring the propensity to be motivated by thoughts in which it is applied. The question of correctness is the question whether the actions they see as worth going in for in that specific way are really worth going in for in that way. We can resolve it into a series of piecemeal questions, whether this or that action is correctly seen as noble. And these piecemeal questions arise *within* the conceptual and motivational outlook that, according to Aristotle, ethical upbringing imparts. They can be perfectly adequately settled from that standpoint.

It is undeniable that, to many modern readers, there seems to be a question of correctness that such an approach cannot address, precisely because the approach does not seek a foundation for the outlook as a whole. But I think the very idea of such a question reflects a kind of anxiety that is distinctively modern. In that case, it is anachronistic to suppose Aristotle thinks he has an answer to it. Moreover, it is disputable whether the question is anything but confused. If the question is confused, we do Aristotle no favour by reading a foundational thought into him—any more than we do by crediting him with the deductivistic prejudice about the very idea of applying a universal that we are now equipped to see as partly sustained, in this application, by the wish for a foundation for ethical thinking.[15]

Aristotle says that the end of the deliberation that is characteristic of practical wisdom is living well *in general*, and that may seem to point to the sort of thing I am rejecting: an exercise of the intellect that might serve a validating function, starting from some totality of indisputable goods and reasoning towards a conception of a way of living that combines them optimally. But this would be a misreading. The formulation "living well in general" merely contrasts the relevant kind of deliberation with deliberation directed at a narrower end than a life plan (such as health: 1140a27). The presence of the phrase "in general" does not dislodge the earlier glossing of "well", in a similar formulation of "the" end, as "in accordance with excellence" (1098a16–18). Aristotle is not talking about an "all things considered" kind of reasoning, in which some weight is given to all the independent goods that are in the offing, and a verdict is reached that somehow combines all their claims. What he calls "deliberation with a view to living well in general" is controlled by the value of nobility, the value that guides action in accordance with excellence; it is not deflected by the claims of other goods. (It is worth remarking that the Greek word, "*bouleusis*", does not have the link to the idea of weighing possessed by the English "deliberation", which is the best we can do for an equivalent.)

9. I said that the result of habituation, properly conceived, can be seen to be already a perhaps primitive form of practical wisdom. Why primitive? Because Aristotle depicts the ethical thinking of members of his audience, at least to begin with, as an unquestioning acceptance of the ethical outlook (or its piecemeal deliverances) that they find themselves with because of their upbringing. They have the *that* but not the *because* (see 1095b4–9). Moving to the *because* would presumably come with reflection.

It would naturally belong with the conception I am questioning to take it that the *because* is the supposed external foundation for the ethical outlook. But nothing in Aristotle requires this reading; and if I am right, it is actually

---

15. I do not mean to suggest that the goodness of other goods is irrelevant to the shape taken by a correct conception of The Good. (*A fortiori*, I do not mean to credit Aristotle with a "Stoicizing" devaluation of the goodness of other goods.) But there can be relevance without the sort of rational derivativeness that would be required for a relation of grounding.

excluded, on pain of anachronism. It is not as if there is nothing else he could mean by the difference between the *that* and the *because*. Here is an alternative: moving beyond the *that* to the *because* is moving from unreflective satisfaction with piecemeal applications of the outlook to a concern with how they hang together, so that intelligibility accrues to the parts from their linkage into a whole.

As far as that goes, moving beyond the *that* to the *because* might leave the *that* undisturbed. In fact I do not believe Aristotle suggests otherwise. He proceeds as if the content of a conception of doing well is fixed once and for all, in the minds of the sort of people he assumes his audience to be, by their upbringing; as if moral development for such a person is over and done with at the point when his parents send him out into the world to make his own life. There is no suggestion that an increase in reflectiveness and explicitness will alter the substance of the conception. Even so, there is nothing to prevent us from seeing the result of habituation as a genuinely intellectual excellence, even if only in a primitive form so long as the concept of the noble is applied unreflectively.

However, even if it is not explicitly part of Aristotle's own picture, it seems consistent with the spirit of Aristotelian ethics to allow for further moral development. It is open to us to suppose that reflection towards the *because*, aimed at an accrual of intelligibility from seeing how elements of the *that* hang together, might issue in a reasoned modification of an inherited outlook. Elements of what has hitherto passed for the *that* might not hang together satisfactorily, on reflective consideration in which one tries to integrate them so as to equip them with a *because*. And situations might turn up that one cannot read, with one's present repertoire of thick concepts, as warranting any satisfying judgment as to what to do—satisfying in that one can see how it could be integrated with other such judgments, to make up a plurality of expressions of what one can regard as a coherent conception of doing well.[16] One way or another, setting out to apply a conception of doing well in a reflective way can throw up reasons—according to the conception's own more or less inchoate lights—to modify its content,

---

16. Perhaps the case is a tragic one, and no available action can count as doing well by the lights of one's conception of doing well. (There is no reason to saddle Aristotle with thinking practical wisdom can find an instance of doing well in any predicament whatever.) If the problem is in the situation, rather than the ethical outlook, there is no need to modify the outlook. But the judgment that the problem is in the situation rather than the outlook would itself have to stand up to critical reflection.

even to the extent of forming new thick concepts for dealing with novel kinds of predicament.[17]

This makes it even less problematic to combine the conviction of correctness (at least in the main, we would now have to say) with not envisaging an external grounding for an ethical outlook. Reflection towards the *because* can put what has hitherto passed for grasp of the *that* at risk. In that case, if some putative grasp of the *that* survives the test, that is some ground for supposing that it is correct.

10. There is an Aristotelian idea that we can capture, misleadingly but appropriately for purposes of comparison with Kant, by saying that good willing has a value that is unconditioned. Of course Aristotle has nothing like a Kantian conception of the will. For Aristotle, what has the unconditioned value I want to point to is *doing* well, and that is not something that is in place independently of what happens in the objective world. Aristotle's analogue to the unconditioned value of the good will is not something that is actual no matter what favours are afforded to an agent by stepmotherly nature. Nevertheless, there is a point of resemblance to Kantian thinking, and that is what I want to bring out by saying that the value of doing well is unconditioned. In Aristotle's thinking, the goodness of doing well is self-standing; it is not owed to the goodness of some other goods, in a relation of dependence that would be traced by the sort of external validation of Aristotle's own conception of doing well that I have been urging that Aristotle does not envisage. We might say that when one sees an action as an instance of doing well, one takes it to be dictated by an imperative that is not hypothetical.

This stands in opposition to a common reading of Aristotle, according to which it is a task for the intellect to ground the correctness of one specific conception of the end, and the intellect can execute that task by exploiting the idea of an optimal combination of goods, with their goodness, and the goodness implicit in "optimal", available independently of any specifically ethical convictions. I have suggested that such readings are partly motivated by a distinctively modern thought: that ethical thinking stands in need of a

---

17. Barbara Herman suggests that the place of tradition in an Aristotelian ethic precludes this kind of flexibility, but I see no ground for that. (See "Making Room for Character".) I think it is a deep truth that all thinking, just as such, is anchored in traditions. Reflection has nothing to go on, anywhere, but a putative grasp of the *that*, which (at least to begin with) is merely inherited. This cannot condemn reflection to inflexibility.

foundation. If the very idea of this kind of foundation is distinctively modern, it is out of place in a reading of Aristotle.

There is an irony here. Reading Aristotle in the framework of a modern anxiety, an anxiety that he cannot have felt if I am right, blots out a similarity between his ethical thinking and Kant's. This is not to play down the dissimilarities. In the context of what I have been urging in this essay, the main divergence can be put like this: about Aristotle, it cannot even be a question, as it notoriously is about Kant, whether his ethical thinking can genuinely make provision for substantive content. Aristotle has no inkling of the idea that one might squeeze content out of formal conditions for there to be such a thing as the good will. For Aristotle, substantive ethical content is in place already, the product of habituation, before philosophical ethics begins. Ethical reflection is controlled by substantive convictions that predate it and shape its course; reflection brings them into question only piecemeal, and when one is questioned, that is only on the basis of others. The very idea of ethical theory takes on a different look in this context. But if we frame the contrast correctly, we can hold on to the idea that categorical imperatives, or something like them, are not alien to Aristotelian ethics.

Incontinence and Practical Wisdom in Aristotle[1]

1. David Wiggins has written important and deeply sensible works in an impressive array of fields. In this essay, I shall try to show my admiration and affection for this best of teachers and colleagues by airing one of my few disagreements with him. I hope this will not seem strange; it should not seem strange to anyone who knows how philosophy proceeds.

Wiggins has written illuminatingly on Aristotle's understanding of practical thinking, and, although only a couple of his papers deal directly with Aristotelian texts, an Aristotelian spirit informs his own conception of practical reason. But although Wiggins applauds and exploits Aristotle's reflections about the intellectual excellence that is operative when excellence of character is put into practice, he sees just about nothing to be said for Aristotle's treatment of cases where there is an approximation to the thought that would find expression in virtuous behaviour, but that thought is not realized in action: cases of *akrasia* (incontinence or "weakness of will").[2] In Wiggins's view, this is a missed opportunity for a satisfying completion of the Aristotelian picture; Aristotle is equipped to be aware that we can acknowledge our rationality without playing down the possibly recalcitrant elements in our make-up as rational animals, but here he lapses into a primitive "Socratic" faith in the controlling power of the intellect.

I think this criticism rests on a rare failure of charity. We can find Aristotle's picture of *akrasia* attractive without losing the insights that drive Wiggins's negative estimate of it.

2. When we consider thinking directed at what to do in general, and its expression in behaviour, realism dictates a healthy sense of how human beings

---

1. This essay was written for a Festschrift for David Wiggins.
2. See "Weakness of Will, Commensurability, and the Objects of Deliberation and Desire".

can fail to live up to the results of their practical intelligence. This is where Wiggins begins his discussion of "weakness of will".

The first aim of practical thought is to equip a prospective agent with a focused awareness of which considerations speak rationally for or against the options he contemplates, and with what force. Practical thought may or may not resolve the reasons that come to its notice into a conclusion to the effect that one thing rather than another is, all things considered, the thing to do. But even when practical intelligence cannot effect such a resolution, it aims at a decision to do something that is backed by a reason for doing that.

Now even when practical thought does arrive at a view of how the balance of the reasons points, it is another question whether the agent will act on that verdict. No doubt the very idea of lively awareness that reason speaks in favour of some action would lose its intelligibility if we tried to abstract it away from the idea of a propensity, at least, to be motivationally swayed by that thought. But why should we expect a guarantee that when different motivational propensities are in the offing, associated with reasons that point in different directions, thought's resolution of the competing reasons into a judgment as to where the weight of the reasons lies—if thought manages such a thing—will ensure that a corresponding motivational force beats out all competitors for control of the agent's behaviour? Still less does it seem realistic to expect decision, the product of practical thought, to eliminate the possibility that a competing motivation might control action in the other sort of case, where thought has to settle for a decision to follow one set of rational considerations rather than others without managing an "all things considered" judgment. Thus: even though the very idea of thought directed at action requires more than merely external connection to motivational susceptibilities, it shows a strange confidence in the intellect's capacity to control the life of an intelligent animal—of which much else is true besides that it is intelligent—if someone supposes that the internal connections are perfectly rigid, so that an agent's best judgment as to how the reasons lie, or his decision in the absence of such a judgment to follow one set of reasons rather than another, is sure to reach expression in action.

All this is simply accentuated if there is a temporal gap between decision and action. Considerations that shone vividly for prior thought may lose motivational efficacy when the time comes to put a decision into effect.

It seems common sense, then, to suppose that even the perfect operation of a perfectly tuned practical intelligence is not enough to ensure that action will accord with its results. If an agent is to act in accordance with his own best judgment, or to execute a reasoned decision made in the absence of a best judgment, he needs executive virtues like firmness of will. (That is to be distinguished from pigheadedness in the face of possible grounds for re-thinking one's decision.)

Now consider Aristotle's characterization of *akrasia* in *Nicomachean Ethics* VII.3. As he remarks (1147b13–17), it concedes a great deal to Socrates' re-ported doctrine that there can be no such phenomenon. Aristotle allows for incontinence only where something has gone wrong with the agent's prac-tical thinking. He does not acknowledge cases where the thinking is in good order, but there is a failure of executive excellence between the thinking and the action it endorses. Indeed the opposite condition, continence (*enkrateia*), figures in Aristotle not as an executive virtue that anyone needs, however excellent the disposition and activity of his practical intellect, but, like incontinence, as a falling short of true virtue: that is, a falling short of temperance, for the paradigmatic cases of continence and incontinence. So far from needing what Aristotle discusses under the head of continence, a temperate person does not have the bad appetites that a continent person has to strain to keep unsatisfied (1151b32–1152a3).

Aristotle makes great contributions to our understanding of practical rea-soning. But he does not complete his reflections by explicitly noting the space between thought and action, and the consequent need for executive virtues to ensure that excellent deliberation finds expression in behaviour. This is the ground for Wiggins's disappointment with what Aristotle says about incontinence.

3. In the account of incontinence that figures in the central sections of VII.3 (1174a24–b5), Aristotle seems to be aiming to represent a state of motiva-tional conflict. The conflict lies in the opposition between a practical syllo-gism not acted on, capturing the thought that would be operative in the be-haviour of a temperate person placed as the incontinent person is, and the appetite, embodying a motivationally active thought of pleasure, that is ac-tually operative in the behaviour of the incontinent person (1147a35–b3).

But Wiggins reads the remarks with which Aristotle introduces this pas-sage in such a way that they rule out such conflict; the result is that Aris-totle looks seriously confused. Wiggins finds in the introductory remarks a claim that when the premises of a behaviour-directed syllogism are put to-gether in the mind, the action they enjoin follows of necessity. If this were

Aristotle's view, he would be committed to supposing that, since the action (abstention) that would be characteristic of a temperate person is not forthcoming from a person who displays incontinence, the thought (the practical syllogizing) that would be characteristic of a temperate person cannot be in the person's mind either. The premises can be there, but only separately, not understood together in their rational bearing on what the agent is to do. As Wiggins remarks ("Weakness of Will", p. 250), this would abolish the struggle that Aristotle elsewhere associates with incontinence.

In Wiggins's "translation-cum-paraphrase", the relevant lines (1147a25–8) go like this (pp. 248–9):

> The one premise [the major] is universal, the other premise is concerned with the particular facts, which are the kind of thing to fall within the province of perception. When a single proposition results from the two premises, then [in the case of scientific or deductive reasoning] the soul must of necessity affirm the conclusion; while in the practical sphere it must of necessity act.

But as the brackets signal, the allusion to scientific or deductive reasoning is an importation; and "in the practical sphere" may be a mistranslation.

What Aristotle actually says, in the second sentence here paraphrased, is this:

> When a single opinion results from them, there is a necessity that the soul in one kind of case [or perhaps: at once][3] affirm the conclusion, and, in the case of premises concerned with production, that it immediately act.

Wiggins's reading finds here a contrast between theoretical reasoning, where the result is an affirmation by the soul, and practical reasoning, where the result is an action. But there is no explicit allusion to theoretical reasoning.

---

3. Sir David Ross (*The Nicomachean Ethics of Aristotle*) translates *"entha men"* by "in one type of case", and glosses this as an allusion to scientific reasoning. This matches Wiggins's interpretation. The suggestion that *"entha"* means "at once" is due to Anthony Kenny, in "The Practical Syllogism and Incontinence", and again in *Aristotle's Theory of the Will*, p. 157. It is not crucial to decide between these; contrary to what Kenny implies, we can take the structure, with Ross, to be "in one kind of case . . . in another kind of case . . ." without saddling ourselves with what Kenny wants to avoid, "an irrelevant contrast between theoretical and practical reasoning". On Ross's translation of *"entha"*, everything turns on what the contrast between the two kinds of case is supposed to be; and Aristotle's specification of the second case casts doubt on the Ross/Wiggins gloss on the first (see the text below).

(Indeed, the announced overall topic is reasoning that combines universal and particular premises, and Aristotle's official account of theoretical reasoning does not even accommodate this structure.) Moreover, "in the case of premises concerned with production" (*en de tais poiētikais*, not *praktikais*) is strange wording for practical reasoning in a general sense, behaviour-directed thinking of any kind, set in contrast with theoretical reasoning. This wording might do in an informal and context-free mention of practical as opposed to theoretical thinking. But here, soon after 1139b1–4 and 1140b6–7, it is more naturally taken as a reminder of the contrast, *within the sphere of the practical in a general sense*, between production (*poiēsis*) and action in a strict sense (*praxis*). In that case the passage restricts the claim that action (in the general sense) must ensue to one kind of behaviour-directed thinking, the productive, and allows other cases *of behaviour-directed thinking* where the most that is necessary if the premises are put together is an affirmation.

Thought directed towards production posits an end that is instrumentally remote from anything the agent can do here and now, and seeks a means. It may select among means that are merely practicable, on the basis of ease of achievement and other desiderata (1112b16–17). No doubt practical thinking can solve a problem of this kind without issuing in the action that constitutes the solution. But this can happen only if the agent decides after all not to pursue the posited end. Perhaps he revises his view of its desirability when he realizes what it will cost to achieve it. This decision revokes the major premise of the reasoning, that such-and-such is to be achieved. If, however, the elements of the reasoning stay in place, then the agent's motivational orientation, for purposes of this reasoning, is simply defined by the posited end. In that case, barring phenomena like paralysis or forcible prevention, the completion of a piece of practical thinking of this kind cannot but lead to realization in action. If what happens is under the sway of the agent's motivations at all, it will be controlled by the nisus towards the posited end; if considerations that appeal to some other motivation are allowed any relevance, besides the subordinate one of selecting among different ways of satisfying the primary motivation, that just means that the terms of the agent's practical problem are not as given by the elements of the productive deliberation.[4]

---

4. Admittedly the example Aristotle offers, to illustrate his claim about the case in which action must follow (1147a29–31), is (to say the least) not a clear case of a syllogism of production. But the point of singling out production here is not that the posited

On this reading of what Aristotle means when he says that certain com-
pleted reasonings issue of necessity in action, the remark reflects no general
prejudice about the efficacy of practical intelligence. Aristotle does not
claim, implausibly, that when any behaviour-directed thought is brought to
completion, it necessarily finds realization in action. His thesis simply registers, innocuously, that in deliberation directed to a problem of production,
the very terms in which the predicament is conceived eliminate all motivations other than pursuit of the posited end.

But it is not problems of production that are solved by the intellectual excellence operative in acts of virtue. For this case, all that Aristotle's remark insists on is that if the premises of the syllogism that a virtuous person would act
on are put together in an agent's mind, there must be an affirmation of the
conclusion. This precisely leaves room for the premises to be put together
without issuing in appropriate action. And Aristotle exploits this later in the
central passage of VII.3. In setting out the opposition between the syllogism of
temperance and the incontinently felt appetite, he says (1147a34): "the
former *says* to avoid this, but the appetite drives." Strictly speaking, "the
former" should refer to the universal premise that prevents tasting, mentioned
at 1147a31–2. But a universal premise can "say to avoid *this*" only if what it
says is mediated by a minor premise, directing the universal prohibition at a
particular object. So it is really the whole syllogism that Aristotle must mean to
describe as "saying to avoid this". Contrary to Wiggins's reading, we can see
the point of the introductory remarks as being precisely to make room for syl-
logisms that do such saying (which requires that the premises are present and
put together), but get no further than that towards realization in action.

4. But this reinterpretation at most removes what looks, in Wiggins's picture
of Aristotle, like a blemish of exposition; it does not address the central

---

end is instrumentally, as opposed to specificatorily, remote from what the agent can immediately do; but rather that, if a practical problem is of the productive kind, the agent's
motivational stance, for the problem's purposes, is defined by the posited end. What matters is not the mode of remoteness of the end from the agent's immediate possibilities of
action, but the fact that the major premise can appropriately contain "must", whereas if
a major premise says merely that something is good, we do not need to regard it as re-
voked if the agent ends up pursuing some different good. The point about production is
that productive deliberation, by its mode of focus on an end, defines a deliberative situation in such a way that a "must" is appropriate in the major premise. That *is* exemplified
in Aristotle's illustrative example.

issue. Given this reading, Wiggins is wrong to suppose Aristotle commits himself to a doctrine that practical thought of necessity achieves realization in action, a doctrine that would have the effect of eliminating any possibility of weak *akrasia* (as opposed to the rather uninteresting impetuous variety: 1150b19–22). Still, Aristotle does take it that, if the premises of the syllogism of temperance are put together in the mind of an agent who nevertheless pursues some pleasure that he should not pursue, that calls for special explanation. The drift of VII.3 seems to be that something must have gone wrong with the agent's purchase on the minor premise of virtue's syllogism, so that although the agent in a way sees things as a temperate person would, the match between the relevant part of his practical thought and that of a temperate person is imperfect. If the match in thought were perfect, there would also be a match in behaviour. We need not saddle Aristotle with a doctrine that would commit him to concluding, from the failure of match in behaviour, that the premises of the syllogism of temperance can be present only in blank separation from one another, so that there is no room even for an approximation to a match in respect of the practical conclusion that a temperate person would draw. But Aristotle still implies that in cases of weakness there can be at most an approximation to such a match; and in Wiggins's view this is evidently an insufficient acknowledgment of the possibilities of failure to put thought into practice:

> [T]he *Nicomachean Ethics* . . . describes, elucidates, and amplifies the actual concerns of human life, and makes transparent to theory the way in which these concerns necessitate, where they do necessitate, the actions or decisions in which they issue. Those who find that this is enough in practice to retain their interest in the subject will discover that they can drop Aristotle's doctrine of the akrates' ignorance of the minor premise . . . ("Weakness of Will", p. 261.)

"Ignorance of the minor premise" may need to be nuanced, if we are to avoid all risk of overstating what Aristotle envisages. (Aristotle indeed speaks of ignorance, for instance at 1147b6, but it is clear that he is straining to avoid alleging an outright failure of grasp.) But no toning down, so long as it leaves in place the basic idea that there is some breakdown in the incontinent person's practical thinking, will help to meet Wiggins's point. Wiggins thinks Aristotle ought to have allowed that even perfectly executed practical thinking may need executive virtues if it is to show itself in action; the thought alone does not suffice. In that case it cannot be correct to infer a defectiveness in thinking (whether we call it "ignorance" or not) from a defectiveness in behaviour.

I think it is quite wrong to object to Aristotle on these grounds, and the materials for seeing that it is wrong are all in Wiggins's paper.

5. The essential thing is to realize that Aristotle's aim in connection with *akrasia* is to characterize a person whose practical thought comes as close as possible, consistently with a failure of action, to matching the practical thought, not of a possessor of just any kind of practically oriented intellectual excellence, but specifically of a person who has "practical wisdom" *(phronēsis)*. Aristotle's conception of the relations between practical wisdom, continence, and incontinence reflects a deeply attractive view of the efficacy of a quite specific kind of practical thinking, when present in its perfect or ideal form. There is no implication that practical deliberation generally, regardless of its type, flows smoothly into action without any need for executive virtues: that is, no unrealistic conviction of the power of practical thought in general to eliminate recalcitrant motivations and control action. This undercuts the basis for Wiggins's disappointment.

Practical wisdom is the intellectual excellence that is operative in the behaviour of a fully-fledged possessor of virtue of character, a possessor of virtue of character in the strict sense (see VI.13). It is a correct conception of the end of human action (1142b31–3). Aristotle does not believe that such a conception can be spelled out in general rules of conduct (1094b11–27, 1109b12–23). We cannot encapsulate the content of practical wisdom in a general formula that could be abstracted away from the concrete details of life. A correct conception of the end is accordingly inseparable from a kind of perception (1142a23–30, 1143a5–b5), which Wiggins helpfully glosses as "situational appreciation":[5] a capacity to discern which of the potentially action-inviting features of a situation is the one that should be allowed to call into operation one of the standing concerns whose being put into practice on the appropriate occasions constitutes living out a correct conception of the sort of life a human being should live.

Now consider a situation that calls for the most striking sort of exercise of temperance, namely abstaining from an available but excessive bodily plea-

---

5. See "Deliberation and Practical Reason", at p. 231. My sketch of how practical wisdom should be conceived closely follows that beautiful essay; I want to bring out how easily it can be separated from what Wiggins takes to be its natural continuation, his negative evaluation of Aristotle's treatment of *akrasia*.

sure. That the pleasure is available is within the awareness of a temperate person no less than anyone else. And facts of that shape, that there is an opportunity for pleasure, can engage a motivational susceptibility that is one of the standing concerns of a virtuous person. (Too little interest in the pleasures of appetite is a defect of character: see *NE* III.11.) But on this occasion what matters about the situation, as the practically wise person correctly sees it, is not that the pleasure is there to be had, but whatever it is that marks out this potential pleasure as excessive.

By separating temperance from continence as he does, Aristotle implies a picture on these lines: on an occasion like this, what is characteristic of a practically wise person, which a possessor of temperance in the strict sense must be, is not simply that he counts as irrelevant to the question what to do an instance of a kind of consideration (the potential for pleasure) that is relevant to that question in other circumstances, but that his counting it as irrelevant is completely realized in how his motivational make-up responds to the situation. It shows in his feeling no appetitive pull towards the potential pleasure. So he stands in sharp contrast with people who are continent or (weakly) incontinent. Such people in such a situation would in a way share the practically wise person's view of the status of the opportunity for pleasure as a candidate reason for acting, namely that it counts for nothing in the face of the fact that the pleasure is excessive. But in them the opportunity for pleasure would trigger an appetite, which would need to be overcome to yield continent behaviour, and would issue in incontinent behaviour if not overcome. Fully-fledged practical wisdom is a "situational appreciation" that not only singles out just the right one of the potentially action-inviting features of a predicament, but does so in such a way that none of the agent's motivational energy is enticed into operation by any of the others; he has no errant impulses that threaten to lead him astray, so that he would be at best continent even if he managed to avoid being led astray. His "situational appreciation" is such as to insulate the attractions of competing courses of action from generating actual urges to pursue them.

This picture simply requires the thesis that a person who is continent or incontinent can achieve at most an imperfect approximation to the "situational appreciation" of a person who is temperate in the strict sense, in a situation where temperance requires refraining from an opportunity for pleasure. The picture is that full achievement of that "situational appreciation" would prevent the attractions of competing courses from actually exerting any motivational force. If the attractions of competing courses do exert a motivational force, as they do in cases of incontinence or continence, it follows that the "situational appreciation" that is characteristic of fully-fledged practical wisdom cannot have been fully achieved. The most we can find in such cases is something less: something that yields a similar selection of what matters about the situation, but without the singleness of motivation that fully-fledged practical wisdom would achieve.

There need be no implication that the attractiveness of the competing course goes dim, in the view of the situation that the practically wise person achieves. The pleasure is there to be had, by the practically wise person no less than by anyone else.[6] He can be completely aware of the attractiveness of the competing course; it is just that he is not attracted by it.

If the course that is not to be followed retains its attractiveness, there is nothing surprising in the fact that ordinarily "good" people are liable to feel an appetitive attraction towards it, so that their action will be continent at best. This is especially unsurprising in the young; there must be stages in ethical upbringing at which it is too soon to hope that a correct conception of how to live can have been perfectly ingrained into someone's motivational make-up, in the way that is characteristic of fully-fledged practical wisdom.

The picture leaves this kind of lapse looking only natural. No thesis of Aristotle's clashes with a common-sense recognition that most people do not achieve the singleness of motivational focus that figures in his picture of the

---

6. At 1151b 34–1152a2–3, Aristotle says: "Both the continent person and the temperate person are such as to do nothing contrary to the *logos* on account of bodily pleasures, but one of them has and the other does not have bad appetites, and the latter is such as not to be pleased contrary to the *logos*, whereas the former is such as to be pleased but not such as to be led." The last clause restates the claim that the temperate person, unlike the continent person, lacks the bad appetites that respond to opportunities for pleasure that are not to be pursued. He lacks any active motivation that would be gratified by pursuing such a pleasure, so there is nothing to make it true that he would take pleasure in that action. But this is surely consistent with supposing that the physical pleasures of such action are there to be had, for him as much as for anyone. It seems ridiculous to suppose that a temperate person is such as simply not to feel the physical pleasures of, say, illicit sex. There is a difficulty about imagining him engaging in such activity, and that is a way of putting Aristotle's point here. But if we contrive to imagine that, what we contemplate is a possible world in which he feels those pleasures, though no doubt he is not pleased to be doing so. David Pears offers a different reading of this passage, in "Aristotle's Analysis of Courage", at p. 276, and in "Courage as a Mean", at p. 173; but Pears's reading is based on a gratuitously assumed connection between potential feelings of physical pleasure and awareness of opportunities for physical pleasure, on the one hand, and felt appetites, on the other.

ideal. What he insists is that where such singleness of motivational focus is not achieved, there cannot be a perfect cognitive match with the ideal case. But this leaves plenty of room for approximations to the ideal, falling short of the unobstructed transition to action that the ideal would guarantee: cases in which the undimmed attractiveness of the course that, with his approximation to practical wisdom, the agent sees is not to be followed generates a felt temptation to follow it. Aristotle's picture leaves plenty of room for cases where continence might figure, not exactly as an executive *virtue*, but as an executive disposition that is required if the agent is to act as, in a way, he realizes he should: this realization being, from the terms of the case, less perfectly meshed with his motivational susceptibilities than in the ideal case.

6. Wiggins appreciates the beauty of this conception of practical wisdom. As he puts it, someone who fully appreciated the end that practical wisdom has in view would find the associated reasons for acting *"distinctively compelling"* ("Weakness of Will", p. 254). It would be impossible to make sense of someone's fully possessing a practical understanding so conceived, and grasping what it dictates in a particular situation, but nevertheless allowing himself to be moved by the attractiveness of some different course of action.

But this special compellingness figures in Wiggins's treatment of Aristotle only by way of diagnosis of a supposed failure on Aristotle's part to leave *any* room for gaps between fully achieved results of practical thinking and action in accordance with those results. Wiggins's Aristotle extrapolates from the distinctive compellingness of the considerations that appeal to practical wisdom in particular, to the idea that *any* fully achieved conclusion of practical thought must flow smoothly into action without any need for executive virtues.

But there is no need to saddle Aristotle with this extrapolation. Aristotle's point about *akrasia* need not be anything over and above a corollary of the fact that he credits the conclusions of practical wisdom, in particular, with that distinctive compellingness. This leaves him no option but to suppose that if someone in a way achieves one of those conclusions but does not act accordingly, what he achieves can be at most a flawed approximation to the conclusion. But that implies nothing to the detriment of the picture that Wiggins gives, and supposes that Aristotle is committed to rejecting, of the gaps between practical thought *in general* and action. Aristotle does not botch the general case, as opposed to the special case of practical wisdom, as Wiggins suggests. The general case is simply off-stage as far as Aristotle is concerned; his interest is in the special case, and there is no particular reason for him to bother with the general case at all.

In "Deliberation and Practical Reason", Wiggins extracts a convincing picture of practical reason in general, at least outside its merely technical employment, from things Aristotle says about the operation of practical wisdom. Here extrapolation to the general case yields treasure. But that should not make us forget that it is extrapolation. Aristotle's chief concern, at least in the *Ethics*, is—as is appropriate there—with the deliberation that is characteristic of practical wisdom; he is interested in other manifestations of behaviour-directed intelligence only in order to differentiate them from practical wisdom, or perhaps, in the case of technical deliberation, in order to get as much as he can out of modelling the operations of practical wisdom on it. We are bound to do him an injustice if we forget the restrictedness of his topic, and read his insistence, *for that special case*, that failures in action must betray flaws in thought to imply a denial that there is a role in the explanation of action for anything besides the way the agent thinks—a denial of any role for factors like firmness of resolve, in an account of how practical thought in general flows into action.

That is just how Wiggins reads Aristotle. This shows when he writes ("Weakness of Will", p. 251) of "the distinction that Aristotle is obliged to postulate between the continent man's and the incontinent man's knowledge and perception of a situation". Reasonably enough, Wiggins is sceptical of such a distinction: "How . . . can it be maintained, even in the face of all the phenomenological findings, that the continent and incontinent man see different things, or must see things differently?" But the supposed obligation to postulate this difference is a product of not allowing Aristotle his restricted topic. From Aristotle's insistence, *for the special case of practical wisdom*, that a clear seeing of a situation in the light in which practical wisdom casts it leaves no room for defective action, Wiggins has inferred a doctrine that the quality of an agent's vision is *always* a complete explanation of how he acts. Thus, since a continent person and an incontinent person act differently, there must be a difference in how they see things. But there is no such doctrine, and no obligation to invent a cognitive difference between the continent and the incontinent person. The only cognitive difference that Aristotle is obliged to postulate is a difference between, on the one hand, a possessor of practical wisdom and, on the other, indifferently, a continent or an incontinent person, who are alike shown not to see things exactly as the practically wise person does by the fact that they feel an appetitive pull towards action other than what, as they in a way realize, virtue requires. Once we have in view the lapse in vision that allows conflicting motivations to be felt, so that the best that can be achieved is continence, it is quite another matter, on which Aristotle leaves his options open, what determines whether the agent acts continently or incontinently.

7. The end of human action, of which practical wisdom is a correct conception, is what Aristotle also refers to as "the good and the chief good" (1094a22) and identifies, in Book I of *Nicomachean Ethics*, with *eudaimonia*: that is, living well and doing well (1095a14–20). Modern commentators often suppose that Aristotle conceives this end of living well in terms of the optimal combination of a bundle of intrinsic goods, marked out as such by their natural appeal to human beings. This style of reading is partly sustained by Aristotle's claim that *eudaimonia* is self-sufficient (1097b6–20), in the sense that "on its own it makes life worthy of going in for and lacking in nothing" (1097b14–15); this is read as saying that nothing that human beings are naturally disposed to find worth pursuing can be missing from a life of *eudaimonia*. It is also partly sustained by a wish to equip Aristotle with a way to establish the pursuit-worthiness of a life of virtue from first principles, by claiming that it optimally secures what human beings are anyway bound to regard as worth securing, without any need for this justification of virtue to exploit the tendencies to delight in virtuous activity as such that the members of Aristotle's audience have acquired in their ethical education (see 1104b3–13, 1095b4–6).

On this sort of reading, the thesis that *eudaimonia* is self-sufficient would risk making it especially difficult to understand how someone could act contrary to what he sees that *eudaimonia* requires, in order to enjoy physical pleasure. This would be to pursue something that would have to be an element in the bundle of goods that is supposedly all that can make life worth living at all, but at the known expense of a better arrangement of that very bundle of goods. The conception of practical reason that is operative here risks looking like a less crude version of the conception that, in the closing pages of Plato's *Protagoras*, serves to obliterate the very possibility of acting contrary to knowledge of how the reasons for acting lie.

But we should not take the claim of self-sufficiency like this. No doubt the valuations of actions that are characteristic of the propensity to delight in virtuous activity for its own sake cannot simply cut loose from dispositions to find things worth pursuing that human beings have anyway, independently of ethical upbringing. That would make a mystery of how ethical upbringing, whose prospects must be conditioned by the prior nature of its recipients, can impart such a scheme of values. But it does not follow that the scheme of values that is characteristic of delighting in virtuous activity for its own sake must be a construct out of the idea of an optimal combination of goods that naturally appeal to human beings as such, so that the genuine pursuit-worthiness of such activity can be defended as conducive to the best arrangement of those goods. These acquired values can have a sort of autonomy with respect to what naturally appeals to human beings. And the claim that *eudaimonia* is self-sufficient can be read in terms of standards for pursuit-worthiness set by these acquired values. So, as Wiggins puts it ("Weakness of Will", p. 260):

> In the definition of self-sufficiency, we need not take "lacking in nothing" to mean "lacking in nothing at all that would be found valuable by anybody pursuing whatever course", only "lacking in nothing that a man who had chosen the great good of eudaimonia would regard as worth bothering with".

This takes us completely away from the idea that the attractiveness of the course that the incontinent person pursues is merely an inferior quantity of some single kind of attractiveness, of which the virtuous action possesses a superior quantity. It allows us to see that the incontinent person can be tempted by a "peculiar or distinctive charm" in the course he follows: something that cannot be regarded as merely a smaller amount of the very same kind of worthwhileness that he denies himself when he declines the virtuous action. This rejection of what Wiggins calls "the principle of compensation in kind" (pp. 259–60) is essential if we are to make room for a common-sense picture of incontinence, a picture that is immune to the difficulties concocted in the *Protagoras* passage.[7]

---

7. Wiggins suggests ("Weakness of Will", p. 260) that Aristotle may have "some occasional slight tendency to believe something rather like the principle of compensation in kind". But this is gratuitous. Nothing like the principle is needed in order to make sense of Aristotle's taking the line he does about incontinence. The Aristotelian thesis (see for instance *De Anima* 433b8–10) that "even the purely pleasurable appears to us under the aspect of good", which Wiggins cites as perhaps resting on the principle, simply says, rightly, that pleasurableness appears as a reason for acting, something to be said in favour of courses of action that promise it. The idea of apparent goods no more implies the sort of homogeneity that the principle affirms than does the idea of reasons for acting.

But this leaves untouched the thesis that incontinence is possible only on the basis of a flawed approximation to the view of a situation that practical wisdom would achieve. What dictates that thesis is the distinctive compellingness of the verdicts of practical wisdom; the argument needs no help from the principle of compensation in kind. Wiggins suggests that when we see our way past the difficulties that the *Protagoras* passage extracts from an unrealistically monolithic conception of reasons for acting, we thereby see how we can "drop Aristotle's doctrine of the akrates' ignorance of the minor premise" (p. 261, already quoted above). But if we allow Aristotle the restricted scope of his doctrine, this rebuke stands revealed as misplaced.

8. Wiggins is admirably hostile towards pictures of practical reasoning in terms of weighing quantities of a homogeneously conceived worthwhileness. But I think he understates the distance between this sort of thing and Aristotle's conception of deliberation with a view to *eudaimonia*. He takes Aristotle to hold that "wherever a man has to act, he can subsume the question at issue under the question of eudaimonia and discern which course of action is better from that point of view" ("Weakness of Will", p. 258). He bases this on *De Anima* 434a5–10, which he paraphrases like this:

> Sensory imagination is found in other animals but deliberative imagination only in those which have reason. For whether one shall do this thing or do that thing it is the work of reason to decide. And such reason necessarily implies the power of measurement by a single standard. For what one pursues is the greater good. So a rational animal is one with the power to arbitrate between diverse appearances of what is good and integrate the findings into a unitary practical conception.

But there are two things wrong with this as a basis for the attribution.

First, the passage does not say that a rational animal can *always* integrate its conceptions of the apparent good, in a given situation, into a unified practical verdict, but just that rational animals can do that (perhaps only in some cases), whereas non-rational animals cannot. The passage is consistent with supposing that some situations may defeat the integrative efforts of practical reason. This is a good thing. As Wiggins reads him, Aristotle would here be casting doubt on the very possibility of tragic predicaments.

Second, the passage does not mention *eudaimonia*, and I doubt that that is its topic. This passage is about practical rationality in general, and I have already suggested that we should distance that from the kind of susceptibility to reasons that is characteristic of practical wisdom in particular. When a situation calling for temperance is seen in terms of doing well, the agent's decision what to do does not supervene on a judgment that sets one apparent good, seen as greater, against another, seen as smaller. The pleasure promised by the course that the agent realizes is not to be pursued is recognized, indeed, as an instance of something that is in general a good. But the prospect of pleasure is not taken to be, here and now, a good, on the dimension of goodness marked out by the idea of *eudaimonia*, but a smaller one than the virtuous action; it is not taken to tell in favour of pursuing the pleasure, by the lights of *eudaimonia*, but more weakly than the reasons for abstention. Rather, by the lights of *eudaimonia*, the prospect of pleasure does not speak at all in favour of pursuing it in these circumstances.

If we conceive the correct practical verdict, on which the incontinent person fails to act, as based on allowing the apparent good constituted by the promise of pleasure to tell in favour of pursuing the pleasure, but not as strongly as the considerations that speak in favour of abstention, we make it harder to comprehend incontinence. On this picture, the attractiveness of the promised pleasure is allowed to count towards the agent's practical judgment; it is simply outweighed. On the different picture I am urging, that attractiveness is not conceded any relevance to the question what to do, and it becomes easier to understand how, denied any bearing on the question of reason, it should insist on making itself felt by triggering an appetite.

9. As I have remarked, Aristotle notes a convergence between the view of incontinence that he is led to and the view that Socrates took (1147b14–15). This convergence encapsulates Wiggins's complaint ("Weakness of Will", p. 251): "When what I might almost venture to call a more Aristotelian account than Aristotle's promises to be possible . . . , why did Aristotle give such a Socratic account of the phenomena of weakness?" Calling Aristotle's account "Socratic" means that it is too optimistic about the power of practical thought to unify motivational direction, and about the control of practical thought over what people do.

I have urged, however, that Aristotle's concern in his discussion of *akrasia* is exclusively with a special kind of action-directed thought, whose perfect operation Aristotle has good reasons for associating with a perfection of moulded character that leaves no room for the agent to be pulled by conflicting motivations. There is no slighting the way reasons for acting, in general, can resist resolution by thought into an overall verdict as to how one should act, and no slighting the way motivational propensities can resist control by thought. Even when *eudaimonia* fixes the nature of the practical attention that an agent directs at a situation, there is no assurance that his practical thinking can resolve the relevant considerations into an overall verdict: no assurance that an action is available that will count as doing well (*eu prattein*, that is, *eudaimonein*). And even where a correct conception of *eudaimonia* does yield a clear identification of one action as doing well, Aristotle allows for cases where an agent approximates to such thinking without acting accordingly. There is no naive intellectualism here.

This raises the question whether we can exploit the coincidence with Socrates the other way round, to begin on a rehabilitation of Socrates from the common charge of unrealistic intellectualism.

It is at worst a salutary exaggeration to say that all we really *know* about Socrates—apart perhaps from something about his method—is that he propounded the famous puzzling theses: that virtue is knowledge, that no one does wrong "voluntarily", and that virtue is one. Our best sources, the early dialogues of Plato, do not lay down slabs of moral theory; they come across, rather, as undoctrinaire explorations of those evidently dark sayings, and of obviously cognate issues such as whether and how virtue can be taught, and in what sense one has a reason for right conduct.

Many modern commentators have counted the closing argument of the *Protagoras* as authentically Socratic, not on the basis of any compelling textual ground, but rather because it fits a philosophical reconstruction: this is supposed to be the sort of thing Socrates *must* have thought if he was to connect knowledge with virtuous action as he seems to have done. The result is to saddle Socrates with a pitifully unrealistic picture of the connection between reason and motivation.[8] But if I am right about Aristotle, who notes his own convergence with Socrates, there is no "must" about it.

In that case, what is going on in the *Protagoras* argument?

The apparently Socratic idea that virtue is a kind of knowledge that ensures living well can be interpreted in two contrasting ways. The first we

8. In Terence Irwin's version (*Plato's Moral Theory*), the picture purports to depict human beings as they are. In Martha C. Nussbaum's variant (*The Fragility of Goodness*), the picture depicts how human beings should aim to be, in order to allow reason a prospect of carrying them safely through life. Nussbaum's Socrates is not blind to plain facts as Irwin's Socrates is, but just as unrealistic, though in a different way. Both versions leave Aristotle's "Socraticism" quite mysterious.

can associate with the sophists (at least as Plato pictures them). According to this interpretation, the advantages that virtue brings are recognizable as such independently of the special propensities to value and disvalue courses of conduct that are acquired in ethical upbringing, so that a claim to be able to teach virtue holds out a promise of something that anyone, whether virtuous or not, will count as living well. The second is the one that I believe we should associate with Socrates. According to this interpretation, the attractions of a virtuous life are real, but recognizable only from within a commitment to that life. What we find in the *Protagoras* is a version of the first of these. At the end of the dialogue, Socrates suggests that he and Protagoras have changed places; we can take this to tell us, almost in so many words, that the position propounded in the closing argument is not the authentic Socratic view, but a sophistic travesty of it.[9]

Perhaps what Aristotle does in his discussion of practical wisdom and its expression in action is simply to recapture what Socrates was really driving at. If I am right about Aristotle, this can liberate Socratic moral psychology from the strange want of realism that much recent commentary has found in it.

9. This undercuts Gregory Vlastos's suggestion (*Plato's Protagoras*, p. xl; cited by Nussbaum, op. cit., p. 451) that the argument is likely to be authentically Socratic, since it argues to a Socratic conclusion. It is questionable whether the conclusion is Socratic, even though the words that express it can also express a Socratic thought.

PART II

Issues in Wittgenstein

Are Meaning, Understanding, etc., Definite States?

1. In his essay "Wittgenstein on Understanding", Warren Goldfarb writes: "Wittgenstein's treatments in the *Philosophical Investigations* of the cognitive or intentional mental notions are evidently meant to persuade us that, in some sense, understanding, believing, remembering, thinking, and the like are not particular or definite states or processes; or (if this is to say anything different) that there are no particular states or processes that constitute the understanding, remembering, etc."[1]

To be fair to Goldfarb, I should stress how he hedges the thought he attributes to Wittgenstein with "in some sense". And he immediately goes on to say: "Such a dark point desperately needs clarification, if it is not to deny the undeniable. For surely we may (and Wittgenstein does) speak of a *state* of understanding, or of thought-*processes*; surely when one understands—understands a word, a sentence, or the principle of a series—one is in a particular state, namely, the state of understanding the word, sentence, or principle."

But that is the only appearance of such admittedly undeniable points in Goldfarb's essay. He devotes the rest of it to elaborating how he reads the passages in which Wittgenstein discourages us from thinking in terms of definite or particular states and processes. The acknowledged sense in which Wittgenstein had better have nothing against such talk gets no further attention.

In this essay I want to try to redress the balance somewhat. I think we can learn something from Wittgenstein about how to picture understanding and so forth as definite or particular states without having the picture reflect a confusion.

---

1. This quotation and the next are from p. 109.

But first (in §§ 2, 3, and 4), I shall say something about the strand in Wittgenstein that Goldfarb focuses on, which deals with a way of being confused by such a picture.

2. There are certainly passages in *Philosophical Investigations*[2] that point in the direction Goldfarb indicates. Perhaps most explicitly, at §154 Wittgenstein says: "Try not to think of understanding as a 'mental process' at all.—For *that* is the expression that confuses you."

Why is it thinking of understanding as a "mental process" (or perhaps "occurrence" [*Vorgang*]), rather than as a "mental state", that Wittgenstein discourages here? In this region of the text, he is considering exclamations like "Now I know (how to go on)!" or "Now I understand!" (§151). Here understanding is apparently "something that makes its appearance in a moment" (ibid.). One grasps the meaning of a word "in a flash" (§138). It is these onsets of understanding at definite moments that, at §154, Wittgenstein is advising us to try not to conceive as mental occurrences. But the advice naturally carries over to states; its counterpart would be advising us to try not to think of what sets in at those moments as mental states.

In the context of this passage, Wittgenstein is considering a temptation to conceive, say, understanding a number series, or knowing its principle, as "a state of a mental apparatus (perhaps of the brain) by means of which we explain the *manifestations* of that knowledge" (§149: here the thought is applied to knowing the ABC).[3] This figures as a gloss one is tempted to put on this thought: "To have got the system (or again, to understand it) can't consist in continuing the series up to *this* or *that* number: *that* is only applying one's understanding. The understanding itself is a state which is the *source* of the correct use" (§146).

About this idea Wittgenstein remarks (still in §146): "What is one thinking of here? Isn't one thinking of the derivation of a series from its al-

2. Citations henceforth will be from this work unless otherwise indicated.

3. If knowing the ABC is as good an example for the point Wittgenstein wants to make as the examples involving number series, we can conclude that the point is not, as commentators sometimes make it seem, essentially connected with the fact that there is no application for the idea of getting to the end of extending a number series. There *is* such a thing as getting to the end of reciting the ABC. Wittgenstein's point is not about infinity. It is about the relation between knowing the ABC, or understanding the principle of a number series, on the one hand, and the actions one performs in reciting the ABC, or extending the number series, on the other.

gebraic formula? Or at least of something analogous?—But this is where we were before. The point is, we can think of more than *one* application of an algebraic formula; and every type of application can in turn be formulated algebraically; but naturally this does not get us any further.—The application is still a criterion of understanding."

The suggestion is that when one thinks of the understanding of a number series as a state from which the correct use flows, one is picturing the state as an embodiment (or perhaps we should say "enmindment") of an algebraic formula. Considered as a mere piece of notation, a formula "stands there like a sign-post" (§85)—that is, like a thing that is in fact a sign-post, but considered in abstraction from what it means in people's use of it, in abstraction from its pointing the way: perhaps considered merely as a board of a certain configuration fixed on a post. Like a sign-post so considered, a formula so considered is normatively inert. These items do not themselves sort behaviour into what accords with them—writing down the right numbers in the right order, going in the direction the sign-post points in—and what does not. Suppose, now, that one tries to conceive understanding the series as an embodiment of a formula in some suitable medium ("perhaps . . . the brain"). Given the normative inertness of the formula itself, that ensures that over and above the state one is picturing, there would need to be something that selects a specific interpretation of the formula that the state embodies, from among several that it is capable of bearing ("we can think of more than *one* application of an algebraic formula"), if we are to have in view something in the light of which what the person whose state it is does, purportedly extending the series, is correct or incorrect. An embodiment of a formula, conceived on these lines, could not contain within itself resources to determine which numbers it is correct to write down if one is to extend the series of whose principle the state is supposed to constitute an understanding. This is made vivid, in our context, by Wittgenstein's remark that the criterion for the presence of the pictured apparatus ought to be "a knowledge of the construction of the apparatus, quite apart from what it does" (§149). If we conceive the pictured state like this, it cannot be the state itself—what was supposed to be the person's understanding of the series—in the light of which the numbers the person writes down are correct or not.

3. There is already enough here to indicate that something is going wrong. The state we are picturing does not stand to the performances we want to

be able to see as manifestations of the person's understanding in the relation in which the person's understanding would need to stand to those performances—the relation of being something they accord with, or not if there is mistake, deception, or whatever.[4] If we are to conceive understanding the principle of a series as a state, it should be the state itself, not the state reinforced with one from among many possible interpretations of the formula it embodies, in the light of which the performances are assessed as correct or not. But this does not exhaust the trouble we fall into if we try to conceive understanding on the lines Wittgenstein is considering.

The idea of following a rule or acting on a principle, for instance the principle of a series, can be spelled out in terms of the idea that what one does *accords* with the rule or principle. If we fall into supposing that this concept of accord can be in play only thanks to an appeal to the concept of interpretation, we put pressure on the very idea of following a rule or acting on an understanding. (This is now familiar in discussions of Wittgenstein, though I think the significance of his moves in this area is still often not properly appreciated.) We start with, say, a statement of a rule—perhaps an algebraic formula, giving the rule for extending a number series—and we suppose that someone could follow the rule, act on an understanding of what it requires, only by putting an interpretation on the statement of it. But if the original statement of the rule and behaviour aimed at conforming to the rule's requirements are related only across a gap, which would seem to need to be bridged by an interpretation, then exactly the same goes for the interpretation that we hoped would bridge the gap. It can only be another statement, or at any rate another expression, of the rule. It is as much in need of interpretation, before the idea of acting in accord with the rule can have determinate content, as the original

---

4. Goldfarb resists making much of this kind of point—that the pictured state does not have "the 'grammar' of understanding" (p. 110)—on the basis that it would involve attributing to Wittgenstein an "essentialism" that is out of line with the hostility to "a priorism" expressed in passages like §131. I think this resistance is excessive. Wittgenstein's unmasking of a certain sort of preconception about how things *must* be does not carry over to such thoughts as that understanding, say, the series of even numbers is (must be, if you like) something in the light of which only writing "1000" when one gets to "996, 998, . . ." would be correct; so no state of which that was not true could be a person's understanding of the series. But there is certainly more than this to be said against the picture that Wittgenstein is starting to discuss in passages like §146.

statement of the rule was.[5] This is obviously the beginning of a regress. If we cannot find anything wrong with the assumptions that lead us into the regress, we shall be deprived of the very idea of behaviour that accords or not with a rule, or a principle, or an understanding. And that means we shall be deprived of the very idea of a determinate understanding. (See, of course, §201.)

Now it is natural to respond to this threat by saying that that in the light of which one's behaviour, in, say, extending a number series, is correct or incorrect is of course not, for instance, a formula, considered as a mere piece of notation, but the *meaning* of the formula, or perhaps *the formula as one understands it*. And there must be a way of taking this response in which it is correct and innocuous.

But there is a risk of being tempted to conceive the *meaning* of the formula, as it figures in this response, as an item of the same character as the interpretations that succeed one another when one embarks on the regress—"one interpretation after another, as if each one contented us at least for a moment, until we thought of yet another standing behind it" (§201)—except that it is somehow not itself susceptible to interpretation. Ordinary interpretations, on reflection, turned out to be themselves susceptible of being interpreted otherwise than as determining the right series. That was what seemed to require another interpretation behind each one we might offer. And that was what ensured that on these lines we can never reach a genuine determination of how the series is to be continued. Each successive interpretation can still be interpreted askew, and moving to another interpretation is just moving to another case of the same predicament. The temptation now is to conceive the *meaning* of the formula as something that allows us to take the first step, but relieves us of the need to take any further steps, in this threatened regress. This conception of meaning as just like an ordinary interpretation, except that it is somehow not itself susceptible to interpretation, is expressed by Wittgenstein in the *Blue Book* in this passage (p. 34):

> What one wants to say is: "Every sign is capable of interpretation, but the *meaning* mustn't be capable of interpretation. It is the last interpretation."

5. In the course of the pivotal §201, Wittgenstein notes that "there is an inclination to say: every action according to the rule is an interpretation". (So there is no gap; the "interpretation" is already on the far side of what threatened to be a gap.) He responds: "But we ought to restrict the term 'interpretation' to the substitution of one expression of the rule for another."

I said "*somehow* not itself susceptible to interpretation". "Somehow" sounds a note of mysteriousness, and that is in a way the point. On this conception, a formula's meaning, or perhaps a person's understanding of the formula or of the principle of a series, is an interpretation that terminates the regress. This converts an idea we ought to be able to take in our stride—the idea of writing down, say, numbers in a way that is in accord with an understanding of the principle of a series—into an idea that incorporates a mystery. We have gone through the motions of giving ourselves a regress-proof conception of acting on an understanding. But really all we have equipped ourselves with is a quasi-magical conception of how the understanding determines what we are to do in acting on it. We have replaced the idea of an embodiment (or enmindment) of, say, an algebraic formula with the idea of an embodiment (or enmindment) of something just like a formula except that, unlike an ordinary formula, it mysteriously cannot be interpreted otherwise than as requiring just the right numbers at all points in the extension of the series.

The idea of an embodiment of a formula yielded a picture of an arrangement in a mental apparatus. The trouble was that such an arrangement could no more be something in the light of which performances of writing down numbers are correct and incorrect than a bit of mere algebraic notation, considered in abstraction from its employment in mathematical practice, could be. The criterion for the presence on a page of a bit of mere algebraic notation is independent of what it would be correct to do if one were told to extend a series in accordance with the principle it expresses. Just so, the criterion for the presence of a state conceived in the corresponding way is "the construction of the apparatus, quite apart from what it does" (§149, quoted earlier); the presence of the state would be independent of what it would be correct to do in order to act on the understanding that the state is supposed to be. The relation of such a state to the performances that issue from it could be at best brutely causal.

Now when we conceive meaning as the last interpretation, we replace the idea of an embodiment of a mere bit of notation with the idea of something conceived as just like an embodiment of a bit of notation, except that performances of writing down numbers flow from it in a way that is somehow bound up with its setting determinate standards for which numbers it is correct to write down. So we picture a criterion that still relates to the construction of the apparatus, but mysteriously contrives to incorporate standards for correctness and incorrectness in performances. This is a way into picturing what one acquires, when one grasps a sense, as something that "determines the future use" not causally, at any rate not by way of any ordinary causation, but in a quasi-magical way—as something in which "in a *queer* way, the use itself is in some sense present" (§195).

This brings out how the confusions Wittgenstein considers in this context, in connection with following a rule or acting in the light of an understanding, lead naturally into a version of the idea that phenomena of meaning and understanding involve states and happenings in the mind, with the mind conceived as "a queer kind of medium" (*Blue Book*, p. 3). This conception of the mind as the mysterious seat or origin of meaningfulness is encouraged in a general way by the thought that words or other signs, considered in themselves, are mere "dead" sounds or marks (see *Blue Book*, ibid.). Breathing life into otherwise dead signs is pictured as an occult feat, of which only something as special as the mind could be capable. (See §454, on the question how it is that a schematic arrow points in a certain direction. Wittgenstein captures a superstitious conception of what makes it the case that the arrow points with the words "a hocus-pocus which can be performed only by the soul".)[6]

What we now have before us is a particular version of this picture. It is not just that meaningful signs are conceived as infused with life by motions in the mind, but also that successive performances in the course of, say, extending a number series reflect a quasi-magical efficacy exerted by a configuration in the same mysterious medium. The occult medium of the mind is pictured as the locus of configurations from which performances that manifest understanding flow, in a way that is like the way events flow from states of regular mechanisms or bits of apparatus except that this machinery is mysteriously capable of placing its output in the normative light constituted by the output's being correct or incorrect in the light of the configuration from which it flows.

Near the start of these reflections of Wittgenstein's, the conception he is concerned with shows up in the guise of an idea of "a state of a mental apparatus (perhaps of the brain)" (§149, quoted earlier). We can now see that that can be at best a provisional attempt at expressing the conception. Once it is clear that nothing but a configuration in an occult medium could seem

---

6. On the temptation to conceive the mind as the origin of meaningfulness and so as a "queer" or "occult" medium, see the opening pages of Barry Stroud, "Mind, Meaning, and Practice", and also his "Wittgenstein on Meaning, Understanding, and Community".

to meet the requirements we are tempted to place on a state of understanding, the idea that the brain might serve as the locus of the required configurations must surely emerge as unsatisfactory. The brain is no doubt very remarkable, but not in a way that amounts to its being capable of quasi-magical feats ("hocus-pocus").[7]

Goldfarb's main focus is on what he calls "the scientific objection". An expression of "the scientific objection" comes when, after failing to find a state that conforms to the requirements we are putting on a state of understanding (or, in a related case, the ability to read), we are led to respond on these lines: "But isn't that only because of our too slight acquaintance with what goes on in the brain and the nervous system?" (§158). And of course it is undeniable that Wittgenstein finds it worthwhile to tackle the inclination to say this. (Though, as Goldfarb notes, §158 is the only place in the *Investigations* where Wittgenstein's explicit topic is the idea that knowing more about the brain and the nervous system might help.) But once it is evident that only something occult could even seem to meet the supposed need, it is clear that it would be merely point-missing to suppose neuroscience, say, might help with the difficulty. It does not seem a good idea to centre our account of what Wittgenstein is doing, as Goldfarb does, on fending off "the scientific objection".

4. Exclamations like "Now I understand!" make it look as if understanding is "something that makes its appearance in a moment" (§151, quoted earlier). "So"—Wittgenstein says—"let us try and see what it is that makes its appearance here" (ibid.). Predictably, given what we have seen about the requirements we are shaping up to placing on the pictured state of understanding, nothing that turns up in consciousness at the relevant moments— for instance, a formula's occurring to one—seems to be sufficiently peculiar to satisfy our felt need. At this point we fall into conceiving the events we find when we ask ourselves what makes its appearance in consciousness at the relevant moments—for instance, a formula's occurring to someone—as *accompaniments* of the understanding. The understanding itself must be hidden behind these episodes in consciousness, still needing to be looked for. But when we give this idea a little further thought, it stands revealed as a dead end (§153):

---

7. At *Blue Book* p. 5, Wittgenstein remarks: "It was in fact just the occult character of the mental process which you needed for your purposes."

. . . how can the process of understanding have been hidden, when I said "Now I understand" *because* I understood?! And if I say it is hidden—then how do I know what I have to look for? I am in a muddle.

It is in this predicament that Wittgenstein issues the advice to stop looking for a "mental process" (§154, quoted earlier). Instead, he suggests (ibid.):

. . . ask yourself in what sort of case, in what kind of circumstances, do we say, "Now I know how to go on," when, that is, the formula *has* occurred to me?

We are to remind ourselves of how these expressions are used. That will disabuse us of the felt need to look for an occurrence in consciousness that such an utterance can be understood to report.

And when he returns to the main line of his reflections after the interpolated discussion of reading (§§156–78), he suggests a positive alternative to supposing that the exclamations announce the occurrence of a "mental process", the onset of a mental state. He describes a case in which the only thing that occurs in the mind of a person who says "Now I know how to go on", after being shown an initial segment of a number series, is "a feeling of relief", and the person then goes on with the series. "And in this case too", Wittgenstein says, "we should say—in certain circumstances—that he did know how to go on" (§179). By this point we are on guard against the temptation to say the onset of the understanding is a happening hidden behind, in this case, the feeling of relief. And now he says (§180):

This is how these words are used. It would be quite misleading, in this last case, for instance, to call the words a "description of a mental state".—One might rather call them a "signal"; and we judge whether it was rightly employed by what he goes on to do.

There is something to the same effect in §323, in a context in which Wittgenstein is again discouraging the question "What happens when a man suddenly understands?" (§321):

"Now I know how to go on!" is an exclamation; it corresponds to an instinctive sound, a glad start.

This is a suggested partial account of what we learn to do with forms of words like "Now I understand". It is clearly intended to be as far away as possible from the idea of describing mental states, saying how things are in an inner region of reality.

5. But that is not the whole of the story. I shall now consider parts of Wittgenstein's text in which he shows, in effect, how the picture of meaning, understanding, and so forth as definite states of mind can after all be innocuous.

In the last few pages of Part I of the *Investigations*, Wittgenstein returns to self-ascriptions of understanding and meaning or intention (and thoughts, wishes, and so forth), but with a new twist, in that his pervasive concern is now with saying, for instance, what one meant at some time in the past. In §666 he introduces a case in which one is in pain and simultaneously bothered by the sound of a piano being tuned, and one says "It'll soon stop". As he says, "It certainly makes quite a difference whether you mean the pain or the piano-tuning!" In §682, this set-up, including one's saying "It'll soon stop", has receded into the past, and the question is "Were you thinking of the noise or of your pain?" (Or one might ask "Did you mean the noise or the pain?") Parallel questions arise about the ability to say what one was going to say, when one has been interrupted in the midst of saying something (§633 and ff.). And at §660 Wittgenstein brings into play, as requiring parallel treatment, a past-tensed counterpart to the exclamation "Now I can go on!":

> The grammar of the expression "I was then going to say . . ." is related to that of the expression "I could then have gone on."
>
> In the one case I remember an intention, in the other I remember having understood.

Shifting to a retrospect over the relevant occasions already, by itself, complicates the picture considerably. Instinctive sounds, glad starts, surely do not have past-tensed forms. There is no past-tense counterpart to a sigh of relief. The idea of a signal, as a clear contrast to the idea of describing a state of mind, no longer seems appropriate once we take note of the fact that self-ascriptions of understanding and so forth have past-tensed forms.

One main thrust of Wittgenstein's reflections here is in line with the thought expressed at §154, that we should be focusing on the circumstances in which the words in question are correctly used, rather than looking for an inner happening that we could as it were point to in order to explain what the words mean. Thus at §654 he writes: "Our mistake is to look for an explanation where we ought to look at what happens as a 'proto-phenomenon'. That is, where we ought to have said: *this language-game is played*." (This echoes, for instance, §180, quoted earlier: "*This is how these words are used*.") And again, at §655, he writes: "The question is not one of explaining a language-game by means of our experiences, but of noting a language-game."

Suppose we ask what state or happening in the mind is alluded to by saying "At that point I intended to say such-and-such" or "At that point I understood the series". If we take such a question as a request for something that would *explain* the language-game of saying such things, it is no good citing one's intention to say such-and-such or the onset of one's understanding of a series. Invoking such things would just be making moves within the language-game—not stepping outside it, as one would need to do in order to explain it.

Now suppose we hold on to that explanatory aspiration, and search the contents of our memories of the relevant moments for something that is not thus ruled out. What we are allowed to find in our memories, if we are not allowed to cite the intention itself or the onset of the understanding itself, is incapable of discharging the explanatory need. What happens here is reminiscent of what happened when we searched the contents of our consciousness at the relevant moments, in §151 and its sequel, with—as we can now see—a parallel restriction in force. In those earlier passages, the result was a temptation to suppose that the state of understanding itself, or its onset, was something hidden behind the occurrences to which our attention was restricted by the explanatory aspiration. Here the result is a temptation to suppose that if one can answer the question what one was going to say when one was interrupted (to stay with one of Wittgenstein's instances), that is because one *interprets* the fragmentary materials that are all we can suppose memory yields, if in saying what memory yields we are restricted by the explanatory aspiration. The restriction makes it look as if what memory yields is limited in a way Wittgenstein describes like this (§635):

> "I was going to say . . . ."—You remember various details. But not even all of them together shew your intention. It is as if a snapshot of a scene had been taken, but only a few scattered details of it were to be seen: here a hand, there a bit of a face, or a hat—the rest is dark. And now it is as if we knew quite certainly what the whole picture represented. As if I could read the darkness.

Hence the temptation to say that knowing what one was going to say must come from interpreting what one finds in one's memory.

In those earlier passages, Wittgenstein unmasks as hopeless the picture in which the understanding is hidden behind the fragmentary phenomena that are the most one can find in the way of occurrences in the mind—if the onset of the understanding itself is excluded, on the ground that citing it would not be a contribution to explaining the language-game but would merely exploit the language-game. What corresponds to that here is that Wittgenstein firmly rejects this picture of what memory yields when the time has receded into the past. Thus (§634):

> When I continue the interrupted sentence and say that *this* was how I had been going to continue it, this is like following out a line of thought from brief notes.
>
> Then don't I *interpret* the notes? Was only one continuation possible in these circumstances? Of course not. But I did not *choose* between interpretations. I *remembered* that I was going to say this.

As he says at §660 (quoted earlier): "In the one case I remember an intention, in the other I remember having understood."

"I remember having understood." If we stop restricting what we are allowed to find in memory of the past occurrence to something that we could cite to explain, from outside, the language-game that includes "Now I understand!" and its past-tensed counterpart, we make it possible to acknowledge that what we recall as having happened at the time includes not just those fragmentary details—having a formula occur to one and the like—but the onset of the understanding itself. What we are able to remember having happened at the time depends in part on which language-games, of a sort that include provision for past-tensed utterances that give expression to memory, we are competent in. Learning the language-game that includes "Now I understand!" and its past-tensed counterpart gives us a new possibility of saying, straight off without needing to interpret what we can recall, how it was with us on suitable past occasions.

And surely in just the same way the present-tensed regions of the language-game can be seen as yielding new possibilities of saying, straight off, how it is with us on suitable present occasions. When we say what makes its appearance on an occasion when our command of the language-game enables us to say "Now I understand!", we are not restricted to occurrences we could conceive as there in our consciousness anyway, independently of our command of the language-game, so that we might hope to appeal to their presence in order to explain what it is for moves in the language-game to be correct. It is no more than an exploitation of the language-game to say that what makes its appearance in the moment, on these occasions, is the understanding itself. What happens is that the understanding sets in.

In a discussion of saying what one meant, Wittgenstein engages with how command of the language-game makes a difference to what one has it in one to report. In §682, reverting to the case where one is bothered both by pain and by the noise of piano-tuning (§666), he writes:

> "You said, 'It'll stop soon'.—Were you thinking of the noise or of your pain?" If he answers "I was thinking of the piano-tuning"—is he observing that the connexion existed, or is he making it by means of those words?— Can't I say *both?* If what he said was true, didn't the connexion exist—and is he not for all that making one which did not exist?

"Observing that the connexion existed" is not the best choice of words here. It is not by observation that one knows what one means, or meant. But this is irrelevant to the point Wittgenstein really wants to make. The point is that one's having meant, say, the piano-tuning can be more than a shadow or reflection of one's saying that that is what one meant, a connection one effects by saying that. No doubt one does make a connection when one says that one meant the piano-tuning—if only that the piano-tuning becomes what one has said one meant. But Wittgenstein is anxious that that should not seem to exclude the possibility of its being a fact that one meant the piano-tuning, whether one says so or not. §689 goes, in part, like this:

> "I am thinking of N." "I am speaking of N."
>
> How do I speak *of* him? I say, for instance, "I must go and see N today."— But surely that is not enough! After all, when I say "N" I might mean various people of this name.—"Then there must surely be a further, different connexion between my talk and N, for otherwise I should *still* not have meant HIM."
>
> Certainly such a connexion exists. Only not as you imagine it: namely by means of a mental *mechanism*.[8]

If what is in one's mind when one says "It'll stop soon", or when one speaks of someone, is limited to items that might be candidates for *explaining* the language-game of saying what or whom one means or meant, then when one considers the connection implied by forms of words like "meaning the piano-tuning" or "meaning N", one will seem to face a choice between supposing the connection is put in place by one's actually saying what one means, or meant, on the one hand, and picturing it as an actualization of an occult power of the mind (a mental mechanism), on the other. But a space

---

8. I have corrected the punctuation.

opens between these options when we realize there need be nothing more to the connection's existing than the fact that, in the cases we are envisaging, "I meant the piano-tuning" and "I mean N" are correct moves in a language-game in which the protagonist of the examples is competent. It can be true, in given cases, that they would be correct moves whether or not they are actually made. So if they are correctly made, we can understand them to report a connection that exists anyway, independently of their being made, though not independently of the subject's being competent in the language-game in which such moves are made.

This makes room for a much less hard line, on the availability in this kind of context of the idea of describing mental states, than is suggested by the passages we were considering before. In §180 (quoted earlier), about "Now I know how to go on", Wittgenstein says it would be "misleading" to use the phrase "description of a mental state". Contrast §662, where, about a clearly parallel case (though now in the past tense), he says:

> One can now say that the words "I wanted N to come to me" describe the
> state of my mind at that time; and again one may *not* say so.

One had better not say so if that is going to lead one to picture the described state of mind as a set-up in an occult mechanism. ("Not as you imagine it: namely by means of a mental *mechanism*.") But it is now clear that we have a different way of picturing the state of mind that we can after all say the words describe. We can see the state of mind of wanting N to come as no more than what is correctly attributed by moves in a language-game that we know how to play. And the same goes for the state of mind of understanding the principle of a series.

6. What I am urging may come into sharper focus if I end by briefly directing it against a certain tendency in the interpretation of Wittgenstein. I shall consider a very explicit expression of the tendency, in the writings of David Pears.

Pears starts from a point he puts like this: "According to Wittgenstein, the distinction between following a rule and violating it cannot be wholly independent of the difference between the way we find it natural to develop the series and other ways of developing it."[9] That seems undeniable.

---

9. *Ludwig Wittgenstein*, pp. xxi–ii.

But what Pears makes of the point is not so straightforward. According to Pears, Wittgenstein's thought is that to follow a rule requires, over and above anything one gets into one's mind when one grasps the rule (perhaps at a moment at which one can correctly say "Now I understand!"), a "contribution from the rule-follower himself" (p. xx). The rule-follower's "mental equipment"—what he has at the moment when he says "Now I understand!"—gives only "incomplete guidance" as to what he is to do in the future, when he reaches a certain point in extending the series (p. xxi). This incomplete guidance needs to be supplemented, in an "unavoidable leap from language to the world" (p. xx), by the rule-follower's propensity to find it natural to write one number rather than another at the relevant point in the series. Nothing "genuinely contemporary in his mind" (p. xxi) can determine what he should write at some point in the future. "The correct solutions to his future problems cannot possibly be contained in anything that is in his mind now" (p. xx).[10]

The thought that Pears's Wittgenstein is here putting in question is that a present understanding, say of the principle of a number series, already determines what number it is going to be correct to write when one gets to a certain point in extending the series. Now if there were no way to persuade oneself that one could make sense of that thought except by picturing the current understanding as a set-up in an occult mechanism, a configuration in an occult medium, then we ought indeed to have no truck with the thought. Bringing that out is one of Wittgenstein's main points. And if this point required us to give up the idea that one's understanding of the principle of a series is itself sufficient to determine what it is correct to do, it would indeed seem that we would have to resort to something on the lines of Pears's account, in which what one finds natural serves as a needed supplementation, over and above the only partial guidance provided by what one acquires when one comes to understand the principle of the series.

But to attribute a thought on these lines to Wittgenstein is to miss the character of his objection to the idea of the occult mechanism. To echo Cora Diamond, it is to read his "criticism of . . . mythology or fantasy . . . as if it

---

10. For something similar to Pears's reading, consider Crispin Wright's claim, on Wittgenstein's behalf, that "there is nothing for an intention, conceived as determining subsequent conformity and non-conformity to it autonomously and independently of its author's judgements on the matter, to be" ("Wittgenstein's Later Philosophy of Mind: Sensation, Privacy, and Intention", p. 146). See my discussion of Wright in "Intentionality and interiority in Wittgenstein", especially at pp. 314–21.

were rejection of the mythology as a *false* notion of how things are".[11] If we read Wittgenstein like this, it will seem that the supposedly rejected false notion needs to be replaced with a true one. And then it will seem that the true notion must have something like the shape of the picture Pears attributes to Wittgenstein. But in fact Wittgenstein has no objection to supposing that what one acquires when one comes to understand the principle of a series—one's mental equipment as it stands at that time—already suffices to determine what it is going to be correct to write when one gets to some point far on in the development of the series. He objects only if we fall into mythology, and picture that contemporary mental equipment as a configuration in the occult medium of the mind.

§195 (partly quoted earlier) is very suggestive in this context:

> "But I don't mean that what I do now (in grasping a sense) determines the future use *causally* and as a matter of experience, but that in a *queer* way, the use itself is in some sense present."—But of course it is, 'in *some* sense'! Really the only thing wrong with what you say is the expression "in a queer way". The rest is all right; and the sentence only seems queer when one imagines a different language-game for it from the one in which we actually use it.

Suppose I say: "The correct solution to my future problems (in extending a series) is contained in something that is in my mind now (namely what I acquired when I grasped the relevant sense)". That is a fairly direct negation of what Pears says Wittgenstein holds. But it is surely a good counterpart to "The future use is in some sense present", which Wittgenstein, so far from denying it, says is "all right". What Wittgenstein says is not at all what Pears says he holds, that it cannot possibly be right to say such things. What Wittgenstein says is that if we place saying such things in the right language-game, we can see that they are innocuous. Compare §689 (quoted earlier): "Certainly such a connexion exists. Only not as you imagine it: namely by means of a mental *mechanism*." There is nothing wrong with saying the connection with the person one means exists, just as there is nothing wrong with saying that how to extend the series is present in the understanding that sets in at a moment. The problem is only in supposing that these connections have to be queer. This goes completely missing in Pears's reading, which proceeds as if such connections could not but be queer, and hence need to be rejected.

11. *The Realistic Spirit: Wittgenstein, Philosophy, and the Mind*, p. 6.

Of course it is true that what we find natural, primitively, and what we can be induced to find natural by being suitably schooled are an essential element in an account of the language-game, in particular of how it is viable at all. But the point is not that our propensities to find things natural help out our understanding, which gives only incomplete guidance, when we need to decide what to do. Rather, our propensities to find things natural are partly constitutive of what it is that we ascribe to ourselves when we say, exercising our competence in the language-game, "Now I understand!". And it is no more than taking the language-game seriously to rephrase that like this: our propensities to find things natural are partly constitutive of the identity of the definite state that we come to be in when we come to understand the principle of a series—a state that sets in in its entirety at the relevant moments, and in the light of which it is completely settled what number it is correct to write when one reaches a certain point in extending the series.

How Not to Read
Philosophical Investigations:
Brandom's Wittgenstein[1]

1. In *Making It Explicit*, Robert Brandom appeals to Wittgenstein's discussions of rule-following as part of a motivation for his own treatment of conceptual contentfulness.

Brandom traces to Kant the idea that concept-involving goings-on must be understood in distinctively normative terms. And he credits Wittgenstein with two master arguments that relate to this Kantian idea (p. 28).

One of them gives bite to the insistence that conceptual activity is essentially norm-governed. The target of this argument is *regularism*, which purports to understand norm-governed activity in terms of mere regularities in performance. Against this, Brandom's Wittgenstein exploits a possibility Brandom calls "gerrymandering" (p. 28). For any series of performances, there are indefinitely many ways it can be seen as going on doing the same thing. Whatever the performer does next, it will continue some regularity that characterizes the previous performances. So whatever one does is correct on a conception of correctness determined by some regularity or other. Regularism has no resources for selecting one regularity as the one that is supposed to determine correctness. This obliterates the very idea of a determinately correct way of going on.

The other argument attacks *regulism*, which Brandom says is a feature of Kant's conception of normativity. Regulism identifies norms with rules, and it understands rules as discursively explicit. Brandom's Wittgenstein argues that regulism cannot capture what it is for performances to be governed by norms. Rules need to be applied. So "correctnesses of performance are de-

---

1. An earlier version of this essay was given at a Wittgenstein conference in Delphi, Greece, in June 2001. This version has benefited from comments by Bob Brandom, for which (as for much else) I am grateful to him.

termined by rules only against the background of correctnesses of application of the rule" (p. 20). If this background correctness itself consists in conformity to rules, it is conformity to rules for applying rules. And given that rules need to be applied, to suppose that all correctness is conformity to rules is to begin an interminable regress. The rules for applying rules need to be applied in turn, and so on without end. Brandom's Wittgenstein concludes that "norms that are *explicit* in the form of rules presuppose norms *implicit* in practice" (p. 20)—that norm-governedness is not "rules all the way down" (ibid.).

More generally, Brandom takes Wittgenstein to show that "the norms involved in properly understanding what is said by rules, or in properly understanding any explicit saying or thinking, must be construed in terms of practice" (p. 30).

2. This last formulation yields a picture in which, below the level at which speech can be described by saying which concepts are made explicit in it, it can be described as subject to norms specifiable in terms that do not require an understanding of the idea of explicitly expressing this or that concept. The norms at this more fundamental level are proprieties implicit in linguistic practice.

What Brandom attributes to Wittgenstein is the idea that understanding explicit saying and thinking requires a background of norms implicit in linguistic practice. Brandom's own conception goes beyond this, to claim that there is nothing to understanding the normativity that is constitutive of explicit saying and thinking over and above making those implicit proprieties explicit. For Brandom, norms implicit in practice are not just a necessary background for norms explicit as expressed concepts, but constitutive of them. So making implicit proprieties explicit emerges as the central topic for the philosophy of language and the philosophy of thought.

We can bracket this divergence and still identify a way in which Brandom avowedly goes beyond Wittgenstein as Brandom reads him. Brandom's Wittgenstein argues against regulism in a way that invites the question what it is for norms to be implicit in practices. Brandom acknowledges, of course, that Wittgenstein does not address that question. He says "Wittgenstein, the principled theoretical quietist, does not attempt to provide a theory of practices, nor would he endorse the project of doing so" (p. 29). Brandom himself, however, does offer a theory of norms implicit in practice in general, and an account of the implicit proprieties that govern linguistic practice in particular. The suggestion is that this discharges a philosophical need brought into view by Wittgenstein's regress argument, though Wittgenstein's "quietism" prevents him from doing the work himself. And this suggestion does not depend on treating norms implicit in practice as more than a necessary background for norms explicit as expressed concepts.

I think it is open to question whether Brandom's story works on its own terms. But that is not my topic in this essay. Here I want to object to Brandom's exploitation of Wittgenstein to motivate these moves, which turns on representing them as further steps in a direction Wittgenstein starts in. I shall argue that Wittgenstein does not even start in the direction of the sort of theory Brandom offers. There is no reason to suppose there must be a level of normativity below the level at which linguistic practice is described in terms of explicitly using this or that concept, and it is no concern of Wittgenstein's to suggest that there is. Brandom gives his philosophy an illusory cachet by claiming that Wittgenstein's thinking about rules opens into it.

It is true that Brandom's master arguments—in particular the regress argument, which is what is supposed to point to implicit proprieties to be made explicit—can be framed so as to sound roughly Wittgensteinian. But that is quite misleading. In Brandom's reading, "quietism" is a pretext for not doing constructive work that Wittgenstein reveals as obligatory for others, not constrained by his scruples. Though Brandom calls it "principled", "quietism" so understood looks like an excuse for laziness. I think this is a paradigm of how not to read Wittgenstein. And I hope contrasting Brandom's Wittgenstein with Wittgenstein himself will help bring into focus what Wittgenstein is actually doing in his discussions of rule-following.

3. In an Appendix on "Wittgenstein's Use of *Regel*" (pp. 64–6), Brandom distinguishes three ways in which he says Wittgenstein uses the concept of a rule. The first is the use that figures in regulism, according to which a rule is an explicit statement of what is to be done. The second identifies as a rule "*whatever* guides or is consulted by those whose behavior is being assessed, whether or not it is discursively or conceptually articulated" (p. 64). Here rules, or expressions of rules, include sign-posts, colour-tables, and the like. In the third use, behaviour counts as rule-following if observers subject it to normative assessment, even if it is not undertaken in the light of a conception of what is to be done.

This third conception of rules is not relevant to Wittgenstein's regress argument as Brandom understands it. The first two are, because unlike the third they are specifications of the Kantian idea that norm-governed action is undertaken in accordance with a *conception* of a norm (p. 30), and as Brandom reads the argument, it shows that regulism is not an acceptable way to spell out that idea.[2]

To tell against regulism, the regress argument would need to single out the first of these conceptions of rules. In fact Wittgenstein formulates his regress argument in terms of the second, with expressions of rules including sign-posts. Amazingly enough, this does not deflect Brandom from his account of what Wittgenstein is aiming at; he reads it as mere ineptitude on Wittgenstein's part. He says "It should be admitted that Wittgenstein's terminology in some ways obscures the very point he is after in the regress-of-rules argument" (p. 64). But sign-posts are a perfectly good case for the point Wittgenstein is after. His practice with the concept of a rule, which Brandom treats as lax, simply shows that the aim of his argument is not to attack regulism in Brandom's sense. Not that he would accept regulism in Brandom's sense; it is simply irrelevant to what he is doing in his reflections about rule-following.

Wittgenstein uses "following a rule" as a gloss on the idea of acting in the light of a conception of correctness. Following a sign-post serves for him—perfectly reasonably—as a case of acting in the light of a conception of correctness, acting on an understanding of something. His concern is to free us from a conceptual bind we can easily fall into when we think about acting on an understanding. The threat, which takes shape as a regress, is completely general; it does not arise only where what is understood is discursively explicit.

Consider *Philosophical Investigations* §85: "A rule stands there like a sign-post." For "a rule" here, we might substitute "an expression of a rule", in a sense that fits the second of Brandom's three uses, a sense in which expressions of rules need not be discursive. For example, we might say "A

2. Brandom cites, as exemplifying the third use, *Philosophical Investigations* §54, where Wittgenstein speaks of rules that "an observer can read . . . off from the practice of the game—like a natural law governing the play". But this seems wrong. Brandom does not notice Wittgenstein's allusion in this context to the behaviour characteristic of correcting a slip of the tongue. That makes it clear that what the observer reads off from the practice of the game is a conception of correctness in the light of which the players do what they do. This case is in the scope of the Kantian idea. I doubt that the third use is as prevalent in *Philosophical Investigations* as Brandom suggests. But it is the first two uses that matter for my present purposes.

sign-post—an expression of a rule for following a trail—stands there like a sign-post". How could it be wrong to say a sign-post stands there like a sign-post? Well, the formulation is dangerous, because "stands there" suggests a conception according to which the rule, or its expression, considered in itself, is normatively inert. It stands aloof from those who encounter it: a mere arrangement of matter, not something that as it were speaks to people, telling them which way to go.

That threatens the idea that a sign-post points the way to go. One might hope to preserve the idea of a right way to go—even while conceiving a sign-post as something that stands there, mute and aloof—by supposing that what tells people which way to go is not a sign-post considered in itself, but a sign-post *under an interpretation*. A sign-post under an interpretation sorts responses into those that are correct in the light of it and those that are not. But now whatever made it seem right to say a sign-post stands there, mute and aloof, will equally make it seem right to say, of anything one might want to conceive as an expression of the interpretation that for a moment (compare *PI* §201) seems to get normativity back into the picture, that *it* stands there like a sign-post. (Consider for instance a pointing gesture, or an utterance of the words "Go to the right".) The thing that was supposed to be an expression of an interpretation lapses into normative inertness just as the thing that was originally supposed to tell us which way to go did. And if we suppose we can recover a normative sorting by considering the thing that was supposed to be an expression of an interpretation under an interpretation in its turn, we are obviously starting on an infinite regress.

That is Wittgenstein's regress. The temptation to start on it, and its disastrous consequences, are the same whether we are considering non-discursive expressions of rules, such as sign-posts, or discursive expressions, such as—for the same rule—someone saying "To follow the trail at this point you must go to the right". Regulism in Brandom's sense is neither here nor there.

4. What do we learn from this regress?

We learn that it is disastrous to suppose there is always a conceptual gap between an expression of a rule and performances that are up for assessment according to whether or not they conform to the rule, a gap that is made vivid by saying the expression of the rule stands there, on the construal I have suggested. We must not acquiesce in the idea that an expression of a rule, considered in itself, does not sort behaviour into performances that follow the rule and performances that do not. Once we start thinking like that, it can seem for a moment that an interpretation can bridge the gap—that adding an interpretation can yield something, the expression of the rule under an interpretation, that does effect the required normative sorting of behaviour. But only for a moment, until we realize that the same thought will be just as plausible about whatever we try to conceive as an expression of the interpretation. If we let the gap open at all, it will be unbridgeable. This way, we lose our grip on the idea of an expression of a rule, or an expression of an interpretation. In the end we lose our grip on the idea of an expression of anything.

In a famous passage (*Philosophical Investigations* §201), Wittgenstein puts the lesson of his regress like this: "What this shews is that there is a way of grasping a rule that is *not* an *interpretation*, but which is exhibited in what we call 'obeying the rule' and 'going against it' in actual cases." To paraphrase: we must not suppose that, say, a sign-post can tell someone which way to go only under an interpretation. We must insist on not being deprived of the thought that a sign-post itself points the way, tells people which way to go.

Of course not everyone who encounters a sign-post gets told which way to go. Sign-posts do not speak to those who are not party to the relevant conventions. Perhaps Martians use things that look like our sign-posts to point in the opposite directions. If that is so, our sign-posts would not point the way to Martians. To be capable of being told what to do by a sign-post, one needs to have been initiated into an appropriate practice. One needs to have learned, for instance, that one is to go to the right when, in following a footpath, one comes across a sign-post of a certain familiar configuration. Going to the right in such a situation, on the part of someone who is party to the relevant practice, would be an example of "what we call 'obeying the rule' in actual cases". It would manifest an understanding, a grasp, of the rule—the rule for following a footpath that the sign-post expresses—that is not an interpretation. It would reflect the fact that the subject is such that the sign-post itself, not the sign-post under an interpretation, tells her which way to go.[3]

---

3. It is important that these remarks are about someone who is party to the practice, someone who understands sign-posts. What is in question is not a mere uncomprehending disposition to react to what are in fact sign-posts in "appropriate" ways. See *Philosophical Investigations* §198.

5. Brandom quotes §201 as if it supported his idea that Wittgenstein is attacking regulism (p. 21). But the passage does not say what Brandom would like it to say. It does not say the regress stops at a level below that at which correctness consists in following rules. The idea of a way of grasping a rule that is not an interpretation functions at a level at which correctness is still conformity to rules. According to Wittgenstein, the regress shows there must be cases of following rules that are not cases of acting on interpretations. The regress is inescapable if we suppose "acting on an interpretation" always fits where "following a rule" fits. Or, better: if we suppose what makes it look as if that must be right—that in any case of rule-following, what we follow is, in itself, normatively inert, something that stands there like a sign-post on the dangerous understanding of that description.

Brandom implies that the moral of §201 is this: "The rule says how to do one thing correctly only on the assumption that one can do something else correctly, namely apply the rule" (p. 21). Here he is invoking the two kinds of correctness that figure in his regress argument against regulism: correctness that can be understood as conformity to rules, and the background correctness that on pain of regress cannot. But §201 envisages only one kind of correctness. Its point is not that correctness that consists in following a rule presupposes another kind of correctness. Its point is that we must avoid a regress-generating misconception of the one kind of correctness it considers, following a rule—a misconception according to which following a rule is always acting on an interpretation of something.

This fits a claim I made earlier, that for Wittgenstein "following a rule" serves as a gloss on the idea of acting in accordance with a conception of correctness. Nothing in this pivotal text, or—so far as I know—anywhere else in Wittgenstein's discussions of the topic, warrants Brandom's view that for Wittgenstein normativity is not "rules all the way down". In fact, in *Remarks on the Foundations of Mathematics* (VI-28), Wittgenstein says "Following according to the rule is FUNDAMENTAL to our language-game", and it seems a good paraphrase of that to say the normativity of linguistic practice is precisely rules all the way down.

Brandom is equipped to set aside these points about the texts by appealing to his claim that Wittgenstein's use of "rule" is lax. For Brandom's Wittgenstein, normativity is rules all the way down in the sense that it is proprieties, not necessarily explicit, all the way down. But the point Wittgenstein is supposedly after is that what is fundamental is proprieties that are implicit in practice, not explicit in rules in the sense in which regulism understands rules.

However, the texts afford no justification for discounting Wittgenstein's own wording in this way. The thrust of his regress argument is not that what is fundamental is norms implicit in practice, but that what is fundamental is the ability to act immediately on an understanding—to act in a way that is not mediated by an interpretation of what is understood. As I have stressed, this point applies in the same way whether or not what is understood and acted on is something discursively explicit. For Wittgenstein's purposes here, the difference between discursive and non-discursive expressions of rules has no particular significance.[4] Wittgenstein's regress has no particular connection with regulism in Brandom's sense.

It is not that Brandom's argument against regulism is a special case of Wittgenstein's regress argument. That would involve accepting that Wittgenstein argues for two levels of normativity: one at which norms are expressed and one at which they are only implicit in practice. The idea would be that Brandom's reading goes wrong only in restricting the first level to one at which norms are *discursively* expressed, whereas the argument also applies where norms are non-discursively expressed, as in the case of sign-posts. But Wittgenstein's argument does not add another level of normativity. Wittgenstein's regress shows that acting on an understanding cannot in general be acting on an interpretation of what is understood. When Wittgenstein's regress is applied in the case of norms that are discursively explicit, its moral is not that that normativity presupposes normativity implicit in practice, but that there must be such a thing as a capacity to act immediately on an understanding of that normativity. Brandom's argument is not even as close to Wittgenstein's as a special case of it would be; it is simply different.

6. Brandom's Wittgenstein addresses a question with no particular context, about what it is for behaviour to be norm-governed. He considers a particular answer, regulism, and rejects it in favour of the thesis, supposedly

---

4. That is why I have had no qualms in speaking of sign-posts as telling one what to do. There is an extra layer of metaphor here, over and above what would be involved in speaking of a board inscribed "Go to the right" as telling one what to do. (There would be no metaphor in speaking of someone who says "Go to the right" as telling one what to do.) But Wittgenstein's argument is indifferent to this difference.

established by the regress argument, that "the fundamental form of norm" (p. 21) is norms implicit in practice. At this point the concern to give an account of normativity as such would seem to require an account of what it is for norms to be implicit in practice. But here "quietism" supposedly kicks in, and Brandom has to do the constructive work necessary to finish the job merely begun by Wittgenstein's rejection of regulism. As I noted, Brandom says Wittgenstein's "quietism" is principled, but in this picture it should seem mysterious what its principle might be. As Brandom reads him, Wittgenstein shows a need for some constructive philosophy but pleads "quietism" as a pretext for leaving the job of providing it to others.

On the reading I have outlined, it is easy to see how it can be simply right that the regress argument does not call for constructive philosophy. And this puts Wittgenstein's "quietism" (so called) in a different light. Wittgenstein is not trying to give an account of norm-governedness as such, for its own sake and independently of any specific difficulty about it. He is not trying to supply a theory of norm-governedness to replace regulism. He uncovers a conception that can make acting in the light of a conception of correctness, acting on an understanding, seem mysterious, and he exposes it as a misconception. That dispels the appearance of mystery, and there is nothing further that philosophy needs to do in this connection.[5]

If we conceive, say, sign-posts as in themselves normatively inert, so that only under an interpretation could a sign-post tell anyone which way to go, we lose our hold on the very idea that sign-posts can be understood and followed. To avoid this, we need to retrieve a bit of common sense: that people who are party to the relevant practice are told what direction to go in by sign-posts themselves, not by sign-posts under an interpretation. If there is more work to be done, it is to loosen the grip of the conception according to which an expression of a rule, for instance a sign-post, is, in itself, normatively inert. To do that, we need to administer what Wittgenstein calls "reminders" (*Philosophical Investigations* §127), not put forward philosophical theses. Theorizing about different levels at which practices can be seen as norm-governed would be beside the point.

Wittgenstein's invocations of practice in this context serve not as openings into a theoretical pragmatism, but as reminders for this therapeutic

---

5. Contrast how Brandom (pp. xiii–xiv) talks as if normativity is mysterious anyway, independently of any particular reason why it should be, so that there is a standing philosophical obligation to render it less so, which he undertakes in his book.

purpose. We fall into the bind that concerns him if we abstract sign-posts (for instance) from their place in the lives of those who use them. For someone who is party to the relevant practice, a sign-post is something that points the way. And that is what a sign-post as such is. It is true that for someone who is not party to the practice, an object that is a sign-post might be merely a board of a certain configuration affixed to a post. But it is disastrous to conclude that what points the way, to someone to whom a sign-post does point the way, is such a thing—a board on a post—under an interpretation. On the contrary, what points the way is a sign-post, something that is what it is by virtue of its involvement in the relevant practice. And it points the way, to those who are party to the practice, without their needing to put an interpretation on it.

Of course the practice with sign-posts is essentially norm-involving. Going to the right, for instance, is what accords with—what is correct in the light of—sign-posts of a certain configuration. Brandom seizes on this normativity, and takes Wittgenstein's appeals to practice to reveal a concern with a theoretical question, what it is for behaviour to be norm-governed. Pleading "quietism", Brandom's Wittgenstein goes no further with this concern than a gesture in the direction of the idea of norms implicit in practice. Properly executing the philosophical task Wittgenstein supposedly reveals would require a theory about that supposedly fundamental level of normativity. But for the actual Wittgenstein's purpose, no more is needed than the advice that when we reflect about the capacity of sign-posts to sort behaviour into what accords with them and what does not, we should avoid abstracting the objects themselves from what we do with them. To follow this advice, we need only to remind ourselves of obvious facts about what we do with sign-posts. We do not need a theory of normativity.

It would reveal a misunderstanding if someone complained here that this makes Wittgenstein uninteresting, because there is nothing surprising or controversial in saying that sign-posts, or meaningful items in general, need to be conceived in terms of what we do with them. That it is not controversial is just the point. (See *Philosophical Investigations* §128: "If one tried to advance *theses* in philosophy, it would never be possible to debate them, because everyone would agree to them.") Wittgenstein does not amass philosophical doctrine, or point to areas where it would be a good thing for others to do that, though "quietism" debars him from doing so. He uncovers tendencies to forgetfulness, which lead to trouble when we engage in philosophical reflection, but which can be counteracted by suitable reminders of the obvious.

7. If one is wedded to the idea that starts the regress—the idea that a sign-post (say) can point the way only under an interpretation—it can be tempting to disarm the threat on these lines: "Admittedly, any *expression* of the interpretation that I want to credit with bridging the gap will just as appropriately be said to stand there like a sign-post, and appealing to such a thing will be merely taking the first step in an infinite regress. But my idea is that what bridges the gap is *the interpretation itself*—not the expression, but what the expression expresses. That does not need interpreting before it can tell us what to do. The regress terminates here."

In *The Blue Book* (p. 34), Wittgenstein puts this thought like this: "What one wants to say is: 'Every sign is capable of interpretation; but the *meaning* mustn't be capable of interpretation. It is the last interpretation.'" If we start with the idea that expressions of rules stand there in the dangerous sense, we fall into a regress of things that momentarily look as if they bridge the gap, but then are revealed as needing interpretation in their turn, so that the gap is after all not bridged. The thought is that meanings stop the regress. Meanings do not need interpretation.

No doubt in some contexts it is correct to say that the meaning of an expression of a rule—which will be the same as the meaning of an expression of an interpretation of it, if the interpretation is a good one—does not need interpretation. But here the point of saying that is to make it safe to suppose, say, that a sign-post points the way only under an interpretation. The meaning is construed as an interpretation, but one immune to what dashes the hope that a regular interpretation will bridge the gap—the realization that we have merely shifted our attention to something that, on the principles that required the shift, could itself tell us which way to go only under an interpretation. This picture of meaning as the last interpretation is the germ of the imagery—a familiar target in Wittgenstein's later work—in which understanding a meaning is gearing oneself up to a super-rigid mechanism that keeps one's meaning-involving behaviour in line.[6] The right thing to say is that a sign-post does not need interpretation either. Then we shall not be tempted to this mythology of meaning. We cannot make it all right to say an expression of a rule does not tell us what to do by

6. See my discussion in "Wittgenstein on Following a Rule", at pp. 230–2.

saying its meaning does. An expression of a rule does tell us—those who understand it—what to do.

Brandom (pp. 13–15) treats Wittgenstein's engagements with this mythology of meaning as reaffirming Frege's attacks on psychologism. He treats the imagery of super-rigid mechanisms as a version of the psychologism that is Frege's target—a reflection of not realizing that to make sense of acting in the light of meanings we need to be thinking in normative as opposed to, say, brutely causal terms. But this is exactly wrong. The point of appealing to interpretation, in the move that starts the regress, is precisely to *preserve* the normative distinction between behaviour that accords with a rule and behaviour that does not, even while we are conceiving the expression of the rule as in itself normatively inert. The thought is that although considered in itself a sign-post, say, does not distinguish correct from incorrect behaviour, the sign-post under an interpretation does. What the regress actually shows is that this attempt to keep normativity in the picture, by appealing to the idea of interpretation, does not work. The idea of meaning as the last interpretation, and the imagery that grows out of it, are wrung from one in a desperate attempt to avoid that conclusion—an attempt to *keep* normativity in the picture, as the idea of interpretation seemed to do, even in the context of seeing sign-posts, and expressions of meaning in general, as normatively inert. If one is tempted by the imagery of super-rigidity, it is because one is on the anti-psychologistic side of Frege's divide.

Brandom is in general too ready to find restatements of Frege's attacks on psychologism in this region of Wittgenstein's thinking. The supposed gerrymandering argument against regularism is part of this tendency. In fact the relevant material in Wittgenstein's texts belongs with the regress of interpretations, which Brandom sees as a different master argument with a different target. We start by supposing an expression of a rule could tell us what to do only under an interpretation. Then we realize that any expression of the interpretation that for a moment seemed to bridge the gap would itself, on the same principles, stand in need of interpretation before it could bridge the gap. Gerrymandered interpretations, interpretations that would bridge the gap otherwise than as we intended, make it vivid that on these lines the gap cannot be bridged at all. This is a way of capturing the point of the regress argument, which is what Brandom misreads as an attack on regulism. The gerrymandered formulations (say "Add 2 until you get to 1000, then add 4 until . . ."; see *Philosophical Investigations* §185) are not descriptions of different mere regularities that can be found in rule-conforming behaviour so far, but different interpretations of the norm it conforms to, which are live candidates to be the norm it conforms to on the assumption that the expression of the rule itself (say "Add 2", or an initial segment of the series) does not tell one what to do. There is only one master argument. And it is not an attack on regulism, not a pointer to a supposedly fundamental level of normativity, but an enforcement of the point that, whether or not what is understood is discursively expressed, it must be possible to act on an understanding immediately, not in a way that is mediated by an interpretation.

Of course in refusing to read passages that exploit gerrymandering as arguing against regularism, I am not suggesting that Wittgenstein would have any sympathy with regularism. The point is that in his reflections on rule-following he presupposes, rather than argues for, the "Fregean" point that the concept of acting on an understanding involves the concept of correctness and incorrectness. What he does argue is that this required normativity cannot be captured by invoking the idea of interpretation.

8. I have been urging that Wittgenstein's regress argument does not point to a fundamental level of normativity, norms implicit in practice which it might take work on the part of philosophers to uncover and make explicit, even if the philosophers are comprehending participants in the practice in question. Consider linguistic practice in particular. Concepts are, in the Kantian conception, rules for judging. After the linguistic turn, we can say they are rules for making claims. The contents of these rules for judging and claiming are explicit in speech acts: for instance, in saying that something is a cat. The core, at least, of the norm that governs the concept of a cat is that it is all right, at least so far as truth is concerned, to say or think something is a cat just in case it is a cat. Making that norm explicit is no problem for anyone who understands the word "cat". Wittgenstein says nothing to suggest that speech and thought are subject to norms describable below the level at which we simply say what concepts are employed.

It does not help to bracket my claim that what Brandom credits to Wittgenstein is not Wittgenstein's argument. There is no convincing argument for Brandom's picture in what he purports to find in Wittgenstein, whether it is in Wittgenstein or not.

Brandom's argument against regulism turns on this claim: "For any particular performance and any rule, there will be ways of applying the rule so as to forbid the performance, and ways of applying it so as to permit or require it" (p. 20). But this seems simply wrong. Suppose we found ourselves shaping up to thinking someone who was plainly in the presence of a cat, and not confused, hallucinating, or whatever, thought the rule for judging that constitutes the concept of a cat was to be applied here and now so as to forbid judging *this is a cat*. That would not be recognizable as a way of applying that rule. It would just force us to reconsider the belief that it was that concept—that rule for judging—that was being applied.

In fact Brandom's formulation seems to be merely a version of the paradox-generating thought that Wittgenstein argues we must avoid: the thought that any rule confronts attempted conformity to it across a gap, which needs to be bridged by a substantive act of application. Brandom's "applying" is a mere variant on "interpreting", in the way of thinking that Wittgenstein—so far from making it the basis of an argument against regulism—displays as a disastrous misconception.

9. Brandom says "Rules do not apply themselves" (p. 20). This might be a way of saying the idea of a rule telling someone what to do presupposes that the person can understand the rule, which requires familiarity with a practice. A rule that applied itself would be a rule that guaranteed its own intelligibility, independently of conditions on its addressees—as if words, say, could be understood without anyone's needing to learn a language. Of course that is a fantasy.

To say it is a fantasy is not to say correctness that consists in following a rule presupposes correctness that does not. That is how Brandom glosses the remark that rules do not apply themselves. To quote again a passage I quoted before: "The rule says how to do one thing correctly only on the assumption that one can do something else correctly, namely apply the rule" (p. 21). But there is no warrant for this picture of two correctnesses. A rule says how to do something correctly only to someone who understands its expression. She has to be a competent participant in the relevant practice. That is not to say she has to be able to do something else, besides follow the rule, in order to have the rule tell her what to do. The only correctness we need to consider is correctness that consists in following the rule.

The fantasy of rules that suffice of themselves for their own intelligibility might be described as a fantasy of explicitness. If one is gripped by this conception of what it would be for a rule to be explicit, it can seem a deficiency that human means of giving expression to rules make themselves understood only to audiences who satisfy particular conditions: having learned a language, having mastered a practice. This fantastic conception of explicitness fits some of the turns in Wittgenstein's treatment of the pathologies we fall into in thinking about rule-following; consider for instance the image of stopping up all the cracks (*Philosophical Investigations* §84). But this is not how explicitness figures in Brandom's reading. His regulism involves explicitness ordinarily understood.

No rule applies itself in this supposed sense. In some cases knowing what a rule tells one to do requires discretion or judgment; in other cases it is routine. Alternatively, we could rework the idea of judgment so that to say following a rule requires judgment is just another way to say rules do not apply themselves. If we use the term this way, we have to say the exercise of judgment can be routine, though in other cases people who understand a rule can be better or worse at following it because their judgment is better or worse.

Here we may be reminded of a passage where Kant finds a regress in the idea that determining how to follow a rule is following another rule, and invokes judgment to avoid the regress.[7] Brandom mentions Kant's regress argument "parenthetically" in an endnote (p. 657). He acknowledges that it raises a question about his taking Wittgenstein's regress to correct a Kantian conception. But he nevertheless frames his main text in terms of "the lesson Wittgenstein has to teach Kant", on the ground that "very little is made of [the point of the regress argument] in the first two Critiques". I think his idea is that to make much of the point would be to do what he does—to offer theory about a level of normativity below that at which correctness can be conceived as conformity to rules. In fact nothing is done in that direction in Wittgenstein's texts either (this is the absence Brandom attributes to "quietism"), and that puts Brandom's idea of a lesson from Wittgenstein to Kant on a shaky footing, even given Brandom's account of Wittgenstein.

Anyway, I have been urging that Wittgenstein's regress does not direct our attention to another level of normativity, and I think the same goes for Kant's. Brandom's picture must be that exercising judgment is Kant's candidate for the other ability supposedly presupposed by the ability to follow rules. But even where the need for judgment is substantial—where it is not routine to know what a rule requires of one here and now—it is surely wrong to conceive the exercise of judgment as subject to a further norm, over and above the norm specified by the rule. Judgment as to what a rule requires is better or worse according to how well its results accord with what the rule requires. The only relevant norm is the one prescribed by the

7. *Critique of Pure Reason*, A132–4/B171–4.

rule. A need for non-routine judgment in following a rule shows something about the character of the norm prescribed by the rule; it does not point us to another norm that governs exercises of judgment. It would be absurd to suggest that in this kind of case we could make explicit some supposedly separate norms governing the exercise of discretion, thereby codifying prescriptions for judgment. Judgment in the relevant sense is essentially uncodifiable. Kant's regress does not go well with Brandom's controlling theme of making previously implicit norms explicit.

10. Brandom represents his work as emerging from a reading of a tradition whose key figures are Kant, Frege, and Wittgenstein (p. xi). Of course there is precedent for a philosopher's rereading his predecessors to as to depict his own work as the culmination of their efforts. And the scope of Brandom's enterprise, and the confidence with which he executes it, cannot but be impressive. I think there is a danger that it will give currency to a travesty of his predecessors—for present purposes, Wittgenstein in particular. Brandom acknowledges that his ancestor portraits take unusual angles on their subjects (p. xii). But the figure who can be seen in Brandom's portrait labelled "Wittgenstein" is not Wittgenstein from an odd angle, but someone else—a philosopher, not very insightful on these topics, of Brandom's own invention.[8]

8. Perhaps Brandom's Wittgenstein is closer to Sellars; see pp. 23–6, where Brandom cites a regress argument against regulism from Sellars's "Some Reflections on Language Games". Sellars's argument assumes without discussion that the rule for the use of a word would have to be something one could consult in order to find out how to use the word, so rules such as "It is legitimate to call red things 'red'" are excluded from the start. The effect is that something like Brandom's required patternings of behaviour, describable below the level of specifying what concepts are in play, are presupposed at the very beginning of Sellars's argument, not argued for in it.

Sellars's regress argument palpably diverges from Wittgenstein's, in that it is supposed to require going to a level at which behaviour is produced because of its place in a pattern, but without the agent envisaging the pattern and acting so as to realize it—not, then, a level at which behaviour is animated by a grasp of a rule, as in Wittgenstein's "a way of grasping a rule that is not an interpretation".

Sellars's argument may not be as congenial to Brandom as Brandom supposes. Sellars imagines a philosopher called "Metaphysicus", who construes the norms that govern linguistic practice as "entities of which the mind can take account before it is able to give them a verbal clothing" (p. 323). Sellars mentions this conception only to dismiss it. Brandom's invocation of norms implicit in practice prior to their explicitation seems to add a pragmatist variant of this conception to the nominalist and conceptualist versions Sellars considers.

PART III

Issues in Davidson

Scheme-Content Dualism
and Empiricism

1. Donald Davidson has credited scheme-content dualism with an important role in setting the agenda of modern philosophy: "To a large extent this
picture of mind and its place in nature has defined the problems modern
philosophy has thought it had to solve."[1] That means that to deconstruct the
dualism, as Davidson has undertaken to do in a number of writings, is potentially to transform philosophy's conception of itself. If we can rid ourselves of the dualism, we shall no longer think we have those problems—
which is not the same as taking ourselves to have solved them.

I think Davidson is profoundly right in attaching this kind of significance
to scheme-content dualism. But in what follows I want to suggest, with
help from his own writings, that his diagnosis of the dualism's hold on
modern thinking does not quite go to the roots; and hence that his recipe
for a transformation of philosophy is not quite the one we need.

2. What is the dualism of scheme and content?

I take it that the parties to the dualism are supposed to determine the significance of, say, bodies of belief or theories. The picture can be encapsulated in the familiar Kantian tag: "Thoughts without content are empty, intuitions without concepts are blind."[2] So "scheme" is, more fully, "conceptual
scheme", and "content" is, more explicitly, "intuitions" or sensory intake. The
idea is that beliefs or theories are significant, non-empty, because of an interaction between the conceptual and the sensory. (Perhaps we should say
"empirical beliefs or theories"; but it is a central Kantian thesis that this would
not be to add anything.)

1. "The Myth of the Subjective", p. 161.
2. *Critique of Pure Reason*, A51/B75.

Now "dualism", as a term of philosophical criticism, implies more than just duality. In a *dualism* of scheme and content, the two putative determinants of significance are initially separated so far from each other that it becomes a problem how they can come together in the interaction that is supposed to yield significance.

Thus on the scheme side of the dualism concepts are supposed to come into view in abstraction from any connection with the deliverances of the senses. So considered, employments of concepts would indeed be empty, just as the Kantian tag says. If we conceive a subject's employments of "concepts" (so called) in this way, we do not yet have in view anything we could recognize as the embracing of beliefs or theories, the adoption of determinate stands or commitments as to how things are in the world. (We could say "the empirical world", but with the same doubt about whether that would be to add anything.)

Similarly on the content side of the dualism sensory intake is supposed to come into view in abstraction from ("without") concepts. And so considered, sensory intake would indeed be blind, just as the Kantian tag says.

If abstracting it from content leaves a scheme empty, what can be the point of identifying this side of the dualism as *the conceptual*? It is not a routine idea that concepts and their exercises, considered in themselves, are empty, and it is not obvious why it should seem that we can abstract them away from what makes the embracing of beliefs or theories non-empty, but still have concepts and their exercises—what they essentially are—in view.

In the dualism, the relation between scheme and content is evidently a case of the relation between form and matter. So we can put the question like this: why should it seem right to equate the formal with the conceptual, given that we are using the idea of form in such a way that form without matter is empty? We can find an answer to this question in two thoughts. First, that the linkages between concepts that constitute the shape, so to speak, of a conceptual scheme are linkages that pertain to what is a reason for what. Second, that if matter, in this application of the form–matter contrast, is supplied by the deliverances of the senses, then the structure of reason must lie on the other side of the matter–form contrast, and hence must be formal; reason is set over against the senses. No doubt exercises of concepts, as we ordinarily conceive them, are not empty, since they already incorporate content as well as scheme. But if we can see how those two thoughts might be attractive, we can see how it might seem that the conceptual comes into view in a pure form only if we strip content away.

I think the first of those two thoughts, which connects the idea of a conceptual scheme with the idea of reason, need be no more than a determination of the relevant idea of the conceptual. (By itself, without the second thought, this is innocent of the dualism.) The second thought, in which reason is kept pure of contamination by the mere matter yielded by the deliverances of the senses, is more problematic, and I shall return to it. Meanwhile, perhaps that rephrasing can begin to make it intelligible how the thought could be attractive, and so how one might be induced to take in one's stride the surprising idea that the conceptual, considered in itself, is devoid of empirical content.[3]

3. Why is this dualism of scheme and content a suitable case for deconstruction? There are no doubt several things one could say in response to this question, but I shall focus on one glaring problem.

Considered by themselves, employments of elements of a scheme—exercises of a conceptual repertoire—are empty; they are not yet recognizable as cases of adopting commitments concerning how things are in the world. If we take in only this one side of the dualism, we have not yet entitled ourselves to the idea that employments of concepts are determinately answerable to how things are. We do not yet have the resources to see moves within a scheme as open to favourable assessment if things are a certain way and unfavourable assessment otherwise.

Now the other side of the duality is supposed to supply this missing requirement: to entitle us to the idea that a move within a scheme is determinately answerable to the world, and so intelligible as the adoption of a stand about the world. A move within a scheme is answerable to the deliverances of the senses ("the tribunal of experience", in W. V. Quine's phrase);[4] that is supposed to supply the missing requirement, because being answerable to the tribunal of experience is being answerable to the facts that impress themselves on the senses.

But the dualism reflects the idea that the linkages recognized by reason are the linkages that constitute the organization of schemes, and it places the deliverances of the senses outside schemes. And that makes it *incoherent*

---

3. It would miss the point to protest that the connection of reason with form limits rational connections to those that would be exploited in inferences whose excellence is owed to their *logical* form. That is not the application of the concept of form that is in play here.

4. W. V. Quine, "Two Dogmas of Empiricism", p. 41.

to suppose that sensory intake, on this conception, can mediate answerability to the world. If rational relations hold exclusively between elements of schemes, it cannot be the case that what it is for something within a scheme to be rationally in good shape, and so worthy of credence, is its being related in a certain way to something outside the scheme. "Intuitions without concepts are blind," Kant said. But for present purposes, a more suggestive metaphor for the point would be that intuitions without concepts are mute. They cannot intelligibly constitute a tribunal, something capable of passing favourable verdicts on some exercises of concepts and unfavourable verdicts on others.

4. Davidson has identified the dualism of scheme and content as "the third dogma of empiricism", and accordingly he has suggested that when we abandon the dualism, as we must, we are thereby discarding the last vestige of empiricism.[5] By "empiricism" here, he means the thesis that the deliverances of the senses are epistemologically significant: they stand in relations of justification or warrant to world views or theories. He writes:

> Empiricism, like other isms, we can define pretty much as we please, but I take it to involve not only the pallid claim that all knowledge of the world comes through the agency of the senses, but also the conviction that this fact is of prime epistemological significance. The pallid idea merely recognizes the obvious causal role of the senses in mediating between objects and events in the world and our thoughts and talk about them; empiricism locates the ultimate evidence for those thoughts at this intermediate step.[6]

This crediting of epistemological significance to sensory intake is exactly what I have represented the dualism as wanting but, by the way it places intuitions outside the domain of rational linkages, making unavailable.

Suppose we want to give the deliverances of the senses an ultimate evidential role. Are we thereby committed to the dualism, with its conception of the deliverances of the senses as "intuitions without concepts"? If that is so, then empiricism in the non-pallid sense Davidson distinguishes

5. "On the Very Idea of a Conceptual Scheme". (The allusion is, of course, to Quine's "Two Dogmas".)

6. "Meaning, Truth and Evidence". (I quote from the beginning of the essay, and Davidson says "This characterization will undergo modification in what follows"; but the modification does not matter for my purposes.)

is self-defeating, since the dualism is, and Davidson is right to declare empiricism defunct. I shall come back to this.

5. My sketch of the dualism and my account of why it must be rejected have diverged from what Davidson says about it on a couple of points that I shall mention.

First, where I have identified a scheme as one of two putative determinants of, say, a world view, Davidson (at least sometimes) equates world view and scheme. Quine wrote:[7]

> We can investigate the world, and man as a part of it, and thus find out what cues he could have of what goes on around him. Subtracting his cues from his world view, we get man's net contribution as the difference. This difference marks the extent of man's conceptual sovereignty—the domain within which he can revise theory while saving the data.

Davidson quotes this, and remarks: "World view and cues, theory and data: these are the scheme and content of which I have been speaking."[8] But on the account of the dualism that I have given, world view or theory would not itself be one side of the dualism, as this remark of Davidson's makes it. World view or theory would be the result of the supposed interaction between the two sides of the dualism. A scheme would be, not a world view, but what is left when content is subtracted from a world view—what Quine speaks of as "man's net contribution" (we might say "reason's net contribution").

By itself this may not seem much of a divergence. All three items that are present in one version—world view, reason's contribution, the contribution of the senses—are equally present in the other. Perhaps it is just a question of taste which pair one picks to figure in what one attacks as a dualism. I find it neater to let the parties to the dualism be the two contributions, rather than one of the contributions on the one side and the supposed result of the two contributions on the other.

If this is indeed a neater fit to the idea of a scheme-content dualism, that may account for some cross purposes between Davidson and Quine. Davidson first cast Quine as an adherent of scheme-content dualism in "On the Very Idea of a Conceptual Scheme". In a later essay Davidson writes: "What I had in mind as the scheme was language, with its built-in ontology

---

7. *Word and Object*, p. 5.
8. "The Myth of the Subjective", p. 162.

and theory of the world, the content being supplied by the patterned firing of neurons."[9] In a footnote about Quine's "On the Very Idea of a Third Dogma", he says: "In this reply, Quine mistakenly took my picture of his dualism of scheme and content to involve a separation of conceptual scheme and language."[10] But perhaps Quine was simply understanding the accusation of dualism in the natural way. According to the dualism as it is most naturally understood, we have something with a "built-in ontology and theory of the world" only *after* content has made its contribution. If conceptual scheme is the other contributor, and language does indeed have a "built-in ontology and theory of the world", then conceptual scheme must be distinguishable from language, as "man's net contribution" is distinguishable from the world view to which it is a contribution.

The second divergence is more immediately striking. The trouble with the dualism as I have depicted it is that it is *incoherent*. The world's impacts on the senses are given the task of making it intelligible that moves within a conceptual scheme, taken to be such that considered in themselves they are empty, can nevertheless be adoptions of stands as to how things are. But there can be so much as an appearance that this works only if we can see the world's impacts on the senses as a tribunal, something capable of passing verdicts on moves within a scheme. Only so can we conceive an answerability to the world's impacts on the senses as a mediated answerability to the world itself. But when we distance content from scheme, in a way that reflects the idea that rational interrelatedness is confined to elements in schemes, we ensure that we cannot see experience as a tribunal. "Intuitions without concepts" are mute; they can pass no verdicts.

Contrast the problem Davidson most prominently urges about the dualism. When he finds the dualism in Quine, his complaint is not that Quine lapses into incoherence, but rather that Quine makes himself vulnerable to a familiar sort of scepticism. Here is a succinct formulation of the thought:[11]

> Quine's naturalized epistemology, because it is based on the empiricist premise that what we mean and what we think is conceptually (and not merely causally) founded on the testimony of the senses, is open to standard sceptical attack.

9. "Meaning, Truth and Evidence", p. 69.
10. "Meaning, Truth and Evidence", p. 78.
11. From p. 136 of "Afterthoughts".

This remark blames empiricism for the vulnerability to scepticism that Davidson finds in Quine, but given Davidson's identification of scheme-content dualism as "the third dogma of empiricism", that comes to the same as blaming the dualism for it.

On the reading of the dualism that I have offered, this is a curiously muted objection. (I do not mean to be suggesting that vulnerability to standard scepticism is a comfortable condition.) This objection would fit if an epistemology organized in the terms of the dualism made it intelligible that the senses tell us *something*—with the trouble being that it represents them as not telling us *enough* to warrant our world view. But on my reading, the trouble with the dualism is rather this: the very idea that the senses provide testimony becomes unintelligible. "Intuitions without concepts" are mute. If one nevertheless cannot see how anything but answerability to intuitions could ensure that thoughts are not empty, one's predicament is more unnerving than any standard scepticism. Standard scepticism takes for granted that we have a world view, and merely questions whether we are entitled to it. The dualism, on my reading, generates a much more radical anxiety about whether we are in touch with reality. Within the dualism, it becomes unintelligible that we have a world view at all.

My claim that the dualism is incoherent depends on the thought that the domain of rational interrelatedness is coextensive with the domain of the conceptual. Suppose one wants to conceive the impacts of the world on us as "intuitions without concepts", but nevertheless wants those impacts to constitute a tribunal that world views must face. One will then be under pressure to avoid the threat of incoherence by denying that the domain of rational interrelatedness is coextensive with the domain of the conceptual.[12] But the thesis of coextensiveness is a way of putting a fundamental conviction of Davidson's. (He is giving expression to it when he claims that "nothing can be a reason for holding a belief except another belief".)[13] The materials for the claim of incoherence come directly from Davidson himself.

12. Note that one is not already committed to the thesis of coextensiveness if one accepts the stipulation about how to understand the idea of the conceptual that I considered above. That involved no more than that conceptual linkages are included in rational connections, and left open the possibility that the inclusion is proper.

13. "A Coherence Theory of Truth and Knowledge", p. 141.

6. If Davidson is right, as I believe, in claiming that the dualism has set much of the agenda for modern philosophy, something deep must account for its attraction. What might that be?

Davidson answers this question in a way that belongs with the curiously muted objection. Summarizing a survey of the dualism, he writes: "What matters, then, is . . . that there should be an ultimate source of evidence whose character can be wholly specified without reference to what it is evidence for." He goes on:

> It is easy to remember what prompts this view: it is thought necessary to insulate the ultimate sources of evidence from the outside world in order to guarantee the authority of evidence for the subject. Since we cannot be certain what the world outside the mind is like, the subjective can keep its virtue—its chastity, its certainty for us—only by being protected from contamination by the world. The familiar trouble is, of course, that the disconnection creates a gap no reasoning or construction can possibly bridge.[14]

Now I would not dream of disputing that Davidson here captures a motivation that is familiar in modern philosophy, and reminds us of how the motivation defeats itself. But do these remarks adequately account for the grip of scheme-content dualism?

This question becomes especially pressing when we note that the survey of scheme-content dualism to which these remarks are appended culminates in Davidson's citing Quine as an adherent. This is not the first time I have mentioned this Davidsonian reading of Quine. I do not want to question it; on the contrary, I think it is very perceptive. But surely Quine does not belong in the context of the temptation that these diagnostic remarks of Davidson's appeal to: the admittedly familiar temptation to "interiorize", or "subjectivize", the ultimate evidence for world views, so that whatever the fate of the world views, at least the ultimate evidence is (supposedly) proof against sceptical challenge. A page further on, Davidson writes, summarizing the thought about trying to guarantee the authority of ultimate evidence:

> Instead of saying it is the scheme-content dichotomy that has dominated and defined the problems of modern philosophy, then, one could as well

14. "The Myth of the Subjective", p. 162.

say it is how the dualism of the objective and the subjective has been conceived. For these dualisms have a common origin: a concept of the mind with its private states and objects.

Surely this concern with privacy or subjectivity does not fit Quine. When Quine espouses his version of scheme-content dualism, his concern is to stress the freedom of play that our "cues" leave us when we build or remodel a world view. What Quine wants to bring out is "the extent of man's conceptual sovereignty". There is nothing in Quine's thinking that would lead him to hanker after a peculiarly solid authority for beliefs corresponding to the "cues", an authority supposedly achievable by insulating the subject matter of those beliefs from the external world. On the contrary, Quine is unperturbed by the familiar epistemological anxiety to which that move is an intelligible, though, as Davidson rightly points out, unsuccessful response.

Davidson's suggested source for scheme-content dualism is bound to be unsatisfying if one focuses on the fact that the dualism is incoherent, in the way it tries to conceive experience as a tribunal while distancing it from the domain of rational interrelatedness. If we follow Davidson's suggestion that the dualism responds to an anxiety about our *entitlement* to our world view, the sort of worry that might seem to be met by securing a solid authority for some supposedly basic evidence on which the world view is founded, then it becomes mysterious why that should have as its outcome a way of thinking in which the putative ultimate warrants for world views are pushed out of the domain of rational interrelatedness altogether—a move that in fact makes them incapable of intelligibly constituting warrants at all. This would be a much more radical case of a motivation's defeating itself than the one Davidson considers. In the case Davidson considers, the case of ordinary empiricism, we trade informational strength for immunity to sceptical challenge, and so secure the authority of the evidence only at the price of a vividly obvious gap between it and what it was supposed to be evidence for. The dualism is worse; it undermines the capacity of the supposed evidence to be seen as evidence at all, weak or strong.

Of course if the dualism of scheme and content is incoherent, it will fail to satisfy any motivation that is operative in embracing it. I am not suggesting we should look for a motivation that the dualism would satisfy, as it does not satisfy the one that Davidson offers. The point is that a quest for epistemic security cannot explain why one might be led beyond the mere failure of ordinary empiricistic epistemologies—in which the senses yield items of the right kind to be evidence, and the problem is just that the evidence falls short of warranting an ordinary world view ordinarily understood—into the incoherence of scheme-content dualism, in which the deliverances of the senses are simultaneously required to constitute a tribunal and rendered mute. To explain how this incoherence could stay hidden, and how the incoherent way of thinking could seem compulsory, we need something deeper than the motivation that Davidson considers.

7. In order to understand scheme-content dualism, I think we need to forget, for a while at least, that familiar anxiety about whether we are sufficiently entitled to our world view. If we allow ourselves to feel that anxiety, we simply presuppose that we have a world view. But part of what underlies the dualism is something that lets that presupposition come into question. The felt need to conceive experience as a tribunal derives, not from what Davidson focuses on, a concern to give our possession of a world view—which we simply assume—a secure warrant, but from an interest in the conditions of its being intelligible that we have a world view (or theories, or beliefs) at all. How is it that some moves we can make, moves we would like to think of as exploitings of concepts, are takings of stands as to how things are in the world? This is intelligible only if we can see the moves as answerable, for their rational acceptability, ultimately to the facts themselves. And part of what underlies the dualism is the thought that this required answerability to the world can be realized only as an answerability to the way the world puts its mark on us; that is, an answerability to the deliverances of our senses.

Once the question "How is it possible that there are world views at all?" is in view, this thought is not easy to dismiss. Consider the thesis that responsiveness to reason is part of the content of the idea of exploiting conceptual capacities. I suggested that we can take that thesis simply to define a useful notion of conceptual capacities. Now it is a Kantian idea that responsiveness to reason is a kind of freedom. (The note of freedom sounds in Quine's talk of "the extent of man's conceptual sovereignty".) We cannot gloss this freedom in terms of an unlimited absence of constraint; exactly not, since it consists in undertaking one's moves in allegiance to—if you like—restrictions, constituted by what is a reason for what. But if these restrictions are conceived as wholly formal, in that responsiveness to reason does not extend as far as answerability to impacts the world makes on us, then it becomes a live question how, in exercising such a freedom, we could be adopting commitments as to how things are in the world. If "man's conceptual sovereignty" has no limits set by the facts themselves, it becomes unrecognizable as what it is meant to be, the power to make up our minds *about how things are*. And it is open to question whether we enable ourselves to see "man's conceptual sovereignty" as constrained in the right way if—like Davidson when he rejects empiricism—we say that impacts from the world exert a *causal* influence on how the sovereign power is exercised, but deny that they set *rational* constraints. If we say that, we preclude ourselves from pointing to rational answerability to the world's impacts on our senses as the way in which employments of concepts are ultimately rationally answerable to the world itself, and then it becomes mysterious how these exploitations of freedom can be otherwise than empty, just as "thoughts without content" are in the Kantian tag.

It does not help to say that impacts from the world cause beliefs, which can then serve as a tribunal for world views to face. These beliefs would be just more elements of world views. The question we have allowed to arise is how there can be anything of that kind, if not because some things of that kind are answerable to a tribunal constituted by experience, and it is unresponsive to help ourselves to some things of that kind. The causal ancestry we cite for the ones we help ourselves to makes no difference to this.

That is to say that empiricism, even in Davidson's non-pallid sense, is not easy to dismiss. This is perfectly consistent with accepting his insistence that an ordinary empiricism, which "interiorizes" the supposed warrants for world views in order to make the warrants safe from sceptical challenge, yields a quite unsatisfying picture of our entitlement to our beliefs. Empiricism is separable from that "interiorizing" move, and the obsession with epistemic security that directly motivates it. We can concur with Davidson in rejecting that kind of epistemology, without threat to this thought: empiricism, in the non-pallid sense, captures a condition for it to be intelligible that thoughts are otherwise than empty.

Scheme-content dualism is incoherent, because it combines the conviction that world views are rationally answerable to experience—the core thesis of empiricism—with a conception of experience that makes it incapable of passing verdicts, because it removes the deliverances of the senses from the domain of the conceptual. According to the dualism, experience both must and cannot serve as a tribunal. Davidson's treatment of the dualism would resolve this contradiction by rejecting its first limb, its basic empiricism. But I am suggesting that this basic empiricism is not easy to dismiss. What holds it in place is not the concern with entitlement that Davidson discusses, but a concern with the very idea of content, which he seems not to consider as a motivation for it.

Here we can perhaps find a deeper significance in the first of the two divergences I noted between my reading of the dualism and Davidson's. The divergence was that in Davidson's reading what stands over against sensory intake in the dualism is already a world view; not, as in my reading, what Quine calls "man's net contribution". If the other party to the dualism is already a world view, before it comes into relation with sensory intake, then it cannot owe its being a world view (at all) to an interaction with sensory intake—not even according to the dualism, on this Davidsonian identification of its elements. The idea that the deliverances of the senses might matter for securing non-emptiness thus goes missing, in this reading of the dualism; they are left with no apparent role except the one Davidson considers, that of putatively supplying warrants for world views, taken to be anyway and independently constituted as such. So perhaps the divergence is not just a matter of taste about how best to organize the triad of world view, reason's contribution, and sensory intake. Davidson's identification of scheme with world view belongs with the fact that his discussion of the dualism addresses only the epistemological unsatisfyingness of ordinary empiricisms (which of course I acknowledge), and never considers empiricism as a way of not being beset with a mystery over the fact that there are world views at all.[15]

I remarked that Quine is immune to the sort of anxiety that tends to issue in "interiorizing" the warrants for world views, so as to make them safe from sceptical challenge. It would be in the spirit of Davidson's remarks about that sort of epistemology to say that this immunity is desirable, since nothing but bad philosophy results from letting oneself feel the anxiety. What I am saying now is that Davidson is immune to any anxiety about how it is possible that there are world views at all. Is that not similarly a good way to be? Well, certainly I am not suggesting we should take ourselves to have the option of deciding that it is *not* possible that there are

---

15. This absence is quite strange, in view of the fact that "content", in Davidson's label for the dualism that he discusses, is plainly an echo of the Kantian tag. The Kantian tag surely gives content the role of securing the non-emptiness of thoughts; not that of supplying a warrant for accepting them.

world views, any more than we should take ourselves to have the option of deciding that we know nothing about the external world. There is no real question whether world views are possible. But that leaves it open that entitlement to this absence of worry may depend on accepting the core thesis of empiricism. If that is so, then someone who rejects empiricism, like Davidson, thereby deprives himself of the right to his immunity to anxiety over the non-emptiness of thoughts. In this context, the immunity is not a philosophically desirable condition.

8. In Davidson's treatment, the diagnostic question that the dualism raises is this: why is it tempting to suppose that the deliverances of the senses would have to constitute a tribunal for our world views to face? Davidson suggests an answer in terms of the craving for epistemic security. I have been urging that that answer is unsatisfying, because it falls short of accounting for the temptation to fall into the dualism's incoherence, as opposed to the mere failure of ordinary empiricistic epistemologies. An empiricism with the different motivation I have pointed to cannot be dismissed on the grounds of vulnerability to standard scepticism. Perhaps there is nothing wrong with such an empiricism. In that case the diagnostic question that the dualism raises is rather this: why is it difficult to see how the deliverances of the senses could constitute a tribunal for our world views to face? Why is it tempting to suppose that the world's impacts on us would have to be "intuitions without concepts"?

With the intellectual development that we can sum up as the rise of modern science, there became available a newly sharp conception of the proper goal of the natural sciences, as we can (significantly) call them: namely, an understanding of phenomena as interrelated perhaps causally, but certainly (this becomes a tempting gloss on what it is to see phenomena as causally interrelated) within a framework of laws of nature. This supersedes a pre-modern outlook, which did not sharply differentiate a natural-scientific mode of understanding from one that places its objects in rational relations with one another, and so works with categories like meaning. In this pre-modern outlook, it was sensible to look for meaning in phenomena like the movement of the planets—phenomena that we are equipped, with modernity's conception of a special mode of understanding, the natural-scientific, to see as appropriately brought within its scope, and so as exactly not something to look for meaning in. In step with the emergence into clarity of this idea of a special mode of understanding, to be radically contrasted with finding meaning in things, it is only to be expected that there was an increasing sense of how special—by comparison with the framework of natural law—are the patterns or structures within which things are placed when they are understood in the contrasting way: how special are the linkages that constitute the domain of rational interrelatedness.

Now the idea of the world making its impact on a sentient being is the idea of a causal transaction, an instance of a kind of thing that takes place in nature. And that differentiation of modes of understanding can easily make it seem that once we conceive a happening in those terms, we are already thereby conceiving it in a way that is distanced from placement in the domain of rational interrelatedness. Succumbing to that appearance, we might say something on these lines: "The idea of the world's impacts on us is the idea of something natural. And we moderns now see clearly how the structure of rational linkages contrasts with the structure of the natural, the topic of natural-scientific understanding. Hence, given that the domain of the conceptual is the domain of rational interrelatedness, it must be that intuitions as such are without concepts."

That suggests how a familiar feature of modern thinking might explain the idea that the sensory stands opposed to the conceptual, as it does for Davidson as well as in the dualism of scheme and content. And it is not that this line of thought uncovers a mistake in the idea that I have suggested underlies the empiricism that figures, inconsistently with the conclusion of this line of thought, in the dualism: the idea that thought can be intelligibly non-empty only by virtue of answerability to experience. There are two independently tempting thoughts here: a thought about the conditions for it to be intelligible that we have world views, suggesting that experience must constitute a tribunal, and a thought about the naturalness of the idea of an impact on the senses, suggesting that experience cannot constitute a tribunal. If we can see how these two influences might both shape reflection, we have an explanation of how one might be tempted into the incoherence of scheme-content dualism.

I have suggested that there is no obvious way to avoid the idea that empiricism captures a condition for thought not to be empty. (Davidson does not even consider that recommendation for empiricism.) Of course it cannot be obligatory to think incoherently. So if empiricism is compulsory, there must be a flaw in the line of thought I have just rehearsed, the one that makes it look as if intuitions as such are "without concepts".

It is indeed an achievement of modernity to have brought into clear focus the contrast between two modes of understanding: one that involves placing phenomena in the framework of natural law, and one that involves placing things in the domain of rational interconnectedness. But to give proper credit to that achievement, we do not need to accept that when we see something as a happening in nature—as the world's making its mark on a sentient creature would indeed be—we are *eo ipso* placing it in the sort of frame that is characteristic of the natural sciences. If that were so, then, given the contrast, the fact that something is a happening in nature would be a ground for supposing that—at least in itself, viewed as the happening in nature it is—it is "without concepts". But it is not so. We need not accept what might seem to be implied by the label "natural sciences", that phenomena are conceived in terms of their place in nature only when they are conceived in terms of their place in the framework of natural law. If we reject that, we make room for supposing that the world's impacts on us, even considered in themselves as just that, the world's impacts on us, are not "without concepts". That would allow the tension within scheme-content dualism to be resolved in the opposite direction to the one Davidson suggests: in the direction of a coherent empiricism.[16]

9. What Davidson considers under the head of scheme-content dualism is an attempt to achieve security against sceptical challenge for evidence on which world views are putatively founded. This leads to a shrinkage in the informational content of the putative evidence. I have contrasted this with the more radical failure that, exploiting argumentative materials supplied by Davidson himself, I find in the dualism: namely that it disqualifies what it requires us to conceive as a tribunal from being a tribunal at all. Now I have acknowledged that the quest for epistemic security that Davidson focuses on is fundamental to modern epistemology. I have also said that I think Davidson is profoundly right in placing scheme-content dualism at the root of what is unsatisfactory about modern philosophy. How can this hang together? How can what is in fact a disqualification of putative evidence from being evidence at all—with the upshot that, in the context of an empiricism that I suggested is hard to dismiss, our very possession of a

16. I do not mean this lightning sketch to suggest that this resolution of the tension is easy. I discuss these issues slightly less breathlessly (to echo Davidson, "The Myth of the Subjective", p. 162) in *Mind and World*.

world view becomes a mystery—be at the root of a philosophical tradition that is, as I acknowledge, driven by an obsession with the authority of our evidence for our world views, and takes it for granted that we have a world view and evidence for it?

No doubt the full story of why modern epistemology takes the course it does is complex, but I think this part of it can be told quite simply. The dualism is the outcome of a pair of independently intelligible temptations. It is intelligible that reflection should be shaped both by the genuine credentials of empiricism (which are not undermined by Davidson, since he considers empiricism only in the context of the quest for security, not in the context of the very idea of a world view), and by the conception of nature that I have depicted as underlying the idea that the world's impacts on us are "intuitions without concepts". Now consider someone who is susceptible to both those influences. Such a person is thereby *en route*, as it were, to a frame of mind in which it is a mystery how thought bears on the world at all. The outcome of the first influence sets a requirement for thought to bear on the world; the outcome of the second is that the requirement cannot be met. But it is not to be expected that the destination would be obvious at all stages in the journey; especially not if the reflection is undertaken early in the evolution of the conception of nature whose finished product, in this context, is the idea that experiences are "intuitions without concepts". (That the destination is not obvious is surely a condition of continuing to let oneself be subject to both influences.) At a primitive stage in such reflection, a sense of where it is headed need not take any clearer shape than something to this effect: thought's hold on the world is coming into question. And a disquiet that can be expressed like that is just what is responded to—ineptly given this account of its origin, but not at all surprisingly—by the sort of philosophy that is obsessed with the authority of our warrant for our world views; the sort of philosophy on which Davidson focuses, without this conception of what underlies it.

It is a familiar thought—I have concurred with Davidson in a form of it—that philosophy in this vein does not succeed in its own explicit aim, that of reassuring us as to our epistemic security in our world views. I am suggesting another respect in which this sort of philosophy is unsatisfying. It does not even correctly identify the drift of the submerged philosophical anxiety by which it is driven.

Scheme-content dualism figures in this picture as the conclusion to which a pair of influences that shape traditional epistemological reflection would take one if their tendencies achieved explicit formulation together. There is no need to look for outright adherents of the dualism among proponents of the sort of traditional epistemology that Davidson rightly deplores.

We come perhaps as close as possible to an outright adherent of the dualism in Quine, and he is certainly not a proponent of traditional epistemology. He is not vulnerable to the disquiet about thought's hold on the world that I have suggested underlies the anxieties of traditional epistemology, and is ineptly responded to by its characteristic moves. (I exploited that fact when I pointed to a tension between Davidson's account of the source of scheme-content dualism and his reading of Quine as an adherent of it.) The pull of empiricism on Quine (in Davidson's interesting, non-pallid, sense of "empiricism") is almost vanishingly small. It is reflected only in his rhetoric about "the tribunal of experience", and that is out of line with the dominant feature of Quine's epistemological thinking: namely, a naturalism that cheerfully casts experience as "intuitions without concepts", and rejects questions about the warrant for world views altogether, in favour of questions about their causation. It is tempting to resolve this tension by discounting the empiricist rhetoric. In one way that would do Quine a favour, just by eliminating the tension; but if I am right about the credentials of empiricism, in another way it would not, since it would involve expunging the vestigial expression of a real philosophical insight.[17]

10. I suggested that with the modern achievement of clarity about a distinctive sort of understanding—now available to be cited as the defining aim of a distinctive intellectual endeavour, the natural sciences—there comes an appreciation of how special, by comparison, is the sort of understanding that involves placing things in rational relations to one another. The sense of specialness is expressed in a genre of philosophical questions that we can sum up, exploiting the connection between reason and freedom, like this: how is

17. In "Epistemology Externalized", Davidson claims that "Quine's naturalized epistemology, while it makes no serious attempt to answer the skeptic, is recognizably a fairly conventional form of empiricism" (pp. 192–3). But the vestigial empiricism in Quine is very far from conventional, just because its motivation has nothing to do with responding to ordinary sceptical challenges. And the empiricism is not an aspect of the naturalized epistemology; it is a trace of an insight that cannot genuinely find a home in the environment of Quine's naturalism, which removes experience from the category of warrant altogether.

freedom related to the natural world? This wording points to familiar questions about action and responsibility as paradigms of the sort of thing I mean. But the problems posed by the tendency towards a dualism of scheme and content belong in this genre of philosophy too. Underlying the dualism of scheme and content is a dualism of freedom—the freedom of reason—and nature.

In "Mental Events" and kindred writings, Davidson has undertaken to defuse philosophical anxieties of this genre, anxieties about integrating freedom into the natural world. He endorses the sense of specialness: he puts forward on his own behalf a quasi-Kantian picture of, as we might say, the realm of freedom, according to which it is organized by a "constitutive ideal of rationality", wholly distinct from the organizing structure of the world as viewed by the natural sciences. But he aims to prevent this sense of specialness from generating metaphysical anxiety, by arguing that the distinction between freedom and nature reflects a duality of conceptual apparatuses and not a duality of ontological realms.[18]

Now I have cast the dualism of scheme and content as crystallizing a cognate philosophical anxiety: the question "How are world views possible?" is a form of the question "How is freedom possible?" But here Davidson's way with other forms of the anxiety does not help. Davidson's invocation of a duality that is conceptual, and not ontological, does not undermine the thought that the world's impacts on us are "intuitions without concepts". That is a thought that Davidson accepts. And it is a thought that, I have claimed, leaves the freedom of "conceptual sovereignty" a mystery.

Davidson misses this, because he misidentifies the incipient philosophical anxiety that is crystallized in scheme-content dualism; he takes it to be a concern about entitlement to world views, and he does not see that the familiar anxiety about freedom, applied in this context, takes shape fully only as a concern about how it is possible that exercises of "conceptual sovereignty" are world views at all. This concern rests in part on a recommendation for empiricism that does not come into view in Davidson's thinking at all. If we are to defuse the anxiety while respecting this quite different attraction for empiricism, something that Davidson does not give us reason not to want to do,

18. Just because it involves endorsing the sense of specialness, this is a much more promising programme for disarming the philosophical anxiety that the sense of specialness risks generating than that of Richard Rorty, at least in *Philosophy and the Mirror of Nature*. There Rorty pooh-poohed the sense of specialness, in debunking the idea of a philosophically significant contrast between the *Naturwissenschaften* and the *Geisteswissenschaften*.

we need to find a way to resist the idea that the impacts of the world on our senses are "intuitions without concepts". And for that we need a more radical counter to the underlying dualism of reason and nature than the one that Davidson supplies. On this view, the sources of what is unsatisfactory about modern philosophy include something that lies deeper than the interiorizing conception of subjectivity pointed to by Davidson. A more fundamental source is a misconception of the intellectual obligations of naturalism, to which Davidson himself—in his willingness to accept that the deliverances of the senses are "intuitions without concepts"—seems to be subject.

ESSAY 8

Gadamer and Davidson on
Understanding and Relativism[1]

1. That I might pay a small tribute to Hans-Georg Gadamer by considering the comparison indicated in my title was suggested to me by some remarks of Michael Friedman.[2]

In my *Mind and World*, I wrote in terms of a conceptually mediated openness to reality, partly constituted by inheritance of a tradition. My invocation of tradition was, as I indicated, inspired by Gadamer. The idea of inheriting a tradition helps us to understand what is involved in possessing conceptual capacities, in a certain demanding sense: capacities of freedom, capacities whose paradigmatic actualization is in cognitive activity that is under its subject's control, centrally judgment. I urged that conceptual capacities can also be drawn into actualization in operations of sensibility, outside the subject's control. My aim was to allow us to see perceptual experiences as events in which, in operations of their sensibility, subjects take in facts—elements of the world, in the sense determined by the opening remark of Wittgenstein's *Tractatus*: the world as everything that is the case. With this conception, we can hold that operations of our sensibility exert a rational influence on our formation of belief, impinging on our capacities for judgment from within the conceptual sphere. And since in experience—at any rate when they are not misled—perceivers take in elements of the world, experiences allow the world itself to figure in the rational background of the fixation of belief. I contrasted this with Davidson's picture, in which the operations of sensibility make only a brutely causal impact on belief-formation, from outside the conceptual sphere.

1. This essay was written for a collection in honour of Gadamer.
2. "Exorcising the Philosophical Tradition: Comments on John McDowell's *Mind and World*"; see especially pp. 464–7.

134

Friedman thinks this contrast places me close, at least, to "the traditional idealist doctrine that the world to which our thought relates is a creature of our own conceptualization" (p. 464). And he thinks Davidson is immune to any such charge, just because of the difference between his picture and mine. The occasion for this essay is that Friedman thinks he can reinforce this accusation by exploiting my Gadamerian invocation of tradition. About the accusation in general, I am inclined to echo Gadamer's remark: "It is a sheer misunderstanding if one appeals against idealism—whether transcendental idealism or 'idealistic' philosophy of language—to the being-in-itself of the world. This is to miss the methodological significance of idealism, the metaphysical form of which can be regarded, since Kant, as outmoded."[3] We shall see how this misunderstanding shapes Friedman's critique.

As Friedman notes, Davidson exploits the so-called principle of charity to avoid any threat of linguistic or conceptual relativism. On the ground that I follow Gadamer in insisting that any understanding consciousness is situated in tradition, Friedman suggests I cannot share Davidson's invulnerability to relativism. After citing my Gadamerian claim (*Mind and World*, p. 155) that "languages and traditions can figure not as '*tertia*' that would threaten to make our grip on the world philosophically problematic, but as constitutive of our unproblematic openness to the world", he goes on (p. 465): "One might wonder, accordingly, how McDowell himself would respond to the threat of cultural or linguistic relativism. Are we not faced, in particular, with the threat that there is not one space of reasons but many different ones—each adapted to its own cultural tradition and each constituting its own 'world'?" The implication is that where Davidson is protected against relativism, Gadamer's thinking positively exacerbates the threat. And the further implication is that Gadamer thereby slides towards the "traditional idealist" picture of the world as a creature of our conceptual activity. Friedman implies this when he characterizes his comparison between Davidson and Gadamer on relativism as "further elucidat[ing] the sense in which McDowell's own position is actually more idealistic than Davidson's" (p. 464). The sense he means, as he has already made clear, is the sense in which idealism depicts the world as a creature of our mental activity.

In this essay, I shall begin (in §2) by explaining why I think this is wrong. In the respects in which it follows Gadamer's, my thinking is no doubt more

---

3. *Truth and Method*, p. 448, n. 84. All subsequent page references to Gadamer will be to this work.

idealistic than Davidson's, but not in a sense that has anything to do with representing the world as a product or reflection of our intellectual activity. I am sorry to have drawn Friedman's fire in Gadamer's direction, and I shall try to deflect the attack, in order to begin a renewed expression of the admiration for Gadamer's work that I meant to signal in my book. I shall go on (in §3) to consider the contrast between Davidson and Gadamer over the philosophical significance of tradition in its own right, without the supposed connection with idealism in that sense.

2. Davidson averts the threat of relativism by justifying a refusal to make sense of a certain supposed idea, the idea of a repertoire that is meaning-involving, and so intelligible, but not intelligible to us.[4] As he remarks, "it is tempting to take a very short line indeed" (p. 185) with that supposed idea—namely, blankly rejecting it. The principle of charity is central to a less blunt treatment, which displays the rejection as warranted. The argument undermines a conception of a language, or a conceptual scheme, as something that enables a certain sort of confrontation with the world conceived as "something neutral and common that lies outside all schemes" (p. 190). Against this, Davidson insists that when we make play with a conception of languages as confronting the world, we can conceive the world only as the world that we understand our own practice to engage with. Accordingly he says (p. 198): "In giving up the dualism of [conceptual] scheme and world [this is the world conceived as "something neutral and common that lies outside all schemes"], we do not give up the world, but re-establish unmediated contact with the familiar objects whose antics make our sentences and opinions true or false."[5]

Now this is perfectly in line with Gadamer's thinking.

Davidson argues that we are entitled to refuse to make sense of the idea of a case of intelligibility that is radically inaccessible to us. What matches

4. See "On the Very Idea of a Conceptual Scheme".

5. This paragraph gives a compressed summary of salient points in a rich and complex article. But I think the only substantial divergence from Davidson's text is that I have replaced Davidson's specification of his target, as the idea of languages untranslatable into ours, with a specification in terms of languages unintelligible from our standpoint. This does no harm to the argument, and it is a better fit with Davidson's usual focus on interpretation, rather than translation, as a focus for reflection on understanding. In a limiting case we simply adopt into our own linguistic repertoire our subjects' means of giving expression to thoughts we have contrived to understand, in order to say what it is that we have come to understand them as saying; this is hardly translation.

this in Gadamer is his contention that "each [worldview] potentially contains every other one within it—i.e., each worldview can be extended into every other" (p. 448). The "horizon" constituted by a specific situatedness in tradition is not closed. On the contrary, it is always open to "fusion" with the horizon constituted by a different specific situatedness.[6] Friedman registers Gadamer's appeal to the possibility of fusion of horizons, but, as we shall see, he does not properly acknowledge its force.

Again, the target of Davidson's argument is a conception of the world as "something neutral and common that lies outside all schemes". What matches this in Gadamer is his contention that the openness of every view of the world to every other "makes the expression 'world in itself' problematical" (p. 447). Gadamer writes (ibid.): "Those views of the world are not relative in the sense that one could oppose them to the 'world in itself,' as if the right view from some possible position outside the human, linguistic world could discover it in its being-in-itself." There is no relativism in saying we cannot draw a distinction between the world itself and the topic of our world view. As Gadamer says (p. 447): "In every worldview, the existence of the world-in-itself is intended." And the world-in-itself, as it figures in this thought, is not Davidson's target but the topic of our world view—the familiar world with which Davidson says we re-establish unmediated contact when we give up the dualism of scheme and something outside all concepts.[7] Our world view, precisely because it is, *qua* world view, open to every other, has as its topic the world itself, not some supposed item constituted by just what we think. (Such an item would be, at least in part, no better than notional, since we are certainly wrong about some things, and would differ from the corresponding item associated with a different world

6. On the fusion of horizons, see *Truth and Method*, pp. 300–7. This passage is concerned in particular with historical understanding, directed at our own cultural precursors, and in this context Gadamer can use the image of a single horizon that shifts with the passing of time. But the idea of horizons being fused easily transposes to any case where the occurrence of understanding involves overcoming an initial alienness.

7. That the contact is unmediated, in the sense Davidson intends, is perfectly consistent with what I mean by talking of conceptually mediated openness. Davidson's point is to rule out mediation by epistemic intermediaries, on the lines of sense-data as often conceived—objects of a direct awareness that yields indirect awareness of things in the environment. In the picture of perceptual awareness I recommend, nothing intervenes like that between us and things in the environment. Part of the point of the conceptual mediation I talk of is precisely that it allows us a picture of experience in which it is environmental things themselves, not stand-ins for them, that are "given to the senses".

view.) Our world view includes its own receptiveness to the possibility of correction, not only by efforts at improvement that are internal to our practices of inquiry, but also through coming to appreciate insights of other world views in the course of coming to understand them.

As I said, on the conception of perceptual experience that I recommend, experience lets the world itself figure in the rational background of our fixation of belief. In experience worldly states of affairs themselves exert a rational influence on belief-formation, working within the conceptual sphere. I expressed this in *Mind and World* (p. 26) by saying we should not picture the world as lying outside an outer boundary that encloses the conceptual sphere. This image, which is avowedly idealistic in one sense, is part of what prompts Friedman to accuse me of embracing idealism in the sense of representing the world as a creature of our conceptual activity. He writes (p. 462): "In Davidson's picture the world that our beliefs and judgments are about is, at least in principle, characterizable wholly independently of the conceptual-psychological domain of human intentionality. Indeed, the causal (as opposed to rational) relations between our thinking and the world must ultimately be supported by the entirely nonintentional characterization of the world as the domain of physical natural fact. In this sense, experience relates thought to an independent objective reality across an outer boundary; and it is precisely such a boundary that McDowell himself is most concerned to erase." But this is a travesty of my image. The boundary Friedman insists on is not the one I am concerned to erase.

Of course the facts that constitute the world (apart from facts about human intentionality) are characterizable "independently of the conceptual-psychological domain of human intentionality". It would be crazy to hold that characterizing an object as cubic (for instance) requires concepts of intentionality—in the sense, not of concepts employed in thought, but of concepts whose satisfiers are thinkers or acts of thinking. As Gadamer says (p. 447): "No one doubts that the world can exist without man and perhaps will do so. This is part of the meaning in which every human, linguistically constituted view of the world lives." No one doubts that the world exists for the most part outside a boundary that can be drawn around the domain of intentionality. (For the most part only, because of course there are facts to the effect, for instance, that someone thinks such-and-such a thought.) But consistently with its being true, as it obviously is, that facts typically do not concern thought, we can understand the world's impacts on belief-formation as being already within the conceptual sphere, not impingements from outside it. The world's impacts on belief-formation are the actualizations of conceptual capacities that constitute experiences.

In sustaining the mere sanity of refusing to picture the world as a creature of our conceptual activity, it certainly helps that we can see our thinking as causally influenced by the world we think about. Friedman is wrong to imply that this is unavailable to me, as if the rational relation I discern between operations of sensibility and belief-formation—enabling a rational relation between the world itself and our thinking—excluded a causal connection. My objection to Davidson's picture is not that it takes the impact of sensibility on our thinking, and thereby the impact of the world on our thinking, to be causal, but that it takes the impact to be *brutely* causal—causal to the exclusion of being rational. That a relation's being rational can cohere with its being causal—that not all causal relatedness is brutely causal—is of course a doctrine of Davidson's own.[8]

The thought that causal relations "must ultimately be supported by a characterization of the world as the domain of physical natural fact", which Friedman suggests is essential to the way Davidson sustains the world's independence from our intellectual activity, is in fact superfluous to the possibility I am exploiting, the possibility of pointing to a causal connection between thinking and the world in order to disclaim an idealism that depicts the world as a creature of our conceptualizations. This physicalism about causal relations reflects a scientistic hijacking of the concept of causality, according to which the concept is taken to have its primary role in articulating the partial world view that is characteristic of the physical sciences, so that all other causal thinking needs to be based on causal relations characterizable in physical terms. This might be warranted if there were a reason to credit physical science with a proprietary capacity to penetrate to the real connectedness of things. But I follow Gadamer in holding that there is no such reason.[9] And I think this is Davidson's view too, though he slips from it in his conception of causal relations. The thought that causal relations between mental activity and the extra-mental world require an ultimate anchorage in physical nature, so far from being necessary for Davidson's common-sense realism, as Friedman suggests, is out of line with Davidson's best thinking.

8. See "Actions, Reasons, and Causes". Davidson there discusses reasons for action, but his considerations apply equally well to reasons for belief.

9. See, e.g., *Truth and Method*, p. 449: "the truth that science states is itself relative to a particular world orientation and cannot at all claim to be the whole." See also the elaboration of this thought at pp. 450–3.

As I said, Friedman concedes (p. 464) that for Gadamer the possibility of a fusion of horizons is supposed to save us from relativism. But he juxtaposes this concession with saying that for Gadamer, unlike Davidson, the "cultural and linguistic traditions" that account for the initial positions of horizons "can certainly be conceptually divergent from one another" (ibid.). I think this contrast is a misreading of Gadamer. When Davidson attacks the very idea of conceptual divergence between languages, his target is the thought that there might be a way of thinking, a conceptual scheme, constituted as such by the fact that its exercises are suitably directed at the world, with this relation to the world conceived as independent of whether the exercises are intelligible to us. (At p. 191 of "On the Very Idea of a Conceptual Scheme", he describes the target like this: "The idea is . . . that something is a language, and associated with a conceptual scheme, whether we can translate it or not, if it stands in a certain relation (predicting, organizing, facing, or fitting) to experience (nature, reality, sensory promptings).") Rejecting this conception, or supposed conception, is perfectly compatible with acknowledging, as Davidson of course does (pp. 183–4), that different languages can express different, even strikingly different, ways of thinking. When Gadamer writes of different "worlds" corresponding to different horizons (e.g. at p. 447, in a passage Friedman quotes), his point—precisely because this talk of different "worlds" comes in a context in which Gadamer is insisting that "the multiplicity of these worldviews does not involve any relativization of the 'world'" (ibid.)—cannot be more than what Davidson thus acknowledges. This talk of different "worlds" is only vivid imagery for the undisputed idea of striking differences between mutually accessible views of the one and only world. There is not the contrast that Friedman draws.

This matters for Friedman's suggestion that my aligning myself with Gadamer leaves me without a response to a relativistic challenge. With this suggestion Friedman implies that Gadamer's appeal to the possibility of fusing horizons cannot, as Gadamer supposes, genuinely protect him from problems of relativism. About coming to understand an initially alien thinker, I wrote (*Mind and World*, pp. 34–6) in terms that were intended to recall Davidson's conception of the standpoint of a radical interpreter, who takes note of how the alien subject's expressions of thought relate to the world the subject lives in. I sounded a Gadamerian note by urging that what the radical interpreter aims at is coming to share a horizon with the other. About this, Friedman writes (p. 466): "In what sense, however, is the world *with which the alien thinker is engaged* open to our view? For Davidson . . . the principle of charity guarantees that there is only one such world. . . . For McDowell, by contrast, the realm of the conceptual is absolutely unbounded . . . . If the conceptual contents of an alien thinker's engagements with the world are not yet available to us, therefore, how can the world corresponding to these conceptual contents be so? Are we not faced—*before* a fusion of horizons—simply with two different conceptual systems together with two different 'worlds' constituted by these systems?" This reflects Friedman's misreading of my image of the unboundedness of the conceptual, and his misreading of Gadamer's talk of different "worlds", as if these bits of imagery made unavailable the commonsense point that there is only one world. The world with which the alien thinker is engaged, in a way that is open to our view, is simply the world, which—this is a point that Davidson and Gadamer share—we cannot distinguish from the topic of our world view. What we are faced with before a fusion of horizons is the world, together with a candidate for being understood as another way of conceiving it, and we have a guarantee—if what confronts us really is another thinking subject—that it will be possible to understand the other's engagements with the world as expressive of another view of the world we had in view all along. (Here we see how the idea that horizons can be fused can be expressed in what amounts to a formulation of the principle of charity.) When we come to understand the other subject, that can involve a change in how we view the world. When the horizons fuse, the horizon within which we view the world is no longer in the same position. But what is in view, now that the horizon is in its new position, is still the world, everything that is the case, not some supposed item constituted by this particular new positioning of the horizon—everything that seems to be the case from within a horizon so positioned. There is no devaluing of reality's independence from thinking here.[10]

3. My main point so far has been that Davidson's exploitation of the principle of charity (at least in this connection) matches Gadamer's exploitation

10. Friedman in effect refuses to allow Gadamer and me to distinguish a change in our view of the world from a change in the world. See p. 466, n. 50, where, besides his misreading of Gadamer's talk of "different 'worlds'", he also tries to justify this conflation—from which he concludes that "the possibility of fusion does nothing to diffuse the threat of idealism"—by citing from me a remark to the effect that when we are not misled in perception, there is no difference between how we perceive things and how they are. But that is a truism. It cannot dislodge me (or Gadamer) from the thought that every world view has the world in view as everything that is the case, not as everything that it takes to be the case.

of the possibility of fusion of horizons. Friedman is wrong to suggest that the divergence between them—about whether or not there must be something shared, language or tradition, in the background of the very idea of an understanding consciousness—reveals a difference in respect of vulnerability to a threat of relativism, and thereby to a threat of being unable to pay sufficient respect to the independence of reality. A way to bring this out is to note that Davidson's argument against relativism, in "On the Very Idea of a Conceptual Scheme", predates his even raising (at least in print) the question whether idiolects or shared languages should be primary in our reflection about the meaning of linguistic expressions, let alone settling it in favour of idiolects.[11] Davidson's argument against relativism turns on the thought that—to put it in a way that emphasizes the correspondence with Gadamer—any linguistic practice is intelligible from the standpoint of any other. Put like that, the thought is neutral on what the primary context for the intelligibility of linguistic items is: a community's language or the linguistic practice of an individual. The former might have seemed to cohere with Davidson's early essays on meaning and understanding.[12] In more recent essays he has urged the latter. The argument against relativism works equally well either way; the divergence Friedman tries to exploit is simply not relevant to the argument's success.

But the divergence is surely worth discussing in its own right. I do not believe Davidson has addressed considerations of the sort he would need to address if he were to engage with Gadamer on the significance of shared languages and traditions. And if that is right, there is at least an incompleteness in Davidson's defence of his attribution of priority to the practice of individuals. In fact I believe Davidson's disparagement of sharing deprives him of a wealth of insight that we can find in Gadamer, though I shall not be able to substantiate that properly in this essay.

Davidson plays down the significance of shared languages in the course of reacting against a certain conception of linguistic competence. According to this conception, mastery of a language is "the ability to operate in accord with

11. For this latter doctrine of Davidson's, see, among other essays, "A Nice Derangement of Epitaphs", and "The Social Aspect of Language". It may not be quite accurate to describe Davidson's position as giving priority to idiolects; see Michael Dummett, "A Nice Derangement of Epitaphs: Some Comments on Davidson and Hacking", at p. 469. But Davidson does not dissent from this characterization, and it is a convenient way to bring out the flavour of his thinking.

12. See, e.g., "Truth and Meaning".

a precise and specifiable set of syntactic and semantic rules", and "verbal com-munication depends on speaker and hearer sharing such an ability, and it re-quires no more than this" ("The Social Aspect of Language", p. 2). Mala-propisms (see especially "A Nice Derangement of Epitaphs") provide clear counter-examples—cases where understanding is not disrupted by mis-matches between speaker and hearer in respect of anything we might see as rules to which they conform their linguistic behaviour. In what he himself de-scribes as "a leap" ("The Social Aspect of Language", p. 7), Davidson moves to the thesis that there is "no reason, in theory at least, why speakers who un-derstand each other ever need to speak, or to have spoken, as anyone else speaks, much less as each other speaks" (ibid.). Of course he does not deny that we have a use for the idea of languages spoken by several people. But he suggests ("The Social Aspect of Language", p. 3) that this familiar idea can be reconstructed in terms of speakers tending "to use the same words to mean the same thing", and that the definitional transition from individual practice to shared language is "a short, uninteresting step". Mutual understanding is mas-sively easier if one shares ways of using words and constructions with one's in-terlocutors. This merely practical utility is the only importance Davidson is willing to concede to shared linguistic practice. Because sharing makes mutual understanding easier to arrive at, people who live together are in practice brought up into conformity with one another in their linguistic behaviour, but Davidson suggests that in principle there need not be any such sharing.

By Gadamer's lights, Davidson is surely right to deny that a shared ability to produce linguistic behaviour in conformity to specifiable rules could suf-fice for mutual intelligibility. Even restricted to people who, as we would ordinarily say, speak the same language, this is unacceptable. Looking back over his inquiry into what sharing a language might amount to, Davidson says ("A Nice Derangement of Epitaphs", p. 445): "We have discovered no learnable common core of consistent behaviour, no shared grammar or rules, no portable interpreting machine set to grind out the meaning of an arbitrary utterance." And this chimes well with Gadamer. Nothing could be further from the spirit of Gadamer's reflections about hermeneutics than to suppose there could in principle be a method, in a narrow sense, for ar-riving at an understanding of another person's linguistic productions—something that could be followed mechanically, or, in Davidson's image, a "portable interpreting machine".

Davidson is also surely right that people who understand each other need not share a language with each other in the ordinary sense. Suppose after a disaster two monoglot survivors from widely divergent linguistic communities encountered each other. Surely they could in principle, given sufficient imagination and good will, come to understand each other's linguistic performances. We could concoct an extraordinary sense in which, in making sense of each other, they would share a language, one defined by specifying what counts as speaking in the same way in terms of the translation scheme they use for each other's utterances (see "The Social Aspect of Language", p. 7). But as Davidson says (ibid.), "this is not what anyone would call sharing a language, nor what anyone has meant by a common practice or a shared set of rules or conventions".

In this thought experiment, we envisage mutual understanding between people neither of whom speaks as the other speaks. But Davidson's "leap" goes further, to the claim that understanding does not require anyone ever to *have spoken* as anyone else speaks. Now we could make "speaking as someone else speaks" imply the conception of a sharing that suffices by itself for understanding, and then it would be simply a way of putting Davidson's main point to say that no one needs ever to have spoken as anyone else speaks in that sense. I have suggested that this coincides with a fundamental thought of Gadamer's. Mutual intelligibility is never a matter of the parties having internalized an interpreting machine, and that holds in particular for previous abilities of the parties in our thought experiment to come to an understanding with fellow speakers of their divergent mother tongues. But this just emphasizes that on a more ordinary interpretation of "speaking as someone else speaks", our thought experiment as it stands involves people who previously spoke as others did—say, one speaks German and the other speaks Xhosa, and before the disaster they spoke these languages in interacting with others who spoke them too. If Davidson is to sustain his doctrine that shared practice is of no philosophical interest beyond what derives from its utility in facilitating communication, he must suppose this feature of the thought experiment is inessential. Davidson's claims commit him to denying that one needs to learn to speak as others do, in the ordinary sense, in order to become a human subject, a potential party to an encounter with another that leads to mutual understanding, at all.

Gadamer says (p. 443): "man's being-in-the-world is primordially linguistic." A follower of Davidson might want to appropriate these words, glossing "linguistic" in terms suitable to Davidson's devaluing of shared languages. But Gadamer is discussing Humboldt's reflections on the differences between languages—languages in the ordinary sense, in which they are shared by their speakers and have histories: languages in the sense that Davidson claims has only practical importance and is devoid of philosophical interest. Gadamer's wording is meant to capture the real significance of Humboldt's doctrine that "languages are worldviews" (ibid.). The thought is that the being-in-the-world of any human subject is shaped by one or another language in the ordinary sense.

I do not believe Davidson ever considers the thought that shared languages might matter for the constitution of subjects of understanding. His target is always the conception of a sharing that would suffice of itself for communication. His implied denial that shared languages might matter in another way is ungrounded by argument. Perhaps it is unintentional, and it may seem harsh to hold him to it. But the fact remains that, focusing exclusively on what is required for communication, he draws a conclusion that is generally disparaging to shared practice. He proceeds as if shared practice could be philosophically interesting only if it were true that it suffices, of itself, for mutual understanding between parties to it. This looks like a blind spot for an alternative possibility.

Davidson writes ("The Social Aspect of Language", p. 10): "It . . . seems to me important to emphasize that much successful communing goes on that does not depend on previously learned common practices, for recognizing this helps us appreciate the extent to which understanding, even of the literal meaning of a speaker's utterances, depends on shared general information and familiarity with non-linguistic institutions (a 'way of life')." This seems well placed against his standard target, the idea that shared linguistic practice might suffice for mutual understanding. But in pointing in the other directions it points in, the remark opens the question whether shared languages might be philosophically significant in a different way. A world view, with the same world in view as one's interlocutor has in view ("shared general information"), and familiarity with a human way of life are surely not just aids to arriving at understanding, but conditions for being potential subjects of understanding at all. And can we make sense of subjects meeting these conditions without having been initiated into languages in the ordinary sense, shared linguistic practices?

A human way of life is pervasively shaped by language, not just on occasions of verbal behaviour but also in its "non-linguistic institutions". ("Man's being-in-the-world is primordially linguistic.") A "language-game" cannot be confined to bursts of speech. It is a whole in which verbal behaviour is integrated into a form of life, including practices that if considered on their own would have to be counted as non-linguistic.[13] In one sense, we might say, there are no non-linguistic human institutions. Does it make sense to suppose there could be this pervasive shaping of life by language if everyone's verbal behaviour was completely idiosyncratic? Surely the understanding baulks if we are asked to envisage initiation into and maintenance of a distinctively human way of life in a context in which there is no such thing as simply hearing the meaning in another's words—in which all communicative interactions require the parties to work at interpreting one another, as they would have to if the ordinary idea of a shared language had no application.

Humboldt considered the differences between human languages in terms of different forms of a universal faculty. Conceding that such an approach yields insights, Gadamer writes (p. 441): "Nevertheless this concept of language constitutes an abstraction that has to be reversed for our purposes. *Verbal form and traditionary content cannot be separated in the hermeneutic experience.* If every language is a view of the world, it is so not primarily because it is a particular type of language (in the way that linguists view language) but because of what is said or handed down in this language." (Gadamer's emphasis.) Humboldt already had a thought that Gadamer puts like this (p. 443): "language maintains a kind of independent life vis-à-vis the individual member of a linguistic community; and as he grows into it, it introduces him into a particular orientation and relationship to the world as well." But Humboldt understood this thought in terms of "the formalism of a faculty" (pp. 440, 442), whereas Gadamer, reversing that abstraction, understands it in terms of "the unity between language and tradition" (p. 441). Here the very idea of having the world in view is made intelligible in terms of having grown into a tradition, which is part of what it is to have learned to speak a language in the ordinary sense. In learning to speak a language in the ordinary sense, one does not just acquire propensities to respond verbally to aspects of the passing show. One learns what to say, which in the first instance coincides with what *we* say, about general features of the world,

---

13. This is one of the ways in which Wittgenstein uses the expression "language-game"; see *Philosophical Investigations* §7: "I shall also call the whole, consisting of language and the actions into which it is woven, the 'language-game'." See also §19: "to imagine a language means to imagine a form of life." Davidson must mean to sound this Wittgensteinian note with his use of "way of life". *Truth and Method* antedates Gadamer's encounter with Wittgenstein, but its conception of the linguistic character of human life resonates with Wittgenstein's later work.

including, importantly, the past—though it can become clear to one that this is what one is learning only when one is already some distance into the development. Can we keep an application for this idea of growing into a tradition while we try to suppose that no two individuals share a way of speaking? (What becomes of, for instance, listening to the stories of the elders, or more sophisticated counterparts to that?) Or can we dispense with the idea of having grown into a tradition and still make sense of possessing a world view? Does it make sense to suppose an individual might acquire a world view by his own efforts of concept-formation and investigation? It cannot help to bring in the efforts of others, if one must already have a world view in order to be able to interpret their attempts to tell one what they have found out.

Davidson accepts that the very idea of speaking meaningfully presupposes "the distinction between using words correctly and merely thinking one is using them correctly" ("The Social Aspect of Language", p. 10). He argues against the thesis that the required use of "correctly" involves norms of a shared practice. Instead he urges that the relevant norm is determined by a speaker's intention to be understood in a certain way. A speaker uses words correctly, in the only sense that matters, if he uses them in such a way as to be understood as he intends. Depending on one's audience, this may involve using words incorrectly by the lights of grammarians of languages in the familiar sense.

Davidson is surely right in this resistance to elitism in our reflections about meaning. But without claiming that one can make oneself understood only if one uses some common language in ways that would be approved by a certain sort of authority, we can wonder if the conceptual apparatus that Davidson here helps himself to would be available if there were no such thing as a shared language. The ability to intend some performance to be understood in one way or another has to be learned, like the ability to intend to trump one's right-hand opponent's ace. Such an intention is not a purpose that might simply start to animate a creature's activity in the course of its animal life, as the purpose of grooming itself can start to govern the behaviour of a cat. Is it only a superficial fact, a reflection of mere practicalities, that as things are we acquire the ability to have such intentions at all by learning to speak a language in the ordinary sense—by acquiring a repertoire of potential actions that belong to such a practice, much as trumping one's opponent's ace belongs to the practice of certain games? Does it make sense to suppose that the repertoire of actions whose acquisition enables the formation of such intentions in the first place might be specific to an individual? This is not to suggest that in uttering a string of words one can mean, and be understood to mean, only what the words mean in some shared language. But it is one thing to agree with Davidson that that is not so, and quite another to abandon the thought that the primary form of the ability to mean something by verbal behaviour is the ability to mean what one's words mean, independently of the particularity of one's communicative situation—that is, what they mean in the language, in the ordinary sense, that one is learning to speak.

Davidson holds that "verbal behaviour is necessarily social" ("The Social Aspect of Language", p. 5). And, since he takes language and thought (in a certain sense) to be interdependent, this necessary sociality embraces thought as well: "there must be an interacting group for meaning—even propositional thought, I would say—to emerge" ("The Social Aspect of Language", p. 15). Unsurprisingly given how he disparages the significance of shared practice, the sociality he has in mind is minimal: there must be at least a pair of subjects who interpret each other, and there is no necessary role for shared practices. When there are more than two parties to linguistic interaction, each encounter is in principle similarly confined to its participants, with no need for communal practices in the background. This is to depict the sociality of language as *I-thou* sociality, in contrast with *I-we* sociality—to use terminology introduced by Robert Brandom.[14] Davidson only sketches an *I-thou* conception of the sociality of language, but Brandom undertakes a detailed *I-thou* picture, culminating in provision for making objective purport explicit, that hinges on the idea that the participants in the language-game keep score of one another's deontic statuses, their commitments and entitlements.

It would be impossible to do justice in a few sentences to Brandom's mammoth enterprise, which includes far more than just elaborating this Davidsonian inspiration. But without going into detail, we can see that the scepticism I have expressed, starting from Gadamerian considerations, about Davidson's conception carries over to Brandom's, in the shape of the question whether an *I* and a *thou* can be intelligibly in place without a shared language—something that belongs to a *we*—to enter into consti-

---

14. *Making It Explicit: Reasoning, Representing, and Discursive Commitment*; see the Index, under "*I-thou/I-we* sociality". See in particular p. 659, n. 50, for an approving citation of Davidson as taking the sociality of "linguistic practice and therefore intentionality" to be of the *I-thou* variety.

tuting them. It is mysterious how the appeal to scorekeeping can help here. How can a pair of items neither of which is on its own intelligible as a perspective on the world—this is why the construction is supposedly necessary—somehow become perspectives on the world by means of the inclusion, in what they are not on their own intelligible as perspectives on, of stretches of each other's behaviour? There is no such difficulty about the Gadamerian *I-we* picture. Here familiarity with a natural language, in which verbal form and traditionary content are inseparable, constitutes an individual stance that is perfectly intelligibly all on its own an orientation towards reality. As Gadamer can put it (p. 449): "In language the reality beyond every individual consciousness becomes visible." All on its own: not, of course, that a permanently solitary individual could intelligibly have such an orientation towards reality—the language that makes the orientation possible is essentially the possession of a *we*; but there is no reason to accept that the way sociality underlies the possibility of objective purport is by way of multiple individuals keeping tabs on one another.

Brandom suggests that *I-we* pictures are bound to be objectionable. A picture of a linguistic practice has to incorporate subjection to norms, and Brandom suggests that *I-we* pictures, if they undertake this burden, speak of "the community" as acting in norm-involving ways in which only persons can intelligibly act, such as assessing the performances of speakers. Thereby such approaches unacceptably treat "the community" as a superlative individual.[15]

We should not be misled here by a verbal divergence between Brandom and Davidson. The norms involved in this argument of Brandom's are not the expediencies that figure in Davidson's gloss on "correctly", when Davidson undertakes to provide for the distinction between merely thinking one is using words correctly and using them correctly. What Brandom has in mind is, ultimately, norms embodied in the very idea of objective purport. ("Ultimately": he has an idiosyncratic conception, which I am bypassing for these purposes, of norms whose formulation does not involve talk of objective purport, in terms of which he thinks the possibility of objective purport is to be understood.) For instance: the fact that "red" on my lips has the meaning it has involves its being *correct* for me to use the word in saying how a thing is only if the thing is *red*. The normativity this exemplifies makes contact with Davidson's thinking at the point at which he

15. See *Making It Explicit*, pp. 38–9.

undertakes to provide for objective purport, a separate point from that at which he acknowledges "norms" put in place by a speaker's intention of being understood. Davidson considers the need to distinguish merely thinking one is using words correctly from using them correctly only in connection with being mistaken about what uses of words will get one's meaning across, but the need for a distinction that we can formulate in those terms arises equally in connection with saying how things merely appear to be, as opposed to how they are. I think it does not indicate any substantive divergence from Brandom that Davidson talks of correctness in the use of words only in connection with successfully expressing one's mind and not in connection with whether the mind one expresses is in line with how things are. (See "The Social Aspect of Language", pp. 10–14, for "normativity" as communicative expediency, and pp. 14–15 for objectivity, which Davidson treats in a way that does not involve acknowledging a role for an idea of correctness.)

Brandom's argument against *I-we* conceptions certainly tells against some philosophical appeals to "the community". But there is no super-person in the picture I have been recommending. I have not credited the *we* who share a language with a super-personal counterpart to the deontic attitudinizing by individuals that is central to Brandom's picture. It might seem that the point of invoking a *we* must be to ensure that there is someone—if not other individuals then a super-individual—to hold speakers to the norms (in Brandom's rather than Davidson's sense) of their linguistic practice. But this reflects a metaphysical scruple about the very idea of subjection to norms, a scruple that finds comfort in seeing norms as instituted by personal activity—if not on the part of ordinary persons, then, in a version of the picture that would certainly be confused, on the part of a super-person. And I think the scruple is baseless.[16] If that is right, there is no ground for Brandom's suggestion that anyone who refuses to reduce the necessary sociality of language to interactions between individuals must make a super-person out of a *we*. Languages are among what Gadamer calls (p. 460) "the suprasubjective powers that dominate history". They give a normative

---

16. At p. 661, n. 64, Brandom mentions without comment (citing Heidegger) the kind of considerations that show the scruple to be baseless. But this does not deter him from letting its effects control his own thinking about normativity. Consider the implication, at pp. xiii–xiv, that normativity is "mysterious" unless seen as instituted by activities on the part of those who are subject to the relevant norms.

shape to our life-world, in a way that is not to be reduced to the activities of subjects, but saying that is not crediting personal performances to super-persons.

I have barely scratched the surface of Gadamer's thinking about language. My purpose in this section has been no more than to urge that its basic ori-entation stands up well to comparison with the *I-thou* orientation of Davidson and Brandom. Thereby I hope to have removed one obstacle that might blind philosophers of "analytic" formation to the riches of the third part of *Truth and Method*.

Subjective, Intersubjective, Objective[1]

1. For several decades now, Donald Davidson has been steadily producing an amazingly rich and—even though it has been presented in self-contained papers—systematic body of work. In this volume, we have another instalment of his creative output, the fruits of his reflections on central topics in epistemology and metaphysics, shaped by his distinctive and influential approach to issues in the philosophy of language and the philosophy of mind. It goes without saying, but I shall say it anyway: it is a fine thing to have these vintage essays in easily accessible and portable form, to put beside the first two volumes, with a place of honour reserved on the shelves for the eagerly awaited fourth and fifth.

But I think the best way to celebrate Davidson's work is not to praise it, but to find it controversial. Nobody gets everything exactly right, and what is most fruitful in philosophy is work that is worth taking issue with.

2. I want to start by raising some questions about themes that are signalled by the title of this collection and brought together in the final essay, "Three Varieties of Knowledge". Davidson argues that knowledge of the non-mental world around us, knowledge of the minds of others, and knowledge of our own minds are mutually irreducible but mutually interdependent. To me that seems exactly right; my uncertainty is about the details of his picture, not its broad outlines.

To begin with, Davidson argues that the very idea of the objective is inseparable from the idea of the subjective. Concepts of features of objective

---

1. These remarks were written for a symposium that was originally planned to honour Davidson's work in general, but reframed, at his request, as a discussion of the third volume of his papers.

reality require more than mere differential responsiveness to those features. For a creature to have concepts of the objective, and hence for it to have beliefs and knowledge about the objective, it must be aware that in general there can be a difference between how things objectively are and how things seem to it. For there to be mental states with objective content, their possessor must have the idea of objectivity, which is the idea of that potential gap between how things are and how one takes them to be. That puts in place a dependence of objective knowledge on at least a potential awareness of the state of one's own mind, how one takes things to be. And if the subjective comes into view in the first instance like that, in the guise of one's own take or perspective on objective reality, that ensures a dependence in the other direction, of the subjective on the objective. The primary case of the subjective is a subject's take on the objective. (That is not exactly how Davidson secures the connection in this direction, but I think it is Davidsonian in spirit.) So the objective and the subjective are interdependent. So far so good; that seems just right to me.

What links the package as we have it so far, the objective and the subjective, to the intersubjective is the fact that according to Davidson it is language that makes possible the genuinely conceptual engagement with the world that requires a subject to have the idea of objectivity and the idea of its own take on the world. And language is essentially public. It is essential to language that it enables us to make ourselves intelligible to others and to find others intelligible, that it enables us to make our own minds known to others and to know the minds of others. This mutual intelligibility between ourselves and others requires us to conceive objective reality as common ground between ourselves and our interlocutors, potential and actual.

This connection too seems right to me, at least at this level of abstractness. I agree that language is essential for a conceptual engagement with the world, and that language has to be public. I do not want to join those who think, against Davidson, that creatures without language have a subjective orientation towards objective reality, at any rate in the interesting sense that gives rise to the familiar problems of epistemology. In general I find Davidson's human chauvinism on this question perfectly congenial. (Though I wish he would say more about how we should talk about brutes, who are, as he concedes (pp. 101–2), much more like us than they are like guided missiles. We need more than just the insistence, which I applaud, that our ways of understanding brutes differ crucially from our ways of understanding ourselves and one another. We need a positive line about our ways of understanding brutes, and it is not satisfying to suggest that crediting them with intelligent engagements with their environment is just a convenience, called for only by the fact that we lack detailed knowledge about their internal control machinery.)

What bothers me in this region of Davidson's thinking is the way he ascribes a *priority* to intersubjectivity in the interconnected triad of subjective, intersubjective, and objective. It is "through having the concept of intersubjective truth", Davidson suggests, that we "come to have the belief-truth contrast"—that we "arrive at the concept of an objective truth" (p. 105). Certainly given that language, conceived as essentially public, matters for objectivity in the way Davidson says it does, it follows that one cannot have the concept of an objective truth without at least taking oneself to be able to come to an understanding with others. That is, there cannot be a concept of objective reality without a concept of intersubjective truth. But to say that the concept of mutual understanding is a *route to acquiring* the concept of objectivity goes beyond that. And I cannot see how this suggestion of a way into the circle coheres with the thesis that objective and intersubjective, like any pair of the triad, are mutually interdependent. If they are—which I think is right—then surely one could not have the concept of intersubjectivity first, without yet having the concept of objectivity. But that is what the idea of a way of acquiring the concept of objectivity implies. Surely one has either all or none of the three ideas: the idea of subjectivity, the idea of objectivity, and the idea of intersubjectivity. If they are interdependent, one of them cannot be that through which one arrives at the others.

What *can* be the case before the concept of objectivity is on the scene, and hence, granting Davidson's conception of concepts, before any concepts at all are in hand, is that one sentient being is linked to another sentient being by the fact that each is differentially responsive to the other's differential responses to some feature of objective reality. That non-conceptual, perhaps pre-conceptual, relatedness, to a feature of reality and one another's responses to it, is the structure that I think Davidson usually has in mind when he talks about triangulation (see, e.g., pp. 117–21). Getting into such relations to others might be a way to arrive at the concept of objectivity. But as Davidson himself insists, being parties to non-conceptual triangulation does not make creatures possessors of the idea of intersubjectivity. It does not even make them instances of it. So even if we grant that triangulation might be essential for objectivity, that does not warrant the suggestion of a priority for intersubjectivity.

Anyway, I am not sure about Davidson's claims for triangulation. Davidson urges that the triangular structure of responses to one another's responses to the world is necessary for there to be an answer to the question what the responses to the world are responses to (see, e.g., p. 119). He talks about dogs conditioned to salivate when a bell rings. Are they responding to the bell, or to the vibrations in the air, or to a pattern of stimulation of nerve endings? We have no natural way to describe the stimulus that elicits the response except in terms of the bell, and Davidson suggests that that is one side of a structure that, when it gets to have two sides, provides for determinacy in the identification of stimuli. Now I am not sure I understand the problem to which this is supposed to be a solution. Dogs do not respond to configurations in their own nervous systems—that is not a live candidate. (Their nervous systems do.) Dogs do respond to sounds. In the case we are considering, they have been conditioned to expect food at the sound of the bell. However produced, that sound would trigger the same expectation. That is, the response is to the sound—the bell is merely what usually produces the sound. In thus discounting the bell, am I identifying the stimulus as a certain vibration in the air? That would be a superfluous bit of metaphysics. In fact, if someone said "When you say it doesn't matter that the sound is produced specifically by the bell, you're saying that what they respond to is the vibration in the air", it would be a fair—though no doubt annoying—answer to say "No, I'm saying that what they respond to is the sound".

When I say all that, I am giving expression to a conception of how we make sense of the behaviour of animals. (Here is a point at which, as I suggested, it would be good to have more to say about that.) As far as I can see, the classifications we find natural are not to the point—except, of course, that if we could not recognize items as instances of the same sound, we could not have the conceptual resources to say that what the dogs respond to is the sound. But given that we have the conceptual resources to do so, we say it is the sound they respond to because that is what makes the dogs' behaviour intelligible, in the distinctive way in which we can find animal behaviour intelligible. Making sense of what dogs do is a partial analogue to making sense of what concept-possessors do, which centrally includes speaking. That is, it is an analogue to, or perhaps a simple form of, interpretation, which is the master theme of Davidson's philosophy of language and philosophy of mind. Identifying "the" cause—the target—of a response, if the response is a bit of animal behaviour, is an exercise in interpretation in a broad sense, and we may as well focus on the narrow sense in which the response is informed by conceptual capacities and understanding behaviour is inseparable from interpreting a language. Certainly this connection with interpretation implies that thinking about the targets of responses involves envisaging two perspectives, that of the responder and that of an interpreter. But these are not the same as the base points of Davidson's triangle. Even if we focus on the primary case of making sense, the interpretation of language, surely interpreters do not need to be in communication with their subjects.

Davidson argues that in the most fundamental cases, the meaning of an observational sentence is given by what normally causes the disposition to assent to it (see, e.g., p. 151). We might put this thought by saying that the target of a linguistic response is its normal cause. I think that is right, but it risks being misleading if it suggests that an interpreter must first identify "the" cause of a linguistic response—a task that, if approached in the abstract, might seem to raise questions like the one about the dogs—and then, on the basis of having independently settled such questions, declare that cause to be the target. Identifying "the" cause, where the definite description gets its point from Davidson's thought about the meaning of occasion sentences, is itself already an exercise of interpretation, and the identification of target and cause does not establish that interpretation in general faces questions like the one about the dogs.

In Davidson's picture, subjects "take cognitive advantage" of the triangular situation (p. 120); they "make use of the triangular situation to form judgements about the world" (p. 130). I do not dispute that my having the concept of a table (say)—a condition for my being able to make judgments about tables as such—is inextricably connected with my knowledge that I can make myself intelligible to others, and understand others, as talking about tables. But that is not to say that I somehow use my confidence that I could come to an understanding with others as a means to project my thinking to a determinate place in objective reality when I make a judgment about a particular table. I have to admit that I find this imagery of exploitation (taking advantage, making use) a bit mysterious.

I want to end this part of my remarks by mentioning a different connection between the publicity of language and the possibility of coming to a view of the world, which—following Davidson—includes a view of oneself and others as oriented to the world. Learning to talk is not just acquiring habits of verbal response to features of the passing show. It is also acquiring propensities to assent to sentences that might be said to give expression to fundamental propositions about reality, such as that there were things that happened a very long time ago—sentences of a sort that Wittgenstein talks about in *On Certainty*, though because of their status as hinges on which our practices of deciding what to say turn, he tends to suggest we should not suppose utterances of such sentences give expression to propositions at all. At first this element in learning to talk must be just acquiring propensities to vocalize, or react to the vocalizations of others, in ways that pass muster with one's elders. None of this proto-linguistic output is understood until a great deal is understood; as Wittgenstein says (§141), "Light dawns gradually over the whole".

I cannot find any acknowledgment of anything in this area in Davidson, and I think this may not be an accident. Focusing on the requirements for communication between beings that are already full-fledged subjects, Davidson is sceptical about whether speaking a language requires doing as others do (see pp. 114–5; and there will be more about this in the fifth volume). I think this scepticism would make it hard for him to acknowledge the importance, in acquiring a conception of the world with oneself and others in it, of simply learning what to say at that fundamental level, which to begin with—before light has dawned—surely cannot be anything but learning to vocalize in ways that pass muster in a group that one is being initiated into.

3. I am going to end by briefly reopening a conversation about "A Coherence Theory of Truth and Knowledge". In his Introduction (pp. xv–xvi) Davidson says this is the essay he would most like to rewrite. He chastises himself for giving the impression that he disallows any role for the senses in "serious commerce between world and mind". For my part I do not see how any reader of that wonderful essay could miss the fact that Davidson credits the senses with a substantial role in our acquisition of knowledge about the world. His claim is, perfectly clearly, not that the senses play no role in knowledge-acquisition, but that their role is causal and not evidential. I cannot see how rewriting could make that any clearer.

My problem with "A Coherence Theory" is not that it leaves the senses out of the picture, but precisely that it thus restricts their role to the merely causal. The only sensory episodes that figure in Davidson's picture of perception are sensations, which are the sort of thing Kant must have meant by "intuitions without concepts" when he remarked that intuitions without concepts are blind. I think Davidson is clearly right that such things could be only causally, not rationally, relevant to the formation of belief. That is a way of capturing the point Kant makes when he says they are blind. The trouble by my lights is that Davidson's picture has no room for intuitions in the sense in which Kant is talking about intuitions by the time we get to the Transcendental Deduction in the first Critique—episodes that are them- selves cases of our sensory capacities at work, as opposed to being merely caused by operations of our sensory capacities, but which are like beliefs in being actualizations of conceptual capacities and so able, consistently with the basic principles that underlie Davidson's thinking here, to be rationally and not just causally relevant to our thinking. Davidson has no room for the availability of facts to subjects in their sensory consciousness itself.

When we have reached this point in the conversation on earlier occa- sions, Davidson has expressed a puzzlement about what this is that I find missing from his picture. He claims to accommodate perceiving that such- and-such is the case, in the guise of acquiring the belief that such-and-such is the case in a way that is caused, through the operation of the senses, by such-and-such's actually being the case (see p. xvi). What more do I want?

Well, I think it is wrong to think of the significance of "seeing that . . ." (say) as exhausted by the fact that seeing is standardly a mode of belief- acquisition. Seeing that P is not the same thing as acquiring the belief that P in a visual way, though no doubt usually people who see that P do acquire the belief that P, and no doubt if that were not so it would not be possible for there to be such a thing as seeing that P. The difference between seeing that P and visually acquiring the belief that P can be brought out by noting that one can realize later that one was seeing that P, though one did not know it at the time and so did not at the time acquire the belief that P. "I thought I was looking at your sweater under one of those lights that make it impos- sible to tell what colours things are, but I now realize I was actually seeing that it was brown." In saying this, one registers that one had, at the relevant past time, an entitlement that one did not then realize one had. One was in a position to acquire a bit of knowledge about the world, but because of a misapprehension about the circumstances, one did not avail oneself of the opportunity. One did not form the relevant belief, let alone get to know that that was how things were. This past entitlement, possessed without one's then realizing it, is a case of the sort of thing I find missing from Davidson's picture—the availability of a fact to a subject in an episode or state of sen- sory consciousness.

Davidson's so-called coherentism is encapsulated in the claim that "nothing can count as a reason for holding a belief except another belief" (p. 141). The case I have described violates this dictum; it is a case in which there was an entitlement that was not a belief. Of course it is precisely because the entitlement was not a belief that the subject did not form the belief that the entitlement in fact warranted. But it was an entitlement even so, as the subject later realizes. Taking the modality one way, we might say the subject *could* cite the entitlement even at the time—her conscious state was constituted by the presence to her of the relevant fact. Taking the modality another way, she could not cite the entitlement, because her misapprehension about the lighting prevented her from recognizing her conscious state as the entitlement it nevertheless was. Davidson's "coherentist" dictum would be vindicated if it were right to restrict the entitlements a subject has to those she can cite on this second way of taking the modality. But why should we make this restriction? It amounts to a first person (and present tense) approach to epistemic entitlement, and it looks out of line with the sympathy Davidson expresses, in a different context, for a "resolutely third person approach to epistemology" (p. 194). That remark of mine is merely *ad hominem*, and there is no time now to address the issue itself. But I think there is plenty to be said for the idea that epistemology's topic should be not what subjects know, but what they are in a position to know, which is separated from the first topic precisely by cases in which opportunities to know are not taken—cases in which subjects have entitlements that are not beliefs.

PART IV

Reference, Objectivity, and Knowledge

Evans's Frege[1]

1. It helps to start with Russell. In the Theory of Descriptions, Russell gives an account of the logical form of sentences with definite descriptions in what might intuitively be thought of as subject position—sentences of the form "The F is G". Russell's parsing amounts to "There is exactly one thing that is F, and it is G".[2]

This distinguishes the logical form of such sentences from the logical form of sentences with genuinely referring expressions—"logically proper names"—in what, in this case, really is subject position.

In Russell's conception, sentences with logically proper names in subject position express thoughts (or propositions) whose availability to be thought or expressed depends on the existence of the objects referred to by the logically proper names.

Suppose someone sets out to express a thought by uttering a sentence containing a definite description. Russell urges that lack of an object that uniquely satisfies the description cannot imply absence of a thought expressed. Definite descriptions owe their capacity to contribute to the thought-expressing powers of sentences to the fact that they are constructed in a familiar way out of independently significant words. Their significance, like that of a specification, should be independent of whether or not there is anything the specification fits.

Admittedly there is a superficial parallel between the form "The F is G" and the form "a is G" (where "a" marks a place for a logically proper name). If there is an object that uniquely satisfies what replaces "F" in an instance of the former, something is true of the description that is also true of the

---

1. Thanks to José Bermudez for comments on an earlier version of this essay.
2. See "On Denoting". The focus on monadic predications is of course inessential.

logically proper name in an instance of the latter. Both determine a certain object as what the thought that is being expressed concerns, in the sense that the truth or falsity of the thought depends on how it is with that object. Indeed we could use that formulation to define a certain conception of singular reference.

But on Russell's view this superficial parallel masks a deep difference. Where absence of a suitable object would require us to find no thought expressed if we assimilated the two logical forms, the Theory of Descriptions finds a thought that is no worse than false. If we focus on this difference, we shall not be inclined to make much of the conception of singular reference that groups definite descriptions—though only those that do single out objects—and logically proper names together.[3]

2. In Russell's conception, thoughts expressible with the help of logically proper names—genuinely subject-predicate thoughts—are accessible only to thinkers who are "acquainted" with the objects in question.[4] And on his official account of acquaintance, one is acquainted only with things that figure in one's immediate consciousness, conceived in a rather Cartesian way: bits of the sensory given, bits of what is given with similar immediacy in recollection, and (as long as Russell believes in it) one's own self. Outside the range of one's acquaintance, one can direct thoughts at objects only in the way the Theory of Descriptions provides for.

So the apparatus of the Theory of Descriptions cannot have its application limited to sentences that actually contain definite descriptions. The Theory's characteristic form comes to figure also in Russell's account of the thoughts speakers have in mind when they utter sentences containing what would

---

3. This is the questioning of the "traditional grouping" of singular referring expressions for which Evans gives Russell credit, in the Introduction of *The Varieties of Reference*, pp. 1–3. For his own part, Evans goes on to argue that "Russell's criterion *for being a referring expression* simply will not stand up" (p. 53, citing the treatment of "descriptive names" at pp. 46–51; see also pp. 30–8). Accordingly he needs a different ground from the one I have rehearsed here (which he cites as "the most important argument Russell gave", p. 52) for refusing to count pure definite descriptions as referring expressions. For Evans himself, singular terms need not be "Russellian". But since Evans argues that for *Frege* singular terms were "one and all Russellian" (p. 47), I shall suppress this complication here, and work with Russell's original criterion, which is at any rate a criterion for being a Russellian referring expression. If Evans is right about Frege, the conception that underlies Russell's grouping is the only one that matters for him.

4. See, e.g., "Knowledge by Acquaintance and Knowledge by Description".

ordinarily be regarded as singular referring expressions, if the objects in question are outside the range of the speakers' acquaintance, on Russell's restricted conception of acquaintance. This goes for ordinary proper names, say of people other than oneself, and ordinary uses of demonstratives, as opposed to the peculiar demonstratives that Russell identifies as logically proper names. In these cases too we have to suppose that speakers direct their thoughts at objects—if there are objects such that the truth or falsity of the thoughts turns on how it is with them—by exploiting specifications of the objects.

This extension of the apparatus would chime neatly with the original motivation for the Theory of Descriptions. As long as we are confined to objects of acquaintance on Russell's official conception, it would be hard to make sense of a risk that someone might utter a sentence intending to express a genuinely subject-predicate thought, but turn out to have expressed no thought because the belief that there was a suitable object was mistaken. It would be natural to think one cannot be mistaken about the existence of what is given in one's immediate consciousness. But outside the range of one's acquaintance, there is room for scepticism—though perhaps only a hyperbolic Cartesian scepticism in some cases—about the existence of objects one might want to be able to direct one's thoughts at. Here as in the original application, extending the Theory of Descriptions would provide thoughts immune to the fate Russell cannot tolerate in the original case, of turning out to be only illusions of thoughts if the belief that suitable objects exist was mistaken. The worst that could happen is that they would be thoughts all right, but false ones.

It has to be acknowledged that this motivation—avoidance of illusions of thoughts—is not at centre stage when Russell recommends extending the apparatus of the Theory of Descriptions to utterances in which, say, ordinary proper names figure.[5] What Russell urges is not that if one tries to frame subject-predicate thoughts about objects outside the range of one's acquaintance, one runs the risk that the supposed thoughts turn out to be illusory. The attempt to express such thoughts is ruled out directly by the fact that one is not acquainted with their objects; Russell does not appeal to the fact that belief in the existence of their objects is chancy.

In fact, though he thinks such thoughts are beyond the reach of our minds, Russell nevertheless exploits them, somewhat strangely, in his

5. This implies that the way Evans depicts Russell, at pp. 44–5, needs qualification.

picture of how we communicate with the relevant kinds of sentences. If I say something "about Bismarck", perhaps using that ordinary name, the thought in my mind must have the sort of shape that the Theory of Descriptions provides for, since I am not acquainted with Bismarck. But in speaking as I do, Russell holds, I "describe" a subject-predicate proposition about Bismarck—one that only Bismarck himself could get his mind around, since only Bismarck himself was acquainted with the object in question. Someone other than Bismarck who understands me similarly thinks a descriptive thought, with a similar relation to that singular proposition, which neither of us can actually think. It is because each of us thinks a proposition that "describes" that same singular proposition, not thinkable by either of us, that we are in communication with each other.[6]

This comports badly with supposing Russell's motivation for extending the Theory of Descriptions so much as includes, let alone being constituted by, the wish to avoid invoking thoughts of a kind such that their very existence might turn out to be an illusion. If Bismarck is a hoax on the part of historians, the picture Russell thinks I must have of how I can communicate by talking "about Bismarck" involves my purporting to "describe" a thought that by Russell's lights would not exist on that hypothesis.

However, this fact about Russell's thinking need not matter for a broad-brush picture of one way it was widely received, which is all that my present purposes require.

The Theory of Descriptions makes straightforward sense of a way in which thoughts can be targeted on objects. Many philosophers were captivated by this. And they took encouragement from Russell in supposing that that way of directing thoughts at objects need not be restricted to cases where the specification by means of which a thought singles out its object is made explicit in the relevant utterances. There was an intelligible tendency to suppose that the Theory of Descriptions captured the very idea of a thought's or an utterance's being directed at an object. Thoughts that single out objects do so by way of specifications.[7]

6. See *The Problems of Philosophy*, p. 31. There is a fine discussion of this part of Russell's thinking in Mark Sainsbury, "Russell on Names and Communication".

7. For an excellent example of this kind of approach, see John R. Searle's treatment of proper names ("Proper Names"), which is notable for its ingenuity about how to arrive at the content of the specification that, according to Searle, displays how a name singles out its object. Searle conceives his topic as how ordinary proper names refer; his Russell-inspired treatment is not responsive to the Russellian thought that might be put by saying

As I stressed, for Russell himself the idea that a description can single out an object as what a thought concerns, in the sense that the truth or falsity of the thought turns on how it is with that object, marks only a superficial match with the semantical character of logically proper names. In Russell's view, logically proper names enable the expression of thoughts that are about objects in a deeper sense. It is understandable that this should have tended to be forgotten, given how Russell's treatment restricts, almost to vanishing point, our repertoire of the kind of thought we can express with the help of logically proper names. But it remains the case that the extended Theory of Descriptions does not capture Russell's view of genuinely subject-predicate form. In this general "descriptivism", what it is plausible to iden-tify as Russell's own conception of singular reference goes missing.

3. How does this Russellian picture relate to Frege's distinction between sense and reference, as it applies to singular terms?[8] First we need a quick sketch of the point of Frege's distinction.

What difference does the presence of a singular term make to the capacity of sentences containing it, perhaps as uttered on suitable occasions, to ex-press thoughts?[9] Part of the answer is that, at least in primary occurrence, and at least if it does refer to something, a singular term serves to indicate which object the thought expressed by a sentence concerns, in the sense that the truth or falsity of the thought turns on how it is with that object.

But if that were the whole of the answer, we would not be able to dis-tinguish the contributions to the expression of thoughts made by pairs of

---

that "reference" by specification is not genuine reference—not what can be done by ex-ploiting logically proper names. For a conception of this kind applied to the object-directedness of thought in general, not restricted to thought expressed with the help of proper names, see Searle's *Intentionality: An Essay in the Philosophy of Mind*.

8. In this formulation, I have reverted to "reference" for Frege's "*Bedeutung*"— "Meaning" in Evans's exposition, following the more recent translations. See Sainsbury's note, *Departing from Frege*, p. 225. I shall mostly stay with the German term. My formula-tion is designed to allow for the fact that Frege's distinction applies to meaningful expres-sions in general, not just singular terms; the application to whole sentences, in particular, will come up later.

9. The allusion to occasions of utterance is strictly needed to accommodate indexicality and similar phenomena. But my concerns here are at a level of abstractness at which this can pretty much be ignored, and I shall continue to talk often of sentences as (capable of) expressing thoughts.

singular terms that refer to the same object. We would not be able to distinguish the thoughts expressible by sentences that are alike except in that where one has one such term the other has the other. And Frege's idea is that at least sometimes we ought to want to make such a distinction. There is no need for it if the one term differs from the other "only as object"—that is, presumably, if they are merely notational variants.[10] But there can be cases in which a rational subject who understands both terms can, say, believe the thought she understands as expressed by one sentence from such a pair while disbelieving the thought she understands as expressed by the other. To suppose she both believes and disbelieves the same thing would bring her rationality into question, though *ex hypothesi* her combination of attitudes is consistent with her being rational. We can smoothly maintain the hypothesis of rationality if it is not the same thing that she believes and disbelieves. Her understanding of the two sentences associates them with different thoughts. And, since the sentences that express the different thoughts are alike apart from the singular terms they contain, it must be the difference in singular terms that accounts for the difference in thought expressed. It must be that though the singular terms have the same *Bedeutung*, they differ in their contributions to the thoughts expressible by sentences that contain them. That is what a difference in sense (*Sinn*) is, on the part of subsentential expressions. (A difference in *Sinn* on the part of whole sentences just is a difference in thoughts expressed.) Thoughts about the same object can differ in how the object figures in them, how it is presented by singular terms that refer to it in expressions of the thoughts.[11]

On this account, the controlling aim of Frege's introduction of *Sinn* is to provide a conception of thoughts—possible contents of propositional attitudes and speech acts—that, in conjunction with a repertoire of concepts of kinds of propositional attitudes partly explained in terms of rational relations between them (for instance, that rationality precludes believing and disbelieving, or withholding judgment with respect to, the same thing), yields descriptions of ways in which minds are laid out such that the descriptions put a subject's rationality in question only when the subject's

---

10. See "On Sense and Reference", p. 57.

11. This explanation of the point of saying that co-referring singular terms can differ in sense follows Frege's exposition in the letter to Jourdain that Evans cites, *The Varieties of Reference*, pp. 14–15 (the "Afla"-"Ateb" case).

rationality is indeed open to question. If we find ourselves shaping up to crediting a subject with, say, believing and disbelieving the same thing, even though we can find no fault with the subject's rationality,[12] we are to go back and find a way to distinguish what she believes from what she disbelieves. This is what dictates that we find, or postulate, a semantically relevant respect in which coreferring singular terms can differ.

We might say Frege's introduction of *Sinn* reflects an idea on these lines: the very idea of a configuration in a mind needs to be seen in the context of the concept of rationality.[13]

It can be illuminating to draw a connection between this way of spelling out what Frege wants to do with the notion of *Sinn* and his attacks on psychologism about logic. His target there is a conception of logical laws as laws of thought, understood on the model of laws of motion. On this conception, the topic of logic is how minds actually proceed in certain transitions from beliefs to beliefs. (Perhaps how minds normally proceed, but psychologism would understand the invocation of normality statistically, not normatively.) Frege objects that if we conceive our topic as a certain region of facts about how minds work, we shall not get logic into view at all. Logic deals with some of the ways in which minds *must* work, with "must" expressing requirements of reason.

We can put the point here in parallel with the point about the concept of sense. It is not that the concept of deductive inference is alien to the very idea of moves that minds in fact make. The concept of deductive inference is indeed a resource for describing transitions from one layout of mind to another. But the concept makes sense only in the context of an idea of requirements of reason. Just so with the concept of, say, what someone believes. It is a resource for describing certain configurations of minds. But here too, the

---

12. Perhaps a failure to bring the two states together for rational assessment counts as a failure of rationality, in which case the proviso excludes such cases. In any case, they are not what we need to consider in order to understand Frege's point. If it dawns on me that I have contradictory beliefs, what dawns on me is precisely that I believe and disbelieve the same thing, and now rationality requires me to make an adjustment. Frege's point applies to cases where rationality requires no adjustment in attitudes even in a subject who is consciously adverting to both the attitudes in question. If I do not know that Paderewski (the statesman) and Paderewski (the pianist) were the same person, there is nothing irrational about my, say, regarding it as unlikely that Paderewski (the pianist) ever engaged in politics, even though I know a bit about Paderewski (the statesman).

13. Compare Donald Davidson's well-known invocation of the idea of "a constitutive ideal of rationality" in "Mental Events".

concept makes sense only in the context of the concept of rationality. By virtue of its connection with concepts of propositional attitudes, it seems right to say the concept of sense belongs to psychology. But if we say this, we must conceive psychology otherwise than psychologistically.[14]

What I have said so far does no more than locating the notion of *Sinn* in terms of a role it is to play. Thoughts—senses expressible by whole sentences—are to be propositional-attitude contents, individuated in accordance with what Evans (*The Varieties of Reference*, pp. 18–19) calls "the Intuitive Criterion of Difference". Senses of subsentential expressions are to be individuated in a way that allows them to be seen as the contributions made by the expressions to the thoughts expressible by sentences they occur in. And of course this is not yet to say anything specific about what the sense of this or that referring expression might be.[15] But that is nothing to complain about. When we locate the concept of sense in terms of its role, we equip ourselves with a general frame in which to place the detailed accounts of the senses of different types of referring expressions that Evans goes on to offer. Indeed we need something at this level of abstraction in order to appreciate exactly what those detailed accounts are supposed to be accounts of.

4. What we have so far is that singular terms with the same *Bedeutung* can differ in sense, and the difference in sense is a difference in how objects figure in thoughts expressible by sentences containing the singular terms—a difference in "way of being given" (*Art des Gegebensein*), mode of presentation.[16]

---

14. A psychologistic psychology of propositional attitudes could be described as a "physiology of the understanding", echoing Kant's remark about Locke: *Critique of Pure Reason* Aix.

15. As Evans says (p. 18), "Frege never said much about particular ways of thinking of objects".

16. Sainsbury proposes a pared down Fregeanism that discards the idea of mode of presentation as a gloss on the attribution of *Sinn* to singular terms. See *Departing from Frege*, pp. 2–3. Part of his reason is the fact, exploited by Evans, that the idea is hard to reconcile with taking in stride singular terms with *Sinn* but no *Bedeutung*, which is central to Fregean thinking on Sainsbury's reading. But whether the thesis that there can be *Sinn* without *Bedeutung* merits that centrality is just what is going to be at issue here. It is hard to see how the basic Fregean conception, as expounded for instance in connection with the "Afla"-"Ateb" case, could do without an idea of different ways in which an object can figure in thoughts, and "mode of presentation" ("way of being given") need do no more than express that idea. It need not encourage the pressure towards reductivism that Sainsbury, rightly to my mind, resists.

In one place Frege illustrates this idea by suggesting that Aristotle might figure, in some thoughts expressible by using the name "Aristotle", as the pupil of Plato and teacher of Alexander.[17] The words of Frege's gloss here have the form Russell discusses under the head of definite descriptions. And that may have helped to encourage a widespread assimilation of what Frege is aiming at, when he credits singular terms with *Sinn* as well as *Bedeutung*, to the neo-Russellian "descriptivism" that I sketched earlier.

In this reading, Frege's idea that singular terms have *Sinn* anticipates the Theory of Descriptions in its generalized application. Frege and Russell—but, in line with the reception of Russell that I described earlier, Russell deprived of his conception of genuinely subject-predicate form—figure together, for instance, as progenitors of the target of Saul Kripke's influential attack on descriptive conceptions of singular reference.[18]

In the aftermath of the revolt against "descriptivism", in which Kripke's work is a landmark, much theorizing about singular thought and its expression came to focus on certain contextual relations, typically of a causal character, in which objects can stand to episodes of thought and speech.[19] In a newly dominant conception of how singular reference works, directing thoughts at objects by exploiting such relations replaced targeting thoughts

---

17. "On Sense and Reference", 58.

18. *Naming and Necessity*. Remarks like the one about Aristotle are certainly not sufficient ground for concluding that Frege belongs in Kripke's target area. The remark is about how Aristotle figures in certain thoughts (not about how the reference of the name "Aristotle" is fixed). But even though it is not just about reference-fixing, it need not imply that, if Aristotle had died in infancy and someone else studied with Plato and taught Alexander, those very thoughts would still have been thinkable, but would have had that other person as their topic; or that if no one had studied with Plato and taught Alexander, those very thoughts would still have been thinkable, but would have had no one as their topic. Frege's remark is about a way in which, thanks to certain assumed facts, *Aristotle* can figure in some thoughts. It is consistent with supposing that in those envisaged alternative circumstances, there could not have been the thoughts we are considering, thoughts in which Aristotle figures as the student of Plato and teacher of Alexander.

19. Here we should note Evans's chapter 3, where he protests against the way the generalized causal conception of singular reference was supposed to be encouraged by Kripke's own suggestions about how uses of proper names trace back, through the continuation of practices of using them, to their bearers. But the genesis of the general conception that came to replace "descriptivism" as the dominant conception of singular thought and speech need not matter for my purposes here.

on objects as those that conform to specifications. This made room for a kind of recovery of the forgotten parts of Russell's thinking. The relations with objects that are prominent in the new thinking about reference take on something like the role of Russell's concept of acquaintance. But genuine subject-predicate form does not now need to be subject to the tight restrictions that were imposed by the requirement of acquaintance as Russell applied it. Not that Russell is usually conceived in this way, as a forerunner of the newly dominant conception. The forgotten parts of his thinking tend to stay forgotten, and he figures only as a proponent of the "descriptivism" that the new thinking aims to supplant.

With Frege assimilated into the general "descriptivism" that the newly dominant conception defines itself against, the new orthodoxy is conceived as rejecting Frege's apparatus of *Sinn* and *Bedeutung*, or at least as requiring substantial modification in its employment. This has fateful consequences for how philosophers conceive the connection between how thought and speech are directed at objects, on the one hand, and rationality, which provides the frame within which Frege's notion of *Sinn* functions, on the other. At least in the sorts of case that fuel the rejection of "descriptivism", vestigial versions of Frege's notion of *Sinn* come to figure, if at all, only in characterizing configurations in minds that—in a supposedly required divergence from Frege's idea that *Sinn* determines *Bedeutung*—at most partly determine which objects thoughts concern, needing extraneous help, in singling out objects, from causal relations between thinkers and objects, now conceived as obtaining outside the sphere of a subject's rationality.[20]

5. Now the main interest of Evans's exploitation of Frege lies in its rejecting this picture.

Russell formulates his conception of genuinely subject-predicate form by speaking of propositions in which objects themselves figure as constituents. Propositions so conceived would be individuated by their objects, so that there could not be two such propositions in which the same property is attributed to the same object. So in Russell's version of the conception, there is no room for Fregean *Sinn*. If this is what it takes for

---

20. For a splendidly clear expression of a view of this kind, keeping the Fregean terminology but abandoning the thesis that *Sinn* determines *Bedeutung*, see Colin McGinn, "The Structure of Content".

thoughts to be object-dependent, thoughts individuated by Fregean *Sinn* would not be object-dependent.

But Evans points out that what is essential to Frege's notion of *Sinn* has no such implication. Frege's controlling idea, as I said, is that if a rational subject can, say, both accept and withhold acceptance from what we would otherwise need to conceive as a single thought, we must find two different thoughts to be the contents of the two attitudes. Nothing prevents this idea from being applied to thoughts that are "Russellian", in the sense of being dependent for their being available to be thought or expressed on the existence of their objects. So far as singular thoughts are concerned, Frege's aim is to provide for thoughts about objects to be individuated more finely than by the objects they are about, as in Russell's conception. That formulation uses a neutral notion of a thought's being about an object. Nothing stands in the way of its being applied to thoughts that are about objects in the "Russellian" sense that they depend on the objects for their existence.

From this angle, it looks like a mere mistake on Russell's part to think genuinely subject-predicate propositions alike in their predicative material must be identical if they concern the same object. This idea may be encouraged, in Russell's own thinking, by the way his doctrine of acquaintance restricts the range of genuinely subject-predicate propositions. Within the restricted range, it is hard to see how there could be pairs of cases like those Frege exploits to argue that we need a finer individuation of thoughts. But once Russell's restriction is lifted, as in the conception of reference that has supplanted "descriptivism" as the dominant position, it becomes clearer that object-dependence in thoughts is not, of itself, alien to the Fregean framework. There is nothing to prevent us from contemplating rational subjects who combine beliefs and disbeliefs in whose content the same predication is made of the same object—the sort of combination that recommends the Fregean apparatus—even though the contents that Fregean considerations require us to differentiate are contents whose being thinkable at all require the existence of the object. A proposition can be object-dependent even though its identity is determined not by the *Bedeutung* but by the *Sinn* of a singular term used in giving expression to it.

The *Sinn* of a referring expression is the way its *Bedeutung*, the object referred to, figures in thoughts expressible by using it—the way one thinks of the object in thinking such a thought. There can be more than one such way of thinking of a single object, even if each such way of thinking could not be in a thinker's repertoire if the object did not exist. So Fregean fineness of grain simply does not imply object-independence.[21]

This opens the way to a satisfying synthesis, which constitutes the context in which Evans considers, for instance, perceptually demonstrative thoughts. The reaction against "descriptivism" embodies insights about how certain contextual, in particular causal, relations between subjects and objects—which of course have to be actual to stand in those relations to subjects—matter for the directedness of thought at objects. And Evans's point shows that these insights can be, after all, fully integrated with a Fregean stress on rationality, as the frame within which thought about thought and its expression belongs. It need no longer seem that the insights belong with a "Photograph Model" of singular thought—a conception according to which what determines which object a thought concerns is at least partly external to its subject's rationality.[22] We can allow for cases in which reference is partly constituted by the obtaining of the sorts of contextual relations that figure in the new, supposedly anti-Fregean way of thinking, without after all needing to separate such reference from the characteristically Fregean topic, configurations within the minds of subjects understood in such a way that the very idea of such configurations belongs in a framework determined by the requirements of rationality.[23]

21. Evans actually suggests (p. 22) that if we gloss Frege's notion of the *Sinn* of a referring expression in terms of a way of thinking of an object, it is hard to interpret that except as positively *requiring* that such a way of thinking is object-dependent. And there is something to be said for that claim. (This is why Sainsbury wants to drop the notion of modes of presentation; see n. 16 above.) But the present point is just that nothing in the idea of ways of thinking of objects, conceived as individuated on Fregean principles, *excludes* their being object-dependent. Can *Sinn* can in general be glossed in terms of the idea of a way of thinking of the associated *Bedeutung*? This may seem to be threatened by the obvious fact that it cannot be a requirement for understanding a sentence that one know its truth-value. But the "obvious fact" is just that to understand a sentence one need not know that its truth-value is true, or that it is false, as the case may be. That does not prevent us from saying that entertaining the *Sinn* of, say, the sentence "Kant wrote three *Critiques*" is a way of thinking of a truth-value (in fact the truth-value true, though one need not know that that is a correct identification of the truth-value one is thinking of). In entertaining the *Sinn* of the sentence, one is thinking of the truth-value as the truth-value thereof that Kant wrote three *Critiques*. For this locution, see Montgomery Furth, "Two Types of Designation". For the point, made without that locution, see Evans, p. 17, including the discussion of Dummett in n. 17.

22. On the "Photograph Model", see Evans, pp. 73–9, and chapter 4.

23. The synthesis Evans enables needs to be separated from the response to the "new theory of reference" exemplified with great clarity by Searle (see, e.g., *Intentionality*).

Consider uses of demonstrative expressions that single out objects by exploiting their salient availability to perception. Describing the topic like that brings out how the determinate directedness at objects of the thoughts that can be expressed with the help of such expressions depends on contextual, and partly causal, relations between subjects and objects. But even so, "thoughts" in that formulation can be understood in Frege's way. Fregean fineness of grain, held in place by considerations involving rationality, does not need to be conceived as confined to some inner realm, constitutively independent of those real relations to objects. The real relations to objects do not need to be conceived as extra factors, over and above configurations in that supposed inner realm, in the determination of which objects are spoken of in such utterances and thought of in understanding them. Demonstrative senses can be fully Fregean senses that, precisely because they are partly constituted by real relations to actual objects, reach all the way to the objects.

6. As I remarked, Frege's distinction between Sinn and *Bedeutung* is not confined to singular terms. He applies it also to predicates, and, strikingly, to whole sentences. The *Sinn* of a sentence, perhaps on an occasion of utterance, is the thought it can express. Its *Bedeutung* is its truth-value, true or false as the case may be.

Readers are sometimes surprised at this. Surely, they think, the *Bedeutung* of a sentence ought to be a concatenation of the *Bedeutungen* of its significant parts. That is thought to capture an intuitive notion of a state of affairs or situation. So we have a supposed improvement to Frege, in which the *Bedeutung* of a sentence is a situation—conceived as a concatenation of objects and, perhaps, properties—that is actual or not according to whether or not the sentence could be truly asserted. There is a helpfully explicit example of

---

Searle's strategy is to incorporate mention of the causal relations that the new thinking makes much of into the specifications by means of which he continues to argue that singular thought singles out its objects—so that the characteristic concerns of the new thinking are swallowed up into a sophisticated version of "descriptivism". In Evans's synthesis, it is—as in the new thinking itself—not the concept of those relations that carries thoughts to their objects, but the relations themselves. That is the connection with object-dependence; if there is no object, there is no relation. But there is no longer the suggestion, which Searle admirably reacts against, that determining which object a thought concerns is at most partly taken care of by how a subject's mind is configured.

this kind of "correction" to Frege in Jon Barwise and John Perry, *Situations and Attitudes*.[24]

Barwise and Perry assume that "reference" expresses a more or less intuitive semantical idea, and that Frege's use of the concept of *Bedeutung* is a more or less inept attempt to capture it. What controls the supposedly intuitive idea is a principle of "the Priority of External Significance", which stands opposed to conceptions that find the significance of an expression in its connection to something in subjects' minds.[25] Frege acknowledges that in the *Bedeutung* of a sentence, as he conceives it, all specificity is eliminated. All true sentences have the same *Bedeutung*, the truth-value true, and all false sentences have the same *Bedeutung*, the truth-value false.[26] Barwise and Perry take this as an acknowledgment that Frege's apparatus as he uses it cannot accommodate structure in the external significance of language, which they take to be what is supposed to be secured by talk of *Bedeutung*. Their different account of what is "referred to" by sentences is supposed to supply sentences with a kind of external significance in which specific structure is not eliminated.

Evidently they assume Frege cannot preserve specific structure in external significance at the level of *Sinn*. At the level of *Sinn* the specific structure that differentiates the significance of one true sentence from another, or that of one false sentence from another, is not lost. Barwise and Perry must suppose that at the level of *Sinn* the external significance of language, its directedness at objective reality, is no longer in view.

But this is simply wrong about *Sinn*. The *Sinn* expressed in an assertoric utterance is what one says in making the utterance. What one says is, schematically, that things are thus and so, and that things are thus and so is what is the case, if one's assertion is true. And something that is the case is, in a quite intuitive way of speaking, a state of affairs. So an intuitive notion of states of affairs is perfectly available to Frege, but at the level of *Sinn* rather than *Bedeutung*.[27] Talking about the significance of sentences at the

---

24. See especially pp. 20–6. Properties, on any intuitive conception, are no better a fit for what Frege conceives as *Bedeutungen* of predicative expressions than states of affairs, on this kind of conception, are for what he conceives as the *Bedeutungen* of sentences, and the point is connected. But I shall not elaborate it here.

25. See *Situations and Attitudes*, p. 42.

26. "On Sense and Reference", 65.

27. Something that is the case, a fact, is something that can be truly said, or thought, to be the case. A fact is a true thought, in the sense in which a thought is the *Sinn* expressible

level of *Sinn* preserves structural specificity, while in no way retreating from the fact that meaningful utterances are (apart from the special case in which mental realities form the topic) directed at the extra-mental world. Barwise and Perry suggest Frege is confused in choosing truth-values over situations as *Bedeutungen* of sentences.[28] But the Priority of External Significance yields no ground for this extraordinary suggestion. The purpose for which they think he should have opted for situations as the *Bedeutungen* of sentences is served by *Sinn* as Frege conceives it. The point of crediting sentences with *Bedeutung* lies elsewhere, in the needs of a semantical account of logical validity. And for that purpose truth-value is just what is required.[29]

All this can be said without any special attention to singular terms. Advancing from a thought to its truth-value, which is what we do in judgment on Frege's account, cannot be a step that starts from a configuration that is not world-directed and moves to a stance that is world-directed, though with a loss of structured significance. A thought is already to the effect that things are thus and so. It does not acquire its bearing on the world when

---

by a sentence, perhaps on an occasion. Some may find it wrong to call the conception of states of affairs that I am insisting is available to Frege intuitive; it may seem less than intuitive to say that Hesperus's being visible over there (imagine an occasion of utterance) is a different state of affairs from Phosphorus's being visible over there. But whatever the status of this conflicting intuition, it is irrelevant to my point against Barwise and Perry. States of affairs individuated according to the *Sinne* of sentences usable to affirm them are finer-grained than proponents of this intuition would like, but fineness of grain in significance has no tendency to imply that the significance is not external. (This comes out particularly vividly when we see that fineness of grain is consistent with object-dependence in thoughts.) So even if my Fregean states of affairs are too fine-grained for some people's tastes, they are perfectly in line with Barwise and Perry's Principle of External Significance. There is widespread confusion about this, and I am inclined to suspect that it underlies the idea that states of affairs would need to be coarsely individuated.

28. See *Situations and Attitudes*, p. 21.

29. It is a mistake to approach Frege's general picture of *Bedeutung* in the way Barwise and Perry do, as extrapolating, to other sorts of expression, an intuitive notion of how singular terms relate to the objects they enable us to talk about. It would be better to start by appreciating the point of identifying the *Bedeutung* of a sentence with its truth-value, and to see how what is in fact an approximation to the intuitive notion—though it would be wrong to make too much of this—is yielded by a notion of *Bedeutung* for singular terms that is controlled by the requirements of a story according to which, roughly speaking, a singular term's having the *Bedeutung* it has consists in the difference it makes to the *Bedeutung* of a sentence that contains it. See Wolfgang Carl, *Frege's Theory of Sense and Reference: Its Origins and Scope*, p. 116.

someone affirms it inwardly in judgment or outwardly in assertion. And when we do focus on singular terms, it needs no detail of interpretation to see that for Frege, having an object in mind can only be entertaining a thought partly determined by a singular *Sinn*. There is no need for a further step—advancing from a thought to a truth-value—in order to arrive at a position in which one's mind is directed towards the associated *Bedeutung*. One's mind is already directed towards the associated *Bedeutung* just by virtue of entertaining a thought determined by the relevant *Sinn*. But the point becomes especially vivid with Evans's insight that, consistently with Frege's basic principles, a singular *Sinn* can actually be object-dependent. Evans's version of Fregean thinking makes it especially clear that a move from *Bedeutung* to *Sinn* is not a withdrawal from directedness at extramental reality.

The point of Fregean *Sinn* is, as I have said, to provide for a conception of contents that fits smoothly with a conception of what rationality requires of a thinker. Now it needs to be acknowledged that the considerations that are operative here do not make the Fregean apparatus compulsory. We need finer-grained contents if the attitudes we are allowed to work with, in the sorts of case Frege exploits, are restricted to, say, belief, disbelief, and suspended judgment. But we can preserve the rationality of the subjects in such cases even if we equip their attitudes with coarse-grained contents, contents individuated by the objects they concern, as long as we compensate by enriching our inventory of attitudes. Where we find ourselves shaping up to saying that a rational subject both believes and disbelieves the same thing, we can go on identifying the contents of the two attitudes, and protect the subject's rationality by saying she believes a certain coarse-grained proposition under one guise and disbelieves it under another.[30] This might be seen as a sketch for a notational variant of Frege's proposal.

Some people may be tempted to say it cannot be a mere notational variant. It is a substantive improvement, because by allowing us to exploit propositions individuated by the objects that are their topics (like Russell, one might say "having those objects as constituents"), it respects something on the lines of Barwise and Perry's principle of the Priority of External Significance. But what I have urged in this section implies that this supposed ground for preference is illusory. And this becomes especially clear when we take on board Evans's point that a singular *Sinn* can be object-dependent.

---

30. For an elaboration of a position on these lines, see Nathan Salmon, *Frege's Puzzle*.

7. Frege often says expressions can lack *Bedeutung* and still have *Sinn*. Singular terms that lack *Bedeutung* are not thereby shown to be without *Sinn*. And sentences containing singular terms without *Bedeutung* themselves have no *Bedeutung*, no truth-value, though that does not disqualify them from having *Sinn*, from expressing thoughts. On the face of it, this is incompatible with supposing genuine subject-predicate form is Russellian. And of course Evans does not deny that Frege says those things. He does not claim to find Russellian doctrine explicitly espoused in Fregean texts, at least after the introduction of *Sinn*. The claim is rather that the best way to work out what Frege means by attributing *Sinn* to singular terms is to align the Fregean apparatus with Russell's conception of genuine subject-predicate form.[31]

This belongs to a genre of readings in which something a philosopher says is set aside on the ground that the result yields a better version of his thinking.[32] In the simplest variety of such readings, the selection of what to discard reflects only the reader's view of what constitutes a philosophical improvement. In this spirit, someone who thought the best account of how thought is directed at objects is given by the "descriptivism" that finds its inspiration in the Theory of Descriptions might omit, from a reading of Russellian thinking about singular reference, the idea of logically proper names, and the conception of genuinely subject-predicate form that belongs with it. The only question such a reading of Russell could raise would be whether it really opened into a superior account of singular reference. There would be an admitted violence to Russell himself, excused on the ground that it led to better philosophy.

But this is not the sort of line Evans takes about Frege.

Evans insists that Frege's conception of *Sinn* can be understood to fit object-dependent thoughts, and that stands firm independently of speculation about Frege's own attitude to such an idea. This is worth stressing. In the end it is the idea of object-dependent *Sinn* that matters, not whether it can be attributed to Frege himself. But I want to consider Evans's reading of Frege, and not just the use Evans makes of Frege.

31. In Evans's own view genuine subject-predicate form is not restricted to sentences containing "Russellian" referring expressions (see Evans, pp. 30–3, 46–51). But he thinks Frege's conception of singular terms is at bottom Russellian. See n. 3 above, and the text below.

32. For another instance of a "Fregeanism" of this general kind, in which we allow ourselves to improve on Frege's own presentation of his thought, see Sainsbury's *Departing from Frege*.

The ground for going further, and putting the idea of object-dependent singular *Sinn* into a reading of Frege, is not a thesis about genuinely subject-predicate form that is merely imported from outside Frege's thinking. Evans claims that, in spite of Frege's remarks about *Sinn* without *Bedeutung*, the idea of object-dependence as a mark of genuinely subject-predicate thoughts is not alien to Frege's own thinking. There are features of Frege's own thinking that point in this direction.

Before he introduced the idea of *Sinn*, Frege expressed a Russellian line about singular thoughts.[33] However, it does not seem to have occurred to him to query the "traditional" classification of singular terms, which includes definite descriptions. Russell was going to find the "traditional" classification incompatible with taking singular thoughts to be object-dependent, and he was going to conclude that definite descriptions do not belong in a more principled category of singular terms. It is plausible that the considerations that were going to sway Russell made it uncomfortable for Frege to combine the "traditional" classification with the Russellian view of singular thoughts, as expressed in those early texts. So it will have relieved a tension when, after the introduction of *Sinn*, he found himself able to countenance thoughts expressed by sentences containing singular terms that have no *Bedeutung*. But Evans suggests that this apparent relief of a tension can have satisfied Frege only because he did not completely think through what he was doing.

The idea of a thought without a truth-value, which this doctrine commits him to, is problematic by lights that should have been Frege's own. Judging, in Frege's account, is advancing from a thought to the truth-value true. Such advance is correctly undertaken if the thought is true, incorrectly if not. That may seem to allow for cases in which a judgment is incorrect because the thought involved fails to be true, not by being false but by having no truth-value—because an expression of it would contain an expression without *Bedeutung*. But can we really recognize what happens in such a case as judging? Judging is judging something to be so. Supposing there is no

---

33. See the passages from *Posthumous Writings* cited by Evans at p. 12. (It seems clear that the "Seventeen Key Sentences" cannot postdate the introduction of *Sinn*, as in the dating by Scholz that Evans mentions as one that would be better for his reading of Frege. Frege's standard line after the introduction of *Sinn* is the one I am considering, that lack of *Bedeutung* on the part of a singular term does not deprive sentences containing it of *Sinn*.)

condition such that if it is met—if things are indeed so—the judgment is true, how can what we are dealing with be a case of judging? But if there is such a condition, it is either met or not,[34] and we are back to thoughts with one or other of the truth-values, true or false.[35]

As Frege notes, people can be confused into supposing that an expression such as "the least rapidly convergent series" has a *Bedeutung*.[36] Such people will endorse sentences containing such expressions. They will take themselves to be able to make judgments expressible by such sentences. But Frege cannot suppose there is a way things might be such that if things were that way such a supposed judgment would be true. If there were, there would be no alternative to saying things are not that way, so the thought is false. So how does the thought supposedly expressed by such a sentence relate to what such a person is doing when she takes herself to be making such a judgment? In this kind of case specifying the supposed thought cannot be saying *what* the person judges, in the sense of specifying how things are if the person is judging truly. No doubt a person in this situation judges that a certain sentence expresses a true thought. But we cannot get

---

34. Vagueness might require a qualification to this. But it would be quite implausible to suggest that emptiness in a singular term induces vagueness in atomic sentences containing it. The difficulty I am raising arises in connection with sentences that concatenate empty singular terms with non-vague predicates. So we can focus on that case, and ignore any extra messiness that vagueness might bring.

35. Sainsbury, *Departing from Frege*, p. 24, enables himself to talk of conditions for something to be the bearer of a name even in a case in which the name has no bearer ("For all x, 'Vulcan' refers to x iff x is Vulcan"), by employing a free logic, in which atomic sentences with empty names are false. That enables him to see conditions for sentences containing such names to be true ("Vulcan orbits the sun" is true iff Vulcan orbits the sun) as on a par with conditions for sentences containing non-empty names to be true. But this move abandons the link, which is surely central to Fregean thinking, between lack of *Bedeutung* on the part of a singular term and lack of *Bedeutung* on the part of (atomic) sentences containing it. Sainsbury's construction precisely equips an atomic sentence containing an empty name with a *Bedeutung*, the truth-value false. Frege, for whom such sentences were without *Bedeutung*, could not have defended the ascription of *Sinn* to empty singular terms, and consequentially to atomic sentences containing them, like this. See Evans, pp. 24–5, on how free logic is alien to Frege's thought. (It is not alien to Evans's own thought; see n. 3 above. For a discussion of how Evans might employ free logic in a semantics suitable to his conception of referring expressions, see Sainsbury, "Names in Free Logical Truth Theory".)

36. "On Sense and Reference", p. 58.

down from that metalinguistic level to a specific thought from which the person advances to the truth-value true.[37]

Perhaps the idea would be that some thoughts are judgeable—the ones that do have truth-values—and some not. But what is the unity in the concept of a thought, if thoughts are supposed to come in these two varieties—one such that to specify one of its members is to specify how things are according to it, the other not? If it does not belong to a thought as such to be judgeable, Frege's conception of judgment as advancing from a thought to a truth-value lacks the straightforwardness it seemed to have. And we still have the difficulty of saying what happens when someone accepts a sentence that, on this way of talking, expresses a thought that is not suitable for judgment because it lacks a truth-value. It is not a case of accepting a thought, in the sense in which specifying a thought someone accepts is specifying how things are thought by her to be. But surely that is what accepting a thought is, not just one interpretation of "accepting a thought".

We can find a clue to how Frege thinks about all this in the fact that he is happy to describe such cases in terms of unwittingly straying into the sphere of fiction.[38] Of course if "fiction" is just a label for the supposed realm of thoughts that lack truth-value this takes us no further. But in one place in the *Nachlass* where Frege talks head-on about fiction, he shows himself tempted by a certain conception of, say, story-telling, which indeed has its attractions. According to this conception, a story-teller makes a use of language modelled

---

37. This is a version of Evans's argument at p. 24. Carl, *Frege's Theory of Sense and Reference*, p. 24, says Evans identifies thinking with judging (forming a belief), thus losing contact with the indispensable Fregean idea of something from which one needs to advance in order to make a judgment. (See also p. 180, n. 26.) But what Evans identifies with forming a belief is of course not merely entertaining a thought, but *accepting* one; Carl's criticism rests on a crude misreading. Carl goes on to suggest, if I understand him, that Frege's mature conception of judgment, as an advance from a thought to a truth-value, positively requires the idea that sentential *Sinne*, thoughts, may or may not be associated with sentential *Bedeutungen*, truth-values. (See, e.g., p. 117.) But this seems obviously wrong. The thought from which one advances, when one judges truly or falsely, must already have its truth-value—true or false according to whether the judgment is true or false. It does not acquire its truth-value by means of the advance. Carl fails to engage with the difficulty of applying Frege's conception when someone thinks she can make such an advance in connection with a sentence that has no *Bedeutung*.

38. See the passage from "Der Gedanke" that Evans quotes at p. 28. This belongs with the fact that Frege standardly illustrates his *Sinn*-without-*Bedeutung* claims with examples from fiction, ordinarily so called.

on, and imitative of, the making of factual claims, so as to give the appearance of making assertions without actually doing so. And Frege suggests that when he talks of expressing thoughts in fictional discourse, that relates to the thoughts that figure in assertions and judgments only as talk of story-tellers as making assertions would relate to assertions that are expressive of judgment.[39] The cleanest way to capture what Frege seems to be driving at here is to say that there is really only one kind of thoughts, those such that to specify one is to specify how things are according to it, so that it is true if things are that way and false otherwise. Where he allows himself to talk as if there is another kind of thought, whose members lack truth-value, what he really has in mind—at least at some level of his thinking, which never quite surfaces into explicitness—is a kind of case in which someone merely goes through the motions of expressing a thought in the only sense Frege is really committed to, according to which it is part of the very idea of a thought that there is such a thing as how things are according to it. Merely going through the motions is something people do intentionally in fiction, strictly so called, and unintentionally in the sort of case we are considering.[40]

This suggests that when Frege exploits the separation of *Sinn* from *Bedeutung*, thought from truth-value, to alleviate the discomfort that will have resulted from combining his early "Russellian" conception of subject-predicate form with the "traditional" grouping of singular terms, this is not the complete breach with his early "Russellian" way of thinking that it might seem, and perhaps seemed even to Frege himself. In exploiting the idea of an unwitting lapse into fiction, he has confused himself. A conception that would be most cleanly put by talking of a mere appearance of *Sinn* has presented itself to him as if it allowed a kind of genuine *Sinn* that, in connection with indicative sentences, cuts loose from possession of a truth-value. If we pay

39. See the passage from the *Posthumous Writings* that Evans cites at p. 29.

40. Commentators have made great efforts to resist the drift of this passage from Frege. David Bell, in "How 'Russellian' was Frege?", claims (p. 273) that what Frege calls "*Scheingedanken*" are thoughts that "only aim to convey appearance". Sainsbury (*Departing from Frege*, pp. 11–12) acknowledges that *Scheingedanken* figure here alongside *Scheinbehauptungen*, and that *Scheinbehauptungen* are performances that give the appearance of being assertions (*Behauptungen*) but are not. But he strains to avoid the parallel interpretation of "*Scheingedanken*". He suggests, in effect, that the prefix "*Schein*" here means "not to be taken seriously", and, whereas "assertions" that are not to be taken seriously are not really assertions, thoughts that are not to be taken seriously can be really thoughts. But, as against both Bell and Sainsbury, it seems plain that the force of the prefix "*Schein*" is something like "(merely) apparent".

attention to the details of how Frege thinks about fiction, we can find, even in the places where he explicitly rejects the "Russellian" line, traces of a continuing pull towards it, which he may have concealed even from himself.

As Evans puts it (p. 30), Frege's remarks about fiction suggest that

> we may gloss those passages in which Frege says that a sentence containing an empty singular term may express a thought as follows. Yes: a sentence containing an empty singular term may have a sense, in that it does not necessarily have to be likened to a sentence containing a nonsense-word. But no: it does not *really* have a sense of the kind possessed by ordinary atomic sentences, because it does not function properly, it is only *as if* it functions properly. Frege's use of the notion of fiction wrongly directs our attention to just one case in which it is *as if* a singular term refers to something, namely when we are engaged in a pretence that it does, but there are others, and if we think of them, we might speak of apparent, rather than mock or pretend, thoughts.[41]

As Evans acknowledges (p. 28), this reading "does not present Frege in a very good light". That may seem to be the beginning of a principle-of-charity case against it.[42]

But when Evans suggests that Frege's early "Russellianism" is submerged, rather than definitively discarded, by his allowing himself *Sinn* without *Bedeutung*, it does not constitute a response merely to elaborate the characteristic Fregean claim to be concerned only with sentences usable in "science", only in reasoning directed at achieving knowledge.[43] Evans does not miss or

---

41. "Mock thoughts" is the wording in the translation Evans cites; but "apparent thoughts" (which does not embody the implication of pretence) would be a perfectly good translation of Frege's "*Scheingedanken*".

42. For the suggestion that Evans's Frege is not the "profound and powerful thinker" he is usually taken to be, see Bell, "How 'Russellian' was Frege?", p. 276.

43. That is what Carl does, *Frege's Theory of Sense and Reference*, passim. Bell too takes a version of this line. He scores some telling points against Evans's tendency to assimilate Frege's semantical interests to those of, say, Davidson (though it does not inspire confidence when Bell substitutes "explicit" for "implicit" in quoting Evans's claim—which I agree is over the top—that Frege's mature conception of reference is the semantics that is implicit in his earlier works: p. 269). But in the end the credentials of Evans's suggestion of a submerged "Russellianism" are not affected. The alternative picture of Frege's programme that Bell outlines (pp. 276–7) does not remove the difficulty Evans finds in Frege's official *Sinn*-without-*Bedeutung* doctrine, and Evans's suggestion about what underlies the doctrine loses no plausibility by being put in the context of Bell's more accurate account of Frege's general purposes.

ignore that Fregean intention. The trouble he fixes on comes from Frege's proceeding as if a concept for which he gives a proper explanation only in the context of the "scientific" use of language, the concept of thoughts, is straight-forwardly available for talking about cases in which people falsely suppose that sentences are suitable for "scientific" use.[44] And there is the discussion of fiction that Evans exploits, which strongly suggests that the underlying conception, never brought to explicitness by Frege, is that the availability of the concept in those cases is a mere appearance, part of the content of the false supposition.

If Evans's Frege is Frege, of course it would have been better if he had made the submerged thought explicit, to himself and to his readers. Evans's Frege is a thinker one of whose insights he himself only gropes at. But this imputation of unclarity about his own thinking cannot tell against the reading, on principle-of-charity grounds, unless not making it would put Frege in a better light than crediting him with at least groping towards an insight. This depends on the magnitude of the insight, and it would be hard to overestimate that. I gestured towards this earlier by saying that Evans's Frege enables a synthesis between acknowledging that contextual relations between subjects and objects matter for determining the contents of thoughts, on the one hand, and giving full weight to the idea that thinking is an exercise of rationality, on the other. This can be seen as a substantial contribution to a project that goes back at least to Kant, and that is beset with difficulties in the intellectual environment of modern philosophy: in-tegrating our rational powers with our natural situatedness in the world.

---

[44] The explanation is that to determine a thought is to determine a condition for its truth. Defending the idea that singular terms can have *Sinn* without *Bedeutung*, Sainsbury (*Departing from Frege*, p. 208) suggests that the natural counterpart to the idea of deter-mining a condition for a sentence to be true is the idea of determining a condition for a term to refer—a condition that may or may not be satisfied, without threat to its affording a specification of the term's *Sinn*. But a condition for a sentence to be true is not a condi-tion for it to refer *überhaupt*, but a condition for it to have one rather than the other of the *Bedeutungen* that sentences can have. Moreover, the connection of sentential *Sinn* with conditions—for truth in particular—is appropriate precisely because of the special lin-guistic character of sentences: they enable speech acts whose content is *that things are thus and so*, and specifying an instance of that form is specifying a condition for a sentence to be true. It is of course not to be expected that there should be a parallel to this for subsenten-tial expressions. Sainsbury's analogy is not natural at all.

Referring to Oneself

1. In an influential passage in *The Blue Book* (pp. 66–7), Wittgenstein distinguishes "two different cases in the use of the word 'I' (or 'my')", which he calls "the use as object" and "the use as subject". We have the use as object in, for instance, "My arm is broken", "I have grown six inches", "I have a bump on my forehead"; we have the use as subject in, for instance, "I see such-and-such", "I think it will rain", "I have a toothache". Wittgenstein explains the distinction like this:

> One can point to the difference between these two categories by saying: The cases of the first category involve the recognition of a particular person, and there is in these cases the possibility of an error, or as I should rather put it: The possibility of an error has been provided for. . . . It is possible that, say in an accident, I should feel a pain in my arm, see a broken arm at my side, and think it is mine, when really it is my neighbour's. And I could, looking into a mirror, mistake a bump on his forehead for one on mine. On the other hand, there is no question of recognizing a person when I say I have toothache. To ask "are you sure that it's *you* who have pains?" would be nonsensical. . . . And now this way of stating our idea suggests itself: that it is as impossible that in making the statement "I have toothache" I should have mistaken another person for myself, as it is to moan with pain by mistake, having mistaken someone else for me.

And he suggests a conclusion:

> To say,"I have pain" is no more a statement *about* a particular person than moaning is.

That is, "I", at any rate in the use as subject, does not serve to refer to a particular person. It is not the case that the role of an utterance of "I", in

186

helping to determine the significance of an utterance of a form of words like "I have toothache", is to indicate that of which the rest of the utterance is predicated—what the rest of the utterance has to be true *of*, if what one says in making the utterance is to be true.

2. In "The First Person", G. E. M. Anscombe explicitly argues that "I" is not a referring expression:

> Getting hold of the wrong object *is* excluded, and that makes us think that getting hold of the right object is guaranteed. But the reason is that there is no getting hold of an object at all. With names, or denoting expressions (in Russell's sense) there are two things to grasp: the kind of use, and what to apply them to from time to time. With "I" there is only the use (p. 61).

"I"-statements have, as it were, the look of predications, with "I" in subject position. And there is indeed a subject of predication, a target of reference, in the offing: in the case of my "I"-statements, the person John McDowell.[1] If I make an "I"-statement, it is true just in case its apparently predicative material is true of the person John McDowell; and in that specification of a truth-condition, we have a proper predication, with an authentic singular term denoting the item of which the predication is made (see "The First Person", p. 60). But according to Anscombe, it would be wrong to suppose that my "I"-statement is another way of predicating that material of that same item. "I" said by me is not another way for me to refer to that item.

Anscombe does not invoke the passage from Wittgenstein or exploit the distinction between the use as subject and the use as object. Her thesis seems to be quite general: an utterance of "I" does not refer, no matter what apparently predicative material it is concatenated with—"have a broken arm" no less than "have a toothache". Wittgenstein's suggestion, in contrast, seems to leave it open to us to suppose that at least in the use as object "I" is a referring expression. Still, Anscombe's point that "getting hold of the

---

1. Anscombe says that a person is "a living human body" (p. 61). She means to be talking about something that is not "still there when someone is dead". But I do not see how the words "living human body" can be intelligibly construed otherwise than by taking "living" to attribute a property that a human body can lose, *scilicet* without going out of existence. When there is no longer life in it, my body *will* probably "still be there" for a while. (It may not be, but only if the life is snuffed out by the body's, say, being blown to smithereens.) What will not "still be there" is the human being I am—not a human body, though certainly a bodily thing.

wrong object is excluded" is surely a descendant of Wittgenstein's point that no provision is made for a certain possibility of error.[2]

Her treatment of "I" centres on its role in giving expression to "unmediated conceptions (knowledge or belief, true or false) of states, motions, etc." (p. 62), where the truth or falsity of the "I"-statements turns on whether the states, motions, etc. can be truly predicated of (in my case) the person John McDowell. The significance of "unmediated" comes out clearly in her exploitation of an anecdote from William James (pp. 64–5). A person nicknamed "Baldy" had fallen out of a carriage; he had the idea that someone had fallen out of the carriage; and, on being told that Baldy had, said "Did Baldy fall out? Poor Baldy!" This indicates a "lapse of self-consciousness", which Anscombe locates in the fact that Baldy's "thought of the happening, falling out of the carriage, was one for which he looked for a subject . . ." (p. 65). An unmediated conception of the falling, in the relevant sense, would have been one for which that was not so. (Compare Wittgenstein's "there is no question of recognizing a person".)

This connects in an obvious way with the fact that "getting hold of the wrong object is excluded". Getting hold of the wrong object would be going wrong in looking for a subject of which to predicate the content of a conception. If there is no looking for a subject, there is no going wrong in looking for a subject.

We need also to deal with the use as object. There Wittgenstein's point, in the present terms, is that the conceptions expressed are not unmediated: looking for a subject is not excluded. I have a conception of, say, having a broken arm, and in Wittgenstein's accident case I need to look for a person of whom the state that my conception is a conception of could be truly predicated. (In another case I might not need to look for a subject for the predication; but even so, I know which person it is whose arm is broken in the sort of way in which one knows when one came to know by looking for a subject for predication.) But Anscombe's position is that here too, when I say "I have a broken arm", I am not predicating the state, having a broken arm, of a person to whom I refer by my use of "I". And that seems the right line for her to take.

---

2. I am isolating one strand in Anscombe's complex case for her conclusion; I prescind, for instance, from her claim that Frege's notion of sense cannot be made to fit a construal of "I", uttered by a particular person, as a referring expression. I believe Frege had a better view of that question; and he does not hesitate to speak of the "particular and primitive" mode of presentation under which one can figure only in one's own thoughts ("The Thought: A Logical Inquiry", at pp. 25–6).

What do I convey by saying "I have a broken arm", rather than, say, "John McDowell has a broken arm", which would be unproblematically a reference concatenated with a predication?[3] Presumably the point of using the first-person form is to effect a certain association between my mediated conception of the state, having a broken arm, and the unmediated conceptions to which I could give expression in what we can think of as the central uses of "I". By saying "I have a broken arm", I indicate that the person whose possession or not of a broken arm is to determine the truth or falsity of my statement is the one whose states, motions, etc. would determine the truth or falsity of statements I might make in which the first-person form would give expression to unmediated conceptions of those states, motions, etc. But if we must suppose that in the case of these potential other statements, where the conceptions are unmediated, the person in question would not be determined by being referred to, surely we had better suppose that in the associated uses too.

Anscombe says: "The expression 'self-consciousness' can be respectably explained as 'consciousness that such-and-such holds of oneself' " (p. 51). Here "oneself" is the "indirect reflexive", which is intelligible only in terms of the first person. The only explanation of the *oratio obliqua* form, "consciousness that such-and-such holds of oneself", is in terms of an *oratio recta* form containing an expression of the first person: consciousness whose content is given by "Such-and-such holds of me". (See pp. 46–7.) Now this account of self-consciousness is indifferent to whether the conception expressed in a replacement for "such-and-such" is mediated or unmediated. But Baldy's lapse of self-consciousness, in Anscombe's account, lies in his lack of unmediated conceptions of states, motions, etc. of the person Baldy (p. 65). That is surely right; and that is why expressions of unmediated conceptions are the central uses of "I", even though self-consciousness (in the sense of Anscombe's general account) is exemplified also in uses of "I" that express mediated conceptions. If there are no unmediated conceptions, as perhaps in some states of dissociation, then first-person talk and thought lapses altogether. But if first-person talk and thought is available at all, then it—that very thing, and hence self-consciousness—can extend to mediated conceptions (the use as object) as well.

---

3. Perhaps I have forgotten my name in the accident. But then we can ask why I say "I . . ." rather than, say, "The person in this bed . . .", or whatever other (non-first-personal) designation is at my disposal.

3. Anscombe's thinking here starts with an insight. It is indeed fundamental to an understanding of first-person forms that their central use is in expressing unmediated conceptions. But we can acknowledge that, and nevertheless refuse to accept that "I" is not a referring expression. We can block the inference by giving proper weight to this remark of P. F. Strawson's, which formulates the beginning of wisdom on these questions:

> "I" can be used without criteria of subject-identity and yet refer to a subject because, even in such a use, the links with those criteria are not in practice severed.[4]

What Strawson describes as a use of "I" without criteria of subject-identity is what Anscombe describes in terms of unmediatedness, the absence of any need to look for a subject. I do not look for a subject for the unmediated conceptions that I express in some of my "I"-statements (the central ones). Strawson's point is that that is no reason not to suppose that by "I" I refer to the person (in my case John McDowell) whose having the content of those conceptions truly predicable of him or not determines the truth or falsity of the statements (to put the matter in Anscombe's terms).[5]

As the possibility of putting it like that indicates, Anscombe does not simply reject the claim that the links with criteria of subject-identity are not severed. For her too, my "I"-statements are semantically connected to a particular human being: something that can be referred to in a way that is governed by criteria of identity. Where Anscombe diverges from Strawson is that she thinks this semantical connection cannot be a matter of reference. My "I"-statements are indeed true or false according to how it is with a particular human being, a potential target for reference that would be governed by criteria of identity; but not, according to her, because the utterances of "I" that figure in what looks like subject position in those statements refer to that human being.

Anscombe thinks that if one did take one's utterances or thoughts of "I" to be cases of referring, and tried to respect the facts about the use of "I", then the only thing one could find (or invent) for one's "I" to refer to would be a

---

4. *The Bounds of Sense*, p. 165.

5. I follow Strawson in assuming that the criteria of subject-identity are (at least for the subjects we know about) criteria for the identity of human beings; that is, animals of a certain kind. In this connection, Strawson wrote (in 1966): "The topic of personal identity has been well discussed in recent philosophy. I shall take the matter as understood." (*The Bounds of Sense*, p. 164.) This remark looks dated now, but those were better days.

Cartesian Ego: "*if* 'I' is a referring expression, then Descartes was right about what the referent is" (p. 58). She argues for this by imagining herself in a condition of sensory deprivation, telling herself "I won't let this happen again!"

> If the object meant by "I" is . . . this human being, then in these circumstances it won't be present to my senses; and how else can it be "present to" me? But have I lost what I mean by "I"? . . . I have not lost my "self-consciousness"; nor can what I mean by "I" be an object no longer present to me. . . . Nothing but a Cartesian Ego will serve.

We can consider this as an extreme case of unmediatedness, where there is not even a possibility of finding (as a result of looking for) a human being who could be said to have the intention expressed in "I won't let this happen again!" In less extreme cases, finding a subject of which to predicate the content of one's unmediated conceptions is not an outright impossibility; it is just that if one did that, one would not be respecting the fact that the conceptions are unmediated, and the resulting judgments and statements would not be first-personal.

Anscombe's thought here seems to be something on these lines: if "I" were a referring expression, its character as such would need to be entirely securable from within its central uses. The unmediatedness of those uses then precludes crediting "I" with a referent that is subject to the criteria of identity for human beings, since no such criteria are appealed to in those uses.

For another application of that thought, consider the succession of "I"-statements that would give expression to a stream of consciousness (self-consciousness). If "I" refers, how is it that in the course of such a succession no question arises about whether there has been an unnoticed substitution of a new referent for the old?[6] Now suppose one takes it that the resources for responding to such questions must come from within the stream of consciousness itself. In that case one might be tempted to think the answer must be that the continuing referent of "I" is especially easy to keep track of: there is nothing to its persisting as one and the same thing, over and above the experienced continuity within the stream.[7]

This temptation is precisely what leads to the illusion of the Cartesian Ego, according to Strawson's reading of the diagnosis Kant gives in the section of

---

6. See "The First Person", pp. 57–8.

7. If one is tempted by this answer, one ought still to worry about unnoticed substitutions when one picks up one's "I"-thinking after intervals of sleep.

the *Critique of Pure Reason* that deals with the Paralogisms of Pure Reason. It is this line of thought to which Strawson responds, on Kant's behalf, with the remark that the links to criteria of subject-identity are not severed, even in thought and talk where there is no appeal to those criteria. Continuing "I"-thinking involves no keeping track of a persisting referent; but it is nevertheless rightly understood as involving continuing reference, to something whose sameness over time involves satisfaction of those criteria—a particular person. "I" can refer without giving rise to intractable questions about unnoticed substitutions and the like, because understanding "I" requires understanding that the first person is also a third person, an element in the objective world.[8]

This claim also fits the extreme case of unmediatedness that Anscombe tries to exploit. I can think "I won't let this happen again!" in sensory deprivation only against a background understanding, which I cannot suspend on pain of suspending my ability to think first-personally altogether, that the first person is also a third person. It is that third person—who is present to me, in these circumstances, only as the subject of my thinkings, intentions, and so forth—that I mean by "I", even in this condition. Certainly some of the usual materials for bringing that background understanding to bear—for identifying the relevant third person third-personally—are not currently at my disposal. But that does not show that my "I", in these circumstances, cannot refer to the person who, on Anscombe's own account, has those thoughts and forms those intentions. It would show that only on the assumption that a referring role for "I" would need to be fully accountable for within my stream of consciousness. And in the light of the point Strawson finds in Kant, that assumption, which drives Anscombe's argument, looks profoundly Cartesian.

Of course Anscombe is not tempted to postulate Cartesian Egos to be the referents of our uses of "I". On the contrary, she uses the fact that that would be hopeless in order to argue, by *modus tollens*, that "I" is not a referring expression. But we can see something Cartesian in the thought that underlies the conditional premise of her *modus tollens*: the thought that if "I" is a referring expression, its character as such must be able to be wholly provided for from within its use in the articulation of unmediated conceptions. The ultimate Cartesian error is not the postulation of the Ego, but rather an idea to this effect, which underlies the postulation of the Ego: the

---

8. Compare Anscombe's explanation of why "no problem of the continuity or reidentification of 'the I' can arise" ("The First Person", p. 62).

semantical character of the judgments that articulate a stream of consciousness is self-contained, able to be completely provided for within the stream. Certainly Anscombe does not embrace that idea in the unqualified form in which I have stated it: she allows, indeed insists, that the truth or falsity of my "I"-judgments turns on whether their content can be truly predicated of a certain third person, a certain particular element in the objective world. But she thinks avoidance of the Ego requires us to hold that "I" does not refer. Ironically enough, given that anti-Cartesian motivation, this reflects a vestigial form of the Cartesian idea that a stream of consciousness is semantically self-sufficient; she does not let her denial that the judgments in question are semantically self-contained extend to the question whether their logical form is that of reference and predication.

I have already quoted something she says about Baldy's lapse of self-consciousness: it lay in the fact that "his thought of the happening, falling out of the carriage, was one for which he looked for a subject . . .". In a continuation that I omitted, Anscombe implicitly equates that with saying that "his grasp of it" was "one which required a subject" (p. 65). This equation encapsulates her thought that the unmediated conceptions that the central cases of first-person talk express must be "subjectless". To give proper weight to Strawson's point is to see that the equation is a mistake. We must indeed insist that the conceptions exclude looking for a subject, if we are to keep our hold on what is special about the first person. But even so, we can suppose that the conceptions require to be predicated of a subject: the particular person each of us refers to by "I". Of course one does not single out that subject, as if from other candidates, to be what one predicates the content of the conceptions of; but it would be a mistake to think reference must always be a matter of singling out in that sense.[9]

4. Strawson credits the essential point to Kant, but I think this may be generous to Kant. We should not underestimate Strawson's own creativity in what he offers as a reading of Kant. (I do not mean to dispute that his thought is deeply Kantian in spirit.)

As Strawson concedes, Kant "barely alludes" to the fact that we have empirical criteria of identity for persons. Strawson manages to cite only one

---

9. Strawson himself encouraged a step in this direction when he suggested (*Individuals*, p. 100) that one singles the right item out, as from other candidates, at least for others. For a protest, see Gareth Evans, *The Varieties of Reference*, p. 208.

passage, where Kant says: "Its [the soul's] persistence during life is, of course, evident *per se*, since the thinking being (as man) is itself likewise an object of the outer senses."[10]

And it is not just that a topic that is central to the point Strawson finds in the section on the Paralogisms is scarcely mentioned there. That one remark certainly displays Kant as splendidly immune to a familiar Cartesian temptation, the temptation to suppose that what does one's thinking is something other than a certain human being.[11] And the main business of the section is certainly to uncover, at the foundation of rational psychology, a misconstrual of the functioning of "I", in the "I think" that must be able "to accompany all my representations" (B131): "The unity of consciousness, which underlies the categories, is here mistaken for an intuition of the subject as object, and the category of substance is then applied to it" (B421). But Kant can diagnose the misconstrual of that extraordinary use of "I" without needing to take any view about its ordinary uses. Specifically, the diagnosis does not require him to claim that the human being that does one's thinking is the referent of one's ordinary uses of "I".

What Kant's purpose requires him to say about "I" is just that in the "I think" that can accompany all my representations, it does not give expression to "an intuition of the subject as object". This "I", the "I" that expresses "the unity of consciousness", does not refer; the rational psychologists' misunderstanding is precisely to suppose that it refers, and invent a referent for it. Empirical uses of "I", in contrast to that transcendental use, figure in the section on the Paralogisms only for Kant to stress that they are out of bounds for rational psychology. He has no need to offer a doctrine about how they are to be understood. The remark about "the thinking being (as man)" is not made in the context of offering any such doctrine; the thinking being (as man) is not introduced as the referent of its own empirical uses of "I". Anscombe too, of course, has the minimally anti-Cartesian view that the thinking being (as man) is an object of outer sense. As far as I can see, everything Kant says is compatible with her view that it is not by way of reference that one's empir-

---

10. *Critique of Pure Reason*, B415; cited (in a slightly modified form) by Strawson at p. 164 of *The Bounds of Sense*.

11. Contrast the topic of the reflections that include the Cartesian *cogito*, which is not the human being, René Descartes. See Anscombe's perceptive discussion of this, "The First Person", pp. 45–6.

ical uses of "I" relate to the human being one is.[12] And in that case Strawson's reading takes a decisive step beyond what is actually in Kant.

5. The Kantian context in which that insight of Strawson's figures threatens, indeed, to have a positively damaging effect on our understanding of an indispensable thought, which Strawson expresses, in *Individuals*, like this (p. 102): "a necessary condition of states of consciousness being ascribed at all is that they should be ascribed to the very same things as certain corporeal characteristics, a certain physical situation &c."

Strawson's avowedly Kantian treatment of self-reference focuses on that unity of a series of experiences that we can capture by saying that its members "collectively build up or yield, though not all of them contribute to, a picture of a unified objective world through which the experiences themselves collectively constitute a single, subjective, experiential route, one among other possible subjective routes through the same objective world".[13] He (in effect) seeks to preserve the thought I cited from *Individuals* by insisting that this conception—the conception of "a temporally extended *point of view* on the world" (ibid.)—does not contain a sufficient condition for the possibility of self-consciousness. To approach a sufficient condition, we need to make it explicit that the temporally extended point of view is an aspect of the career of an embodied subject of experience—a human being, in the only case we are familiar with. But about the conception of a temporally extended point of view on the world, abstracted from the full conditions for the possibility of self-consciousness, Strawson claims on Kant's behalf that, since that conception provides for the distinction between how things are and how things are experienced as being, it can be recognized to contain "the basic condition for that possibility" (p. 108). And it is easy to read this as suggesting that the conception does, as it were, almost all the work: that in order to build up an adequate (if skeletal) understanding of self-consciousness, we need only put the conception back into the context from which it is abstracted, stipulating (in accordance with the remark from *Individuals*) that the experiences that make up a stream of consciousness are to be attributed to a bodily thing.

I think any such suggestion would be seriously wrong. In order to bring out why, I shall adapt and extend a thought experiment of Anscombe's.

12. It would be wrong to suppose that "the human being one is" already rules out Anscombe's position. She holds, as she must, that "I am E. A.", said by her, "is not an identity proposition"; see "The First Person", pp. 60–1.

13. *The Bounds of Sense*, p. 104.

Anscombe envisages ("The First Person", p. 49)

a society in which everyone is labelled with two names. One appears on
their backs and at the tops of their chests, and these names, which their
bearers cannot see, are various: "*B*" to "*Z*", let us say. The other, "*A*", is
stamped on the inside of their wrists, and is the same for everyone. In
making reports on people's actions everyone uses the names on their chests
or backs if he can see these names or is used to seeing them. Everyone also
learns to respond to utterance of the name on his own chest and back in
the sort of way and circumstances in which we tend to respond to utterance of our own names. Reports on one's own actions, which are given
straight off from observation, are made using the name on the wrist. Such
reports are made, not on the basis of observation alone, but also on that of
inference and testimony or other information. *B*, for example, derives conclusions expressed by sentences with "*A*" as subject, from other people's
statements using "*B*" as subject.

What I want to exploit from this description is the point that "reports on
one's own actions" are made primarily on the basis of observation. (The
other modes of informational access that Anscombe mentions serve as substitutes for observation.) In a central case of a "report on one's own actions",
B (say) observes the clenching of a fist (say) with an inscribed "*A*" visible on
the inside of the wrist to which it is attached, and says "*A* is clenching his
fist". This kind of report can be mistaken in that the fist actually belongs to
a body other than *B*'s. (Perhaps the report could have been truly made; but
only by coincidence, if *B*'s fist was being clenched also.) Such a report gives
expression to an observationally acquired conception of a bodily movement, and the observation includes finding a subject of which to predicate
the movement. Getting hold of the wrong object is not excluded. In short,
the conceptions expressed in these reports are not unmediated. And that is
enough to justify saying that, at least so far, the practice does not provide for
expressions of self-consciousness: "*A*" does not function like "I".[14]

14. This vitiates the use to which Anscombe puts the case. She wants the trouble with
"*A*", as a candidate for a way of giving expression to self-consciousness, to be that it is a referring expression. Thus she suggests that people who treat "I" as a referring expression either represent "I" as "in principle no different from . . . '*A*'" or, seeing the difference between "I" and "*A*", "are led to rave in consequence" (p. 60). But the difference between
"*A*" and "I" is already sufficiently in place when we acknowledge that the conceptions expressed in the "*A*"-language are not unmediated; we do not need to say as well that one

In Anscombe's scenario, the bodily thing whose movements one can correctly report using "*A*" is singled out by the fact that its back and chest are inaccessible to one's vision (ignoring mirrors). The detail depends on the fact that she wants it to be especially clear that the various terms in play function as names: their bearers are actually labelled with them. That is inessential for my purposes. In a variation on Anscombe's case, we can leave out the labels, but preserve the role of the point of view from which one sees. So "*A* is clenching his fist" is said, as before, when one observes a fist clenching, and, now, when one can tell by observation that the fist belongs to the body at the front of whose head is the point from which the observed scene is seen. (As before, one can short-cut observation by relying on testimony, inference, and perhaps just guesswork.) The effect is to turn "*A*" into an indexical expression rather than a label, and, to that extent, to bring it closer to "I". But the conceptions expressed are still not unmediated, so we have still not made provision for self-consciousness.

The "*A*"-language is introduced only in connection with "reports of actions". One obvious addition would be reports on the posture, relation to other objects, and so forth of the singled out bodily thing. (We could hardly countenance "*A* is clenching his fist" while refusing to make sense of "*A*'s fist is clenched".) Nothing essential is altered so long as these reports too are made primarily on the basis of observation. All the reports we are envisaging so far are, we might say, third-personal, just because they are fundamentally observational; it makes no difference that one of the potential referents for third-personal talk is singled out in that special way.[15]

Can the "*A*"-language be extended to psychological predications? We are already contemplating reports made on the basis of observation (which we have tacitly restricted to visual observation). So far we have restricted the topics of observation to the bodily movements, postures, and so forth of the speakers themselves and others of their kind, but that is surely inessential; we can imagine that the language provides for observational reports on other aspects of the passing show. Now let us enrich the range of predications with "*A*" in

---

refers and the other does not. (Anscombe's mistake, which Strawson's insight allows us to expose, is exactly that she does not see that these are two different thoughts. But at this point I mean to have left Anscombe's mistake behind; I am exploiting her thought experiment for my own purposes.)

15. "Third-personal" is not completely felicitous, because there is not the contrast with "first-personal" that that suggests.

subject position like this: when a speaker is in a position to make an observational report of some state of affairs, that very position equally entitles the speaker to produce a statement of a new kind, in which the report of the state of affairs is prefaced by "*A* sees that . . .".

This is radically unlike the predications with "*A*" in subject position that we have so far had in view, in that the basis on which these reports are made does not include identifying an object of which to predicate the rest of the statement. There is no such thing as making sure it is *A* who sees that such-and-such is the case, as one might need to make sure it is *A* who is clenching his fist. These new "*A*"-statements give expression to conceptions that are unmediated.

Does that mean we have brought self-consciousness into the picture? Surely not. These statements attribute seeing that such-and-such is the case to a bodily thing whose movements, posture, and so forth are still reported only on the basis of observation and surrogates for observation. If it was right to conclude that the original "*A*"-language did not provide for one to think of the thing whose "actions" one reported as oneself (indirect reflexive), how can we have brought self-consciousness into the picture by allowing for describing that thing as something that sees as well as "acts"?

We can increase the psychological resources of the "*A*"-language. One obvious addition is a notion of appearance. When one says "*A* sees that P" on the usual sort of observational basis, and it turns out not to be the case that P, let it be correct to say "It seemed to *A* that P". (This presupposes a capacity for a certain sort of memory.) The present-tensed form, "It seems to *A* that P", will be suitable instead of "*A* sees that P" in circumstances in which there is some palpable risk that the latter statement may need to be withdrawn; but we can count it true whenever one has the usual sort of observational entitlement to the less cautious form.

And must we limit the reportable contents of streams of consciousness to perceptual experiences? Statements of the form "It seems to *A* that . . .", like statements of the form "*A* sees that . . .", are made without any need to make sure it is *A* who enjoys the experience. Negation yields "It is not the case that it seems to *A* that . . .", and that cannot import a new obligation to make sure that it is *A* of whom the statement is true. Now suppose a speaker of our expanding language suffers complete sensory deprivation. If what we are describing is a mode of intelligible speech, it must give expression to a possible mode of thought. So why not suppose this speaker can *think* something to the effect of "*A* has no experience at all"—so that the otherwise empty stream of consciousness nevertheless contains occurrent thoughts?

When we introduced "*A* sees that . . .", we already made room for the thought that "*A*" refers to something like a subject of experience, not something with only corporeal properties. With this last move, we might wonder if we have made room for an "*A*"-speaking philosopher who, impressed by the continuing possibility of "*A*"-thinking in sensory deprivation, or perhaps by the susceptibility to hyperbolical doubt of all bodily predications with "*A*" in subject position, argues like this: "Even in sensory deprivation or while entertaining hyperbolical doubt, *A* can be certain of *A*'s existence: *A* thinks, therefore *A* is. This shows that what '*A*' really refers to is not a bodily thing at all, but a thing that thinks—that is, enjoys a mental life. If, as normal sensory experience suggests, there is a body through whose eyes *A* sees, and so forth, that body is something to which *A* has a special relation; it is not what *A* is." And perhaps another philosopher might diagnose this as a paralogism of pure reason, a result of mistaking the purely formal "*A* thinks" that can accompany all *A*'s representations for a genuine reference to a substantial object.

We have, apparently at least, given the "*A*"-language materials for constructing something like the notion of a temporally extended point of view on the world, including the distinction between how things are and how things are experienced as being, which Strawson singles out as the most fundamental necessary condition for the possibility of self-consciousness. With the last development, we seem even to have made room for an analogue to the illusion of rational psychology and its diagnosis. And the diagnosis might continue by insisting that although one does not appeal to criteria of identity when one predicates experiences with "*A*" in subject position, nevertheless the links to such criteria are not severed, and the target of these references is a bodily thing; so we have the unity of consciousness in the required context, as an aspect of the career of a bodily thing.

But surely "*A*" still does not give expression to self-consciousness. In a characteristically Cartesian fashion, our quasi-Cartesian "*A*"-speaking philosopher focuses on the fact that the not purely psychological aspects of what he conceives as "*A*'s biography" can be obliterated, for its subject, by sensory deprivation, or thought away in hyperbolical doubt; he concludes that the real subject of the biography is something whose properties are exclusively psychological. In this case, the composite biography out of which the quasi-Cartesian pure subject is distilled was attributed to a subject whose "actions" are accessible to everyone only by observation (or substitutes for observation). That still seems to ensure that no one can think of this item as himself (indirect reflexive). How could a fantasy of shedding its bodily aspects turn a way of being that is not that of a self into a case of self-consciousness?

6. Clearly the trouble lies in the way "reports on one's own actions" functioned in the original "*A*"-language; what I have been exploiting is the fact that nothing in the enrichments has made any difference to that. What an "*A*"-speaker is entitled to describe as "*A*'s doings" is just a singled-out collection of what observably happens. It is true that these particular happenings are movements on the part of a body that is the point of acquisition of the sensory basis on which the speaker speaks. But they are known about only observationally (and by way of substitutes for observation), not through intention; and that means that, for all their intimate connection to the speaker's point of view on the world, they cannot be conceived as one's doing things. These reports are not reports on actions, one's own or anyone's, except in the sense in which one might report the action of water on a stone.

The behaviour of the singled out bodily thing, not known through intention, is not a case of anyone's exercising agency. Trying to imagine oneself in the "*A*"-practice, one might be tempted to picture those merely observable happenings as the result, in the impersonal objective world, of something else that really is one's doing. I act, in some inner sphere, and thereby somehow bring about those observable motions on the part of the bodily thing that audibly calls itself "*A*". But nothing in the "*A*"-language provides for this conception of the inner I who is a genuine agent, manipulating the bodily thing called "*A*" like a puppeteer. And in any case, if we separate the real agent like this from the bodily thing through whose motions the agent makes its mark in objective reality, we surely prevent ourselves from making real sense of agency.

This must go for the speech behaviour of the singled out bodily thing as much as any other. If that range of activity is likewise accessible to all parties only through observation and substitutes for it, what we have described is a repertoire of activity that is not undertaken, gone in for, by anyone. It would make no difference if we enriched the repertoire with "reports on actions" that are exercises of the repertoire itself, so long as the sole basis for these "reports on actions" was observation and substitutes for it.

If I try to imagine myself looking at the world through the eyes of a participant in the "*A*"-practice, I find no one with whom I can identify myself, no one for me to be. I hear utterances that are intelligible in their way, with "*A*" in subject position, coming from the mouth of the singled out bodily thing. But, not knowing these utterances through intention, I cannot find myself speaking in them; I can conceive them at best as results of my agency, not cases of it. In the fantasy of an inner I, which utterances get made is under my control, and some of them give expression to the content of experience that I undergo, through *A*'s sense organs. But they attribute that experience not to me but to *A*, a bodily thing that I have to distinguish from myself, since it is not what acts when I act, but at best an instrument whereby my agency makes its mark in outer reality.

At least the final stage in my expansion of Anscombe's thought experiment now comes into doubt. If the "*A*"-practice is, from the start, a repertoire for things that are not agents, and so not a language anyone could speak, in a sense in which speaking is an exercise of agency, then we cannot assume that an elaboration of the practice yields a way of giving expression to a mode of thought. This undermines the pretext on which I introduced the quasi-Cartesian "*A*"-speaking philosopher. But the thought experiment, however shaky, can still serve my purpose, which is to point to the basic importance of agency for making self-consciousness intelligible.

A potential for reflectiveness belongs to thought as such; "I" encapsulates that potential into a way individual things can be presented in the contents of thinkings. It would be wrong to put this by saying that one has oneself (indirect reflexive) presented to one, in any bit of "I"-thinking, as the thinker, as well as the object, of this bit of thinking. Of course thinking can be immersed in its ground-level concerns, so that the potential for reflectiveness is merely latent; and this goes for "I"-thinking too (consider "That rhinoceros is about to charge at me"). What we can say is this: if a thought presents an object as oneself, it presents the object in such a way that no further information is required, besides what is already there in the mode of presentation, to warrant the reflective judgment that the object of this reference is the maker of it.

We can understand how something can figure in that way in thought if we can understand how something can figure in that way in speech. It might seem that "*A*" presents its referent in just that way: that the mode of presentation associated with "*A*" itself contains enough to warrant the judgment—whose materials, then, would have to be all at least implicit in the mode of presentation—that the referent is also the maker of the reference. But that misses the point I have been insisting on, that in exercises of the "*A*"-practice there is no speaker, and so no maker of references. If we allow ourselves the fantasy of the inner puppeteer, we have a maker of references in view, at least in the sense of someone who sees to it that references get made; but now the referent is not the maker—the author or originator—of the reference. Contrast how it would have been if reports on one's actions using "*A*" had been introduced as expressions of intention. Then we could indeed have said that the warrant, and materials, for the reflective judgment that the object of this reference is its maker are implicit in the mode of presentation associated with "*A*". But in that case "*A*" would have been, from the start, a first-person form, a mere variant on "I". The materials for the reflective judgment are indeed implicit already in the very idea of an ascription of action that is an expression of the intention being actualized.

When we try to think ourselves into the "*A*"-practice, a certain singled out bodily thing appears at best as an instrument for the will of a self that can only dubiously find a place in our imaginings, a self that recedes inward to the point of vanishing. With bodily agency in the picture, that bodily thing becomes something one can identify as oneself; now there is something plainly present in the world for oneself to be. And it is not clear that we can understand the specific agency exercised in referring—the idea of which is implicit in the potentially reflective mode of presentation under which one is presented as oneself (indirect reflexive)—except by beginning with referring as an element in speaking, a particular mode of physical intervention in the world on the part of the bodily agent that one can identify as oneself. Surely this cannot be less fundamental, in our understanding of self-consciousness, than providing for a distinction between how things are and how things are experienced as being.

Strawson's reading of Kant is revelatory when the question is how self-reference can be reference at all, but it is less helpful towards understanding how self-reference works, what the mode of presentation expressed by someone's use of "I" is. Perhaps I can put the point like this. When it comes to understanding how self-reference works, we are better served by the division into P-predicates and M-predicates, as in *Individuals*, than by the Kantian abstraction of a temporally extended point of view on the world from the career of an embodied subject. P-predications include, from the start, ascriptions of intentionally undertaken bodily movements.[16] In that context, one's being a bodily agent cannot take on the look of an afterthought, a mere frame for something that could sensibly be supposed to be more fundamental to self-consciousness.

[16] See *Individuals*, pp. 111–2.

Towards Rehabilitating Objectivity

1. Richard Rorty is notorious among philosophers for his campaign against epistemology practised in the manner of the Cartesian and British-empiricist tradition. But putting it like that underplays how drastic Rorty's thinking about epistemology is. For Rorty, an activity in that vein is simply what the label "epistemology" means. He has no time for a different, and perhaps useful, kind of reflection that might still deserve to count as epistemological. My main aim in this essay is to urge that what I take to be Rorty's basic convictions, with which I sympathize, do not require so completely dismissive a stance towards the very idea of epistemology. Indeed, I want to urge that Rorty's basic project positively requires a more hospitable attitude to something that may as well be counted as epistemological reflection.

An illuminating context for Rorty's campaign against epistemology is a Deweyan narrative of Western culture's coming to maturity.[1] For Dewey's own growing-up, it was important to disburden himself of the oppressive sense of sin inculcated into him by his mother, and this feature of his own life shaped his picture of what it would be for humanity at large to come of age.

In simple outline, the story goes like this. The sense of sin from which Dewey freed himself was a reflection of a religious outlook according to which human beings were called on to humble themselves before a non-human authority. Such a posture is infantile in its submissiveness to

---

1. Elaborating this context was a central theme in the stimulating lectures Rorty delivered, under the overall title "Anti-Authoritarianism in Epistemology and Ethics", in Girona, Catalonia, during his 1996 tenure of the Ferrater Mora Chair in Contemporary Thought. My formulation of the Deweyan narrative is a simplified version of the way Rorty presented it in those lectures. See also, e.g., "Solidarity or Objectivity?"

something other than ourselves.[2] If human beings are to achieve maturity, they need to follow Dewey in liberating themselves from this sort of religion, a religion of abasement before the divine Other.[3] But a humanism that goes no further than that is still incomplete. We need a counterpart secular emancipation as well. In the period in the development of Western culture during which the God who figures in that sort of religion was stricken, so to speak, with his mortal illness, the illness that was going to lead to the demise famously announced by Nietzsche, some European intellectuals found themselves conceiving the secular world, the putative object of everyday and scientific knowledge, in ways that paralleled that humanly immature conception of the divine. This is a secular analogue to a religion of abasement, and human maturity requires that we liberate ourselves from it as well as from its religious counterpart.

What Rorty takes to parallel authoritarian religion is the very idea that in everyday and scientific investigation we submit to standards constituted by the things themselves, the reality that is supposed to be the topic of the investigation. Accepting that idea, Rorty suggests, is casting the world in the role of the non-human Other before which we are to humble ourselves. Full human maturity would require us to acknowledge authority only if the acknowledgment does not involve abasing ourselves before something non-human. The only authority that meets this requirement is that of human consensus. If we conceive inquiry and judgment in terms of making ourselves answerable to the world, as opposed to being answerable to our fellows, we are merely postponing the completion of the humanism whose achievement begins with discarding authoritarian religion.

The idea of answerability to the world is central to the discourse of objectivity. So Rorty's call is to abandon the discourse, the vocabulary, of objectivity, and work instead towards expanding human solidarity. Viewed in the context I have just sketched, this invitation has a world-historical character. As Rorty sees things, participating in the discourse of objectivity merely prolongs a cultural and intellectual infantilism, and persuading people to renounce the vocabulary of objectivity should facilitate the achievement of full human maturity. This would be a contribution to world history that is, perhaps surprisingly, within the power of mere intellectuals.

2. This phase of the story invites a Freudian formulation, which Rorty gave in his Girona lectures. There are also obvious resonances with Nietzsche.

3. Notice that this is not the same as liberating ourselves from religion *tout court*, as Dewey's own example makes clear.

2. I share Rorty's conviction that we ought to try to get out from under the seeming problems of epistemology in the Cartesian and British-empiricist vein, rather than taking them at face value and attempting to solve them. (It was largely from him that I learned to think like that.) I think, too, that there may be illumination to be had from a parallel between the conception of the world that figures in epistemology in that vein, on the one hand, and a certain conception of the divine, on the other. But it is possible to go that far with Rorty and still dissent from his suggestion that, in order to avoid entanglement in that familiar unprofitable epistemological activity, we need to discard the very idea of being answerable to something other than ourselves.

What gives the seeming problems of mainstream modern epistemology their seeming urgency is not the sheer idea that inquiry is answerable to the world. The culprit, rather, is a frame of mind in which the world to which we want to conceive our thinking as answerable threatens to withdraw out of reach of anything we can think of as our means of access to it. A gap threatens to open between us and what we would like to conceive ourselves as knowing about, and it then seems to be a task for philosophy to show us ways to bridge the gulf. It is this threat of inaccessibility on the part of the world that we need to dislodge, in order to unmask as illusory the seeming compulsoriness of mainstream epistemology. And the threat of inaccessibility is not part of the very idea of the world as something other than ourselves to which our investigative activities are answerable.

This allows us to make the parallel between epistemology and religion more pointed. The world as it figures in mainstream epistemology is a counterpart, not to just any idea of the divine as non-human and authoritative, but to the conception of *deus absconditus*, God as withdrawn into a mysterious inaccessibility. A telling Deweyan protest against epistemology, as practised in the Cartesian and British-empiricist style, can be cast as a protest against the idea of philosophy as priestcraft, supposedly needed to mediate between this *mundus absconditus* and ordinary human beings who aspire to knowledge of it.

The idea that inquiry is answerable to the world does not by itself commit us to believing that there is a need for philosophy as priestcraft. We can accept that inquiry is answerable to the things themselves and still suppose, correctly, that the resources of ordinary investigative activity can suffice to put us in touch with the subject matter of investigation, without need of special philosophical mediation. That is: we can follow Dewey in rejecting philosophy as priestcraft, without needing to abandon the very vocabulary of objectivity. What we need to dislodge is the idea of the world as withdrawn into inaccessibility, and that is quite another matter.

3. If we separate the idea of objectivity from the threat of withdrawal on the part of the world, we can make better sense of the position of Cartesian and British-empiricist epistemology in the history of philosophy.

For one thing, this makes it easier to ensure that a Deweyan protest against an epistemology with priestly pretensions is aimed in an appropriate historical direction. The idea of being answerable to the subject matter of inquiry is surely not new with modern philosophy. Rorty sometimes cites Plato's manipulation of the contrasts between knowledge and opinion, and between reality and appearance, as a paradigm of what goes wrong in the metaphysics of objectivity.[4] But the familiar supposed problems of modern epistemology are not just more of something we already find in Plato. That would make it a mystery that two more millennia had to pass before philosophy began to be obsessed with the anxieties of Cartesian epistemology. It took something further and more specific to make what people wanted to think of as the target of their investigations threaten to withdraw out of reach of what they wanted to think of as their means of access to it.

What figures in Plato as a distance between mere appearance and reality is not the distance that generates the characteristic anxiety of modern epistemology. Perhaps both the Platonic and the Cartesian conceptions can be captured in terms of an image of penetrating a veil of appearance and putting ourselves in touch with reality, but the image works differently in the two contexts. In the Platonic context, appearance does not figure as something that after all constitutes access to knowable reality, although it takes philosophy to show us how it can do so. Philosophy in Plato does not show how to bridge a gulf between appearance and an empirically knowable reality; it does not picture appearance as an avenue to knowledge at all. Correspondingly, the acknowledged and embraced remoteness of the knowable in Plato is quite unlike the threatened, but to be overcome, remoteness of the knowable in modern philosophy. Plato is nothing like a Cartesian sceptic or a British empiricist.

Attacking the vocabulary of objectivity as such, as Rorty does, rather than the conception of the world as withdrawn, distracts attention from a neces-

---

4. See, e.g., "Solidarity or Objectivity?", p. 22.

sary task. If we are to achieve a satisfactory exorcism of the problematic of mainstream modern epistemology, we need to uncover and understand the specific historical influences—which, as I have been insisting, are much more recent than the vocabulary of objectivity itself—that led to a seeming withdrawal on the part of what we wanted to see as the empirically know-able world, and thus to philosophy's coming to centre on epistemology in the sense of the attempt to bridge the supposed gulf.[5] Freeing the vocabu-lary of objectivity from contamination by the threat of withdrawal can be the project of epistemology in a different sense. This is an activity whose very point would converge with the point Rorty is making, when he rejects the idea that philosophy holds the secret to the possibility of empirical knowledge.

If we focus on the threat of withdrawal, we not only enable ourselves to raise diagnostic questions at the right point in history, the beginning of modern philosophy; we also make room, perhaps usefully, for a conception of Kant that differs from Rorty's. Rorty finds figures congenial to his world-historical conception of what philosophers ought to be doing only quite re-cently in the history of philosophy, with the emergence of self-consciously subversive thinkers such as Nietzsche. The only significance Rorty finds in Kant is that Kant's enormous prestige enabled the professionalization of philosophy, in the sense of the activity Rorty deplores as merely prolonging human immaturity.[6] But Kant precisely aims to combat the threat of a with-drawal on the part of the world we aspire to know. Kant undermines the idea that appearance screens us off from knowable reality; he offers instead a way of thinking in which—to put it paradoxically from the point of view of the style of epistemology he aims to supersede—appearance just is the reality we aspire to know (unless things have gone wrong in mundane ways). It is a fundamentally Kantian thought that the truth about the world is within the reach of those who live in the realm of appearance—to use a Platonic turn of phrase that is now rendered safe, deprived of any tendency to encourage the idea that we need philosophical gap-bridging. This is fully in the spirit of a Deweyan protest against the idea that epistemology is

---

5. In *Philosophy and the Mirror of Nature* Rorty did concern himself with the historical question I am pointing to here (though I do not think he got the answer right). In respect of responsiveness to this historical question, more recent writings like "Solidarity or Ob-jectivity?" seem to represent a backward step.

6. See chapter 3 of *Philosophy and the Mirror of Nature*.

needed for a priestly mediation between us and a world that has withdrawn from us.[7] So if we reconceive Rorty's world-historical project, so as to direct it specifically against the epistemological problematic of withdrawal rather than the vocabulary of objectivity, we can see Kant as an ally, not an enemy. For what it is worth, this version of the crusade might do better at engaging professors of philosophy.

4. One aspect of the immaturity that Rorty finds in putting objectivity rather than solidarity at the focus of philosophical discourse is a wishful denial of a certain sort of argumentative or deliberative predicament. On the face of it, certain substantive questions are such that we can be confident of answers to them, on the basis of thinking the matter through with whatever resources we have for dealing with questions of the relevant kind (for instance, ethical questions); there is no need for a sideways glance at philosophy. But even after we have done our best at marshalling considerations in favour of an answer to such a question, we have no guarantee that just anyone with whom we can communicate will find our answer compelling. That fact—perhaps brought forcibly home by our failing to persuade someone—can then induce the sideways glance, and undermine the initial confidence. Rorty's suggestion is that the vocabulary of objectivity reflects a philosophical attempt to shore up the confidence so threatened, by wishfully denying the predicament. The wishful idea is that in principle reality itself fills this gap in our persuasive resources; any rational subject who does not see things aright must be failing to make proper use of humanly universal capacities to be in tune with the world. If we fall into this way of thinking, we are trying to exploit the image of an ideal position in which we are in touch with something greater than ourselves—a secular counterpart to the idea of being at one with the divine—in order to avoid acknowledging the ineliminable hardness of hard questions, or in order to avoid facing up to the sheer contingency that attaches to our being in a historically evolved cultural position that enables us to find compelling just the considerations we do find compelling.[8]

7. See, e.g., *Experience and Nature*, p. 410: "the profuseness of attestations to supreme devotion to truth on the part of philosophy is matter to arouse suspicion. For it has usually been a preliminary to the claim of being a peculiar organ of access to highest and ultimate truth. Such it is not." See the opening remarks in Donald Davidson, "The Structure and Content of Truth", from which I have borrowed this quotation.

8. This theme is central in Rorty's *Contingency, Irony, and Solidarity*.

Here too we can make a separation. This wishful conception of attunement with how things really are, as a means of avoiding an uncomfortable acknowledgment of the limitations of reason and the contingency of our capacities to think as we believe we should, can be detached from the very idea of making ourselves answerable to how things are. We can join Rorty in deploring the former without needing to join him in abandoning the very idea of aspiring to get things right.

I can bring out how these are two different things by looking at a feature of Rorty's reading of Plato.

Rorty follows Nietzsche in suggesting that Platonic conceptions in ethics reflect an inability to face up to the kind of hard choices that are the stuff of an ethically complex life—as if the idea were that getting in touch with the Forms would carry one through life without need for the effort of deliberation.[9] But I think this reading misses the point of Platonic ethics. Being in touch with the Forms is not meant to be a substitute for hard thinking about what to do. On the contrary, the Forms are an image to enable us to sustain the idea that there is such a thing as getting things right, precisely in the absence of ways to make answers to ethical questions universally compelling. It is not a Platonic thought that putting someone in touch with the Forms is in principle a way to compel assent, on disputed questions about how to live, from anybody at all who is rational enough to engage in discussion of the questions.

I think this is brought out by the treatment of Callicles, in the *Gorgias*, and Thrasymachus, in the *Republic*: places where, on Rorty's reading, one would expect to find Plato wheeling in a reality larger than mere human beings, as if it could fill gaps in the arguments that we can come up with apart from resorting to it. That is not what happens in those dialogues. Each of those opponents of ethical orthodoxy is reduced to a sulk, before anything specifically Platonic even appears on the scene, by arguments whose quality is quite uneven, but which are, at the worst, transparently sophistical (so that one can easily sympathize with the sulking). Thrasymachus introduces the question whether one should live in accord with what Socrates would recognize as virtue, but is himself driven into an angry silence in the first book of the *Republic*. Thereafter Plato turns to something that does not look like even a promissory note for a way of rendering an affirmative answer to the question universally compelling, compelling even to people like Thrasy-

9. See "Solidarity or Objectivity?", p. 32.

machus. Instead, with Thrasymachus himself conspicuously taking no part in the conversation, Plato has Socrates characterize the knowledge that matters for knowing how to live as what results from a proper education. And education here is not, as Rorty's reading might lead one to expect, a honing of purely intellectual capacities, to put them in tune with a reality one might conceive as accessible independently of contingencies of cultural position. Plato insists that a proper education is an education of the sentiments no less than the intellect (to put it in eighteenth-century terms). There is a similar structure in the *Gorgias*, with Callicles figuring in the conversation as a patently unconvinced "yea"-sayer—remarkably enough, in view of the fuss Plato has Socrates make, earlier in the dialogue, about how important it is to him to secure the sincere assent of his interlocutors (compare 472b with 501c). I think the moral, in both dialogues, must be meant to be something on these lines: people who raise such questions are dangerous, and should be forced into silence, or acquiescence, by whatever means are available; people whose character is in good order will have confidence in right answers to the questions, a confidence that should not be threatened by the fact that questioners such as Callicles or Thrasymachus cannot be won over by persuasive argument.[10]

It is true, of course, that Plato gives a cognitive slant to his picture of what it is to have one's character in good order; he sees it as a capacity to arrive at the truth about a certain subject matter. But there is no implication that this capacity to arrive at the truth somehow insures one against tragic predicaments, or bypasses the need for hard thinking about difficult questions.

One would not expect Plato to have had the sort of concern Rorty has with contingency. But it is one thing to lack that concern, and quite another to have a metaphysical picture that excludes it. Plato's metaphysical picture can perfectly well accommodate the thought that it is a contingency that certain people can get things right; this formulation smoothly combines an acknowledgement of contingency with an employment of the vocabulary of objectivity, in a way that ought to be incoherent if Rorty were right about the vocabulary of objectivity. There is nothing alien to Plato in supplying,

---

10. Rorty says of Orwell's O'Brien: "Orwell did not invent O'Brien to serve as a dialectical foil, as a modern counterpart to Thrasymachus. He invented him to warn us against him, as one might warn against a typhoon or a rogue elephant." (*Contingency, Irony, and Solidarity*, p. 176.) I think that makes O'Brien pretty much exactly a modern counterpart to Thrasymachus as Plato actually uses him.

say, Glaucon and Adeimantus in the *Republic* with a thought on these lines: "How fortunate we are to have been born Greeks, not barbarians, and thus to have had an upbringing that made us capable of seeing things aright on these matters."

Of course it would be absurd to suggest that one can set aside Rorty's reading of Plato on the strength of a few quick sentences. But I do not need to carry conviction on the alternative I have sketched; it is enough for my purposes here that it should be so much as intelligible. This shows that the very idea of aspiring to get things right, of making ourselves answerable to how things are, has no necessary connection with what Rorty deplores: an inability to face up to contingency, and the fantasy of transferring the burden of hard thinking to the world itself.[11]

5. So far I have been taking issue, at a general level, with Rorty's suggestion that the very vocabulary of objectivity commits us to a wishful denial of contingency, and that it saddles us with the idea that philosophy is needed, in order to supply a guarantee for the capacity of inquiry to make contact with its subject matter. I agree with Rorty that we should be open-eyed about contingency, and hostile to philosophy's claim to be a necessary underpinning for other sorts of intellectual activity, but I have urged that this does not warrant his dismissive attitude to the very idea of making ourselves answerable to the world.

I want now to point to a flaw in the way Rorty treats the vocabulary of objectivity when he goes into analytical detail about it.

Hilary Putnam has argued, to put it in Rorty's words, that "notions like 'reference'—semantical notions which relate language to nonlanguage—are internal to our overall view of the world".[12] Rorty cites Putnam's argument with approval. He writes, giving more examples of the notions to which the argument applies: "From the standpoint of the representationalist, the fact that notions like representation, reference, and truth are

11. "Fantasy" is not the way Rorty would put this; he thinks such terms of criticism concede too much to the metaphysics of objectivity, and he would simply say that such conceptions have not proved useful. This seems to me to be pragmatism gone over the top, depriving itself of a useful critical notion. But this depends on something I am about to argue, that it is only by way of a conflation that Rorty comes to think resisting the kinds of philosophy he rightly sees as unprofitable requires resistance to the very vocabulary of objectivity.

12. *Objectivity, Relativism, and Truth*, p. 6. See, e.g., Putnam's *Meaning and the Moral Sciences*.

deployed in ways that are internal to a language or a theory is no reason to drop them."[13] The figure here labelled "the representationalist" is someone who refuses to give up the vocabulary of objectivity in favour of the vocabulary of solidarity. Of course Rorty is not suggesting we should drop the uses of these semantical notions to which Putnam's argument applies, uses that are internal to a world view. But he thinks "the representationalist" tries to use the notions in a way that is not internal to a world view. It is this supposed external use, according to Rorty, that is in question in the discourse of objectivity. So his view is that we need to distinguish the discourse of objectivity from the innocent internal use of the semantical notions that Putnam discusses.

One could *define* the discourse of objectivity as involving a certain supposed external use of the semantical notions, and in that case I would have no problem with Rorty's attitude to it. But Rorty suggests that rejecting these supposed external uses requires rejecting any form of the idea that inquiry is answerable to the world. I think this deprives us of something that is not inextricably implicated with what Putnam unmasks as illusion, and in depriving us of something we can innocently want, the move is damaging to Rorty's own philosophical project.

Rorty's picture is on these lines. If we use an expression like "accurate representation" in the innocent internal way, it can function only as a means of paying "empty compliments" to claims that pass muster within our current practice of claim-making.[14] Now "the representationalist" finds a restriction to this sort of assessment unacceptably parochial. Recoiling from that, "the representationalist" tries to make expressions like "true" or "accurate representation" signify a mode of normative relatedness—conformity—to something more independent of us than the world as it figures in our world view. This aspiration is well captured by Thomas Nagel's image of "trying to climb outside of our own minds".[15] The image fits a conception, or supposed conception, of reality that threatens to put it outside our reach, since the norms according to which we conduct our investigations cannot of course be anything but our current norms. Recoiling from the idea that we are restricted to paying "empty compliments" to bits of our world view, "the representationalist" tries to conceive the relation between what we want to see as our

13. *Objectivity, Relativism, and Truth*, p. 6.
14. For the phrase "empty compliment", see *Philosophy and the Mirror of Nature*, p. 10.
15. *The View from Nowhere*, p. 9; see *Objectivity, Relativism, and Truth*, p. 7.

world view and its subject matter from sideways on, rather than from the vantage point of the world view—now only problematically so called—itself. This way, it comes to seem that referential relations—to focus on the case that originally figured in Putnam's argument—would have to be intelligible in the "Augustinian" way Wittgenstein considers at the beginning of *Philosophical Investigations*; not, that is, from the midst of an understanding of linguistic practice as a going concern, but as if they could be prior building blocks in an explanation, from first principles, of how language enables us to give expression to thought at all.

This conception is naturally reflected in just the sorts of philosophical wonderment at, for instance, the meaningfulness of language, or the fact that we so much as have an "overall view of the world", that Rorty tellingly deplores. In this conception, being genuinely in touch with reality would in a radical way transcend whatever we can do within our practices of arriving at answers to our questions. Thus a familiar gulf seems to open between us and what we would like to be able to think of ourselves as able to get to know about. And the only alternative, as Rorty sees things, is to take our inquiry not to be subject to anything but the norms of current practice. This picture of the options makes it look as if the very idea of inquiry as normatively beholden not just to current practice but to its subject matter is inextricably connected with the "Augustinian" picture and the impulse to climb outside of our own minds. But a piece of mere sanity goes missing here.

6. It will help to focus on just one of the notions that figure in this line of thought, the notion of truth.

Rorty thinks there are three potentially relevant "uses" of "true": a commending or normative use, a "disquotational" use, and a "cautionary" use.[16]

The "cautionary" use is employed when we say, of some claim that we have so far not managed to find anything wrong with, that it may, even so, not be true. Rorty thinks such a remark is a reminder that, even though the claim's credentials have passed muster in the eyes of all qualified audiences to whom we have so far exposed it, we may in the future encounter an audience who finds fault with it, in a way that, as we shall acknowledge, reflects the fact that the future audience is better qualified.

So far, Rorty thinks, so good. The trouble comes if we take this "cautionary" use to be expressive of a norm. That way, we persuade ourselves

16. See "Pragmatism, Davidson and Truth", at p. 128.

that we understand compellingness to *any* audience as a norm for our activities of inquiry, and for the claim-making that gives expression to their results. And now we are liable to picture this universal compellingness in terms of a conformity to reality that would need to be contemplated from outside any local practice of investigation.

No doubt it is a good thing to aspire to overcome parochiality in the persuasiveness of the warrants we can offer for what we believe; that is part of the content of Rorty's own praise of solidarity. But this does not make universal compellingness intelligible as a *norm*. Rorty writes: "to say something like 'we hope to justify our belief to as many and as large audiences as possible' . . . is to offer only an ever-retreating goal, one which fades for ever and for ever when we move. It is not even what common sense would call a goal. For it is not even something to which we might get closer, much less something we might realize we had finally reached."[17] Trying to identify this "ever-retreating goal", only dubiously conceivable as a goal at all, with truth as a norm for inquiry and judgment is a way into a picture of the obligations of inquirers that has nothing to do with devising arguments in order to convince particular groups of human beings—a picture in which aiming at being genuinely in touch with reality seems appropriately captured by the image of trying to climb outside our own minds. The aspiration to overcome parochiality, then, is all very well; but the only *norm*, at this level of generality, that intelligibly governs inquiry is that of coming up with claims that our peers, competent in the norms of our current practices of claim-making, will let us get away with.[18] If we try to make sense of a further norm, involving responsibility to the subject matter of inquiry, we land ourselves in the "Augustinian" or sideways-on picture of our relation to that subject matter.

Now, to begin with, there is something unsatisfactory about the way Rorty separates the first two of these three uses of "true", the normative use and the "disquotational" use. Rorty claims that the "disquotational" use of "true" is "descriptive", and as such not merely to be distinguished from, but incapable of being combined in a unified discourse with, any use of "true" that treats truth as a norm for inquiry and claim-making.[19] But this makes

---

17. "Is Truth a Goal of Enquiry? Davidson vs. Wright", at p. 298.

18. Rorty writes: "I view warrant as a sociological matter, to be ascertained by observing the reception of S's statement by her peers." ("Putnam and the Relativist Menace", p. 449.) At a different level, we would have to specify the norms of the current practices themselves.

19. See "Pragmatism, Davidson and Truth".

no room for such truisms as the following: what makes it *correct* among speakers of English to make a claim with the words "Snow is white" (to stay with a well-worn example) is that snow is (indeed) white.

The idea of disquotation, literally interpreted, fits the "T-sentences" that are to be provable in a Tarskian theory of truth for a language, formulated in a metalanguage that expands the object language only by adding semantic vocabulary. But we can extend the idea of disquotation to fit the case of a Tarskian theory whose object language is not contained in the metalanguage in which the theory is stated—a theory that might be put to the Davidsonian purpose of capturing an interpretation of one language in another.[20] Here what figures, not quoted, on the right-hand side of a T-sentence is no longer the very same sentence that appears between quotation marks, or otherwise designated, before "is true if and only if" on the left-hand side. But it is a sentence that, if the theory is a good one, has the same effect; its use here cancels the semantic ascent effected by the quotation marks or other method of designation, and so disquotes in an extended sense. A sentence that is true, in the sense of "true" whose conditions of application to the sentences of this or that language Tarski showed how to pin down in a theory (provided that we can find a suitable logical form in, or impose a suitable logical form on, the sentences of the language), is—we can naturally say—*disquotable*. And this idea of disquotability is not separate, as Rorty suggests, from anything normative. For a given sentence to be true—to be disquotable—is for it to be *correctly* usable to make a claim just because . . . , where in the gap we insert, not quoted but used, the sentence that figures on the right-hand side of the T-sentence provided for the sentence in question by a good Tarskian theory for its language (the sentence itself, in the case in which we can exploit the unextended idea of disquotation). Truth in the sense of disquotability is unproblematically normative for sentences uttered in order to make claims.[21]

20. See Davidson's writings on interpretation, collected in his *Inquiries into Truth and Interpretation*. For the extended notion of disquotation (cancellation of semantic ascent), see W. V. Quine, *Philosophy of Logic*, pp. 10–13.

21. Rorty thinks he is following Davidson in glossing disquotation in terms of a causal relation between bits of language and things that are not bits of language, and concluding from the gloss that "the disquotational use of 'true' ", so far from being normative itself, cannot even be coherently combined with normative talk. I think this pretty much misses the point of Davidson's writings about interpretation. (I urged this at pp. 152–3 of *Mind and World*.) I think this feature of Rorty's thinking descends directly from the frequent, and never satisfactory, engagements of Wilfrid Sellars with Tarskian semantics; it would be an interesting exercise to trace the line of descent in detail.

Now let us reconsider Rorty's treatment of the "cautionary" use. In a passage in which he is explicitly wondering whether he suffers from a blind spot, Rorty writes that, apparently unlike Davidson, he sees "no significance in the fact that we use the same word to designate what is preserved by valid inference as we use to caution people that beliefs justified to us may not be justified to other, better, audiences".[22] But what is preserved by valid inference, which is presumably truth as expressed by a commending or normative use of "true", is simply disquotability. That disquotability is normative for conclusions of inference, and hence that disquotability must be preserved by good patterns of inference, is just part of what it means for disquotability to be normative, in the unproblematic way it is, for claim-making. Moreover, disquotability yields a straightforward gloss on the cautionary use of "true" as well. One can express the cautionary point not only with an explicit use of "true", but also with a kind of augmented disquotation: that is, by making a claim in which one modifies a non-quoting use of the words that figure in the original claim, or the words that appear on the right-hand side of a non-homophonic T-sentence for the sentence uttered in making it, by adding a modal operator and a negation sign. Rorty's cautionary use is exemplified in a form of words such as " 'All life forms are carbon-based' may not (after all) be true"; but one could achieve exactly the same effect by saying "There may (after all) be life forms that are not carbon-based". What one warns oneself or others that a claim may not have, in spite of its passing muster so far, is just disquotability. I think this shows that the blind spot Rorty wonders about is indeed there. That we use the same word simply reflects the fact that it is the same status, disquotability, that is, on the one hand, preserved by valid inference and, on the other, possibly lacked by beliefs, or claims, on which there is present consensus among qualified judges.

The same blind spot is operative in a thesis Rorty puts by saying "justification is relative to an audience".[23] Taken one way, indeed, the thesis is obviously correct; whenever one carries conviction by giving reasons, it is some particular audience that one persuades. Now Rorty thinks that is the only way to take the thesis; he thinks the only hygienically available conception

---

22. "Is Truth a Goal of Enquiry?", p. 286. For the belief that the "cautionary" use of "true" "is captured neither by a common-sensical account of its approbative force nor by a disquotational account", see also "Putnam and the Relativist Menace", p. 460.

23. "Is Truth a Goal of Enquiry?", p. 283. See also the passage quoted in n. 18 above.

of what it is for, say, a claim to be justified (or warranted, or rationally acceptable) must be relative to some particular audience, on pain of our purporting to have an idea of justification that is implicated with the sideways-on picture and the aspiration to climb outside our own minds. Failing the sideways-on picture, he suggests, "the terms 'warranted', 'rationally acceptable', etc., will always invite the question 'to whom?' "[24] This idea is what underwrites the argument I rehearsed a few paragraphs back, that, although persuasiveness to audiences other than our peers is a worthy aspiration, the only way justification (or warrant, or rational acceptability) can constitute a *norm* for claim-making is in the guise of ability to pass muster with our peers. But here the norm constituted by disquotability goes missing. An utterance of "Cold fusion has not been achieved, so far, in the laboratory" has (if I am right about the physics) a warrant, a justifiedness, that consists not in one's being able to get away with it among certain conversational partners, but in—now I disquote, and implicitly make a claim—cold fusion's not having been achieved, so far, in the laboratory. Here the terms "warranted", "rationally acceptable", etc., have collected an obvious answer, not to the question "to whom?", but to the question "in the light of what?", and the question "to whom?" need not be in the offing at all.

Notice that in order to insist on these lines that we can make sense of a notion of justification for which the relevant question is "in the light of what?", all I need is my (rather rudimentary) ability to make claims about whether or not cold fusion has occurred. Rorty thinks any purported notion of warrant or justifiedness that is not relative to an audience would have to be implicated with the sort of philosophy that involves trying to climb outside our own minds. But one does not pretend to climb outside one's own mind if one gives expression, as I just did, to the norm constituted by disquotability. One formulates the relevant normative condition on a given assertoric utterance by disquoting (possibly in the extended sense) the words whose assertoric utterance is governed by the norm one is invoking; that is, by using words (for instance, "Cold fusion has not been achieved") that would figure on the right-hand side of the relevant T-sentence, words in whose norm-governed employment one is (more or less) competent.

It is true that we have only whatever lights are at our disposal to go on in bringing such a norm to bear—which involves deciding what to say about, for instance, whether or not cold fusion has occurred. We understand what

24. "Putnam and the Relativist Menace", p. 452.

the norm of disquotability comes to, potential utterance by potential utterance, from the midst of a current practice of claim-making; we understand it by the lights constituted by being a (more or less) competent party to the practice. But it does not follow that nothing can be normative for moves within the practice except ensuring that one's peers will let one get away with them. There is a norm for making claims with the words "Cold fusion has not occurred" that is constituted by whether or not cold fusion has occurred; and whether or not cold fusion has occurred is not the same as whether or not saying it has occurred will pass muster in the current practice. On topics on which there is no dispute, it will always seem from within a practice of investigation that the answers to such pairs of questions coincide, but that should not prevent us from seeing that the questions differ. Moreover, anyone who can be recognized as self-consciously participating in a practice of claim-making must be able to see that the questions differ. Without this difference, there would be no ground for conceiving one's activity as making claims about, say, whether or not cold fusion has occurred, as opposed to achieving unison with one's fellows in some perhaps purely decorative activity on a level with a kind of dancing. The distinguishability of the questions amounts to the availability of the notion of a claim's being justified in the light of how things stand with its subject matter. And the questions are distinguishable from within our practice of claim-making; insisting on the distinction is not an expression of the fantasy that one can conceive the practice's conformity to reality from sideways on.

Seeing how the questions differ, we can see how the thought that some claim is true is not—as in Rorty's "empty compliment" idea—the thought that it would pass muster in the relevant claim-making practice as presently constituted. It is the thought that things really are a certain way: for instance, that cold fusion really has not occurred. To insist on this distinction is not to try to think and speak from outside our practices; it is simply to take seriously the idea that we can really mean what we think and say from within them. It is not just "the representationalist", someone who thinks we need to climb outside our own minds in order to understand how thought and speech relate to reality, who can be expected to recoil from a denial of this.

There are two different things that might be meant by saying, as Rorty applauds Putnam for saying, that norms expressible with notions like that of truth are internal to our world view. Putnam's insight is that we must not succumb to the illusion that we need to climb outside our own minds, the illusion that though we aim our thought and speech at the world from a standpoint constituted by our present practices and competences, we must be able to conceive the conformity of our thought and speech to the world from outside any such standpoint. But to unmask that as an illusion is not to say, with Rorty, that the norms that govern claim-making can only be norms of consensus, norms that would be fully met by earning the endorsement of our peers for our claims. We must indeed avoid the illusion of transcendence that Putnam's insight rejects, but we do not put our capacity to do so at risk if we insist that in claim-making we make ourselves answerable not just to the verdicts of our fellows but to the facts themselves. That is, if you like, to say that norms of inquiry transcend consensus. But this transcendence is quite distinct from the transcendence Putnam unmasks as an illusory aspiration. These norms are internal to our world view, just as Putnam urged that the relevant norms must be. It is just that the world view to which they are internal has the world in view otherwise than as constituted by what linguistic performances will pass muster in our present practice. But that is merely a requirement for us to have the world in view at all—for moves within the relevant practices to be expressive of a world view, as opposed to merely aspiring to vocalize in step with one another. Taking this transcendence in stride requires no more than confidence in our capacity to direct our meaning at, say, whether or not cold fusion has occurred.[25]

7. What I have been urging is that truth as disquotability is a mode of justifiedness that is not relative to some particular audience; the question that this mode of justifiedness raises is not "to whom?" but "in the light of what?" This mode of justifiedness is, innocuously, normative for inquiry and the judgments and claims it aims at. For all the efforts of philosophers

---

25. Rorty makes a helpful distinction between relativism and ethnocentrism, and disavows relativism. (See "Solidarity or Objectivity?") Ethnocentrism is the insistence that we speak from the midst of historically and culturally local practices; it amounts to a rejection of the illusory transcendence involved in the image of trying to climb outside of our own minds. But in refusing to allow the in fact perfectly innocent thought that in speaking from the midst of the practices of our ethnos, we make ourselves answerable to the world itself (for instance, to how things stand with respect to cold fusion), Rorty makes a move whose effect is to collapse his own helpful distinction. The thesis that "justification is relative to an audience" is, as explicitly stated, relativistic, not just ethnocentric. This is at least some excuse for what Rorty complains of (e.g., in "Putnam and the Relativist Menace"), namely Putnam's continuing to count Rorty as a relativist even in the face of Rorty's disclaimer.

to put it in doubt, something we can conceive in terms of satisfaction of such a norm is unproblematically achievable from the local standpoints that are the only standpoints we can occupy in intellectual activity.

Contrast Rorty's picture, in which there is nothing for truth, as a mode of justifiedness that is not relative to a particular audience, to be except the "ever-retreating goal" of being convincing to ever more and larger audiences. Of course the "ever-retreating goal" cannot be achieved, and Rorty says as much. But his blind spot about disquotability leads him to think this correct point can be put by saying something to this effect: if we conceive truth as a mode of justifiedness that transcends consensus, we are conceiving something that would not be achievable. This rejects the innocuous transcendence along with the illusory one. And the effect is to make urgent just the sorts of question that Rorty wants to discourage.

As I said, taking the innocuous transcendence in stride requires no more than confidence in our capacity to direct our meaning at, say, whether or not cold fusion has occurred. Philosophers have contrived to shake this confidence, to make such a capacity look mysterious, by moves whose effect is to make it seem that comprehension of how inquiry, judgment, and claim-making are related to reality would require the other kind of transcendence, the kind that is an illusory aspiration. Rorty's own refusal to countenance norms for claim-making that go beyond consensus is of course motivated by his well placed hostility to this idea, the idea that we need to climb outside our own minds in order to occupy a point of view from which to conceive the relation of thought to reality. But throwing out the innocuous transcendence along with the illusory aspiration has exactly the effect he deplores; it makes a mystery of how we manage to direct our thought and speech as it were past the endorsement of our fellows and to the facts themselves. Rorty is committed to taking imagery on those lines as irredeemably expressive of the hankering after climbing outside our own minds. But the imagery comes to nothing more than an insistence that we speak and think—of course from the midst of our practices—about, say, whether or not cold fusion has occurred. And Rorty's own move makes a mystery of how we manage to do that, in just the sort of way in which he rightly wants not to let philosophy make a mystery of such things.

If one has a steadfast understanding of truth as disquotability, one can be immune to philosophically induced anxiety about how thought and speech, undertaken from the midst of our local practices, can make contact with reality. But consider someone who has a merely inchoate understanding of truth as disquotability, a norm for inquiry concerning which the relevant question is not "to whom?" but "in the light of what?" Suppose such a person is confronted with Rorty's pronouncement that there is no attaining truth except in the guise of convincingness to one's peers. The pronouncement puts in question the achievability of a kind of conformity of thought and speech to the world that—as such a person realizes, though *ex hypothesi* only inchoately—ought to be unproblematic. It would be only natural to recoil into just the kind of gap-bridging philosophical activity that Rorty deplores.

8. Rorty aims to discourage a certain genre of philosophy, and I have been urging that his treatment of truth is counter-productive by his own lights. It is a connected point that this treatment of truth is, I believe, fundamentally un-Deweyan. Philosophers seduce people into the kind of anxiety Rorty follows Dewey in deploring; they induce anxiety by manipulating the thought that we have only our own lights to go on in any inquiry. The thought is actually innocent, but it can be made to seem that having only our own lights to go on is a confinement, something that would threaten to cut us off from reality itself. This makes it seem that we need a special philosophical viewpoint, one that contemplates inquiry's relation to reality from sideways on, so that we can be reassured that ordinary inquiry makes contact with its intended subject matter. On this kind of conception, it is only by the grace of philosophy that truth is attainable in ordinary investigative activity. Rorty follows Dewey in his hostility towards this kind of pretension on the part of philosophy, and as I have indicated, I have no problem with that. But Dewey put the point by saying such things as this: "Truth is a collection of truths; and these constituent truths are in the keeping of the best available methods of inquiry and testing as to matters-of-fact; methods which are, when collected under a single name, science."[26] As Davidson comments: "Dewey's aim was to bring truth, and with it the pretensions of philosophers, down to earth."[27] Dewey insisted that truth is within the reach of ordinary inquiry. Rorty, quite differently, thinks he can achieve the desired effect—cutting down the pretensions of philosophy—by cheerfully affirming that truth in the relevant sense is not within reach at all. That is just

26. *Experience and Nature*; quoted by Davidson, "The Structure and Content of Truth", p. 279.

27. "The Structure and Content of Truth", p. 279.

the sort of pronouncement that triggers the kind of philosophy Dewey and Rorty deplore, and it is not an effective consolation, or deterrent, to add "not even within the reach of philosophy".[28]

What about the idea that the vocabulary of objectivity reflects an intellectual and cultural immaturity? I have been urging that disquotability is unproblematically normative, and that a proper understanding of the point yields a good gloss on the idea that inquiry is answerable to the world. It seems to me that it would be absurd to equate accepting this simple thought with abasing ourselves before the world, so as to fail to live up to our capacity for human maturity. Indeed, I am inclined to suggest that the boot is on the other foot. If there is a metaphysical counterpart to infantilism anywhere in this vicinity, it is in Rorty's phobia of objectivity, and the suggestion that we should replace talk of our being answerable to the world with talk of ways of thinking and speaking that are conducive to our purposes.[29] This fits a truly infantile attitude, one for which things other than the subject show up only as they impinge on its will. Acknowledging a non-human external authority over our thinking, so far from being a betrayal of our humanity, is merely a condition of growing up.[30]

I applaud Rorty's hostility to the sort of philosophy that sets itself up as providing necessary foundations for intellectual activity in general. But I think he is wrong in supposing that the way to cure people of the impulse

28. Rorty writes: "To try to make truth approachable and reachable is to do what Davidson deplores, to *humanize* truth" ("Is Truth a Goal of Enquiry?", p. 298). I think this is a misreading of Davidson's opposition to an "epistemic" conception of truth. Davidson opposes the idea that an account of what it is for a claim to be true needs to incorporate a reference to, for instance, human powers of recognition. That is not at all to say that it is all right to conceive truth as *out of reach* of human powers of recognition.

29. For a sounding of this note in the context of Rorty's anti-authoritarianism, consider the following passage: ". . . my preferred narrative is a story of human beings as having recently gotten out from under the thought of, and the need for, *authority*. I see James's suggestion that we carry utilitarianism over from morals into epistemology as crucial to this anti-authoritarianism of the spirit. For James shows us how to see Truth not as something we have to respect, but as a pointless nominalization of the useful adjective we apply to beliefs that are getting us what we want. Ceasing to see Truth as the name of an authority and coming to see the search for stable and useful beliefs as simply one more part of the pursuit of happiness are essential if we are to have the experimental attitude toward social existence that Dewey commended and the experimental attitude toward individual existence that Romanticism commended." ("Response to Bernstein", p. 71.)

30. This thought too could be put in Freudian terms.

towards that sort of philosophy is to proscribe, or at least try to persuade people to drop, the vocabulary of objectivity, and centrally the image of the world as authoritative over our investigations. I think this policy of Rorty's involves a misconception of an innocuous notion of truth. Once we understand that, we can see why Rorty's attempt to dislodge people from the vocabulary tends to have an effect that is exactly opposite to the one he wants. The way to cure ourselves of unwarranted expectations for philosophy is not to drop the vocabulary of objectivity, but to work at understanding the sources of the deformations to which the vocabulary of objectivity has historically been prone. If we could do that, it would enable us to undo the deformations, and see our way clear of the seemingly compulsory philosophical problematic that Rorty wants us to get out from under. This would be an epistemological achievement, in a perfectly intelligible sense of "epistemological" that does not restrict epistemology to accepting the traditional problematic. It is the deformations, to which Rorty's discussions of truth reveal him to be a party, and not the vocabulary itself, that lead to philosophical trouble.

The Disjunctive Conception of Experience as Material for a Transcendental Argument

1. In *Individuals* and *The Bounds of Sense*, P. F. Strawson envisaged transcendental arguments as responses to certain sorts of scepticism. An argument of the sort Strawson proposed was to establish a general claim about the world, a claim supposedly brought into doubt by sceptical reflections. Such an argument was to work by showing that unless things were as they were said to be in the claim that the argument purported to establish, it would not be possible for our thought or experience to have certain characteristics, not regarded as questionable even by someone who urges sceptical doubts. So the argument's conclusion was to be displayed as the answer to a "How possible?" question. That has a Kantian ring, and the feature of such arguments that the formulation fits is the warrant for calling them "transcendental".

Barry Stroud responded to Strawson on the following lines.[1] Perhaps we can see our way to supposing that if our thought or experience is to have certain characteristics it does have (for instance that experience purports to be of a world of objects independent of us), we must *conceive* the world in certain ways (for instance as containing objects that continue to exist even while we are not perceiving them). But it is quite another matter to suggest that by reflecting about how it is possible that our thought and experience are as they are, we could establish conclusions not just about how we must conceive the world but about how the world must be. Stroud writes:

> Even if we allow that we can come to see how our thinking in certain ways necessarily requires that we also think in certain other ways, and so perhaps in certain further ways as well, . . . how can truths about the world which ap-

---

1. See "Transcendental Arguments". Several other essays in Stroud's *Understanding Human Knowledge* are very helpful in clarifying the picture.

pear to say or imply nothing about human thought or experience be shown to be genuinely necessary conditions of such psychological facts as that we think and experience things in certain ways, from which the proofs begin? It would seem that we must find, and cross, a bridge of necessity from the one to the other. That would be a truly remarkable feat, and some convincing explanation would surely be needed of how the whole thing is possible.[2]

According to Stroud, Kant's explanation is transcendental idealism. As Stroud reads it, transcendental idealism explains how that "bridge of necessity" can be crossed by saying that the world of which the transcendentally established claims are true is "only the 'phenomenal' world which is somehow 'constituted' by the possibility of our thought and experience of it".[3]

Perhaps this might be better put by saying there is no bridge to cross. But then how satisfying a response to scepticism can be provided by such arguments? On this reading transcendental idealism does not so much respond to sceptical worries as brush them aside. Or perhaps it amounts to a concession that they are well placed. As Stroud puts it:

> [T]here is the challenge of saying in what ways idealism is superior to, or even different from, the sceptical doctrines it was meant to avoid. How it differs, for example, from Hume's view that we simply cannot avoid believing that every event has a cause, and cannot help acting for all the world as if it were true, but that it is not really true of the world as it is independently of us.[4]

And even if Stroud does not succeed in raising our suspicions of transcendental idealism, Strawson is anyway suspicious of it. In *The Bounds of Sense*, Strawson claims to preserve fundamental Kantian insights, but outside the idealist frame in which Kant formulated them. So Strawsonian transcendental arguments are expressly not equipped with what Stroud identifies as the Kantian apparatus for explaining how that "bridge of necessity" can be crossed. Stroud suggests, accordingly, that the Strawsonian arguments can yield only conclusions on the near side of the bridge. They uncover structural connections *within* our thought or experience, enabling us to argue that our thought or experience must be a certain way as a condition for the possibility of their being a certain other way.

2. "Kantian Argument, Conceptual Capacities, and Invulnerability", pp. 158–9.
3. "Kantian Argument", p. 159.
4. "Kantian Argument", pp. 159–60.

That need not deprive the arguments of all force against scepticism. Suppose that whether things are a certain way comes within the scope of sceptical doubts. If we can establish that we must conceive things as being that way for it to be possible that our thought or experience has some characteristic that a sceptic would not or could not deny that it has, then we will have made some headway against that sceptical worry. This falls short of claiming to have shown that things must be that way for our thought and experience to be as they are. But with an argument of this more modest kind, we will have shown that, given the characteristic of our thought or experience that is the unquestioned starting-point of the argument, there is no possibility of our being rationally required to discard the conviction that the sceptical argument was supposed to undermine.

Strawson has come to share Stroud's doubts about crossing that "bridge of necessity". It is not that he has given up the Kantian project, an inquiry into how it is possible that our thought and experience are as they are. But he has come to approach the project in something like the way Stroud recommends, as tracing connections *within* how we conceive and experience things, rather than between how we conceive and experience things and how things must be. The aim of the investigation, as Strawson more recently sees it, is to establish "a certain sort of interdependence of conceptual capacities and beliefs; e.g., . . . that in order for self-conscious thought and experience to be possible, we must take it, or *believe*, that we have knowledge of external physical objects or other minds".[5]

2. This territory has been much worked over.[6] I am not going to work over it any more; I have sketched this picture of the state of play, in a certain region of recent discussion of transcendental arguments, only to bring out a contrast. I am not going to consider transcendental arguments of either of the two kinds that have come into view so far: neither the ambitious kind, in which the aim is to establish the truth of general claims about the world; nor the modest kind, in which the aim is to establish only that we cannot consistently go on taking it that our thought and experience are as they are in the relevant respects while withholding acceptance of the relevant claims about the world.

5. *Skepticism and Naturalism: Some Varieties*, p. 21.

6. For a helpful survey, see Robert Stern, *Transcendental Arguments and Scepticism: Answering the Question of Justification*.

Instead I want to consider a different approach to one sort of scepticism. I want to suggest that this different approach can be pursued through a kind of transcendental argument that belongs to neither of those two types.

The scepticism in question is scepticism about perceptually acquired knowledge of the external world. And the approach in question is diagnostic. The diagnosis is that this scepticism expresses an inability to make sense of the idea of direct perceptual access to objective facts about the environment. What shapes this scepticism is the thought that even in the best possible case, the most that perceptual experience can yield falls short of a subject's having an environmental state of affairs directly available to her. Consider situations in which a subject seems to see that, say, there is a red cube in front of her. The idea is that even if we focus on the best possible case, her experience could be just as it is, in all respects, even if there were no red cube in front of her. This seems to reveal that perceptual experience provides at best inconclusive warrants for claims about the environment. And that seems incompatible with supposing we ever, strictly speaking, *know* anything about our objective surroundings.[7] The familiar sceptical scenarios—Descartes's demon, the scientist with our brains in his vat, the suggestion that all our apparent experience might be a dream—are only ways to make this supposed predicament vivid.

Suppose scepticism about our knowledge of the external world is recommended on these lines. In that case it constitutes a response if we can find a way to insist that we *can* make sense of the idea of direct perceptual access to objective facts about the environment. That contradicts the claim that what perceptual experience yields, even in the best possible case, must be something less than having an environmental fact directly available to one. And without that thought, this scepticism loses its supposed basis and falls to the ground.

It is important that that is the right description of what this response achieves. We need not pretend to have an argument that would prove

---

7. Stroud regularly depicts scepticism about the external world as arising like this. See, e.g., "Epistemological Reflection on Knowledge of the External World", p. 131: "[The philosopher] chooses a situation in which any one of us would unproblematically say or think, for example, that we know that there is a fire in the fireplace right before us, and that we know it is there because we see that it is there. But when we ask what this seeing really amounts to, various considerations are introduced to lead us to concede that we would see exactly what we see now even if no fire was there at all, or if we didn't know that there was one there." See also *The Significance of Philosophical Scepticism*.

that we are not, say, at the mercy of Descartes's demon, using premises we can affirm, and inferential steps we can exploit, without begging questions against someone who urges sceptical doubts. As I said, the point of invoking the demon scenario and its like is only to give vivid expression to the predicament supposedly constituted by its not making sense to think we can have environmental facts directly available to us. But if it does make sense to think we can have environmental facts directly available to us, there is no such predicament. And now someone who proposes those scenarios can no longer seem to be simply emphasizing a discouraging fact about our epistemic possibilities. When we reject the scenarios—if we choose to bother with them at all—we need no longer be hamstrung by a conception of argumentative legitimacy controlled by that understanding of their status. An accusation of question-begging need no longer carry any weight. We can invert the order in which scepticism insists we should proceed, and say—as common sense would, if it undertook to consider the sceptical scenarios at all—that our knowledge that those supposed possibilities do not obtain is sustained by the fact that we know a great deal about our environment, which would not be the case if we were not perceptually in touch with the world in just about the way we ordinarily suppose we are.

Similarly, there is no need to establish, without begging questions against scepticism, that in any particular case of perceptual experience we actually are in the favourable epistemic position that scepticism suggests we could never be in. That would similarly be to accept tendentious ground rules for satisfying ourselves in given cases that we have knowledge of the environment. If we can recapture the idea that it is so much as possible to have environmental states of affairs directly presented to us in perceptual experience, we can recognize that such ground rules reflect a misconception of our cognitive predicament. And then our practice of making and assessing claims to environmental knowledge on particular occasions can proceed as it ordinarily does, without contamination by philosophy. There need no longer seem to be any reason to discount the fact that in real life the assessment is often positive.

3. Perhaps most people will find it obvious that reinstating the sheer possibility of directly taking in objective reality in perception would undermine a scepticism based on claiming that perceptual experience can never amount to that. (I shall consider an exception later.)

But what does this have to do with transcendental arguments? Well, it depends on how the undermining move is defended. And it can be defended by an argument that is broadly Kantian, in the sense in which the arguments I was considering at the beginning are broadly Kantian. The argument aims to establish that the idea of environmental facts making themselves available to us in perception must be intelligible, because that is a necessary condition for it to be intelligible that experience has a characteristic that is, for purposes of this argument, not in doubt.

The relevant characteristic is that experience purports to be of objective reality. When one undergoes perceptual experience, it at least appears to one as if things in one's environment are a certain way.

Consider Wilfrid Sellars's discussion of "looks" statements in "Empiricism and the Philosophy of Mind". Sellars urges something on the following lines. In order to understand the very idea of the objective purport of visual experience (to single out one sensory modality), we need to appreciate that the concept of experiences in which, say, it looks to one as if there is a red cube in front of one divides into the concept of cases in which one sees that there is a red cube in front of one and the concept of cases in which it merely looks to one as if there is a red cube in front of one (either because there is nothing there at all or because although there is something there it is not a red cube).

At least implicit here is a thought that can be put as follows. In order to find it intelligible that experience has objective purport at all, we must be able to make sense of an epistemically distinguished class of experiences, those in which (staying with the visual case) one sees how things are— those in which how things are makes itself visually available to one. Experiences in which it merely looks to one as if things are thus and so are experiences that misleadingly present themselves as belonging to that epistemically distinguished class. So we need the idea of experiences that belong to the epistemically distinguished class if we are to comprehend the idea that experiences have objective purport. If one acknowledges that experiences have objective purport, one cannot consistently refuse to make sense of the idea of experiences in which objective facts are directly available to perception.

The scepticism I am considering purports to acknowledge that experiences have objective purport, but nevertheless supposes that appearances as such are mere appearances, in the sense that any experience leaves it an open possibility that things are not as they appear. That is to conceive the epistemic significance of experience as a highest common factor of what we have in cases in which, as common sense would put it, we perceive that things are thus and so and what we have in cases in which that merely seems to be so—so never higher than what we have in the second kind of case.[8] The conception I have found in Sellars can be put, in opposition to that, as a disjunctive conception of perceptual appearance: perceptual appearances are either objective states of affairs making themselves manifest to subjects, or situations in which it is as if an objective state of affairs is making itself manifest to a subject, although that is not how things are.[9] Experiences of the first kind have an epistemic significance that experiences of the second kind do not have. They afford opportunities for knowledge of objective states of affairs. According to the highest common factor conception, appearances can never yield more, in the way of warrant for belief, than do those appearances in which it merely seems that one, say, sees that things are thus and so. But according to the Sellarsian transcendental argument, that thought undermines its own entitlement to the very idea of appearances.

The highest common factor conception is supposedly grounded on a claim that seems unquestionable: the claim that from a subject's point of view, a misleading appearance can be indistinguishable from a case in which things are as they appear. That might be taken as a self-standing claim about the phenomenology of misleading appearance, available to be cited in explaining the fact that subjects can be misled by appearances. So taken, the claim is open to dispute.[10] But the right way to take it is as simply registering the fact that, on that interpretation, it is supposed to explain: the undeniable fact that our capacity to get to know things through perception is fallible.[11]

The claim of indistinguishability is supposed to warrant the thought that even in the best case in which a subject, say, has it visually appear to her that there is a red cube in front of her, her experience could be just as it is even if there were no red cube in front of her. But we need a distinction

8. On the idea of the highest common factor, see, e.g., my *Mind and World*, p. 113.

9. On the disjunctive conception, see J. M. Hinton, *Experiences*; Paul Snowdon, "Perception, Vision, and Causation"; my *Mind and World*, loc.cit.; and my "Singular Thought and the Extent of Inner Space" and "Criteria, Defeasibility, and Knowledge".

10. See J. L. Austin, *Sense and Sensibilia*.

11. I have revised what I first wrote in this connection, partly in response to an objection from Costas Pagondiotis. I have been influenced here by Sebastian Rödl.

here. When we say her experience could be just as it is even if there were no red cube in front of her, we might be just registering that there could be a misleading experience that from the standpoint of her experience she could not distinguish from her actually veridical experience. In that case what we say is just a way of acknowledging that our capacity to acquire knowledge through perceptual experience is fallible. It does not follow that even in the best case, the epistemic position constituted by undergoing an experience can be no better than the epistemic position constituted by undergoing a misleading experience, even one that would admittedly be indistinguishable. The acknowledgment of fallibility cannot detract from the excellence of an epistemic position, with regard to the obtaining of an objective state of affairs, that consists in having the state of affairs present itself to one in one's perceptual experience. This is where the disjunctive conception does its epistemological work. It blocks the inference from the subjective indistinguishability of experiences to the highest common factor conception, according to which neither of the admittedly indistinguishable experiences could have higher epistemic worth than that of the inferior case. And the transcendental argument shows that the disjunctive conception is required, on pain of our losing our grip on the very idea that in experience we have it appear to us that things are a certain way.[12]

4. This transcendental argument starts from the fact that perceptual experience at least purports to be of objective reality, and yields the conclusion that we must be able to make sense of the idea of perceptual experience that is actually of objective reality. I have urged that that is enough to undermine a familiar sort of scepticism about knowledge of the external world.

Now there may be a temptation to object that this argument assumes too much. Should it be left unquestioned that perceptual experience purports to be of objective reality?

There is plenty of room to argue that it is proper to start there. The sceptical arguments Descartes considers, for instance, do not question the fact

---

12. The essential thing is that the two sides of the disjunction differ in epistemic significance, whereas on the highest common factor conception the "good" disjunct can afford no better warrant for perceptual claims than the "bad" disjunct. This difference in epistemic significance is of course consistent with all sorts of commonalities between the disjuncts. For instance, on both sides of the disjunction it appears to one that, say, there is a red cube in front of one. In "(Anti-)Sceptics Simple and Subtle: G. E. Moore and John McDowell", at p. 341, n. 12 and associated text, Crispin Wright makes needlessly heavy weather of this.

that perceptual experience yields appearances that things are objectively the case. Descartes's arguments question only our entitlement to believe that things are as they appear to be. The highest common factor conception owes its attractiveness to the subjective indistinguishability of experiences all of which can be described in terms of the appearance that things are objectively thus and so. This supposed basis for scepticism does not need a more minimal picture of experience.

But what if we do decide that we ought to confront a more whole-hearted scepticism, a scepticism willing to doubt that perceptual experience purports to be of objective reality? Well then, the transcendental argument I have been considering cannot do all the work. But it can still do some of the work. If this is the target, we need a prior transcendental argument, one that reveals the fact that consciousness includes states or episodes that purport to be of objective reality as a necessary condition for some more basic feature of consciousness, perhaps that its states and episodes are potentially self-conscious. Strawson's reading of the Transcendental Deduction in Kant's first *Critique* might serve, or perhaps the Transcendental Deduction itself. It would take me too far afield to go into this here. The point is just that we cannot dismiss an argument that pivots on the disjunctive conception of perceptual appearance, on the ground that it does not itself establish the characteristic of perceptual experience that it begins from.

5. In a recent paper, Crispin Wright argues that as a response to scepticism, replacing the highest common factor conception of perceptual experience with a disjunctive conception is "dialectically quite ineffectual".[13]

Wright starts from a helpful account of why G. E. Moore's "proof of an external world"—at least if taken at face value—is as unimpressive as nearly everyone finds it.[14] Moore moves from the premise "Here is a hand" to the conclusion, which is indeed entailed by that premise, that there is an external world. Wright takes Moore to suppose that his premise is itself grounded on something yet more basic: something Moore could express by saying "My experience is in all respects as of a hand held up in front of my face". And Wright's diagnosis of what goes wrong in Moore's argument is that the warrant this ground supplies cannot be transmitted across the ac-

---

13. "(Anti-)Sceptics Simple and Subtle: G. E. Moore and John McDowell"; the phrase quoted is at p. 331.

14. Moore may intend something more subtle. But I shall not consider this possibility.

knowledged entailment from "Here is a hand" to "There is an external world". The warrant that "My experience is as of a hand" provides for "Here is a hand" is defeasible, and it is defeated if the sceptic is right and we are, for instance, at the mercy of Descartes's demon. We can allow it to warrant the premise of Moore's entailment only if we already take ourselves to be entitled to accept the conclusion of the entailment. So the whole argument is question-begging.

Wright now turns to the disjunctive conception. He sums up his verdict on it as follows (pp. 346–7):

> In brief: whether our perceptual faculties engage the material world directly [the thesis that the disjunctive conception is aimed at protecting] is one issue and whether the canonical justification of perceptual claims proceeds through a defeasible inferential base is another. One is, so far, at liberty to take a positive view of both issues. And when we do, the I-II-III pattern [the pattern of Moore's argument, augmented with a formulation of the ground for the premise of Moore's entailment] re-emerges along these lines:
>
> I *Either* I am perceiving a hand in front of my face *or* I am in some kind of delusional state
> II Here is a hand
> Therefore
> III There is a material world.

It is clear that this is a mere variation on Moore's argument as Wright reconstructs it. In this version too, the support I provides for II is defeasible. That we take it not to be defeated depends on our already taking ourselves to be entitled to accept III. So it would be question-begging to suppose the argument provides any support for III.

But what does this have to do with the disjunctive conception? The point of the disjunctive conception is that if one undergoes an experience that belongs on the "good" side of the disjunction, that warrants one in believing—indeed presents one with an opportunity to know—that things are as the experience reveals things to be. When one's perceptual faculties "engage the material world directly", as Wright puts it, the result—a case of having an environmental state of affairs directly present to one in experience—constitutes one's being justified in making the associated perceptual claim. It is hard to see how any other kind of justification could have a stronger claim to the title "canonical". And this justification is *not* defeasible. If someone sees that P, it cannot fail to be the case that P. So if one accepts the disjunctive conception, one is *not* at liberty to go on supposing that "the canonical justification of perceptual claims proceeds through a defeasible inferential base".

In urging the contrary, Wright constructs an argument whose starting-point is the whole disjunction. Of course he is right that the whole disjunction could provide at best defeasible support for a perceptual claim. But what he has done is in effect to cast the whole disjunction in the role in which the supposed case for scepticism casts the highest common factor. And the point of the disjunctive conception is precisely to reject the highest common factor picture of the justification for perceptual claims.

I do not mean to suggest that a I-II-III argument starting from the "good" disjunct would be any more impressive as an augmentation of Moore's "proof" than the I-II-III argument Wright considers, starting from the whole disjunction. I shall come to that in a moment. The point for now is that Wright is wrong to claim that the disjunctive conception leaves one free to think perceptual claims rest on defeasible inferential support.

What has gone wrong here?

Wright apparently assumes that a dialectically effective response to scepticism would need to be what Moore—again, if we take his performance at face value—tries to produce: that is, an argument that directly responds to the sceptic's questioning whether there is an external world. Such an argument would need to start from a premise available without begging a question against the sceptic, and it would need to transmit warrant legitimately from that premise to the conclusion that there is indeed an external world. And only the whole disjunction is non-question-beggingly available as a premise for such an argument.

But the point of the disjunctive conception is not to improve our resources for such arguments.

At one point (p. 341) Wright acknowledges, in a way, that when I appeal to the disjunctive conception I do not claim to be directly answering sceptical questions. The acknowledgment is backhanded, since Wright describes my disclaimer as "an official refusal to take scepticism seriously". It is worth pausing over this description. The wording would be appropriate if in order to take scepticism seriously one had to attempt direct answers to sceptical questions. But that seems simply wrong. Surely no one takes scepticism more seriously than Stroud. And Stroud thinks "the worst thing one can do with the traditional question about our knowledge of the world is to try to answer it".[15]

---

15. "Reasonable Claims: Cavell and the Tradition", p. 56.

Wright notes my suggestion that the disjunctive conception "has the advantage of removing a prop on which sceptical doubt . . . depends", as he puts it. But he treats this as a mere lapse from the "official refusal", as if removing a prop could only be offering an answer to a sceptical question. Only on that assumption could noting the inefficacy of the re-emergent I-II-III argument, the argument that starts from the whole disjunction, seem relevant to the anti-sceptical credentials of the disjunctive conception.

The disjunctive conception cannot improve on Moore in the project of proving that there is an external world. Wright is correct about that.

This is not, as Wright has it, because the disjunctive conception allows us to go on holding that "the canonical justification of perceptual claims proceeds through a defeasible inferential base". As I have insisted, the disjunctive conception is flatly inconsistent with that thesis. The canonical justification for a perceptual claim is that one perceives that things are as it claims they are, and that is not a defeasible inferential base.

The point is, rather, that if one lets the sceptic count as having put in doubt whether there is an external world in which things are pretty much as we take them to be, it becomes question-begging to take oneself, on any particular occasion, to *have* the *indefeasible* warrant, for a claim such as "Here is a hand", constituted by, for instance, seeing that there is a hand in front of one. In the dialectical context of an attempt to show that the sceptical scenarios do not obtain, the indefeasible warrant for "Here is a hand" constituted by seeing that there is a hand in front of one can no more be transmitted across the entailment to "There is a material world" than can the defeasible warrant Wright considers in his diagnosis of Moore. In Moore's argument as Wright reconstructs it, the fact that the warrant's support for "Here is a hand" is not defeated depends on our already taking ourselves to have grounds for the conclusion supposedly reached by entailment from there. In the argument I am considering now, our conviction that we have the warrant at all depends on our already taking ourselves to have grounds for the conclusion. This, incidentally, suggests a different account, which seems no less plausible than Wright's, of the implicit warrant for the premise Moore actually starts from. In any case, whether or not it is what Moore has in mind, an argument that starts from one's seeing a hand in front of one would be just as useless for Moore's purpose—if, again, we identify his purpose by taking his performance at face value.

But all this is irrelevant to the anti-sceptical power of the disjunctive conception. What the disjunctive conception achieves is indeed to remove a prop on which sceptical doubt depends. That is Wright's wording, but he does not allow it to carry its proper force. The prop is the thought that the warrant for a perceptual claim provided by an experience can never be that the experience reveals how things are. The disjunctive conception dislodges that thought, and a sceptical doubt that depends on it falls to the ground. There is no need to do more than remove the prop. In particular, as I explained before, there is no need to try to *establish* theses like the conclusion of Moore's argument, with the ground rules for doing so set by scepticism. The idea that such theses are open to doubt now lacks the cachet of simply emphasizing an epistemic predicament constituted by its being impossible for experience to reveal to us how things are. There is no such predicament, and now it is perfectly proper to appeal to cases of ordinary perceptual knowledge in ruling out the sceptical scenarios, or—better—in justifying a common-sense refusal to bother with them.

Wright might be tempted to seize on what I have just said as vindicating his talk of my "official refusal to take scepticism seriously". But like Stroud, I hold that the way to take scepticism seriously is not to try to disprove the sceptical scenarios. We take scepticism seriously by removing the prop, thereby entitling ourselves to join common sense in refusing to bother with the sceptical scenarios.[16]

Considering the form "*Either* I am perceiving thus-and-such *or* I am in some kind of delusional state", Wright offers this reconstruction of the sceptical reasoning that, according to him, survives the disjunctive conception (p. 346):

> [I]n this case it is our practice to treat one in particular of the disjuncts as justified—the left-hand one—whenever the disjunction as a whole is justified and there is, merely, *no evidence for* the other disjunct! That's a manifest fallacy unless the case is one where we have a standing reason to regard the lack of any salient justification for a disjunct of the second type as a reason to discount it. And—the sceptical thought will be—it's hard to see what

---

16. In writing here of a common-sense refusal to bother with the sceptical scenarios, I am echoing a remark at *Mind and World*, p. 113 (in the passage Wright cites to document the "official refusal"): "The aim here is not to answer sceptical questions, but to begin to see how it might be intellectually respectable to ignore them, to treat them as unreal, in the way that common sense has always wanted to." Of course it takes work to reach such a position. This attitude can look like a "refusal to take scepticism seriously" only given the picture of what it is to take scepticism seriously that Stroud rejects.

could count as a standing reason except a prior entitlement to the belief that delusions are rare. But that's just tantamount to the belief that there is a material world which, at least on the surfaces of things, is pretty much revealed for what it is in what we take to be normal waking experience. So, the Sceptic will contend, that broad conception once again emerges as a rational precondition of our practice, even after the disjunctive adjustment to the concept of perception; and on its warrantedness depends whatever warrant can be given for our proceeding in the way we do. Since it cannot be warranted by appeal to the warrant for specific perceptual claims—Moore's proof being no better in this setting than before—the Sceptic may now focus on the apparent impossibility of any kind of direct warrant for it, and the dialectic can proceed essentially as before.

It is clearly correct that our practice of assessing the credentials of perceptual claims could not be rational if we were not entitled to the "broad conception" according to which the external world is pretty much the way we take ourselves to experience it as being. But it is tendentious to suppose it follows that the rationality of our practice is in jeopardy unless the "broad conception" can be warranted *in advance of the practice* without begging questions against scepticism. And it is wrong to suppose the disjunctive conception leaves unchallenged the idea Wright here exploits, that the justification for a perceptual claim must go through the whole disjunction, exploiting some supposed standing reason for discounting the "bad" disjunct. The justification for a perceptual claim is an entitlement to the "good" disjunct. What entitles one to that is not that one's experience warrants the whole disjunction, plus some supposed ground for discounting the "bad" disjunct. That would commit us to trying to reconstruct the epistemic standing constituted by perceiving something to be the case in terms of the highest common factor conception of experience, plus whatever ground we can think of for discounting the "bad" disjunct. I think Wright is correct that that is hopeless; if we see things this way, the sceptic wins. But the disjunctive conception eliminates the apparent need for any such project, because it contradicts the highest common factor conception.

What does entitle one to claim that one is perceiving that things are thus and so, when one is so entitled? The fact that one is perceiving that things are thus and so. That is a kind of fact whose obtaining our self-consciously possessed perceptual capacities enable us to recognize on suitable occasions, just as they enable us to recognize such facts as that there are red cubes in front of us, and all the more complex types of environmental facts that our powers to perceive things put at our disposal.

Of course we are fallible about the obtaining of such facts, just as we are fallible about the facts we perceive to obtain. I can tell a zebra when I see one—to take up an example Wright borrows from Fred Dretske (pp. 342–4). If what I believe to be a zebra is actually a cunningly painted mule, then of course I do not recognize it as a zebra, as I suppose, and I do not have the warrant I think I have for believing it is a zebra, namely that I see it to be a zebra. My ability to recognize zebras is fallible, and it follows that my ability to know when I am seeing a zebra is fallible. It does not follow—this is the crucial point—that I cannot ever have the warrant for believing that an animal in front of me is a zebra constituted by seeing that it is a zebra. If the animal in front of me is a zebra, and conditions are suitable for exercising my ability to recognize zebras when I see them (for instance, the animal is in full view), then that ability, fallible though it is, enables me to see that it is a zebra, and to know that I do. My warrant is not limited to the disjunction "Either I see that it is a zebra or my visual experience is misleading in some way". That is the highest common factor conception, and fallibility in our cognitive capacities cannot force it on us.[17]

6. Transcendental arguments of Stroud's ambitious type aim to establish large-scale features the world must have for it to be possible that thought and experience are as they are. Those of his modest type aim to establish large-scale features we must conceive the world to have for it to be possible that thought and experience are as they are.

The argument I have considered belongs to neither of these types. It does not offer to establish anything about how things are, let alone must be, in the world apart from us, so it is not vulnerable to Stroud's doubts about arguments of the ambitious type. But the way it makes itself immune to those doubts is not by weakening its conclusion to one about structural features we must conceive the world to have. The conclusion is rather one about how we must conceive the epistemic positions that are within our reach, if it is to be possible that our experience is as it is in having objective purport.

---

17. A misconception of the significance of fallibility on these lines is the topic of the passage in my *Mind and World* (pp. 112–3) that Wright comments on at p. 341, n. 13. His remarks there seem to me to miss, or ignore, the dialectical context of the passage he is commenting on.

That frees us to pursue our ordinary ways of finding out how things are in the world apart from us. The specifics of what we go on to find out are not within the scope of what the argument aims to vindicate.

That might seem to distance this argument from much in Kant, who is presumably the patron saint of transcendental arguments. In sketching the argument, I have not needed to connect it with the question "How is synthetic *a priori* knowledge possible?", or with an investigation of the principles of the pure understanding. But there is still the fact that the argument displays its conclusion as a necessary element in the answer to a "How possible?" question about experience. Moreover, Sellars's account of how experience has its objective purport, which the argument exploits, is strikingly Kantian, in the way it represents the content of an experience as the content of a claim. Sellars links the fact that experience is of objective reality with the fact that to make a claim is to commit oneself to things being objectively thus and so. This talk of claims is Sellars's counterpart, after the "linguistic turn", to Kant's invocation of judgment. So perhaps the argument I have been considering can be seen as belonging to a minimal Kantianism. In the argument's background is an explanation of the objective purport of experience in terms of the fact that experience exemplifies forms that belong to the understanding. But in the argument as I have considered it so far, we exploit that Kantian thought without needing to concern ourselves either with how the world must be or with how we must conceive the world to be. Of course this is not the place to try to take this any further.

PART V

Themes from *Mind and World* Revisited

Experiencing the World[1]

1. I am going to begin by saying something about the frame in which I want to place a conception of experience as taking in the world.

Such an idea has obvious attractions from an epistemological point of view, and that is not irrelevant to my interest in it. But the main purpose to which I want to put the idea is not to reassure ourselves that we can achieve empirical knowledge, but rather to ensure that we are not beset by a difficulty about the capacity of our mental activity to be about reality at all, whether knowledgeably or not. I suggest that we can understand some of the central preoccupations of modern philosophy by making sense of a wish to ask "How is empirical content so much as possible?" That would give expression to an anxiety about how our intellectual activity can make us answerable to reality for whether we are thinking correctly or not—something that is surely required if the activity is to be recognizable as thinking at all. The question whether some of our thinking puts us in possession of knowledge cannot even arise unless this prior condition, that our thinking can have empirical content at all, is met. I use the word "transcendental", in what I hope is sufficiently close to a Kantian way, to characterize this sort of concern with the very possibility of thought's being directed at the objective world. And it is in this context of transcendental anxiety that I am primarily concerned with the question how we should conceive experience.

It is part of my point that people who are in the grip of the anxiety I am interested in typically do not clearly comprehend what is bothering them. One shape this unclarity can take is that one's problem strikes one as episte-

---

1. This was written as a lecture to introduce the conception of experience that I recommended in *Mind and World*. I have also drawn on thoughts from "Having the World in View".

mological rather than transcendental. An unfocused sense of what is in fact a transcendental difficulty need take no more definite a form than a vague inkling that thought's hold on reality is coming into question. And the image of thought's hold on reality can easily seem to fit knowledge, as contrasted with, say, guesswork or plausible conjecture. This yields a misunderstanding of the difficulty one feels oneself falling into, though *ex hypothesi* only inchoately. In the misunderstanding, it seems that one needs a secure foundation for knowledge—as if one could take the contentfulness of one's empirical thinking for granted, and merely had to reassure oneself as to its credentials. Thus what would be revealed as a transcendental anxiety, if it came into clearer focus, can, through an intelligible unclarity attaching to a merely incipient form of it, underlie the concern with, so to speak, mere scepticism that shapes much modern philosophy. So I suggest that making sense of a transcendental anxiety can cast light on more of modern philosophy than one might at first suppose.

The anxiety in its focused, explicitly transcendental form is perhaps closer to the surface in what Richard Rorty calls "impure philosophy of language" in chapter 6 of *Philosophy and the Mirror of Nature*. There he depicts a concern with how language hooks on to reality as a late-coming counterpart to an anxiety about how thought hooks on to reality, which according to Rorty has been a major deforming force in modern philosophy. Rorty himself, however, sees the deforming anxiety as primarily epistemological, rather than epistemological only in the guise of a defectively understood difficulty that is really transcendental, and that is just what I am resisting.

I understand the wish to ask the transcendental question, "How is empirical content possible?", as expressing an attraction to a pair of thoughts whose implication, if taken together, is that empirical content is impossible. The thoughts impose a requirement for there to be empirical content, but ensure that it cannot be met.

The requirement is that empirical thinking must be subject to what W. V. Quine (in a strikingly Kantian phrase) calls "the tribunal of experience".[2] The idea is that we can make sense of intellectual activity's being correct or incorrect in the light of how things are in the world only if we can see it as, at least in part, answerable to impressions the world makes on us, as possessors of sensibility. But this felt requirement can easily seem impossible to satisfy. The notion of the world's making an impression on a possessor of

---

2. "Two Dogmas of Empiricism", p. 41.

sensibility is on the face of it the notion of a kind of natural happening. As such it can seem to be excluded, on pain of naturalistic fallacy, from the special logical space—what Wilfrid Sellars calls "the logical space of reasons"[3]— that we would have to be moving in when we take things to be related as tribunal and respondent. Sellars introduces this image of the logical space of reasons in a context in which he is precisely warning against a naturalistic fallacy, which he suggests one falls into if one takes it that merely natural happenings can constitute a tribunal. Quine himself seems to succumb to just this pitfall, in trying to conceive experience as a tribunal even while he understands experience in terms of irritations of sensory nerve-endings.

It can thus come to appear that thought's being answerable to impressions is a condition for there to be empirical content at all, which, however, cannot be met because the idea of an impression does not fit in the logical space of reasons. And this leads to the incredible conclusion that there simply cannot be empirical content. This is not a perhaps surmountable difficulty about how there can be empirical content—as if the question "How is empirical content possible?" could receive a response that started like this: "Good question; let me tell you how." "How is empirical content possible?", uttered from the frame of mind I am describing, expresses a temptation to believe the premises of an argument whose conclusion is that empirical content is not possible. Given that empirical content is possible, there must be something wrong with the premises. And once we identify a culprit and dislodge it, we shall be freeing ourselves from the frame of mind that seemed to find appropriate expression in the "How possible?" question. The result will be, not an answer to the question, but a liberation from the apparent need to ask it.

However, it is easy to suppose that the "How possible?" question, even if one's wish to ask it has the kind of background I am considering, expresses a difficulty rather than an impossibility. In this misunderstanding, one thinks one can leave one's background assumptions in place but still take on an obligation to try to force empirical content into one's picture, as it were against some resistance. Here we encounter a deeper sense in which, as I said, people who are in the grip of the anxiety I am considering do not command a clear view of what ails them. Not only do such people often mistake a transcendental anxiety for an epistemological one. The deeper misconcep-

3. "Empiricism and the Philosophy of Mind", §36.

tion is to mistake an impossible conceptual bind for a tractable intellectual problem—something one might set out to solve without shifting one's background assumptions. The predicament is beautifully captured by a remark in Wittgenstein's *Nachlass*: "You are under the impression that the problem is *difficult*, when it's *impossible*. I want you to realize that you are under a spell."[4]

2. I have suggested the spell is cast by the attractions of a pair of thoughts: first, that empirical content depends on answerability to impressions, and, second, that impressions could not be the kind of thing to which something could be answerable, because the idea of an impression is the idea of a natural phenomenon. Dislodging either of these two thoughts would in principle lift the spell. Donald Davidson, for instance, in effect retains the second thought, that impressions could not constitute a tribunal, and discards the first, that empirical content depends on answerability to impressions.[5] That is to say: he discards empiricism, in one obvious sense. One might think of Davidson as offering an implicit argument by reductio, in which the impossibility of accepting that there cannot be empirical content is turned against the transcendental empiricism that is one of the premises from which that impossible conclusion can be derived, in a way that pivots on retaining the other premise.

But I prefer to try to explain away the attractions of supposing that impressions could not be the kind of thing to which something could be answerable. This makes it possible to hold on to the thought that empirical content depends on answerability to impressions.

The idea of an impression is indeed the idea of a kind of occurrence in nature. But only a conflation makes it seem to follow that impressions cannot constitute a tribunal. The idea of intellectual activity being answerable to a tribunal belongs in the logical space of reasons, to stay with Sellars's image. And Sellars is right to depict the logical space of reasons as special, by comparison with a logical space in which we make a quite different kind of move. I think the best way to understand this contrast of logical spaces is in terms of a distinction between two ways of finding things intelligible: on the one hand, placing things in a context of rational considerations for and

---

4. MS 158, p. 37; quoted by Baker and Hacker, *An Analytic Commentary on Wittgenstein's Philosophical Investigations*, vol. 1, p. 228.

5. See Davidson's essay, "A Coherence Theory of Truth and Knowledge".

against them (the sort of thing we do when, for instance, we make sense of behaviour as rational agency), and, on the other hand, finding things intelligible in the ways in which the natural sciences do, for instance by subsuming them under lawlike generalizations. On this view, then, Sellars is right to set the logical space of reasons in opposition to a contrasting logical space, and, given that we can gesture towards an identification of the contrasting logical space, as I have just done, by invoking the natural sciences, it can be almost irresistible to entitle it "the logical space of nature". This chimes with Sellars's warning against a naturalistic fallacy, and this is how it comes to seem that the idea of an impression, as the idea of a natural occurrence, has to be foreign to the logical space of reasons. But we can avoid the appearance by refusing to let the logical space that Sellars rightly contrasts with the logical space of reasons be identified as the logical space of nature.

It is intelligible that this identification should be hard to resist, given that one can mark the contrast of logical spaces, as I just did, by invoking the natural sciences. But in spite of the label, those disciplines need not be conceded ownership of the very idea of natural phenomena. The idea of an impression can be both the idea of a kind of natural happening and an idea that belongs in the logical space of reasons.

Impressions can fit in the logical space of reasons because impressions can be actualizations of conceptual capacities. Sellars glosses the space of reasons as the logical space "of justifying and being able to justify what one says".[6] The implication is that one comes to inhabit the logical space of reasons—to have conceptual capacities in the relevant sense—by acquiring command of a language. We can acknowledge that this enables our lives to contain goings-on warranting characterization in terms that are special, in just the way Sellars aims to capture with the image of the logical space of reasons. But this need not seem to remove those goings-on from the realm of natural phenomena. Acquiring command of a language, which is coming to inhabit the logical space of reasons, is acquiring a second nature. Given that the space of reasons is special in the way Sellars urges, ideas of phenomena that are manifestations of a second nature acquired in acquiring command of a language do not, as such, fit in the logical space of natural-scientific understanding. But there is no reason why that should rule out seeing those phenomena as manifestations of nature, since the nature in question can be a second nature. Actualizations of conceptual capacities,

---

6. "Empiricism and the Philosophy of Mind", §36.

which as such belong in the logical space of reasons, can be natural in a different sense from the one that figures in the admittedly well-drawn contrast with the logical space of reasons.

On these lines, we can acknowledge a correctness in the contrast of logical spaces that seems to make it impossible for impressions to constitute a tribunal, but take that appearance to be after all a mere appearance. There is no need to follow Davidson in discarding the other of the two thoughts that together generate the seeming impossibility of empirical content. We do not, after all, have materials for a reductio of transcendental empiricism, as Davidson implicitly suggests.

It may seem that Davidson's way of avoiding transcendental anxiety is symmetrical with the way of avoiding it that I have begun to sketch. He discards one premise of the inchoate argument that empirical content is impossible, whereas I discard the other. So why should anyone prefer my way to Davidson's? Well, there is, I believe, an intuitive appeal in the idea that empirical thinking must be answerable to impressions if it is to be contentful at all, and Davidson's approach does nothing towards explaining that away. In effect Davidson claims that since transcendental empiricism will not cohere with the status of impressions as natural phenomena, transcendental empiricism must be wrong. He does not offer a suggestion as to why it should nevertheless seem right, so that its attractiveness could stand revealed as an intelligible illusion. Suppose someone is really tempted to think both that empirical thinking must be answerable to impressions and that it cannot be. Davidson does nothing to help such a person. It is not helpful, if someone is really enmeshed in this bind, to say: "Since impressions are natural phenomena, and the members of a tribunal would have to belong in the contrasting logical space of reasons, the transcendental empiricism that you find appealing must, after all, be wrong." Suppose a victim of the bind became clear about its shape. She would know that something must be wrong in her thinking. Helping her would require showing her how some of her thinking *could* be wrong, not just ordering her, as it were, *ex cathedra*, to repress this rather than that bit of it. Whereas on my side, I offer a story whose point is to acknowledge, but explain away, the attractiveness of the other of the two sources of the anxiety, the thought that impressions cannot constitute a tribunal. So there is after all an asymmetry. I explain away the attractiveness of the premise I discard, whereas Davidson merely discards the other premise, as it were by force, without saying anything to help someone who is captivated by it.

3. So much for a general frame; now let me say something about the specifics of the conception of experience, as taking in the world, that my framing move is meant to make room for.

In an experience of the relevant kind, if things go well, some case of how things are impresses itself on a perceiving subject thanks to her possession of some suitable sensibility. Experience is receptivity in operation. To invoke the Kantian idea of receptivity like this is simply to begin elaborating the idea of an impression, in a way that is guided by the etymology of the word "impression". Any concept whose explication begins on these lines would have to be the concept of a kind of state or occurrence in nature. And this brings out sharply the apparent difficulty in conceiving impressions as constituting a tribunal while respecting Sellars's point about the special character of the logical space of reasons. It can seem that if we try to confer a position in the order of justification on experience conceived as receptivity in operation, we must be falling into what Sellars attacks as the Myth of the Given. What Sellars attacks under that label extends more widely than this, but the main form of the Myth he discusses is precisely the attempt to give merely natural phenomena a position in the order of justification. It is common to read Sellars as holding precisely that as soon as one begins explicating a concept of experience by invoking something on the lines of receptivity, one is doomed to fall foul of the Myth of the Given.

Bracketing, for the moment, the question whether this is indeed Sellars's position, I can say that at any rate the thesis strikes me as simply wrong. Starting an explication of the idea of a perceptual experience by invoking sensory receptivity leaves us able, quite coherently, to go on to bring conceptual capacities into the story. Remembering that nature can be second nature, we can immunize ourselves against the idea that the naturalness implied by the idea of sensory receptivity would have to stand in tension with the placement in the space of reasons implied by the talk of conceptual capacities. This allows us a conception of perceptual experience as something we can place in the order of justification, while respecting the point Sellars makes by insisting that the space of reasons is special.

What we need, and can have, is the idea of a case of receptivity in operation that, even while being that, is an actualization, together, of conceptual capacities whose active exercise, with the same togetherness, would be the making of a judgment. This is the idea of a case of receptivity in operation, an impression, that itself has conceptual content, the conceptual content that would be the content of the counterpart judgment—the judgment one would be making if one actively exercised the same conceptual capacities with the same togetherness. There is no more difficulty about placing such a state or occurrence in the order of justification than there would be about placing the counterpart judgment in the order of justification. In particular, there is no question of the hopeless attempt that characterizes the Myth of the Given, to credit something with supplying rational or warranting force into the realm of the conceptually contentful from outside. The warranting item—the experience conceived in these terms—itself already has content that is just as firmly conceptual as the content of a judgment; in fact it just is the content of the possible judgment that I have been calling "the counterpart judgment".

For the idea of judgment as an act in which several conceptual capacities are exercised with a suitable togetherness—the model for this idea of experience—I would cite, in the first instance, a brilliant treatment of judgment offered by P. T. Geach in his book *Mental Acts*. Geach there exploits an analogy between, on the one hand, the combination—the joint exercise—of conceptual capacities in acts of judgment and, on the other, the concatenation of subsentential expressions in a declarative utterance. Conceptual capacities exercised in a single act of judgment have a semantical or logical togetherness that is, on Geach's picture, to be understood on analogy with the semantical or logical togetherness of the corresponding words, in a grammatically structured form of words that would give expression to the judgment. What I am suggesting is that we can amplify Geach's conception of judgment, and understand experience through a second use of analogy. Geach shows how to model acts of judgment on declarative utterances, and we can model experiences on acts of judgment.

In making judgment pivotal, I hope I secure that the conception of concepts that is in play here is palpably Kantian. Our way into the very idea of a concept is through the thought that the paradigmatic actualization of conceptual capacities is their exercise in acts of judgment. Geach shows how we can domesticate this Kantian way of thinking of conceptual capacities within the post-Kantian form of philosophy characterized by what has been called "the linguistic turn". But one might suggest that this much of a linguistic turn is implicit in the already Kantian idea that conceptual capacities are exercised with a logical togetherness in acts of judgment, which are of course not necessarily expressed in language.

Making judgment fundamental to our conception of concepts brings out at least part of the point of saying, with Kant, that conceptual capacities belong to a faculty of spontaneity. Judging is making up one's mind about how things are, as forming an intention is making up one's mind about what to do. Judging is like forming an intention in being an exercise of responsible freedom. But I formulated the Kantian anchoring of the very idea of a concept by saying that acts of judging are the paradigmatic kind of occurrence in which conceptual capacities are actualized. This leaves room for conceptual capacities, in the very same sense, to be actualized in nonparadigmatic ways, in kinds of occurrence other than acts of judging.

There are straightforward cases of this possibility. Consider, for instance, entertaining suppositions. This is perhaps not far removed from what I am describing as the paradigmatic case. For one thing, we should understand the capacity to entertain mere suppositions, in the first instance, in the context of thinking aimed at making up one's mind, and work out from there to the capacity for, say, idle fantasy. And in any case, even in idle fantasy conceptual capacities are exercised. To say that some activity is irresponsible, as one might about daydreaming, is exactly not to remove it from the scope of responsible freedom, but to criticize it as an irresponsible use of one's freedom to exercise one's conceptual capacities.

But with experience conceived as I recommend, we have a more radical departure from the paradigmatic case of conceptual capacities being actualized. An actualization of a conceptual capacity need not be an exercise of the capacity, so it need not be itself within the scope of responsible freedom, as even the exercise of conceptual capacities in daydreaming is. The point of talking of paradigmatic cases is that the kind of actualization of a conceptual capacity we need to focus on first, in order to understand what kind of capacity a conceptual capacity is, is indeed an exercise, an ingredient in an instance of the complex kind of act that judgments are. But once we have thus identified the relevant kind of capacity, we can countenance cases in which capacities of that very kind are not exercised, but are nevertheless actualized, outside the control of their possessor, by the world's impacts on her sensibility. That is just how I recommend conceiving experience.

I hope it is clear that it matters to keep the terms "actualization" and "exercise" apart. Conceptual capacities are capacities of spontaneity, but in one obvious sense there is no spontaneity in perceiving. It is not up to one how things, for instance, look to one. How things look to one does not come within the scope of one's responsibility to make up one's own mind. But this is consistent with understanding experience as actualizing capacities that belong to spontaneity, in the sense that to understand what capacities they are we have to focus on their being exercisable in judgment. It is just that that is not the kind of actualization that is involved in experience.

I introduced impressions, in the relevant sense, as occurrences in which how things are impresses itself on a perceiving subject. The resources I have introduced enable us to give this wording full force. We can see the relevant case of *how things are* as encapsulated into the circumstance of being impressed in the way the subject is. Without these resources, we could conceive the subject's being impressed only as something on the lines of receiving a dent in the mind's wax tablet. (It would make no difference if we replaced that image with some sophisticated physiology.) Perhaps a theorist could recover an aetiology for a dent from its configuration, but it would only be in some such sense that an impression could contain the relevant case of how things are, and such a sense would not make impressions suitable for a transcendental empiricism. This is just Sellars's point; the Myth of the Given, in the relevant form, is the hopeless attempt to make a mere dent in the tablet of the mind—not a fact about the dent but the dent itself—into a rational consideration. But with the conceptual resources I have introduced, an operation of one's receptivity can itself be having certain conceptual capacities passively drawn into operation by the impact of a fact on one's sensibility. So it can be having *that things are thus and so*—the conceptual content of the judgment one would be making if one actively exercised the same conceptual capacities in the same combination—borne in on one. But that things are thus and so can be how things are. So receiving an impression can be having how things are borne in on one.

There are two points here. First, we see how impressions can be no harder to place in the order of justification than judgments are, even while we fully respect Sellars's point about the Myth of the Given. Second, and more specifically, we see how we can take facts themselves to be available to a perceiving subject, as rational considerations relevant to her task of making up her mind. Thus, in the course of seeing how to alleviate a transcendental difficulty, we equip ourselves with an idea that has a directly epistemological interest.

4. I bracketed the question whether Sellars himself thinks sensory impressions would have to be dents in the tablet of the mind. I used to read Sellars that way, but I now think that when, in "Empiricism and the Philosophy of Mind", he elaborates the image of experiences as "containing" claims, he is best understood to be pointing towards a conception of experience on just

the lines I have been sketching, as episodes of sensory consciousness that are constituted by actualizations of conceptual capacities.

This is not the only respect in which I think I am a better Sellarsian than some people give me credit for. In my book *Mind and World*, I allow myself to say the contents of experience are ultimate in the order of justification. In a "Critical Study" of my book ("Exorcism and Enchantment"), Michael Williams takes that to show that I am a foundationalist, in the sense that I hold a position Sellars attacks in passages like this: "One of the forms taken by the Myth of the Given is the idea that there is, indeed *must* be, a structure of particular matter of fact such that (a) each fact can not only be non-inferentially known to be the case, but presupposes no other knowledge either of particular matter of fact, or of general truths; and (b) . . . the non-inferential knowledge of facts belonging to this structure constitutes the ultimate court of appeals for all factual claims—particular and general—about the world."[7] It may help to clarify my picture of experience if I try to say why this accusation misfires.

Sellars himself has a nuanced attitude to the image of foundations. He does not object to the idea of a stratum of knowledge that "constitutes the ultimate court of appeals for all factual claims . . . about the world". The knowledge expressed in reports of observation plays just that role for him. Sellars's objection, in the passage I quoted, is not to that idea on its own, but to combining it with something else: the idea that the knowledge that constitutes the ultimate court of appeal is knowledge one could have all by itself, even without having a world view built on it. Thus Sellars says: "the metaphor of 'foundation' is misleading in that it keeps us from seeing that if there is a logical dimension in which other empirical propositions rest on observation reports, there is another logical dimension in which the latter rest on the former."[8] This is not to object to the idea of a "logical dimension" in which reports of observation are the support for everything else, but only to warn that a natural image for expressing that idea, the image of foundations, tends to make us forget the other dimension of dependence, in which reports of observation depend on the world view that rests on them as a building rests on its foundations. When I say experiences are ultimate in the order of justification, all I mean is that they are ultimate in the "logical dimension" in which Sellars allows that reports of observation are ultimate. I

7. "Empiricism and the Philosophy of Mind", §32.
8. "Empiricism and the Philosophy of Mind", §38.

simply put experiences in the epistemological position in which Sellars puts reports of observation. Experiences, in my picture, have conceptual content, and that means I have just the machinery Sellars does—a holism about the conceptual—to ensure that the other dimension of dependence is not lost. So I am not a foundationalist in Williams's sense.

5. I want to end by making a beginning on a large topic. Philosophers are prone to assume that mental occurrences are, as such or in themselves, *internal* to the person in whose mental life they take place, either quasi-literally internal (as in Descartes, for whom this spatial talk cannot be literal) or even literally internal (as in many contemporaries, who take themselves to be emancipated from Cartesian ways of thinking). Perceptual experiences are mental occurrences, so they come within the scope of such an assumption. The effect is to obliterate the conception of experience I recommend.

The assumption is operative in this expression of puzzlement, by Robert Brandom, about why I find my conception of experience so compelling: "Sense impressions are 'behind' [judgments of observation] in a causal sense, and *facts* are behind them in a normative sense (as well as, in the favored cases, in a causal sense). What is the source of the insistence that there must *also* be some *internal* thing, the experience, that plays both these roles at once?"[9] By "sense impressions" here, Brandom means something on the lines of Quine's conception: irritations of sensory nerve endings, the sort of thing no follower of Sellars would try to conceive as constituting a tribunal.

One might elaborate what Brandom is suggesting on the following lines. If experiences as I want them in the picture are not simply what Davidson calls "perceptually acquired beliefs" under another name (so that their justificatory force is allowed for in Davidson's slogan "nothing can count as a reason for a belief except another belief"),[10] then placing them justificatorily "behind" perceptual judgments or perceptually acquired beliefs can only be a case of a familiar epistemological syndrome, in which we interpose something internal between perceivers and the facts they perceive to hold. On this view, my appeal to experiences is a case of what Davidson calls "the Myth of the Subjective":[11] the hopeless idea that we can start with what is *in here* (here we need a gesture of pointing with both hands into one's head),

---

9. "Perception and Rational Constraint", at p. 257.
10. "A Coherence Theory of Truth and Knowledge", p. 141.
11. See "The Myth of the Subjective".

and entitle ourselves, on the basis of that, to beliefs about what is *out there* (here we need a gesture at the world about us). I protest that receiving an impression, on my account, is (or at least can be) a case of having an environmental state of affairs borne in on one. It is already an entitlement to beliefs about what is "out there", not some inner occurrence from which one might hope to move to an outward entitlement. But the assumption that mental occurrences are internal risks making this protest inaudible. If experiencing, as a mental occurrence, is in itself "in here", then, even supposing we can make sense of describing an episode of experiencing in terms of an environmental state of affairs, as having that state of affairs borne in on one, this mode of description cannot get at what the episode is in itself. We seem to be back with the idea of a dent in the mind's tablet.

My talk of impressions secures that we can see observational judgments as rationally responsive to the states of affairs they judge to obtain. This enables observation to occupy not only the epistemological role of which Sellars gives his nuanced picture, but also the transcendental role I have been concerned to protect, as the point to focus our attention on in order to find it unproblematic that our intellectual activity is answerable to the world. It is exactly not the case that impressions, as I conceive them, intervene between perceiving subjects and the states of affairs they observe to obtain. Rather, at their best impressions constitute an availability, to a judging subject, of facts themselves, which she may incorporate into her world view—perhaps by way of explicit judgment, or perhaps less reflectively—on the basis of the impressions.

I think the real villain here is the assumption that experiences, as mental occurrences, must be in themselves internal to their subjects. Davidson's protest against what he calls "the Myth of the Subjective" is directed against a symptom, the tendency to postulate intermediaries, rather than against the underlying malady, which infects Davidson himself, even though he contrives to free his thinking from the symptom. The fundamental mistake is the thought that a person's mental life takes place in a *part* of her. Descartes thought it would have to be an immaterial part, and it is an improvement on that, at least in some respects, to make the seat of mental life a material part of the person (so that "in here", with the pointing gesture, can be meant literally). But this modification does not fix the real problem. In Davidson's case, the monism that is part of his anomalous monism[12] implies a correctness

12. See "Mental Events".

for the "in here" gesture, taken literally. But I think we need a way of thinking about the mental in which involvement with worldly facts is not just a point about describability in (roughly speaking) relational terms (like someone's being an uncle), but gets at the essence of the mental. The "in here" locution, with its accompanying gesture, is all right in some contexts, but it needs to be taken symbolically, in the same spirit in which one takes the naturalness of saying things like "In my heart I know it", which can similarly be accompanied by an appropriate gesture. If anomalous monism disallows this, then so much the worse for anomalous monism.

If we conceive experience as I recommend, our picture of subjects who are in a position to make observational judgments can take an attractive shape. We can see the facts in question as available to the subjects, as rational constraints on their activity of making up their minds. That is: we can see the facts as behind observational judgments in a normative sense, as Brandom puts it in the passage I quoted. Brandom's puzzlement is this: why do I want to place something else—something internal—normatively behind the judgments, over and above the facts? This leads into the idea of intermediaries, the target of Davidson's protest, but it misses the point. To make sense of how it is that the facts are normatively behind the judgments, we need the facts to be available to the subjects who make the judgments, as the rational constraints on judgment that they are. On my conception, to enjoy an experience in which all goes well is simply to have a fact available to one, so that it can be normatively behind a judgment one might make. Davidson thinks the subjective as such is a myth, and Brandom in effect follows him, because they cannot see anything for the subjective to be except the internal items that threaten to interpose themselves as intermediaries between subjects and the world. But in experience on my conception we have, not only something that is necessary for making sense of the normative connection between facts and observational judgments that Brandom agrees we need, but also a paradigm of a kind of subjective state that is immune to the objections against intermediaries. So without defending what Davidson attacks, we can use the idea of experience to start on recapturing a hygienic idea of subjectivity. The benefits of conceiving experience as I recommend are not restricted to pre-empting transcendental anxiety and opening up a satisfactory epistemology for perception, but extend also into general concerns in the philosophy of mind.

Naturalism in the Philosophy of Mind

1. Modern epistemology is beset by distinctive anxieties. We can base an understanding of them on a remark of Wilfrid Sellars: "In characterizing an episode or a state as that of *knowing*, we are not giving an empirical description of that episode or state; we are placing it in the logical space of reasons, of justifying and being able to justify what one says."[1]

Sellars implies that to say how an episode or state is placed in the space of reasons is not to give an empirical description of it, and I think that is infelicitous. A better way to put the thought might be to say, as Sellars almost does elsewhere, that epistemology is vulnerable to a naturalistic fallacy.[2] On a familiar modern understanding of nature, a contrast opens between saying how something is placed in the space of reasons—a logical space that is organized by justificatory relations between its inhabitants—and saying how something is placed in nature. The contrast is such as to suggest that the content of concepts that belong in the space of reasons, such as the concept of knowledge, cannot be captured in terms of concepts that belong in the contrasting logical space, the space of placement in nature.

The conception of nature that yields this contrast is one whose origins lie in the development of modern science. The contrast Sellars implicitly appeals to was not available before modern times. This can help us understand why modernity brings with it a new tone, distinctively panicky and obsessive, for philosophical reflection about knowledge.

Consider how Aristotle or a medieval Aristotelian would have conceived the relation between the idea of knowledge and the idea of the natural. For

---

1. "Empiricism and the Philosophy of Mind", §36. Richard Rorty quotes the remark *twice* in *Philosophy and the Mirror of Nature*: pp. 141, 389.
2. See §5 of "Empiricism and the Philosophy of Mind" for a formulation on these lines.

such a thinker, the capacities that equip human beings to acquire knowledge could be, as such, natural powers, and the results of their exercise could be natural states of affairs. Not that those pre-modern thinkers were innocent of the connection Sellars insists on, between the idea of knowing and ideas of justification—as if pre-modern people could not entertain the thought that becomes so pregnant in modern epistemology, that knowledge is a normative status. But they did not feel a tension between the idea that knowledge is a normative status and the idea of an exercise of natural powers. Before the modern era, it would not have been intelligible to fear a naturalistic fallacy in epistemology.

But the rise of modern science has made available a conception of nature that makes the warning intelligible. The natural sciences, as we now conceive them, do not look for an organization for their subject matter in which one item is displayed as, say, justified in the light of another item. (This is one interpretation of the slogan that natural science is value-free.) It is tempting to identify nature with the subject matter of the natural sciences so conceived. And now the contrast Sellars draws can set an agenda for philosophy.

Some followers of Sellars, notably Richard Rorty, put the contrast as one between the space of reasons and the space of *causes*.[3] But I think it is better to set the space of reasons not against the space of causes but against the space of subsumption under, as we say, natural law. Unlike Rorty's construal of the contrast, this version does not pre-empt the possibility that reasons might *be* causes. We need not see the idea of causal linkages as the exclusive property of natural-scientific thinking.[4]

If we conceive nature in such a way that delineating something's natural character contrasts with placing something in the space of reasons, we can no longer take in stride the idea that powers to acquire knowledge are part of our natural endowment. Knowing, as a case of occupying a normative

---

3. See *Philosophy and the Mirror of Nature*, p. 157, where Rorty sharply separates "what Sellars calls 'the logical space of reasons' " from "that of causal relations to objects".

4. I am suggesting that we can appeal to the idea of laws of nature in order to express the contrast Sellars insists on, even while we urge that the contrast is essentially modern. I am not thereby flying in the face of the plain fact that the concept of a law of nature predates modernity, just as the concept of nature does. The phrase itself obviously traces back to a time when the idea of laws of nature did not stand in contrast with the idea of a normative organization of a subject matter. This does not undermine the point I exploit, which is one about what the idea of a law of nature has become.

status, can no longer be seen as a natural phenomenon. And now it is easy for knowing to seem mysterious. It is no use expanding our conception of what is real beyond what is natural, if the effect is to make it seem that acquiring knowledge must be a supernatural feat. So with the new conception of nature, the knowing subject threatens to withdraw from the natural world. That is one way in which it comes to look as if philosophical epistemology needs to reconnect the knowing subject with the rest of reality.

2. I began with epistemology, but parallel considerations extend into the philosophy of mind in general. It is not just knowing that threatens to be extruded from nature on the basis of the contrast between nature and the space of reasons.

Sellars says characterizing something as a case of *knowledge* is placing it in the logical space of reasons. Compare Donald Davidson's claim that our talk of *propositional attitudes* is intelligible only in the context of "the constitutive ideal of rationality".[5] We could reformulate Davidson's thesis in Sellarsian terms: the concepts of believing, desiring, and so forth are understood only in the framework of the space of reasons.

And Davidson's thesis is not idiosyncratic. It has, for instance, an obvious affinity with Daniel Dennett's claim that intentionality is in view only from the intentional stance, which organizes its subject matter within a framework put in place by a postulate of rationality.[6] We could reformulate Dennett's position using Sellars's phrase "the logical space of reasons" or Davidson's phrase "the constitutive ideal of rationality".[7] There is an evident resonance with the tradition in which *Verstehen* is distinguished from *Erklären*.

So Sellars's thought about knowledge generalizes into a thought about propositional attitudes. In that case, we can expect the epistemological implications of Sellars's contrast between nature and the space of reasons to be mirrored in implications for our thinking about all of sapient mental life, not just knowledge.[8] Modern epistemology sees itself as under an obligation to reconnect the knowing subject with a natural world from which it seems

5. See especially "Mental Events"; the phrase I have quoted is from p. 223.

6. See *The Intentional Stance*.

7. See the discussion of "the Normative Principle" at pp. 342–3 of *The Intentional Stance*.

8. Some people think sentience is quite another matter, but I do not believe that is right (though I cannot discuss the matter here). For some hints, see my "One Strand in the Private Language Argument". In any case, sapience is enough for my present purpose.

to have withdrawn. Much modern philosophy of mind sees itself as under a parallel obligation to reintegrate the thinking subject into a natural world from which it has come to seem alien.

Rorty famously urges that the supposed gulf-bridging obligation of epistemology reflects an illusion. Anyone sympathetic to this conviction of Rorty's should have a similar suspicion of much modern philosophy of mind.

3. I have suggested that knowledge and intentionality can be in view only in the framework of the space of reasons.[9] When Sellars warns of a naturalistic fallacy, he is implying that the structure of the space of reasons is *sui generis*, by comparison with the kind of structure that the natural sciences find in nature. It is intelligible that the resulting sense that knowledge and thought are *sui generis*, by comparison with what can present itself as a compelling conception of the natural, should generate metaphysical anxieties about them, which crystallize in a felt threat of supernaturalism.

Now we can avoid those anxieties if we can contrive an entitlement to count thinking and knowing as natural phenomena after all, even though Sellars's suggestion raises a question about how they can be. I want to distinguish two ways of undertaking such a project.

The first leaves unchallenged the equation of nature with the realm of law. The idea is that the organization of the space of reasons is not, as Sellars suggests, alien to the kind of structure natural science discovers in the world. No doubt relations of warrant or justification are not visibly present, as such, in nature as the paradigmatic natural sciences depict it. But according to this approach, we can display the concepts of warrant or justification as not, after all, foreign to the natural on that conception. So thinking and knowing can after all be revealed as natural phenomena, even on that conception of what it is for a phenomenon to be natural.

On one version of this approach, the idea is that the structure of the space of reasons can be *reduced* to something else, which is already unproblematically

9. I have exploited a suggestive parallel between Sellars's talk of "the logical space of reasons" and Davidson's talk of "the constitutive ideal of rationality". But we should note a difference between Sellars's point about knowledge and its generalization. A state or episode counts as one of knowing only if it comes up to scratch in the light of norms of justification. If we extrapolate mechanically from that, we shall suppose, quite wrongly, that "space of reasons" understanding of thought and action is unavailable where rationality is less than perfect.

natural on the modern conception. On another version, one might aim to reveal concepts that work in the space of reasons as themselves, after all, directly serving to place things in the realm of law. The details do not matter. The essential point is that this approach, whether reductively undertaken or not, takes Sellars's starting-point to be a mistake. Sellars contrasts the logical space of subsumption under law with the logical space within which the concept of knowledge operates. This is a contrast between the realm of law and the realm of freedom, to put it in a way that makes Sellars's Kantian roots explicit. Against that, this first kind of naturalism holds that we can continue to equate nature with the realm of law but reject the Sellarsian suggestion that nature so conceived cannot be a home for knowing and thinking subjects.

This kind of naturalism would be well motivated if it were the only way to avoid supernaturalism about knowing and thinking. But there is an alternative, still within the project of representing knowing and thinking as natural phenomena. In a Kantian spirit, we can refuse to accept that the structure of the realm of freedom can be naturalized in the sense of the first approach—that is, insist that Sellars's contrast is well-taken—but disown a commitment to supernaturalism by holding that what the modern scientific revolution yielded was clarity about the realm of law, and that is not the same as clarity *about nature*. Sellars's contrast is between the space of reasons and the realm of law, and it need not imply that the space of reasons is alien to the natural.

To avoid conceiving thinking and knowing as supernatural, we should stress that thinking and knowing are aspects of our lives. The concept of a life is the concept of the career of a living thing, and hence obviously the concept of something natural. But there are aspects of our lives whose description requires concepts that function in the space of reasons. We are rational animals. Our lives are patterned in ways that are recognizable only in an inquiry framed within the space of reasons. On these lines, we can see thinking and knowing as belonging to our mode of living, even though we conceive them as phenomena that can come into view only within a *sui generis* space of reasons. Thinking and knowing are part of our way of being animals. Thus the fact that we are knowers and thinkers does not reveal us as strangely bifurcated, with a foothold in the animal kingdom—surely part of nature—and a mysterious separate involvement in an extra-natural realm of rational connections.

The first approach—a restrictive naturalism—aims to naturalize the concepts of thinking and knowing by forcing the conceptual structure in which

they belong into the framework of the realm of law. The second approach—
a liberal naturalism—does not accept that to reveal thinking and knowing
as natural, we need to integrate into the realm of law the frame within
which the concepts of thinking and knowing function. All we need is to
stress that they are concepts of occurrences and states in our lives.

This liberal naturalism enables us, like medieval Aristotelians, to take in
stride the idea that our capacities to acquire knowledge are natural powers.
But unlike medieval Aristotelians, we can combine that idea with a clear
appreciation of the *sui generis* character of the conceptual framework within
which the concept of a capacity to acquire knowledge operates. Similarly,
when we generalize Sellars's point, for the concepts of propositional attitudes and occurrences. We can acknowledge a genuine achievement of the
modern scientific revolution, in firmly separating natural-scientific understanding from the sort of understanding achieved by situating what is understood in the space of reasons. We can accept that concepts that subserve
the latter kind of understanding, such as the concepts of knowledge and the
propositional attitudes, cannot be captured in terms that belong in the logical space of natural-scientific understanding. So Sellars is right that there is
a risk of fallacy. But when he suggests that what we risk is a *naturalistic* fallacy, he implies that the logical space of natural-scientific understanding
can be equated with the logical space of nature. And we can avert the threat
of supernaturalism by rejecting that equation.

For liberal naturalism, the significance of getting the idea of the realm of
law into clear focus is simply to isolate the associated mode of intelligibility.
There is no implication that concepts of the natural are restricted to concepts that subserve that mode of intelligibility. Rejecting that implication
enables us to see the philosophical anxieties I have been considering as
groundless, somewhat as Rorty urges. But this exorcism of philosophy is
combined with acknowledging the *sui generis* character of the concepts of
thinking and knowing. If we see how easy it is to suppose that getting the
idea of the realm of law into clear focus is getting the idea of nature into
clear focus, we can have a lively appreciation of how those philosophical
anxieties arise, even combined with an immunity to them.

4. Both restrictive and liberal naturalism aim to avoid supernaturalism by
finding a way to see knowing and thinking as natural phenomena. That sets
them apart from a different style of response to Sellars's contrast, exemplified by Rorty's attitude to epistemology.

Rorty's reading of traditional epistemology pivots on Sellars's contrast. The concept of knowledge works only in the space of reasons, and the space of reasons is *sui generis* in comparison with nature on the restrictive conception. So a restrictive naturalism about knowledge is ruled out. But for Rorty the natural is what figures on the other side of Sellars's contrast, and that obliterates, for him, the very possibility of a liberal naturalism about knowledge.[10]

With both types of naturalism unavailable, Rorty has no option but to deny that knowing is a natural phenomenon. As Rorty sees it, trying to cast knowing as a natural phenomenon is, precisely, the pervasive defect of traditional epistemology. The result of the attempt is that philosophers try to make the quite different sorts of relation that organize the subject matter of natural-scientific investigation do duty for the relations of justification or warrant that alone provide the proper context for talk of knowledge. Traditional epistemology thus commits exactly the fallacy Sellars warns against. It conceives knowing as a syndrome in "the physiology of the understanding".[11] To avoid this, Rorty suggests that we should not conceive knowledge as a natural phenomenon. Of course that is not to say we should conceive it as a supernatural phenomenon. Instead, Rorty urges that we stop thinking of knowledge as a phenomenon—a feature of actuality—at all, and shift to talking about the social role of attributions of knowledge.

I have urged a parallel between Sellars's thought about knowledge and a thought about intentionality expressed in different ways by Davidson and Dennett. So there is room for a view about intentionality like Rorty's view about knowledge—a denial that talk of intentionality deals with natural phenomena. Curiously enough, Rorty himself does not occupy this position. For Rorty, thoughts and even meanings are, if anything, posits in a naturalistic psychology, where "naturalistic" marks a contrast with the normativity imported by talk of the space of reasons.[12] I hesitate to identify an

10. This is connected with a fact that I noted earlier: Rorty has causation, just as such, on the opposite side of the Sellarsian divide from the considerations about justification or warrant that are the proper environment for classifying states or episodes as cases of knowledge. That means that Rorty lacks a resource that would surely be needed if we tried to put detail into the thought that capacities to acquire knowledge are natural powers.

11. Compare Kant's remark about Locke, *Critique of Pure Reason* Aix, cited by Rorty, *Philosophy and the Mirror of Nature*, p. 126.

12. See chapter 5 of *Philosophy and the Mirror of Nature*.

occupant of the position that mirrors Rorty's view of knowledge with a denial that there are natural phenomena of intentionality.[13] Perhaps there is a whiff of it in the aspect of Dennett's thinking that attracts the accusation of instrumentalism.[14]

I think Rorty's reading of traditional epistemology has much to be said for it. Rorty is very convincing on how useless it is to try to make relations of the sort that organize the realm of law do duty for relations of warrant. Given that, he makes it look compulsory not to think of knowledge as a natural phenomenon. But this merely reflects the fact that he does not consider a liberal naturalism. Liberal naturalism is immune to Rorty's attack on the confusions of traditional epistemology. And the same failure of compulsoriness would infect a structural analogue of Rorty's line of thought, if anyone wanted to produce one, yielding the analogous conclusion that intentionality is not a natural phenomenon.

5. I have stressed that a clear conception of the realm of law was a modern achievement. What underlies a familiar philosophical anxiety about knowing and thinking is the ease with which this conception can be equated with a conception of the natural. That threatens to extrude knowing and thinking from nature, given that the concepts of knowing and thinking belong in a logical space that contrasts with the space of subsumption under law.

Consider now an early stage in the development of modern science. Imagine a dawning sense that the concepts of knowing and thinking are special, by comparison with the concepts that figure in the emerging natural sciences. Such a sense will have begun to influence reflection about the mental before there was a clear appreciation of what it is about the concepts of the mental that makes them special—before there was a clear appreciation of what comes into focus in Sellars as the contrast between the space of reasons and the space of natural-scientific understanding.

This intuition of specialness reflects a conception, putatively of the natural, that, when fully in focus, works to exclude the mental. But the intuition will have been operative before that fact was clear. And before that

13. Kripke's Wittgenstein would be a case: see *Wittgenstein on Rules and Private Language*. But I was looking for an actual occupant of the position, not a fictional character.

14. Consider, e.g., such claims as that "beliefs . . . are attributed in statements that are true only if we exempt them from a certain familiar standard of literality" (*The Intentional Stance*, p. 72). Compare the suggestion that the subject to whom things are said to seem thus and so is "just a theorist's fiction": *Consciousness Explained*, p. 128.

fact was clear, it would be intelligible that one might try to respond by conceiving the mental as a specially marked out part of nature, with nature understood according to a rudimentary form of the very conception that in fact excludes the mental.

This yields a way of understanding Cartesian philosophy of mind, at least on the Rylean reading under which Descartes figures in a common contemporary picture of how modern philosophy of mind developed.[15] On this reading, Descartes wanted the relations that organize the mental to be special cases of the sorts of relations that organize the subject matter of the natural sciences. But the specialness of the mental, to which on this reading Descartes was responding without a proper comprehension of its basis, requires these relations, supposedly suitable for natural-scientific treatment, to do duty for the relations that constitute the space of reasons. That is why Cartesian thinking takes a form to which Ryle's term of criticism "para-mechanical" is appropriate. Cartesian immaterialism is intelligible within the framework I am describing; no part of material nature could be special enough to serve the essentially confused purposes of this way of thinking. If one tries to make connections of the sort that figure in descriptions of law-governed processes do duty for relations of justification or warrant, one will inevitably lapse into an appeal to magic, masquerading as the science of a peculiar subject matter; what one intends to postulate as mechanisms of a special kind will degenerate into what Ryle lampoons as para-mechanisms.

On this reading, Cartesian philosophy of mind is a confused version of the first of the two kinds of naturalism I distinguished, an attempt to integrate thinking and knowing into nature on the modern conception that the second kind of naturalism rejects.

What I have said about para-mechanisms coincides with an element in Rorty's reading of modern epistemology. But Rorty depicts a train of thought that starts from an obsession with the fragility of certainty, and lapses into para-mechanism because of a wish to disclaim the burden of responsibility for one's putative knowledge, which shows up as a wish to represent one's putative knowledge as the result of the world forcing itself on one. I find this reading less satisfactory than the one I have sketched for at least two reasons. First, the onset of the obsession with certainty—which surely does come to characterize epistemology with Descartes—still seems

15. The qualification matters. I make no claims about the historical Descartes in this essay. The reading is that given currency by Gilbert Ryle, *The Concept of Mind*.

to need explanation. In my reading, the obsession with certainty can fall into place, not as a starting-point for a train of thought that issues in the characteristically Cartesian conception of the mental, but as manifesting an explicable anxiety over the felt threat that the knowing subject withdraws from the rest of the world. Second, the peculiarities of the Cartesian subject are not restricted to its role as knower; this is the point about the generalizability of Sellars's contrast, which I have already noted that Rorty misses.[16]

6. In the perspective I am urging, the fundamental mistake of Cartesian philosophy of mind is its failure to take the point of Sellars's contrast. What is special about concepts of the mental is that they make sense only in the framework of the space of reasons. Cartesian thinking intuits a specialness about concepts of the mental, but misunderstands it, taking it to reflect a peculiar mode of belonging to nature, with nature understood according to a conception that, when it comes into clear focus, actually stands opposed to the logical space within which alone concepts of the mental are intelligible.

The idea of para-mechanisms, realized in an immaterial substance, figures in this reading as a mere result of trying to force the specialness of the mental into that unsuitable mould. The fundamental mistake is not the notion of a ghostly mechanism, but the idea that the mental can be in view from a standpoint that organizes its subject matter in the manner of the natural sciences.

But this idea is still widespread in contemporary philosophy of mind. In a common view, at least part of the truth about the mental is the truth about a demarcated region of nature, conceived as the realm of law: specifically, the truth about the internal machinery that controls behaviour in response to impacts from the environment. This is not the whole of the truth about the mental, according to this style of thinking, because on its own this body of truth cannot incorporate the bearing of mental states on objective reality. But it is the whole of part of the truth about the mental.[17]

I want to suggest that this conception of the mind as internal machinery is, in one respect, no advance over the Cartesian conception. Of course this

---

16. I do not mean to suggest that a wish to disburden oneself of responsibility is anything but central to a proper understanding of the genesis of modern philosophy. But I do not believe a supposedly autonomous obsession with certainty is the right context in which to understand such a wish.

17. For a formulation on these lines, see p. 232 of Colin McGinn, "The Structure of Content".

style of thinking has shed the familiar ontological embarrassments of Cartesianism. It does not envisage immaterial substances, and it has no need for the role Descartes attributes to the pineal gland, as the site of a mysterious interaction between an immaterial substance and the rest of nature. But this style of thinking still makes what I have suggested is the fundamental mistake of Cartesianism. It supposes that truth about the mental can be in view when the subject matter of the inquiry is conceived as framed in the realm of law, and not as framed in a *sui generis* space of reasons. On this score, which is separable from the benefit of discarding those ontological embarrassments, looking for regular mechanisms is no better than postulating para-mechanisms.

Indeed in one way the change is for the worse. At least the old Cartesian thinking registers, in its confused way, the intuition that thought and talk about the mental are special. The modern version avoids immaterialism and the pineal-gland mystery by taking as its subject matter something that is not special at all, but just a more or less ordinary part of nature.

Of course there is nothing wrong with having the internal machinery that controls behaviour as one's subject matter. The warmed-over Cartesianism I am describing consists not just in taking an interest in that bit of nature, but in thinking that the truth about it is truth about the mental.

7. I want to illustrate this in connection with a common contemporary attitude to a Fregean conception of intentionality. The idea is that "externalistic" considerations have demolished Frege's apparatus of sense and reference. Versions of this view have been expressed by many people.[18] But I am going to consider a particularly clear expression by Ruth Garrett Millikan, when she directs against Frege her campaign against what she calls "meaning rationalism".[19] I want to suggest that Millikan's argument is vitiated by adherence to the residual Cartesianism I have identified, and that reflecting on her thinking is a good way to see how small an advance is constituted by discarding Cartesian immaterialism.

The fundamental thesis of the "meaning rationalism" Millikan attacks is that samenesses and differences in elements of thought-content are

18. Examples include John Perry, "Frege on Demonstratives", and McGinn, "The Structure of Content".

19. See in particular "Perceptual Content and Fregean Myth"; and "White Queen Psychology". Similar assumptions seem to me to vitiate pp. 570–1 of Robert Brandom, *Making It Explicit*.

transparently available to a rational subject.[20] A stronger version adds that it is transparently available to a rational subject whether or not a putative content-element really is a content-element, so we cannot make sense of the idea that a thinking subject might take herself to be entertaining a thought when there is no thought there to be entertained.

Now Frege's notion of sense is fixed by the principle that we must distinguish senses whenever the price of not doing so would be to leave a possibility that a rational subject could, at the same time, take rationally conflicting attitudes—for instance belief and disbelief—to a single thought (where thoughts are the senses expressible, perhaps in suitable contexts, by utterances of whole sentences). This is indeed a form of "meaning rationalism". Frege's requirement is that senses must be sufficiently fine-grained to secure that we need not describe rational subjects as, say, believing and disbelieving the same thing. And if the difference between the same sense twice over and two different senses is to correspond with the closing or opening, to a rational mind, of possibilities for combining attitudes, the difference must be available to the rational mind in question.

This "meaning rationalism" is weaker than Millikan's fundamental thesis, with its general transparency of sameness and difference in content-elements. (Let alone the further thesis that excludes illusions of existence for content-elements.) Frege's principle forces a difference of sense only if rationally conflicting attitudes to what would otherwise have to be conceived as the same thought are present in a rational mind *at the same time*. Frege says nothing to exclude a subject's losing track of a thought over time, which would make room for holding conflicting attitudes to the same thought at different times without the subject's rationality being impugned.[21] Nor does

---

20. "White Queen Psychology", pp. 286–7, especially p. 287: "Of these . . . claims, the givenness of meaning identity is the most central."

21. See Gareth Evans, "Understanding Demonstratives". Millikan blurs this point by a strange reading of the principle Evans calls "Russell's Principle" (see chapter 4 of *The Varieties of Reference*): that is, the principle that "in order to be thinking about an object . . . one must know which object is in question—one must know which object it is that one is thinking about" (*The Varieties of Reference*, p. 65). Evans shows how this principle fits in a Fregean framework, and Millikan ("White Queen Psychology", pp. 287–8) reads the principle as requiring that a thinker be able to tell when she is thinking of the same object again (or, in a weaker form, that she be able to tell when the object figures in her thoughts later under the same mode of presentation). But contrary to what Millikan's citations imply, the requirement that a thinker be able to tell when she is thinking of the same object again is no part of what Evans means by "Russell's Principle". And even the weaker version, in terms of modes of presentation, goes far beyond Frege's principle, with its "at the same time" qualification.

Frege's principle rule out a subject's taking what is in fact a different thought to be the same as one she entertained earlier, so that she wrongly supposes she is already committed to an attitude to it.[22] But I can ignore this; Millikan's argument against Frege does not depend on crediting him with a stronger "rationalism" than he accepts.[23]

Millikan's argument goes like this. Grasping a sense would need to be an achievement characteristic of the intact mind. But Frege wants grasping a sense of the relevant kind to be having an object—the associated *Bedeutung*—in mind. For this to be so, the rationality that figures in Frege's attempt to place the notion of sense would have to be semantic rationality, a matter of, for instance, what can and cannot be true together. So Frege's picture of sense and reference requires "the assumption that the intact mind is, as such, semantically rational".[24] Millikan argues that this assumption is substantive, and indefensible.

She sees the assumption as substantive because she takes it that for one's mind to be intact is for one to have one's "head . . . intact, in good mechanical order, not diseased, not broken".[25] Her thought is that the only sort of

22. It is remarkable how many philosophers suppose that Frege has a problem with thoughts such as the one that Rip Van Winkle might express, on waking after his twenty-year sleep, by saying "Today is the day I fell asleep".

23. Transparency is really a red herring. At pp. 121–30 of *The Intentional Stance*, Dennett rehearses the usual case against a putatively Fregean construal of propositional attitudes. (Though Frege's *Gedanken* do not actually figure in his catalogue of possible things to mean by "propositions", p. 121.) Dennett casts the argument as a problem for the idea of "grasping senses"—or, as one might say, knowing what one thinks—posed by the fact that one can lose track, be deceived by ringers, and so forth. Would Dennett argue that my claim to know, on a suitable occasion, that it is Dennett whom I see before me is undermined if I could be deceived by a ringer (as I surely could)? Why is knowledge of what one thinks held to a higher standard? (At p. 129 Dennett writes: "One could sum up the case . . . thus: propositions are not *graspable* because they can elude us." Are live chickens not graspable? They can surely elude us.) In the same spirit, at p. 200 Dennett offers another strange reading of Russell's Principle, as expressing the idea "that we can define a kind of aboutness that is *both* a real relation to something in the world *and* something to which the believer's access is perfect". Why must the access be perfect (that is, proof against ringers, losing track, and the like)? This is not Russell's Principle as Evans uses it, which is what Dennett claims to be talking about. It would be an interesting exercise to work out how the strikingly Cartesian conception of self-knowledge that Dennett here foists on Fregeans is connected with Dennett's psychologistic (though certainly non-dualistic) conception of what it would be for something to be otherwise than "psychologically inert" (p. 130).

24. "White Queen Psychology", p. 290.

25. "White Queen Psychology", p. 289.

"rationality" (so called) that is legitimately available for Frege to appeal to, as a context for his talk of sense, is "mechanical rationality"—the head being in good mechanical order. So the substantive assumption is that internal machinery could be so arranged that its states and changes of state track the requirements of semantic rationality.

And Millikan seems right that this assumption is indefensible. We cannot engage in the kind of assessment of semantic rationality that Frege wants to exploit in his account of sense, say in connection with possible and impossible combinations of singular predicative thoughts, until we have secured that the items that are allowed or not allowed to be combined are directed at determinate objects. And there are modes of directedness at determinate objects—for instance, those expressible by perceptually based demonstratives—that we cannot get into our picture without appealing to environmental circumstances—circumstances external to the intra-organismic machinery that Millikan thinks would have to be meant by "the intact mind".[26]

8. Millikan's argument, then, is this: "the assumption that the intact mind is, as such, semantically rational" is substantive, and indefensible; therefore sense and reference cannot hang together as Frege supposes. Now the inferential step here is fine. But surely Frege's line is to contrapose. Sense and reference do hang together as he takes them to; so much the worse for the thesis that intactness in a mind is independent of semantic rationality. The assumption is not substantive. Millikan makes it look as if it is by insisting that "the intact mind" must be healthy machinery in the head; so much the

26. I have shifted from a focus on the transparency of samenesses and differences in sense to a focus on the capacity of a concept of sense to cater for directedness at objects (which is part of the semanticity of singular thoughts) at all. Millikan's basic point against Frege is still formulable in this context: grasping senses would have to be an exercise of "mechanical rationality", and sense and reference could hang together in Frege's way only if "mechanical rationality" sufficed for semanticity, which it does not. The advantage of the shift is that it obviates any need to set foot in the morass of cases like Kripke's Pierre (which Millikan exploits: "White Queen Psychology", pp. 290–1). Just for the record, let me say that Kripke's Pierre poses no problem for a Fregean view; as Frege's principle requires us to say, he has two different modes of presentation for London. It is a gross misconception to suppose this involves segregating a putative notion of rationality from directedness at the objective world ("a relocation of rationality into some inner, purer, safer realm": "White Queen Psychology", p. 348).

worse for that interpretation of mental intactness. Rather, to have an intact mind just *is* to be semantically rational.[27]

Frege is famous for railing against psychologism in logic. His point is that the concept of, say, deductive inference is available only within a normative framework, and an inquiry that restricts itself to transitions minds regularly make, without the normative framework of logic, properly conceived, does not get as far as bringing deductive inference into view. But the thought is not limited to logic. Frege's attack on psychologism is a way of expressing the generalized version of Sellars's point that I have been working with in this essay. (The correspondence is unsurprising in view of how important Kant is for both.) Already in the logical case, it is not just the idea of deductive inference that is available only within a normatively framed inquiry; the very idea of what deductive inferences start from and issue in—beliefs—makes sense only within the normative context that psychologistic logicians deny themselves.

Now Millikan's conception of "the intact mind" is psychologistic in the generalized sense; it purports to have the mind's states and operations as its topic even though the topic is not conceived as framed within a *sui generis* space of reasons. We should not be misled here by her phrase "mechanical rationality". When the machinery in the head is in good working order, that is not to say that its states and changes of state are related by the sorts of relation that constitute the space of reasons, any more than are the states and changes of state in, say, a healthy kidney. This is just a way of putting Millikan's own point. "Mechanical rationality" (so called) cannot ensure semantic rationality, but it is semantic rationality that structures the space of reasons.[28]

---

27. That is, rational enough to count as a thinker (and it would be silly to ask "How rational is that?"). Formulations like the one in the text do not imply that the conceptual apparatus I am talking about becomes unavailable if a subject shows less than perfect rationality.

28. The point is the same as the one that Dennett makes by saying that "the brain . . . is just a *syntactic engine"*: *The Intentional Stance*, p. 61. It is because this is a way of putting Millikan's own thought that I can classify her naturalism about "the intact mind" as a case of restrictive rather than liberal naturalism. She argues that "the biological sciences, including physiology and psychology, are distinguished from the physical sciences by their interest not in lawful happenings . . . but in biologically proper happenings" ("White Queen Psychology", p. 362). But this does not remove the biological, as she conceives it, from what I introduced as the realm of law: it is just that the relevant laws are underwritten by considerations about proper function, rather than inductively based on what actually happens. We still have the contrast with the space of reasons.

A psychologistic conception of the mental is not a promising context in which to look for what Frege, of all people, might have wanted from the notion of sense. No wonder his thinking comes out looking so unsatisfactory. For Frege, grasping a (singular) sense should simply *be* having a *Bedeutung* in mind (under a mode of presentation)—a notion that works only in the framework of semantic rationality. Millikan takes the introduction of sense to be a tool for characterizing the internal mechanics of having one's mind on objects.[29] She rightly concludes that grasping a sense, so construed, cannot be what Frege wants it to be, but she does not see that this might tell against the construal.

This is a blind spot. I think it amounts to not seeing the possibility of a liberal naturalism. The proper home of the idea of "grasping senses" is in describing patterns in our lives—our mental lives in this case—that are intelligible only in terms of the relations that structure the space of reasons. This patterning involves genuine rationality, not just "mechanical rationality" (so called). Liberal naturalism needs no more, to make the idea of "grasping senses" unproblematic, than a perfectly reasonable insistence that such patterns really do shape our lives.

If someone refuses to take the notion of sense as a tool for characterizing the internal mechanisms that underlie having one's mind on objects,[30] Millikan detects a commitment to a spooky idea that, as she puts it, "meanings move the mind directly".[31] The spookiness is that of Cartesian paramechanisms. She recoils into a neo-Cartesian search for regular mechanisms, and supposes Frege must have been after that too, though she finds his attempt inept—rightly, given her construal of Frege's thinking. But Frege's thinking is quite different. It involves, if you like, the thought that "meanings move the mind directly", but in a form that is not spooky at all. The idea of a mind's being moved by meanings involves a metaphor from the logical space of mechanical understanding, but it is an idea whose functioning needs to be understood in the contrasting space of reasons. Trying to take the metaphor literally is a form of the basic Cartesian mistake.

29. See an extraordinary passage in "Perceptual Content and Fregean Myth" (p. 442), in which she takes the idea of "grasping senses" to be a case of "postulating intermediaries", with a view to theorizing about "the underlying nature of the vehicle of thought".

30. Perhaps expressing scepticism about whether there must be any such internal mechanics. Consider, e.g., Wittgenstein's notorious remarks about "the prejudice of psychophysical parallelism" (§611) at §§608 and ff. of *Zettel*.

31. "Perceptual Content and Fregean Myth", p. 442.

9. What ground is there for accepting that it is a mistake? Millikan's position is quite suggestive here. Like ordinary Cartesianism, it poses a threat to a common-sense conception of thinking things.

What is it that thinks? One might suppose it should be what Millikan calls "the intact mind". But the activities of "the intact mind" as Millikan conceives it do not amount to thinking. That is just to affirm her own point that its activities exemplify only "mechanical rationality", and not semantic rationality.

What is it that exercises semantic rationality? Millikan's answer to this question shifts the relevant boundary out from the one around "the intact mind", past the boundary around the animal whose behaviour it controls, to encompass a system that combines "the intact mind" with conditions in the animal's environment: "Rationality is . . . a biological norm effected in an integrated head-world system under biologically ideal conditions."[32] But "externalism" is grotesque if it implies that exercising semantic rationality is an activity of a "head-world system"—as if the environment of what we ordinarily conceive as thinkers is partly responsible for doing the thinking that gets done. The environment is partly responsible for there being a possibility of doing that thinking. But the thinking is done by something that lives in the environment, which includes thinking about it. This piece of mere sanity is obscured by Millikan's concern with the mechanics of thinking (with how rationality is "effected"). If we conceive the animal as a complex mechanism, what we have in view is not a realization of semantic rationality any more than its internal control machinery is, and now it looks as if nothing less than a "head-world system" will do.[33] If the only respectable intellectual orientation towards rationality is inquiry into how it is "effected" in a mechanism, we lose our grip on rationality as something exercised in the activities of an animal.

Millikan's "intact mind" is a counterpart to the Cartesian *res cogitans*. There is a difference; Millikan realizes that her counterpart cannot actually

32. "White Queen Psychology", p. 280.

33. Is it a difficulty that the "head-world system" is itself only a syntactic engine? Millikan must hope that if we describe it in a way that is suitably organized in terms of biological function, we shall be describing it in a way that reveals it as genuinely instantiating rationality—as a semantic engine. This strikes me as a fantasy, but I need not substantiate that impression: my present point is that even if we allow Millikan what she must hope for, it does not yield a satisfactory answer to the question "What thinks (what exercises semantic rationality)?".

be a *res cogitans*, although she still calls it "the mind"—perversely, one might think, since it does not do what minds are supposed to do, namely think (exercise semantic rationality). This is the result of a familiar trade-off; the price of discarding Cartesian immaterialism, while staying within restrictive naturalism, is that one's singled-out part of nature is no longer special enough to be credited with powers of thought.[34] But Millikan's conception, for all its freedom from immaterialism, is like the original Cartesian conception in threatening the sane belief that a *res cogitans* is also a *res dormiens*, a *res ambulans*, and so forth. Millikan's "intact mind" does not exercise rationality, and the "head-world system", which supposedly does exercise rationality, is not the thing that sleeps and walks. The rational animal finds no place in the picture.

Properly understood, the claim that the operations of the intact mind include directing itself at objects, which Millikan cannot make room for, is perfectly acceptable; it is a way to say it is the rational animal that thinks. We do not in any way denigrate the reality of the mental if we say the word "mind" labels a collection of capacities and propensities possessed by a minded being. It is a recipe for intellectual disaster to assume that what we mean by "the mind" must be something more substantial than that, but less than the rational animal itself: an organ in which the thinking we credit to the animal, loosely or derivatively on this view, takes place.[35] That is the original sin of Cartesian philosophy, and it is no redemption to replace the para-organ postulated by Descartes himself with a regular organ, something a more sophisticated contemporary biology can countenance.[36] Of course

34. John Searle is unique among contemporary neo-Cartesians in thinking he can both de-immaterialize the Cartesian *res cogitans* and keep its remarkable powers.

35. See my "Putnam on Mind and Meaning".

36. Dennett's thinking shows this blemish in parts. He endorses Millikan's attack on Frege. And consider this passage from *Consciousness Explained* (p. 41): "Dualism, the idea that a brain cannot be a thinking thing so a thinking thing cannot be a brain, is tempting for a variety of reasons, but we must resist temptation . . . . Somehow the brain must be the mind . . . ." But a brain *cannot* be a thinking thing (it is, as Dennett himself remarks, just a syntactic engine). Dualism resides not in the perfectly correct thought that a brain is not a thinking thing, but in postulating something immaterial to be the thinking thing that the brain is not, instead of realizing that the thinking thing is the rational animal. Dennett can be comfortable with the thought that the brain must be the mind, in combination with his own awareness that the brain is just a syntactic engine, only because he thinks that in the sense in which the brain is not *really* a thinking thing, nothing is: the status of possessor of intentional states is conferred by adoption of the intentional stance

there is a relevant organ, the brain, and none of what I have said casts doubt on investigating how it works. But on pain of losing our grip on ourselves as thinking things, we must distinguish inquiring into the mechanics of, say, having one's mind on an object from inquiring into what having one's mind on an object is.

10. My topic in this essay has been a cultural effect of the maturation of modern science. The associated clarification of the relevant mode of intelligibility, which separated it from the mode of intelligibility revealed by placing things in the space of reasons, was in itself an unqualified intellectual advance. But I have been urging that there is a strand in the philosophy of mind, exemplified alike in Descartes and in the writings of contemporaries who think they are fully emancipated from Cartesian confusions, that should be seen as a toxic by-product of a frame of mind—scientism—made possible only by that intellectual advance.

---

towards it, and that is no more correct for animals than for brains, or indeed thermostats. But this is a gratuitous addition to the real insight embodied in the invocation of the intentional stance. Rational animals genuinely are "semantic engines". (It is irrelevant to this claim that the intentionality of rational animals is a product of evolution, a causal outcome of "intentionality" on the part of "Mother Nature": compare pp. 287–321 of *The Intentional Stance*.) The blemish is detachable: much of the material in, say, *Consciousness Explained* is illuminating independently of Dennett's neo-Cartesian thought that the brain must be the mind. It makes a contribution to the study of "the mechanics of consciousness" in an acceptable sense, not parallel to the sense in which Millikan supposes that Frege must have been concerned with the mechanics of intentionality.

PART VI

Responses to Brandom and Dreyfus

Knowledge and the Internal Revisited[1]

1. In his "Knowledge and the Social Articulation of the Space of Reasons", which is a response to my "Knowledge and the Internal", Robert Brandom claims to agree with everything I say there (and indeed not only there). The fact is that he takes for granted something that contradicts the main point of my essay. With hindsight in the light of Brandom's subsequent responses to my *Mind and World* I have come to see his essay as an episode in an ongoing effort on his part to appropriate my work as a kind of promissory note for his.[2] Brandom writes (p. 895): "I hope at *worst* to clarify some of the key concepts and connections that McDowell appeals to, and at *best* to twist his words into a perverted caricature of their true meaning." I think on this peculiar scale of assessment things are even *better* than Brandom hopes. His representation of me fails to achieve even the status of a caricature—which would require a recognizable likeness. Instead it sets me up as sketching a thought quite alien to what I aimed at, which might indeed seem to need Brandom's work for its proper elaboration. I conceive this note, in which I shall attempt to explain this, as an analogue to the small explosion emitted by a bombardier beetle to avoid being swallowed by a predator.[3]

2. My main point in "Knowledge and the Internal" is to protest against an interiorization of the justifications available to us for claims about the external world. The interiorization threatens to deprive us of the justificatory power of, for instance, the form "I see that . . .". I insist that statements of such forms

---

1. My thanks to Bob Brandom for many conversations and a joint seminar.

2. See "Perception and Rational Constraint: McDowell's *Mind and World*" and "Perception and Rational Constraint".

3. Another image, which I borrow from Simon Blackburn: I am resisting being cast as the hind legs of a pantomime horse called "Pittsburgh neo-Hegelianism".

are proper moves in the game of giving reasons, and their truth fully vindicates entitlement to the embedded propositions. This ought to seem sheer common sense, and it would if questionable philosophy did not put it at risk. Someone who can truly make a claim of that form has an entitlement, incompatible with any possibility of falsehood, to a claim whose content is given by the embedded proposition. The entitlement consists in the visual availability to her of the fact she would affirm in making that claim.

Compare Brandom's §II (pp. 899–901), where he purports to restate my argument. Brandom lists four positions that he says my argument rules out. About one of them, "dogmatism", he writes, supposedly in agreement with me (p. 899): "The dogmatist arrives at the *true* conclusion that knowledge *is* possible by combining the *false* claim that justification must be incompatible with falsehood with the further *false* claim that justification that rules out the possibility of falsehood *can* be had." But both these supposedly false claims are true by my lights. What I urge in my essay is precisely that justification adequate to reveal a state as one of knowing must be incompatible with falsehood and can be had. "Dogmatism", one of the four positions Brandom says I reject, is precisely what I defend.

About the four positions, Brandom says (p. 899): "McDowell rightly does not rehearse at length the difficulties of these views; their unsatisfactoriness is widely acknowledged." But about the fourth—"dogmatism"—I protest at length against a style of thinking that is widely thought to show its unsatisfactoriness. I aim to rescue the position from bad philosophy, and to leave it looking perfectly satisfactory. In particular, though I do not put it like this in my essay, I aim to cast the position in a light in which it should not seem to deserve the label "dogmatism".

Brandom assumes, and, amazingly, takes me to assume, that justification that rules out falsehood cannot be had for empirical claims. That is just the idea that I deplore, and diagnose as resulting from an interiorization of the space of reasons. At p. 902, looking back over his purported restatement of my argument, Brandom says: "You may have noticed that although here and there I helped myself to McDowell's imagery of what is conceived as internal or external to the space of reasons, in my exposition of his core arguments I did not find it necessary to say *anything at all* about *interiorizing* the space of reasons in this sense . . . ." But it is not just that Brandom's purported exposition leaves out my imagery of interiorizing. In purporting to expound me, he actually *makes* the interiorizing move I attack, when he assumes that justification must fall short of guaranteeing truth.

Brandom says (p. 903): "If you are standing in a darkened room and seem to see a candle ten feet in front of you, I may take you to have good reason for believing that there is a candle in front of you, and so take you to be entitled to your commitment. But that may be my attitude even if I know, as you do not, that there is a mirror five feet in front of you, and no candle behind it, so that I am not in a position to endorse or commit myself to what you are committed to." The implication is that the entitlement one can credit to someone who seems to see a candle in front of her, for claiming that there is a candle in front of her, is always indifferent to whether or not there is a candle in front of her. The subject's entitlement in the case Brandom describes cannot be such as to guarantee the presence of a candle at the relevant place, since there is no candle there. And the implicit suggestion is that even if things had been as the subject supposes, the subject's entitlement would not have reached any further. That is, the entitlement in both cases is the highest common factor of the two. Even in the best case, the subject's entitlement does not go beyond the fact that she *seems* to see a candle ten feet in front of her, which of course does not guarantee that there is a candle there.

This is just the move I object to. I insist that in the best case the subject can have an entitlement consisting in the fact that she *sees* that there is a candle in front of her. Or, to put it another way: for a subject in the best case, the appearance that there is a candle in front of her is the presence of the candle making itself apparent to her. This is not a mere seeming, which would be compatible with there being no candle there. The subject in the mirror case does not have an entitlement of this kind, one incompatible with there being no candle there, though she will probably think she does. It is a kind of entitlement that I insist can be had—contrary to what Brandom says I say.

No doubt some notion of entitlement or justification might have application in Brandom's mirror case. It might be rational (doxastically blameless) for that subject—who only seems to see a candle in front of her—to claim that there is a candle in front of her. But this is not the notion of entitlement or justification that should figure in a gloss on the Sellarsian thought that knowledge is a standing in the space of reasons. The right notion for Sellars's point is precisely what Brandom says I reject, a notion for which entitlement and truth do not come apart.

3. Of course one does not *inherit* entitlement to, for instance, "There's a candle in front of me" from a commitment—to which one would have to be

entitled—to "I see that there's a candle in front of me". One could not be entitled to "I see that there's a candle in front of me" while it was still in suspense whether one was entitled to "There's a candle in front of me"—suspense that one would terminate, on this impossible picture, by inferring "There's a candle in front of me" from "I see that there's a candle in front of me". But the impossibility of this picture does not disqualify "I see that . . ." from its status as the form of a proper move in the game of giving reasons, a move that, if one can make it truly, vindicates one's entitlement to a claim with the content of the embedded proposition. The point just brings out the insufficiency of a conception of justification that limits itself to inferential inheritance of entitlement (perhaps with a special story about one's entitlement to the premises of the envisaged inferences).

Brandom writes (p. 904): "A fundamental point on which broadly externalist approaches to epistemology are clearly right is that one can *be* justified without being *able* to justify. That is, one can have the standing of being *entitled* to a commitment without having to *inherit* that entitlement from *other* commitments inferentially related to it as reasons." If one's justification for "There's a candle in front of me" is that one sees that there is a candle in front of one (that the presence of a candle in front of one makes itself visually apparent to one), one's entitlement is, as I have just said, not inherited from a commitment to "I see that there's a candle in front of me". But that is not to say in other words—Brandom's "That is"—that one can be justified without being able to justify. It seems so only because of that insufficient conception of justification. The case is one in which one *is* able to justify, to vindicate one's entitlement, precisely by saying "I see that there's a candle in front of me". Only that insufficient conception of justification makes it look as if there is a point here on which externalist approaches to epistemology are clearly right.

This passage in Brandom's essay belongs in a series of places where he tries to find support for an externalist admixture in epistemology from what is certainly an unsatisfactoriness in Sellars's treatment of the authority of observation reports.[4] Sellars claims that the authority of an observation report "must *in some sense* be recognized by the person whose report it is."[5] And he cashes this out in terms of the idea that the reporter must be able to give evidence of her reliability in reporting the sort of state of affairs in

4. See, in particular, *Making It Explicit*, pp. 213–21.
5. "Empiricism and the Philosophy of Mind", §35.

question. This is certainly quite implausible. Brandom concludes that the internalism of Sellars's claim that observational authority must be ("in some sense") recognized by its possessor is a mistake.[6] But the mistake is in Sellars's proceeding as if the only available sense for the requirement were that the reporter can derive her reliability as the conclusion of an inference. Like most adults, I know that I can tell a green thing when I see one (in the right conditions of illumination)—that is, I conform to Sellars's internalist requirement: I recognize my own authority as a reporter of greenness. But I would be at a loss if pressed for premises for an argument that would have my reliability about greenness as a conclusion. My reliability about that kind of thing has for me, rather, a sort of status that Wittgenstein considers in *On Certainty*. It is held firm for me by my whole conception of the world with myself in touch with it, and not as the conclusion of an inference from some of that conception. If we equip Sellars with something on these lines[7] as a spelling out of his "in some sense", his intuition that observational authority must be self-consciously possessed can stand. The unsatisfactoriness of his gloss on the intuition does not constitute a case in favor of a concession to externalism, as Brandom claims.

4. In "Knowledge and the Internal", I argue against views according to which knowledge is only partly constituted by standings in the space of reasons, with the requirement that what a knower takes to be so is indeed so conceived as an extra condition, over and above her standing in the space of reasons. Brandom purports to respect my point. In his account, an attributor of knowledge attributes a commitment and an entitlement, and herself undertakes a commitment corresponding to the commitment attributed. This third component of knowledge attribution is Brandom's counterpart to the traditional truth requirement for knowledge. Brandom purports to respect my argument by saying that the distinction of perspectives that matters for his account—between the perspective of the one to whom a com-

---

6. Brandom thinks Sellars imposes his internalist requirement with a view to securing that the reporter *understands* her reports. (See "Knowledge and the Social Articulation of the Space of Reasons", p. 905.) But its point is rather to secure that they have a specific kind of *authority*.

7. This is in the spirit of Sellars's own addition, to traditional empiricism, of a second dimension of dependence, in which observation reports depend on knowledge that, in the dimension to which traditional empiricism restricts itself, depends on them: "Empiricism and the Philosophy of Mind", §38.

mitment and an entitlement are attributed and the perspective of the attributor, from which the corresponding commitment is undertaken—is "a distinction of perspectives *within* the space of reasons, not a distinction between what is within it and what is without it" (p. 906). But this appearance of respecting my point is an illusion, generated by an equivocation on the phrase "space of reasons". Brandom's conception of knowledge attributions is squarely in the target area of the argument of mine that he purports to endorse.

I derive the idea of knowledge as a satisfactory standing in the space of reasons from Sellars. Sellars writes: "in characterizing an episode or a state as that of *knowing*, we are not giving an empirical description of that episode or state; we are placing it in the logical space of reasons, of justifying and being able to justify what one says."[8] I think it is clear from Sellars's gloss ("justifying and being able to justify") that this talk of placing in the space of reasons is imagery for assessing the *entitlement* of the putative knower in the episodes or states in question. I might have spoken of standings in the space of entitlements.

What I object to is interiorizing *entitlements*, in the sense of refusing to let the connivance of the world enter into constituting them. Applied to the entitlements that perceptual, for instance visual, experience affords, the interiorizing move restricts them to appearances, conceived as a highest common factor between seeing that such-and-such is the case and having it merely look to one as if such-and-such is the case. I argue that it is not satisfactory to leave entitlements thus interiorized but add that what the putative knower takes to be so is in fact so, conceiving this as an extra condition over and above an interiorized entitlement. Now Brandom's socially perspectival hybrid conception of knowledge attributions has just that shape. It makes no difference that he can take over my phrase, "standing in the space of reasons", and define it so that it includes the satisfaction of the extra condition. The extra condition is still seen as extra to the knower's entitlement, and that is what, according to the argument of mine that Brandom purports to endorse, precludes making sense of the status in question as one of knowledge.

That the connivance of the world cannot enter into constituting perceptual entitlements—the interiorizing move I attack—Brandom takes for granted. His idea that an attributor of knowledge needs to undertake a corresponding commitment, over and above attributing whatever entitlement

---

8. "Empiricism and the Philosophy of Mind", §36.

she can attribute, reflects the assumption that there can be no entitlement such that to attribute it is already implicitly to undertake the commitment to which one is saying someone is entitled (to put things in Brandom's social-perspectival terms). So far from its being the case that the social-perspectival apparatus yields a richer understanding of the point I was driving at, Brandom's employment of it gives expression to a conception of knowledge that has exactly the structure I object to.

Let me reformulate the objection in a way that takes note of the possibility of exploiting a difference of perspectives in giving expression to its target. What I claim yields no satisfactory conception of knowledge is the thought that truth—that is, worthiness of endorsement, which is expressed by the attributor's undertaking the relevant commitment herself—is needed as an extra condition, over and above whatever entitlement can be attributed to the candidate knower. This thought reflects the idea that entitlement incompatible with falsehood in what one is entitled to cannot be had. Thinking on these lines, one will suppose that if one does no more than attribute whatever entitlement one can, one leaves it open that what the putative knower putatively knows is not even true. In that case she certainly does not know it. Given this interiorizing of entitlement, the fact that the putative knower's commitment is to something that is in fact true—that the attributor can go in for the undertaking of a commitment that is the third component in Brandom's picture of knowledge-attribution—looks accidental in relation to the putative knower's entitlement. Not completely accidental, as I concede ("Knowledge and the Internal", p. 403). Given a defeasible entitlement, it is at least likely that things are as the putative knower takes them to be; so if they are that way, they are as the entitlement makes it at least likely that they are.[9] But it is accidental, in relation to the subject's entitlement conceived on these lines, that the case we are considering is not one of the cases in which the supposedly open possibility of falsehood is actual. How does this add up to a picture of knowing that things are thus and so, as opposed to having good but not conclusive reason to suppose that things are thus and so, in a situation in which, *as it happens*, things *are* thus and so? "As it happens" seems appropriate given the avowed defeasibility of the entitlement, and this seems to undermine any possibility that it is intelligibly knowledge that we are pic-

---

9. Given a defeasible entitlement; in the end I think the argument indicates that we are not really entitled to talk about entitlement in the framework of the interiorization, but to get the argument going we can pretend we are.

turing. It does not help at all with this difficulty to apportion the entitlement and the undertaken commitment between two different perspectives. If anything, it accentuates the difficulty.

I do not see why we should be impressed by the possibility of securing a social-perspectival analogue to factiveness, in something one labels "a standing in the space of reasons", by including the attributor's undertaking of a commitment in what we count as attributing the standing. Believing truly that . . . is factive in this sense, even if the belief in question is the result of a wild guess. The thrust of the argument of mine that Brandom purports to accept can be captured by saying that this picture does not discriminate, in a way we need, between the factiveness of knowing that . . . and the factiveness of merely believing truly that . . . .

5. Brandom (p. 899, n. 3) cites conversation with me as an occasion for registering that the Sellarsian conception of standings in the space of reasons does not fit non-linguistic animals or pre-linguistic human beings. This point is already explicit in my paper, where I specify my topic as "knowledge—at least as enjoyed by rational animals" (p. 395).

What Brandom makes of the point is that in the case of these other subjects, "it is common to talk about them loosely as though they were capable of some version . . . of these accomplishments" (centrally, for these purposes, knowledge). And about the sort of state thus "loosely" called "knowledge," he says: "This status has in common with the genuine article what the parrot [trained to utter "red" when shown a red thing] has in common with the reporter of red things: reliable differential responsive dispositions." But I see no reason to think the knowledge of animals without conceptual capacities is only loosely so called, just because it is not the interesting kind of knowledge that the Sellarsian conception fits. I see no reason to think there is nothing really there but actualizations of responsive dispositions. The implication is that, say, a cat's awareness of the prey it stalks is no more genuinely a case of awareness than is an "awareness" of the presence of moisture shown by iron filings in rusting.[10] This is the kind of thing nobody

---

10. The parrot case may be confusing here; parrots, unlike collections of iron filings, are after all complex living beings. But the parrot ability Brandom cites, unlike parrots' ability to locate, say, suitable perches, *is* plausibly conceived as a mere case of a reliable differential responsive disposition. The ability to respond to red things with "red", at least as Brandom describes it, does not fit into a parrot-style purposive life in the way that would differentiate it from the sort of thing iron filings "do".

but a philosopher would suppose. (Descartes, perhaps.) I want no truck with it.

The point here is that it need not be part of the role of the image of the space of reasons to secure for us the very idea of being on to things. The knowledge that Sellars's remark distinctively fits comes into view when what are *already* ways of being on to things—exemplified in the self-moving lives of animals, but not in the "doings" of iron filings—are taken up into the ambit of the space of reasons.

Brandom undertakes, in effect, to do what I am saying is unnecessary: to exploit the image of the space of reasons, cashed out in his social-perspectival terms, so as to secure the very idea of being on to things. (This is why he has to hold that being on to things is only loosely attributable to creatures without concepts.) And he tends to suggest that any disbelief manifests a lingering individualism.[11] The fact is that, as I have tried to explain in this note, Brandom's idiosyncratic way of invoking the social, so far from making explicit the true direction of my argument in "Knowledge and the Internal", is epistemologically unhelpful in just the way my argument aims to uncover. And insisting on this betokens no individualism, no failure to acknowledge that sociality matters for knowledge as possessed by rational animals, and more generally for the very idea of objective purport. A rational animal could not have acquired the conceptual capacities in the possession of which its rationality consists except by being initiated into a social practice. But as I see things, the capacities transform their possessor into an individual who can achieve standings in the space of entitlements by her own efforts. (The point of my "Knowledge and the Internal" is that "by her own efforts" must not be understood to imply that the world's kindness cannot enter into constituting the entitlements that are achievable.) Which is closer to individualism: a position according to which initiation into a social practice yields individuals of a special kind, able to achieve standings in the space of reasons by, for instance, opening their eyes; or a position according to which we supposedly accommodate the very idea of such standings by contemplating subjects individually incapable of achieving them, who somehow nevertheless keep one another under surveillance? At any rate, one can find the second picture unhelpful without denying that sociality is important in understanding our capacities for objective purport.

11. There is a hint in this direction in "Knowledge and the Social Articulation of the Space of Reasons", p. 902; it is more explicit in the two responses to *Mind and World*.

Motivating Inferentialism:
Comments on Chapter 2 of
Making It Explicit[1]

1. One way Brandom tries to motivate inferentialism is by putting it in competition with representationalism, which he describes as "the traditional order of semantic explanation" (p. 92).

Representationalism takes a concept or concepts of representation as primitive, and offers to explain all the features of linguistic practice that are relevant to the fact that expressions are meaningful—for instance, and centrally, proprieties of inference—in terms of that concept or those concepts. Brandom has no difficulty in deprecating that order of explanation. On that basis he recommends an inversion of the order. We are to take the concept of inference as primitive, and explain everything else about the significance of language, including ultimately the capacity for representation, in terms of it.

Brandom focuses especially on a version of representationalism that takes designation as its primitive. According to this approach, we are to start with a supposedly self-standing understanding of the relation between a singular term and its referent (and perhaps also that between a predicate and a member of whatever kind of things a theorist decides to count as the referents of predicates). Next we are to explain, on the basis of that relation (or those relations), the semantic significance of stringing words together into statements. And then we are to go on to explain how statements hang together in rationally sequential discourse, in particular arguments.[2] Brandom

---

1. This essay is a descendant of material I presented to a joint seminar with Brandom in 1998. I am grateful to him for the continuing stimulus of his work, and for much helpful discussion.

2. See p. 69. Brandom's presentation leaves it unclear whether predicates are supposed to be independently treated, and I have paraphrased so as to leave that open.

introduces this as a "particularly unhelpful" version of representationalism, but as he goes on he tends to take it as representative.[3]

2. A supposedly primitive understanding of relations of reference figures as a target in Wittgenstein's *Philosophical Investigations*, especially the early sections. I think it is helpful to compare Brandom's treatment with what happens there.

Wittgenstein's considerations are not, like Brandom's, directed against a "dominant tradition" in philosophical reflection about language. The supposedly self-standing understanding of the name-bearer relation that Wittgenstein considers is not something he depicts as a bad move in answering a good question, perhaps because it approaches things in the wrong order, so that the trouble is to be fixed by inverting the order. On the contrary, he suggests that the supposedly self-standing understanding of designation that he considers both reflects and encourages a characteristically philosophical attitude, in which the meaningfulness of language is experienced as a mystery. And his ultimate target is that attitude itself, rather than a choice of what order to proceed in when one lets it control one's thinking.

In the frame of mind Wittgenstein is concerned with, one supposes the key to the mystery is that words have the remarkable property of being words for things. This property looks remarkable—in a way that fits with seeing it as the key to a mystery—when one tries to focus on, say, the relation between a name and its bearer in abstraction from how cases of the relation figure in human life. That makes one prone to fall into a fetishistic superstition about linguistic expressions, or to think of their possession of meaning as "a hocus-pocus which can be performed only by the soul" (compare *Philosophical Investigations* §454). And when that has happened, it is too late to bring the role linguistic expressions play in human life back into view. What we do with words takes on the appearance of rags and dust, from which one *knows* that a mouse could not come into being, so there is no point in looking at the details (*Philosophical Investigations* §52). The cure for this trouble is to stop trying to consider the relation between a name and an object in abstraction from its role in human life, in hopes of

---

3. See, e.g., p. 94, on "the contemporary way of working out the representationalist order of explanation" as starting with "an independent notion of relations of reference or denotation obtaining between mental or linguistic items and objects and sets of objects in the largely nonmental, nonlinguistic environment".

being able to exploit the idea of the relation in a radical explanation of the very idea of meaning, given from outside the standpoint of our lived familiarity with language. We need to take the measure of the fact that it is only in a language-game that an object can have a name at all (*Philosophical Investigations* §49).

So we should not see what people do with language as a topic to be broached only after we have catered for the fact that expressions have semantic properties. Rather, linguistic practice is a context within which alone talk of expressions as meaningful makes sense.

That might be described as a kind of pragmatism. But there is no whiff of Brandom's proposal to invert an order of explanation. Wittgenstein does not suggest that we must first describe the needed context in a way that avoids the concept we were puzzling over—the concept of a word for something—and then explain the concept we were puzzling over in terms of such supposedly prior concepts of linguistic practice. The idea is not that we need to postpone using the concept we were puzzling over until we have entitled ourselves to it by some such explanation. What made the concept seem mysterious was the attempt to understand it in abstraction from a necessary context. When we put the context back into the picture, there is no need to forswear using the concept of names for objects in the course of describing the area of human life it helps to shape. Our problem was not that we were making the wrong choice of primitive, and the cure is not to fix on some other concepts as primitive.

What we find in Wittgenstein, then, is a well-placed negative response to a supposedly primitive understanding of relations of reference, but with no tendency to motivate an inverted order of explanation.

3. As I said, Wittgenstein's target is not a tradition in philosophy. In fact there is ground for scepticism about Brandom's picture of a dominant tradition, to be superseded by inferentialism.

Brandom is surely on the right track when he depicts the priority of the propositional, the centrality of judgment, as a Kantian innovation, though one anticipated by strands in Leibniz and Spinoza (pp. 79–80, 93–4). Kant here moves towards a conception of logic that comes to maturity in Frege, who insists on abstracting concepts out of judgments rather than building judgments out of concepts (pp. 80–2). Frege definitively supersedes a conception according to which logic starts with terms and works up to judgments.

As Brandom reads this, Kant's move begins to overturn a hitherto dominant representational understanding of "the proper order of semantic explanation" (p. 79). And since Kant situates the idea of judgment in the context of the idea of reasoning, Brandom takes him to be at least incipiently a proponent of the inferentialist order (p. 92).[4]

On this view, Kant points towards the right way to execute a philosophical task his precursors were already engaged on, though, apart from those anticipations in the rationalists, they approached things in the wrong order. But it seems wrong to suppose Kant's move is a new, or nearly new, contribution to an old project. The attribution of centrality to propositional content, which needs to be understood in the context of reason, belongs with the fact that Kant is posing a new question. Kant brings into view a new way of finding philosophical problems in meaningfulness, or—better, since it is anachronistic to treat Kant as a philosopher of language—objective purport, a puzzlement that could not have exercised a medieval logician, who might indeed have begun with a logic of terms. The idea of objective purport first comes into focus as a distinctively philosophical issue around Kant's time, precisely because of the entanglement with an idea of responsiveness to reason that Kant registers by making judgment central. This entanglement poses new questions in modern philosophy, because there is an increasing sense that reason resists integration into nature, on a newly sharp conception of nature made available by the maturation of the natural sciences. Perhaps some of the early modern philosophers have an inkling of this new problem about objective purport, but it does not come properly into view until Kant. So if some early moderns still begin logic with a logic of terms, like medieval logicians, that does not reveal them as accepting a representationalist approach to questions Kant is addressing when he makes judgment central. They are not considering Kant's questions. That is a way of putting a Kantian criticism: his predecessors do not recognize an obligation he envisages for philosophy. He is precisely not urging a different way to perform a task he takes his precursors to be already trying to perform, though they do things in the wrong order.

4. At p. 92, Brandom suggests that Hegel took the incipient inferentialism Brandom finds in Kant to its logical conclusion: "It remained for Hegel, however, to complete the inversion of the traditional order of semantic explanation . . . ." But it seems off-key to read Hegel as having any sympathy with an idea of conceptual primitives. Inferentialism shares with representationalism a linear style of conceptual clarification, starting with something supposedly independently understood. That is surely not a Hegelian way of proceeding.

The puzzlement Kant is addressing is not intelligibly felt unless objective purport is conceived in the context of reason. As with the context of linguistic practice that Wittgenstein insists on, that does not imply that the concepts that figure in delineating the required context are to be taken as primitive. There is no ground here for seeing Kant as incipiently inferentialist. And this account of the Kantian innovation makes it problematic whether we can really understand the frame of mind that would need to be characteristic of Brandom's "majority tradition", whose members supposedly pursue a different order in addressing the very question Kant addresses with the move Brandom reads as proto-inferentialist. The idea would need to be that we can begin on alleviating that felt puzzlement by invoking concepts of representational meaningfulness that we take to be intelligible independently of the role of objective purport in reasoning. But this conception of what primitive concepts might be available conflicts with a condition for even feeling the difficulty about objective purport that Kant addresses. This makes Brandom's "majority tradition" look like a fiction. It is not clear that his foil for inferentialism is anything but a straw man.[5]

Why does this matter? Well, Brandom pays almost no attention to the question whether semantic explanation should be linear, with some concepts selected as primitive. As long as he can make it seem that there is a real school of thought that proceeds in that way, although its choice of primitive concepts is wrong, the assumption that what is called for is the right choice of

5. Perhaps we should look for examples in contemporary philosophy. But where? We cannot attribute a representationalist orientation on the basis of the order in a formal presentation of a semantic theory. It is true, for instance, that a Davidsonian semantic theory of a language would begin with assignments of semantic properties to subsentential expressions. But that is perfectly consistent with endorsing a Kantian priority of the propositional. Davidson makes that clear; see "In Defence of Convention T". And attributing priority to the propositional reflects the thought, which shapes Davidson's thinking about interpretation, that a semantic theory for a natural language would ultimately stand or fall according to whether it made rational sense of speakers. (Among much else, inference would matter for this.) Davidson is certainly not a proponent of Brandom's "representationalist order of explanation". At p. 337, Brandom describes Davidson as conceiving "representational relations as holding in the first instance between propositionally contentful intentional states and facts or states of affairs". This at least acknowledges that Davidson has the Kantian priority of the propositional, though it grossly misrepresents Davidson's thinking, which makes no such play with facts or states of affairs. And the picture Brandom gives in this later passage is still that "most representationalists", unlike Davidson, think they can begin with independently intelligible relations between subsentential expressions and things in the real order. One wonders whom he has in mind.

primitives can look innocent, not in need of defence. But if his competition between orders of linear explanation is unreal, the assumption can no longer go unremarked, and it becomes more evident that from the hopelessness of the representationalism he sets up as inferentialism's competitor, he cannot really derive any recommendation for the inverted order.[6]

4. The designational representationalism that Brandom tends to take as representative starts with semantic relations between subsentential expressions and elements of extra-linguistic reality. Now Brandom casts his inverted order of explanation as matching that but in the opposite order. His own notion of representation, to be reached at the end of the explanatory procedure, mirrors that of a designational representationalist. This shows in the fact that he does not think representation is explicitly on the scene until he has arrived, in chapter 8, at locutions for attributions of commitments in which the attributor explicitly relates the attributee to elements of extra-linguistic reality (as in "Ralph believes of the man he saw at the beach that he is a spy").

Brandom's designational representationalists think of representation as a generic relation, species of which hold between names and objects, predicates and (perhaps) properties (or sets), and—derivatively—sentences and states of affairs (pp. 69–70). This conception is quite suspect. It does not become innocuous just by being reconceived as something we reach at the end of our story rather than something we begin with, with the first two species derivative from the third rather than the other way around. But Brandom seems content to think of the final stage in the inferentialist explanatory procedure—providing for the representational dimension of discursive content—as making explicit just such a conception of representational relations.[7]

6. At p. 669, n. 90, Brandom actually acknowledges something like this point. But he relegates the acknowledgment to an endnote whose text indication comes late in the chapter (at p. 135). It makes no difference to how the main body of the chapter proceeds.

7. In "Replies", at p. 190, n. 1, Brandom rephrases my suggestion that "snow" and snow are so related that concatenating the former with ". . . is white" yields a truth just in case snow is white, by including a relation between ". . . is white" and being white. Contrary to what Brandom implies, this is not an improvement; there is no need for a real thing (or, as Sellars might say, non-thing) to stand to ". . . is white" in an analogue to the relation in which snow stands to "snow". I conjecture that the reason Brandom thinks it is an improvement to add relations between predicates and properties is that he wants the representational relations that are to be brought on to the scene at the end of his progression to match the representational relations with which his designational representationalists are described as thinking they can begin.

This makes a difference to how he conceives what is needed for him to claim a successful completion of the inferentialist project—providing for the representational dimension of meaningfulness in terms of a prior understanding of inference.

To my ear, we have locutions that are explicitly representational as soon as we have "that" clauses, as soon as we have the idea of propositional content. If someone is said to assert that things are thus and so, she is thereby said to represent things as being thus and so. Of course this need not, and should not, be parsed as expressing a relation, representing, that holds between the person, or her words, and a state of affairs—the sort of thing someone might purport to understand as a species of a genus that also comprises the relation of names to their bearers.

Now one could surely have a concept of inference without mastering the explicitly relational locutions that Brandom reaches at the end of his story. So it is a live possibility that the concept of inference is primitive with respect to the concepts expressed in those locutions. But it is quite another matter with the concept of asserting that things are thus and so, and hence representing that things are thus and so in the way one does when one asserts that things are thus and so. Indeed Brandom himself, in chapter 3, seems to concede that the concept of inference is not primitive with respect to the concept of asserting that things are thus and so, when he says not only "Asserting cannot be understood apart from inferring" but also "Inferring cannot be understood apart from asserting" (p. 158). It is only the conception of representation I am questioning, a mirror image of the designational representationalist conception, that can make it look as if these remarks do not yet traffic in a concept of representation. But if they do, the second one amounts to an admission—contrary to the whole thrust of the recommendation for inferentialism—that the concept of inference is not primitive with respect to the concept of representation.[8]

5. Perhaps the moral we should extract from Brandom's acknowledgment that inferring is not prior to asserting is that "inferentialism" is, after all, not a good label for the position he means to recommend. What he really wants

---

8. Even leaving representation out of account for the moment, I do not see how to make the second of these remarks from p. 158 consistent with the implied claim of chapter 2 that the concept of inference is primitive with respect to concepts that presuppose the idea of the semantic (see, e.g., p. 89).

us to see as primitive is the idea of a deontic structure of commitments and entitlements with rationally consequential relations between them. A characterization in those terms does not evidently presuppose any prior grasp of semantic or even language-related concepts. And now the claim is that a description of a practice given exclusively in those terms can suffice to reveal that the practice described is discursive—to display the moves made in the practice as assertions. If the idea of inference is on a level with the idea of assertion, we would become entitled to see the transitions between moves as inferences at the same time. So on this reading of Brandom the idea of inference and the idea of conceptual content are to be understood together, in terms of the prior ideas of commitment, entitlement, and practice-sanctioned consequence.

In his Preface, Brandom says the project of explaining the very idea of discursive linguistic performances is executed in chapters 3 and 4 (p. xxii). In fact his claim (at least sometimes) is that giving sufficient conditions for a practice to be conceptually contentful *überhaupt* is done before he turns, in chapter 4, to specifically empirical and practical conceptual content (pp. 221, 234); so, presumably, in chapter 3.

In assessing this claim, it is important not to let the concept of inference in too soon. If transitions between moves in a practice are inferences, then surely some of the moves are assertions. But that does not vindicate the claim, now that we have it in a form in which the idea of inference is on a level with the idea of discursive performances rather than prior to it. If it is open to question whether, given only the description of a deontic structure, the moves in a practice are displayed as including assertions, it is equally open to question whether the transitions between moves are thereby displayed as inferences. It is the same question, given the acknowledgment that assertion and inference are two sides of a single coin. One cannot justify an answer to one form of the question—"Are these moves recognizably assertions?"—by helping oneself to an answer to the other—"Are these transitions recognizably inferences?"

Now as far as I can see, the deontic structure—involving commitments, entitlements, and rationally consequential relations between them—that Brandom puts in place in chapter 3 is consistent with the possibility that a game describable in those terms is just a game, a behavioural repertoire whose moves do not have a significance that points outside the game, so that the moves are not assertions and the transitions are not inferences. It makes no difference to this if we drop the more demanding version of

Brandom's claim, according to which the material of chapter 3 suffices for discursivity, and bring in a role for experiential input and behavioural output, the topics of chapter 4. Now we have a game in which players' entitlements are partly determined by features of the observable environment, and some of their commitments are discharged in non-linguistic action. But nothing in the description of the deontic structure ensures that these pointers outside the game have anything to do with the sort of meaningfulness that would reveal the practice as linguistic.

To make this vivid, consider a thought-experiment of a kind Michael Dummett has exploited in a related context.[9] Martians convey information to one another in a way extremely unlike ours—so much so that the hypothesis that human vocalizations are, among other things, our way of doing that does not immediately suggest itself to Martian anthropologists. And Martians have a rich repertoire of not necessarily competitive games: rule-governed behaviour with no external point, behaviour they engage in just for fun. Perhaps the fun lies in the intellectual challenge of keeping track of the positions of players. Now suppose they see human vocal behaviour as just such a game. It does not occur to them that the behaviour has meaning, except in the sense in which, say, chess moves have meaning. They realize that the human practice they are investigating includes inheriting entitlements from other players, and deferring to those others the responsibility for vindicating the inherited entitlements, but the Martians do not see inheriting an entitlement as a case of having it affirmed to one that things are thus and so. They see it as just another complexity in how the concept of a position in the game works. They do not see moves in the game as assertions, and (the other side of the coin) they do not see transitions between moves as inferences. But they miss nothing about linguistic behaviour that is capturable with the concepts of commitment, entitlement, and practice-sanctioned consequence.

This connects with a point about the sociality that would be revealed by a description of (what is in fact) a linguistic practice in those deontic-structural terms. In Brandom's depiction of such a practice, players keep score on one another, and make their moves in awareness that others who witness the moves will be keeping score. One can acquire entitlements from others whose moves one witnesses, and one can defer the responsibility of vindicating the entitlements to those others. But moves need not be

9. See *Frege: Philosophy of Language*, pp. 295–8.

addressed to those who acquire entitlements by witnessing them. It is only in the scorekeeping context, for instance in challenges to entitlements and responses to challenges, that Brandom's game specifically provides for moves to be addressed by one player to another. The deontic-structural description does not display players as taking an interest in anything beyond the deontic status of the players (themselves and others). Nothing in the deontic-structural description ties this interest to a concern with how things are outside the game, except in so far as how things are outside the game affects a player's deontic status, specifically her entitlements. A description of the practice in these terms does not reveal the kind of cooperativeness—sociality—that shows itself in a concern to *inform* others of things. And this is not an oversight. Given the character of Brandom's project, the description cannot explicitly provide for informative purposes, on pain of presupposing a concept that already involves an idea of meaningfulness. If the Martians have only the deontic-structural description of the game, nothing in their understanding of it requires them to find that kind of cooperativeness in the communal playing of it. If they must see the practice as cooperative, it is only in that players need to care about making available to one another the intellectual pleasure that the Martians take to be the point of playing. This makes it doubtful that the description suffices to display moves as assertions, and (again, the other side of the coin) that it licenses seeing transitions between moves as inferences.

6. Besides the recommendation for inferentialism—to stay with the official label—that is supposed to lie in the unsatisfactoriness of representationalism, Brandom invokes some authorities.

Unsurprisingly, one is Sellars. Brandom cites (p. 102) a passage from "Inference and Meaning" (p. 265) in which Sellars recommends the strongest of six conceptions of "the status of material rules of inference" that he considers: "Material rules are as essential to meaning (and hence to language and thought) as formal rules, contributing to the architectural detail of its structure within the flying buttresses of logical form."

Now it is indeed plausible that a behavioural repertoire would not be meaningful at all—linguistic, expressive of thought—if it were not characterized by proprieties of non-formal inference. That is a natural reading of Sellars's thesis that material rules of inference are essential to meaning. But it would be quite another matter to claim, with inferentialism, that an expression's meaning what it does *consists in* the fact that certain material-inferential proprieties govern its correct use, so that all semantic concepts, including that of an expression's meaning, can be explained in terms of no more than the concept of such proprieties. One can concede that there would be no meaning without material-inferential proprieties, while remaining sceptical that there need in general be any interesting answer to the question what it consists in that some expression means what it does.

It could not be correct to hear, say, "smoke", on someone's lips, as meaning *smoke* if her use of it did not conform to some suitable material-inferential proprieties. But no specific proprieties are essential to the word's meaning that. Certainly some may seem more central than others. If she does not think it right to derive an expectation she would express with "smoke" from the presence of fire, it might take ingenuity to interpret her word as nevertheless meaning *smoke*. But the interpretation might still be made to fit, by finding in her suitably unorthodox substantive beliefs about smoke. Their unorthodoxy would not by itself show that they could not have smoke as their topic. And similarly with any candidate for being a propriety essential to the word's meaning what it does. There need be no specific proprieties in which it can rightly be said to consist that "smoke" means what it does. The claim Brandom cites from Sellars is plausible, but it is simply wrong to think its plausibility is a recommendation for a general semantic inferentialism.[10]

7. More surprisingly, Brandom's authorities include the young Frege (pp. 94–7, 107–16). Brandom reads Frege's *Begriffsschrift*[11] as an inferentialist tract.

The reading gets off to an unpromising start. Brandom cites a passage from Dummett, which he interprets as deploring a shift in Frege's thinking, from an early semantic inferentialism to a later way of thinking that, in

---

10. Sellars takes himself to have recommended the thesis that "material transformation rules determine the descriptive meaning of the expressions of a language" ("Inference and Meaning", p. 284, cited by Brandom at p. 103). But he gives no good reason to accept anything stronger than that expressions could not mean what they do if they were not caught up in some suitable material-inferential proprieties. That can be accepted by someone who does not believe that the idea of inferential proprieties—or, to accommodate the possibility I considered in §5, proprieties of transition between commitments and entitlements—is primitive in the order of semantic explanation.

11. I shall use "*Begriffsschrift*" for Frege's book, and "conceptual notation" for the "formula language" it proposes.

Brandom's words, "makes truth, rather than inference, primary in the order of semantic explanation".[12] But what Dummett is deploring as retrograde, in the passage Brandom appeals to, is not a shift from an early inferentialist to a later representationalist period in Frege's thinking about semantic explanation, but a shift from pre-Fregean thinking about logic, which, rightly in Dummett's view, conceived logic as the study of logical consequence, to Frege's thinking, which—early no less than late—conceives logic as a science that arrives at a body of truths, of a quite special sort in that truth is not just the goal of this science, as of other sciences, but its object of study. Brandom can cite Dummett in support of reading the young Frege as a semantic inferentialist only by misreading Dummett.

There is certainly something right about taking the Frege of *Begriffsschrift* to be interested in making inferential proprieties explicit, on some interpretation of that idea. As against, say, Boole and Schröder, Frege prides himself on devising a notation that does not merely enable a codification of the forms of logical inference, leaving content to be taken care of elsewhere. With Frege's conceptual notation, one is to be equipped to make contentful claims in a way that makes it clear exactly what one is committing oneself to. And of course that is a matter of what follows from one's claims, what inferences to consequential commitments they license.

But there is something amiss with taking this to signal an anticipation of Brandom's semantic inferentialism. That begins to come out in some remarks Brandom is constrained to make about Frege's conditional. In Brandom's picture, the conditional is a device for making explicit, in the form of claims, material-inferential proprieties that characterize a linguistic practice anyway, independently of the availability of a conditional locution, and determine the content of the concepts involved in the inferences they license. But Frege explains his conditional by saying it is to be denied only in the case in which the antecedent is to be affirmed and the consequent is to be denied.[13] Thus it

---

12. *Making It Explicit*, pp. 96–7; citing Dummett, *Frege: Philosophy of Language*, pp. 432–3.

13. In *Begriffsschrift* the conditional is explained on these lines, rather than in terms that amount directly to the familiar truth-table, as in Frege's later presentations. (What Frege actually says is that the conditional is denied only if the antecedent is affirmed and the consequent denied. But this would be strictly true only of someone who never used the conditional incorrectly. My rewriting in the gerundive form seems appropriate.) Brandom tries to connect the move from the earlier to the later style of explanation with the shift he misreads Dummett as complaining of (p. 111). But it is surely clear that the difference of presentation is not significant.

would be correct to affirm the counterpart, in Frege's notation, of "If Hegel was Hölderlin's roommate, then 43 is prime" (Brandom's example, p. 113). As Brandom has to acknowledge, this makes Frege's conditional "an alarmingly bad choice for making explicit actual proprieties of inference" (p. 113). There would be nothing proper about inferring the consequent of that conditional from its antecedent, but the conditional is fine by Frege's lights.[14] Brandom says this "tend[s] to obscure the crucial expressive role in explicitating inferences (and therefore conceptual contents) that [Frege] assigns to" the conditional (p. 111). But Frege's conditional is so patently a bad instrument for the purpose Brandom says Frege assigns to it that charity recommends finding a different purpose for it. Frege is not blind to the peculiar features of his conditional. On the contrary, he parades them. It would be extraordinary if he intended the conditional for Brandom's purpose, making material goodnesses of inference explicit in the form of claims, and simply failed to see that his explanation allows correct uses of it that do no such thing.

In fact Frege's conditional, in combination with his notation for generality, is perfect, just as he explains it, for doing what he prides himself on making it possible to do, namely giving expression to complex contents in such a way as to make perspicuous what one is committed to in being committed to them. Frege's notation allows one to make explicit what one is committed to when one says, for instance, that a property is hereditary in a series, in such a way that the consequences that follow from the commitment can be derived in formally valid proofs, leaving no gaps needing to be bridged by intuition—a defect Frege famously complains of, in the inferential practice of mathematics conducted without his conceptual notation.[15]

The consequences that matter for Frege here are consequences he displays as following logically from contents expressed in the conceptual notation. All the inferences in *Begriffsschrift* are formally valid. Indeed they are all of the same form, and Frege draws attention to that. What his

---

14. Brandom suggests the point turns on the fact that Frege's conditional is two-valued. But a many-valued conditional, incorrectly affirmed only if the antecedent has a designated value and the consequent an undesignated one, would surely be just as bad by Brandom's lights. Adding more truth-values would not ensure an inferentially relevant connection between antecedent and consequent.

15. For an extended example of such a derivation, see "Boole's Logical Calculus and the Concept-Script", at pp. 27–32.

conditional serves to make explicit is not, as in Brandom's picture, material proprieties of inference, in the sense of excellences of inference that
can be brought within the scope of logic only by the suspect move of
counting the inferences as enthymematic and supplying an extra premise.
(See §8 below for more on this.) The explicitation Frege achieves consists
in articulating the *premises* of certain inferences in such a way that their
conclusions can be displayed as following from the premises *by logical reasoning*, needing no leaps of intuition or assumed further premises.

Brandom acknowledges, after a fashion, a point in this area (pp. 113–4).
What it reflects, according to him, is that in *Begriffsschrift* Frege only partly
executes the task he sets himself. The ultimate aim is "to use logical vocabulary to make explicit the inferential involvements in virtue of which *non-
logical* claims have the conceptual contents they do" (p. 113; my emphasis).
Frege's ambitions for his conceptual notation extend outside the territory
covered by his logicism, according to which logic accounts for not only the
form but also the content of certain mathematical statements. But in *Begriffsschrift* Frege only gets as far as spelling out the inferential roles of "the logical concepts themselves, and those mathematical concepts that turn out to
be definable from them" (p. 113). According to Brandom's suggestion, if
Frege had gone beyond this "first stage of his grand project of clarification of
nonlogical concepts through their explicitation in logical terms" (p. 113),
and tried to apply his ideas in areas such as geometry and mechanics, where
logic accounts only for form and not also—as he thinks it does in
arithmetic—for content, he would have been forced to realize that his conditional is inappropriate for the general case of the expressive purpose he
assigns to it.

Brandom here in effect admits that his own conception of the conditional,
according to which it makes proprieties of material inference explicit in the
form of claims, is at best off-stage in *Begriffsschrift*. But in fact there is no
reason to suppose Brandom's conditional is even waiting in the wings. It is
beside the point that the contents Frege explicitly treats in *Begriffsschrift* are
limited to those that come within the scope of his logicism. What Frege
achieves with his conceptual notation is, quite generally, a way of articulating logical structure in such a way that the consequences in virtue of
which claims have the content they do can be formally derived from the
claims as expressed in the new notation. As he says, this is achieved by ensuring that "the content is not just indicated but is constructed out of its constituents by means of the same logical signs as are used in the computation"

(that is, in the formal derivation).[16] It is true that in the cases he considers in *Begriffsschrift* logic is supposed to account ultimately not only for the structure revealed by such an articulation of the content of a concept but also for the constituents, to stay with that way of putting things. But the same expressive powers of the logical notation—including the conditional as Frege explains it—would enable him similarly to display the logical structure of contents whose constituents are definitely non-logical, in such a way as to allow formal derivation of commitments consequential on committing oneself to those contents. And that is Frege's claim about the expressive utility of his conceptual notation, now formulated in a way that allows it to apply in other exact sciences besides those that come within the scope of his logicism. It is still, in this general case, a matter of articulating premises so as to reveal consequences as formally derivable from them, not of making explicit proprieties of inference governing inferences that are not formally valid at all.

Frege takes pride in the superiority of his conceptual notation to those of Boole and Schröder. They already have resources for laying open to view structure in the content of concepts with certain kinds of logical complexity. To take an obvious case: if we suppose being H is defined as being F or G, Boolean apparatus displays how the concept of being H is inferentially connected to the concept of being F and the concept of being G. But Frege provides resources for making explicit a different kind of concept formation, engaged in, with at best partial articulateness before his innovation, in mathematics and no doubt other exact sciences. Here the complex concepts do not merely exploit boundaries already drawn by the simpler concepts out of which they are formed, as in the cases that can be handled with Boolean resources.[17] The novelty consists in the fact that Frege's apparatus makes it possible to do, in cases of this kind, what Boole and Schröder could already do in cases of the kind they could cope with—to make the content of logically complex concepts explicit by enabling formal derivations, from premises in which those concepts figure, of conclusions involving only the simpler concepts from which those complex concepts are formed. As before, the only inferences that matter for making sense of Frege's pride in his innovation are formally valid inferences. There is no reason why he should interest himself at all in the material goodnesses of inference that figure at the foundation of Brandom's construal of semantics. In citing Frege as a

16. *Posthumous Writings*, p. 35.
17. See *Posthumous Writings*, pp. 33–5.

precursor of his inferentialism, Brandom simply misreads the expressive purpose of Frege's conceptual notation.

8. It is a mistake to assimilate material goodness in inference to formal validity by insisting that those who engage in such inferences tacitly supply extra premises. Moves that display inferential rationality need not themselves be cases of logical reasoning. Brandom makes considerable fuss about rejecting this mistake, under the label "formalism" (pp. 97–102).[18]

Brandom's conception of logical vocabulary definitively precludes any tendency to fall into this mistake. According to Brandom, the point of logical vocabulary, centrally the conditional, is to make explicit inferential proprieties that characterize a linguistic practice anyway, independently of its even containing logical vocabulary. So there could be a practice that was linguistic, in the demanding sense of being governed by norms including norms for inference, but that did not yet contain means for formulating inferences of a specifically logical kind. (See, e.g., p. 383: "There is nothing incoherent about a language or stage in the development of a language in which the only vocabulary in play is nonlogical.") Participants in such a practice would show rationality in their inferential behaviour, but they would not yet be able to engage in logical reasoning.

I have been urging that Brandom has no basis for his claim that this conception of logical vocabulary is Frege's. In fact nothing in Frege's thinking tells against the thought that a practice could not be indicative of rationality at all, as it would need to be in order to be linguistic in that demanding sense, unless it already enabled its participants to engage in logical reasoning. On this view there could not be a language without logical vocabulary. A position on these lines would not have the firewall against "formalism" that Brandom's thinking supplies. But such a position is nevertheless perfectly compatible with recognizing that "formalism" is a mistake. (So the wrongness of "formalism" is no ground for rejecting it, as Brandom seems to suggest at p. 383.) The idea would be that nothing subjects do can count as inferring, even inferring whose excellence is material rather than formal, unless something they do—which can be something else—can be understood as inferring logically. The idea that there is no rationality without

---

18. He makes the point in large part by way of a massively uncharitable reading of a passage from Daniel C. Dennett. But the point is certainly right, and I shall not quibble with the details of his presentation of it.

logic need not imply that all exercises of rationality are themselves cases of logical reasoning.

In a striking phrase, Brandom says "Logic is the organ of semantic self-consciousness" (p. xix). In his book, this slogan expresses an implication of the thesis I have been considering, that logical vocabulary enables prior inferential proprieties that determine the semantic properties of expressions to be made explicit in the form of claims. What connects this with self-consciousness is that only by being thus made explicit can the proprieties become subject to criticism and reasoned modification. Semantic self-consciousness requires the ability to contemplate, so to speak as objects, the determinants of the semantic properties of the expressions one uses, as opposed to merely living within the normative constraints they impose. And this stepping back from one's practice is achieved by making its norms explicit as claims, about which one can ask whether they are correct.

Now if we discard the idea that prior inferential proprieties determine the semantic properties of expressions, we can no longer embrace Brandom's slogan as he means it. But we can say logic is the organ of rational self-consciousness. We can say that an explicitly conditional locution is required if supposed inferential proprieties—features of the supposed topography of the space of reasons—are to be possible objects of contemplation, so that the shape of a subject's supposed responsiveness to reasons can be an object for her, as it must be if her responses to reasons are to be self-conscious.[19] The picture diverges from Brandom's in that these inferential proprieties, these shapings of rationality, are no longer seen as constituting an independently available foundation for a semantic theory of a language.

This leaves untouched the thought—which is surely congenial to Brandom's basic outlook—that awareness of oneself as subject to semantic norms, in self-conscious participation in a discursive practice, is awareness of oneself as subject to rational requirements of a specific kind. Semantic self-consciousness is a case of rational self-consciousness. And now, combining that thought with the thought that logic is the organ of rational self-consciousness, we can recover an interpretation for Brandom's slogan, even without his semantic foundationalism. In this conception no less than in Brandom's, logic is the organ of semantic self-consciousness.

19. Frege's conditional will serve in this inquiry, to the extent that if the answer to the question "Is it true?" asked about a Fregean conditional is "No", the associated inferential practice is revealed as needing critical attention. Of course we had better not suppose that if the answer is "Yes", that suffices for a supposed inferential propriety to pass muster.

Given this reinterpretation of Brandom's slogan, the thought that a practice is not recognizable as linguistic unless it already contains logical vocabulary can be rephrased by saying there is no discursiveness, no genuine trafficking in meanings, without semantic self-consciousness. This stands in contrast with Brandom's picture, in which self-consciousness *überhaupt* is a late-coming extra (he undertakes to provide for it only in chapter 8), not a necessary condition for a practice to be discursive, with its performances expressive of conceptual content. It is, to say the least, not obvious that this really respects the intuitive connection, which is fundamental to Brandom's thinking (see, e.g., pp. 1–3), between the idea of having one's life shaped by meaning and the idea of being responsive to reasons. Surely the responsiveness to reasons that figures in this connection should be responsiveness to reasons *as such*. Can that really be in place in the absence of the capacity to raise questions about whether what one finds oneself inclined to be swayed by, in forming a belief or deciding to act, really constitutes a reason for the belief or action one is contemplating? And that imports rational self-consciousness, and hence—by Brandom's own lights—command of logical vocabulary. There is something to be said for the view that logic, as the organ of rational and hence semantic self-consciousness, is more deeply implicated in the very idea of a distinctively conceptual kind of content than Brandom's story allows.

9. When I previously expressed doubts about how he undertakes to motivate inferentialism, Brandom's response was to suggest that in the end it does not matter whether he succeeds in making inferentialism antecedently attractive. Even if the inferentialist project might not have seemed a good idea in advance, the proof is in the pudding.[20]

That can easily sound reasonable. But it is really not clear how much pudding there is, if we discount the considerations that are supposed to recommend inferentialism in the first place.

Given the enormous size of Brandom's book, that may seem a crazy remark. But much in the second part of *Making It Explicit* depends essentially on the first. If we grant that propositional content—the objective purport of utterances of whole sentences—has been provided for in the first part, it is indeed plausible that the semantic properties of subsentential expressions, their contribution to the semantic properties of whole sentences, can be

---

20. See "Replies", p. 191.

isolated by attending to substitutional inferences. (See, in particular, the pivotal chapter 6.) But that is not a vindication of inferentialism unless the provision for propositional content that it assumes has itself been genuinely achieved by inferentialist means. The conception according to which the meanings of subsentential expressions are what they contribute to the meanings of whole sentences is in itself neutral. (It is fundamental to the thinking of the mature Frege.) So a great deal of weight rests on the first part of the book.

Now I have already (§5 above) sketched a scepticism about the claim that a description of a behavioural repertoire in the deontic-structural terms Brandom elaborates would suffice to display its moves as including assertions. To repeat a crucial point, the label "inferentialism" must not be allowed to confuse the issue here. If the concept of inference is on a level with the concept of assertion, as Brandom seems to say it is (p. 158), we cannot presuppose that the transitions between moves in a practice so described are inferences, on pain of begging the question whether the construction has really provided for a role for the concept of assertion.

In a part of chapter 2 I have not yet considered, Brandom offers possible ingredients for an inferentialist pudding taken from the work of a third authority, Dummett (pp. 116–32). Dummett draws attention to explanations of logical constants in terms of introduction and elimination rules, that is, specifications of canonical forms of inference in which the constants figure in the conclusions and premises respectively. He proposes to generalize this. He suggests we can explain the meanings of other sorts of expressions in terms of circumstances that license using them and consequences of the commitments undertaken in such uses. The star illustration of this is the case of pejorative terms such as "Boche". It is indeed plausible that the expressive work "Boche" does for those who use it can be captured in terms of an inference from someone's being German to that person's being barbarously cruel, or something on those lines. Someone who calls Kurt "a Boche" aims to convey that he is German—the circumstances of application—and *therefore* barbarously cruel—the supposed consequence.

Now the case of logical constants is of course fine, but quite special. It is not a distinctively inferentialist thought that the very essence of logic lies in certain inferences. Someone who is doubtful about the general credentials of inferentialism can acknowledge that the meanings of the vocabulary that is special to logic can be captured in terms of inferences, and refuse the invitation to generalize.

For different reasons, words like "Boche" are special too. Why should we suppose the significance of predicative expressions in general—let alone expressions of other kinds—can be modelled on the expressive role of ethnic or racial slurs? As I acknowledged before (§6), it is plausible that predicative (or any) expressions would not mean what they do if their use were not subject to suitable inferential proprieties. But that is not to say their meaning what they do can be exhaustively explained in inferential terms. It is peculiar to terms like "Boche" that their expressive role can be captured by a paraphrase that includes an occurrence of "therefore".

Inferentialism is nothing if not a general thesis. That semantic insights can be achieved in this or that particular area by focusing on inferences does not vindicate inferentialism. It is compatible with the view that semantic concepts come in a package, each intelligible partly in terms of the others, rather than conforming to the foundational structure that inferentialism envisages. Brandom's talk of the proof being in the pudding would be to the point if he had actually given a semantic account of a language in inferentialist terms. But what he has given is really only an advertisement for such a thing. The question whether his proffered motivation is convincing matters more than he acknowledges.

What Myth?

1. I have urged (e.g. in *Mind and World*) that our perceptual relation to the world is conceptual all the way out to the world's impacts on our receptive capacities. The idea of the conceptual that I mean to be invoking is to be understood in close connection with the idea of rationality, in the sense that is in play in the traditional separation of mature human beings, as rational animals, from the rest of the animal kingdom. Conceptual capacities are capacities that belong to their subject's rationality. So another way of putting my claim is to say that our perceptual experience is permeated with rationality. I have also suggested, in passing, that something parallel should be said about our agency.

In his Presidential Address, Hubert Dreyfus argues that in taking this line I bend over backwards to avoid one myth, the Myth of the Given, and fall into another, the Myth of the Mental. I focus exclusively on "the conceptual upper floors of the edifice of knowledge", and ignore "the embodied coping going on on the ground floor". Or—worse—I deny the very existence of embodied coping, "in effect declaring that human experience is upper stories all the way down".[1] That lands me in an analogue to what Merleau-Ponty calls "intellectualism". Intellectualism holds that "judgment is everywhere pure sensation is not, which is to say everywhere".[2] Just so, for me, as Dreyfus puts it, "*mind* is everywhere the pure *given* is not, that is to say, 'all the way out'".[3] That is what Dreyfus stigmatizes as the Myth of the Mental, and diagnoses as overreaction to the Myth of the Given.

---

1. "Overcoming the Myth of the Mental: How Philosophers Can Profit from the Phenomenology of Everyday Expertise", p. 47.

2. *Phenomenology of Perception*, p. 34; cited by Dreyfus at "Overcoming the Myth of the Mental", p. 52.

3. "Overcoming the Myth of the Mental", p. 52.

But what is mythical about the claim that mind is pervasive in our perceptual experience? Dreyfus thinks the sphere of the conceptual in my sense, the sphere of the rational, cannot include embodied coping. He thinks embodied coping skills are, just as such, non-conceptual.[4] It would follow that if conceptual rationality is everywhere, there is no room anywhere for embodied coping skills. And our perceptual experience needs to be understood in the context of our embodied coping skills. But why should we accept that embodied coping skills are, just as such, non-conceptual? If they are not, Dreyfus has no ground for his claim that to find mind everywhere in a distinctively human perceptual engagement with the world is to fall into a myth. I do not have to ignore embodied coping; I have to hold that, in mature human beings, embodied coping is permeated with mindedness. And that is exactly what I do hold.

2. Dreyfus pictures rationality as detached from particular situations—as able to relate to particular situations only by subsuming them under content determinately expressible in abstraction from any situation. He makes a compelling case for the claim that the skills exercised in embodied coping cannot be characterized in such terms. If rationality is essentially situation-independent, that feature of embodied coping establishes that it cannot be permeated with rationality. But I think we should reject the picture of rationality as situation-independent.

This picture of rationality is clearly in play in the way Dreyfus handles my exploitation of Aristotle. I invoked Aristotle's view of practical wisdom as an exemplar of how to think about determinate shapings of conceptual rationality. In a passage Dreyfus quotes, I wrote:

> Imposing a specific shape on the practical intellect is a particular case of a general phenomenon: initiation into conceptual capacities, which include responsiveness to other rational demands besides those of ethics.[5]

Now on the ground that I describe Aristotle's notion in terms of responsiveness to reasons, Dreyfus concludes that I read Aristotle in a way that conflicts with the insights of Heidegger's reading. Heidegger depicts Aristotelian practical wisdom as, in Dreyfus's words, "a kind of understanding

---

4. See "Overcoming the Myth of the Mental", p. 47.

5. *Mind and World*, p. 84; cited by Dreyfus at "Overcoming the Myth of the Mental", p. 50.

that makes possible an immediate response to the full concrete situation".[6] Dreyfus quotes Heidegger saying this:

> [The *phronimos*] . . . is determined by his situation in the largest sense . . . . The circumstances, the givens, the times and the people vary. The meaning of the action . . . varies as well . . . .
>
>   It is precisely the achievement of *phronēsis* to disclose the [individual] as acting *now* in the *full* situation within which he acts.[7]

But that is just how I understand Aristotelian practical wisdom. Dreyfus's idea that my reading conflicts with Heidegger's reflects his interpreting my talk of responsiveness to reasons in terms of an assumption I dispute: the assumption that to involve reason in action could only be to apply to the situation in which one acts some content fully specifiable in detachment from the situation.

In the place in my work that Dreyfus cites from, my aim was only to introduce the idea of second nature, and it was not to the point to discuss the specifics of Aristotle's conception of *phronēsis*. But when, elsewhere, I consider the specifics, I reject the understanding of Aristotle's conception that Dreyfus thinks I accept. I reject the idea that the content of practical wisdom, as Aristotle understands it, can be captured in general prescriptions for conduct, determinately expressible independently of the concrete situations in which the *phronimos* is called on to act. Purporting to set me straight, Dreyfus quotes this from Aristotle: "*Phronēsis* . . . involves knowledge of the ultimate particular thing, which cannot be attained by systematic knowledge but only by 'perception' . . . ."[8] But my reading of Aristotle is precisely centred on the thought expressed in that passage.[9]

It was from David Wiggins that I learned to understand Aristotelian *phronēsis* as concretely situation-specific discernment. But, curiously enough, it is conceivable that some of my formulations of Aristotle's view as I see it have been influenced by Heidegger, indirectly through Gadamer. I first read Gadamer on Charles Taylor's recommendation; he urged me to read *Truth and Method* because he was struck by an affinity between things he had

---

6. "Overcoming the Myth of the Mental", p. 51.

7. *Plato's Sophist*, p. 101, cited by Dreyfus at "Overcoming the Myth of the Mental", p. 51.

8. *Nicomachean Ethics* 1142a25–7, cited by Dreyfus at "Overcoming the Myth of the Mental", p. 51.

9. See "Some Issues in Aristotle's Moral Psychology".

heard me saying about *phronēsis* and Gadamer's treatment, which is of course quite Heideggerian.

In a passage Dreyfus cites, I describe acquiring *phronēsis* in terms of having "habits of thought and action" inculcated into one.[10] This encourages Dreyfus in saddling me with the detached conception of rationality that, as I have said, I reject, and in reading such a conception into my understanding of Aristotle. Dreyfus interprets my talk of habits in terms of following *general* reasons—reasons that can be expressed in abstraction from particular situations. He says:

> One can easily accept that in *learning* to be wise we learn to follow general reasons as guides to acting appropriately. But it does not follow that, once we have gotten past the learning phase, these *reasons* in the form of habits still *influence* our wise actions.[11]

But that is not my picture at all. No doubt the very idea of a habit implies a generality of content. But conceiving *phronēsis* as a habit, or a set of habits, is consistent with holding that the only way one can register the generality of *phronēsis* is by a description on these lines: "the habit of responding to situations as *phronēsis* requires." And that leaves *what* response a particular situation calls for from the *phronimos* still needing to be determined by situation-specific discernment.

To say what I have just said, I did not need to go beyond an ordinary understanding of the word "habit". But it may be worth remarking that the word comes from the Latin "*habitus*", which is the standard equivalent in philosophy for the Greek "*hexis*". *Phronēsis* is a virtue—the paramount virtue of the practical intellect. As such it is certainly, in Aristotle's view, a *hexis*, a *habitus*, a habit. This cannot conflict with anything that could figure in a correct reading of Aristotle.

Dreyfus quotes me saying this: "I construe Aristotle's discussion of deliberation as aimed at the reconstruction of reasons for action not necessarily thought out in advance."[12] He reads this, too, as giving expression to a conception according to which the actions of a *phronimos* are guided by reasons

---

10. *Mind and World*, p. 84, cited by Dreyfus at "Overcoming the Myth of the Mental", p. 50.

11. "Overcoming the Myth of the Mental", p. 51.

12. "Virtue and Reason", p. 66; cited by Dreyfus at "Overcoming the Myth of the Mental", p. 51.

that relate to particular situations only by way of applying situation-independent content to them. If such reasons are not explicitly adverted to in deciding what to do, Dreyfus thinks I think, then they must be retrospectively postulated as having been implicitly followed by the agent.

Here again, the connection Dreyfus assumes between rationality and situation-independence is alien to my understanding of Aristotle. My thought was that the practical rationality of the *phronimos* is displayed in what he does even if he does not decide to do that as a result of reasoning. So the structure of what Aristotle offers as an account of deliberation should be relevant more widely than where action issues from reasoning. There is no implication that the reconstruction I envisage, for displaying actions that do not issue from prior deliberation as nevertheless cases of a properly formed practical intellect at work, involves rational structures in which the concrete details of the situation figure only in specifying what some situation-independent conception of how to act was implicitly applied to. That would be to picture the practical reasoning of a *phronimos*, and correspondingly the rationality that there is in action that manifests *phronēsis* even if it does not issue from reasoning, in terms of subsuming cases under rules expressible in abstraction from particular situations. And that picture is exactly what I oppose in my reading of Aristotle.[13]

Dreyfus cites from Heidegger the claim that the "pure perceiving" that is the characteristic accomplishment of the *phronimos* "no longer falls within the domain of *logos*".[14] Dreyfus reads this as a formulation of the contrast he assumes, between the situation-specificity of the kind of competence exemplified by *phronēsis*, on the one hand, and, on the other, conceptual rationality conceived as situation-independent. Conceptual rationality is what language enables us to express, so it belongs with this reading to interpret "the domain of *logos*" as the domain of language, and to understand Heidegger to be equating the domain of language with the domain of rationality conceived as detached and situation-independent.

But that is a hopeless conception of the domain of language, and thereby of the domain of the conceptual. A requirement of situation-independence

---

13. Dreyfus reads me as holding that "there must be a maxim behind every action" ("Overcoming the Myth of the Mental", p. 52). If rationality is as such situation-independent, this is the only possible reading of the claim that rationality permeates action. But it does not fit my thinking at all. In my picture rationality is *in* action, and just as situation-dependent as action is—not *behind* action, in the guise of a "maxim".

14. *Plato's Sophist*, p. 112, cited by Dreyfus at "Overcoming the Myth of the Mental", p. 51.

would exclude what might be meant by an utterance of, say, "This one is beautiful" from the domain of the linguistically expressible and so of the conceptual, since there is no telling what thought such an utterance expresses in abstraction from the situation in which the thought is expressed.

There is no call to foist such an idea on Heidegger. The word "*logos*" can accept many different interpretations. Aristotle explains the "perception" of the *phronimos* partly in terms of a comparison with theoretical intuition, which immediately grasps indefinables (things of which there is no *logos*).[15] On a more charitable interpretation, Heidegger is picking up on that comparison. The domain of *logos* in Heidegger's remark is not, as Dreyfus thinks, the space of reasons, the domain of conceptual articulation. Contrary to what Dreyfus implies, the domain of conceptual articulation includes thoughts that are not intelligible in abstraction from particular situations, so that interpretation of "the domain of *logos*" would not secure the contrast Heidegger wants with the "pure perceiving" of the *phronimos*. The domain of *logos* that is relevant to Heidegger's point is the domain of the definable, which is not the same thing at all.

What Heidegger insists is that in Aristotle's view the *phronimos* determines action by situation-specific discernment. And as Heidegger of course knows, Aristotle has no problem combining that with glossing the practical knowledge of the *phronimos* in terms of the idea of correct *logos*.[16] Here—in contrast with what "*logos*" must mean when Heidegger locates *phronēsis* outside the domain of *logos*—*logos* must be situation-specific conceptual articulation.

3. As Dreyfus emphasizes, we share basic perceptual capacities and embodied coping skills with other animals.[17] That may seem to yield a quick argument that those capacities and skills, as we have them, cannot be permeated with rationality, since other animals are not rational. But the quick argument does not work. The claim that the capacities and skills are shared comes to no more than this: there are descriptions of things we can do that apply also to things other animals can do. For instance: any animal—rational or not—with suitable sensory equipment, engaged in getting from

---

15. *Nicomachean Ethics* 1142a25–7 (the passage Dreyfus cites at "Overcoming the Myth of the Mental", p. 51).

16. See, e.g., *Nicomachean Ethics* 1138b20. Such talk of correct *logos* pervades Aristotle's ethics.

17. See "Overcoming the Myth of the Mental", p. 47.

one place to another, can be expected, other things being equal, to respond to the affordance constituted by a sufficiently large opening, in a wall that otherwise blocks its path, by going through the opening. But the truth about a human being's exercise of competence in making her way around, in a performance that can be described like that, need not be *exhausted* by the match with what can be said about, say, a cat's correspondingly describable response to a corresponding affordance. The human being's response is, if you like, indistinguishable from the cat's response *qua* response to an affordance describable in those terms. But it does not follow that the human being's response cannot be unlike the cat's response in being the human being's rationality at work.[18]

Dreyfus says that when I talk of perception as openness to the world I seem "to agree with the phenomenologists that perception has a function more basic than justification".[19] But he thinks this is unmasked as mere appearance when one puts my talk of openness in the context of my adherence to the allegedly mythical view that mind is everywhere in our lives. The most basic function of perception, Dreyfus says, is this:

> We directly perceive affordances and respond to them without beliefs and justifications being involved. Moreover, these affordances are interrelated and it is our familiarity with the whole context of affordances that gives us our ability to orient ourselves and find our way about.[20]

But the suggestion that I cannot accommodate what is right about this is, I think, just a sophisticated version of the quick argument, which, as I said, does not work.

To explain this, I need to consider Heidegger's distinction between being open to a world and merely inhabiting an environment. Dreyfus relegates a mention of this to an endnote. He says: "This is an important difference between human beings and animals, but since we are focusing on the role of perception in giving us a background on the basis of which we can perceive objects and justify our beliefs about them, we need not go into it here."[21]

18. For a hint, at least, at the quick argument, see "Overcoming the Myth of the Mental", p. 56, with note 39 (which belongs with note flag 37 in the text; the notes are plainly misnumbered).

19. "Overcoming the Myth of the Mental", p. 58.

20. "Overcoming the Myth of the Mental", p. 59.

21. "Overcoming the Myth of the Mental", p. 65, n. 54. (The relevant note flag in the text is 51, at p. 59.)

But the role of perception in giving us a background is its giving us familiarity with that context of interrelated affordances. And what is in question between Dreyfus and me, once we are focusing on that aspect of what perception does for us, is precisely whether our perceptual openness to affordances, which I agree is necessarily bound up with our embodied coping skills, is permeated with rationality. That cannot be set aside as something we need not go into. I do not dispute that perceptual responsiveness to affordances, necessarily bound up with embodied coping skills, is something we share with other animals. And I can accept that there is a sense in which familiarity with affordances is a background for our openness to objects. But I can still hold that our openness to affordances is part of the way of being that is special to rational animals.

What perception discloses to human beings is not restricted to affordances. That is a way of beginning to spell out the thought that human beings are different from other animals in that they do not just inhabit an environment, but are open to a world. What is right about describing openness to affordances as providing a background is this: the fact that perception discloses the world to us is intelligible only in a context that includes the embodied coping competence, the responsiveness to affordances, that we share with other animals. But as I have urged, this sharing comes to no more than that there are descriptions that apply both to our competence and to the competence of other animals. I can acknowledge that, and still claim that there are further descriptions that fit our case only. There is more to our embodied coping than there is to the embodied coping of non-rational animals. Becoming open to the world, not just able to cope with an environment, transforms the character of the disclosing that perception does for us, *including* the disclosing of affordances that, if we had not achieved openness to the world, would have belonged to a merely animal competence at inhabiting an environment. When familiarity with affordances comes to be a background to what there is, over and above openness to affordances, in being oriented towards the world, which is a distinctively human way of being, a human individual's relation *to affordances* is no longer what it would have been if she had gone on living the life of a non-rational animal. Affordances are no longer merely input to a human animal's natural motivational tendencies; now they are data for her rationality, not only her practical rationality but her theoretical rationality as well. (Remember that I have rejected the conception of rationality as situation-independent.)

Openness to affordances is in a way basic in the picture of rational openness to the world that I am urging, and this corresponds to something Dreyfus claims. As I said, openness to the world, which is rationality at work, is intelligible only in a context that includes embodied coping skills. But on the view I am urging, the point is not, as Dreyfus has it, that our embodied coping skills are independent of any openness in which rationality figures—a ground-floor level, supporting a distinct upper story at which openness involves rationality. If that were right, it would follow that our embodied coping skills cannot themselves be permeated with conceptual mindedness. But that is not the right interpretation for the thought that openness to affordances is basic. No doubt we acquire embodied coping skills before we acquire concepts, in the demanding sense that connects with rationality. But when our embodied coping skills come to constitute a background for our openness to the world, the openness to affordances that is an element in what it is for us to have embodied coping skills becomes *part* of our openness to the world. Openness to affordances draws on the rationality of subjects who are open to the world just as much as any other part of openness to the world does.

I cited a passage in which Dreyfus excludes *justification* from the proper account of "the basic function of perception".[22] Now it is true that Sellars explains the logical space of reasons as the space "of justifying and being able to justify what one says".[23] And this talk of justification needs to be taken with care in connection with the claim that our perceptual openness to the world is our rationality at work. If we put the claim in terms of the justification of beliefs, that can encourage interpreting it to say that our perceptual experience yields items—experiences—that justify some of our beliefs in that forming the beliefs is responding rationally to those items. And then it looks as if a proponent of the claim can be embarrassed with a question on these lines: granting that belief-formation, on the part of a rational animal, is an exercise of the animal's rationality, why should we suppose rationality must be operative also in the constitution of that to which perceptual belief-formation is rationally responsive? But this construal of what Sellars's thought would have to be, as applied to perceptual openness, is anyway out of line with Sellars's insistence that observational knowledge is non-inferential. Perceptual experiencing, on the part of a rational animal,

---

22. "Overcoming the Myth of the Mental", p. 59, quoted above.
23. "Empiricism and the Philosophy of Mind", §36.

is not just something that can elicit rational responses in the shape of perceptual beliefs. What Sellars's thought comes to in this context is that the perceptual experiencing of rational animals is itself rational openness to the world—which includes openness to affordances, as I have been insisting. So capacities that belong to a subject's rationality must be operative in the subject's experiencing itself, not just in responses to it.

4. Embodied coping skills are essential to a satisfactory understanding of our orientation to the world. And we falsify the phenomenology of embodied coping if we describe it in terms of applying situation-independent knowledge of how to act. Those claims are central to Dreyfus's argument against me.

What I have been urging is this: accepting those claims is perfectly consistent with holding that our orientation towards the world, including our orientation towards the affordances we respond to when we exercise our embodied coping skills, is permeated with mindedness. Dreyfus dismisses the thesis that mind is pervasive in a distinctively human life as a myth, on the ground that the thesis cannot be combined with a proper phenomenology of embodied coping skills and a proper placement of embodied coping skills in an account of our orientation towards the world. But I have been arguing that this is wrong. Acknowledging the pervasiveness of mind in a distinctively human life is consistent with appreciating those phenomenological insights.

This is nicely illustrated by Gadamer's version of the distinction between being oriented towards the world and merely inhabiting an environment. (A version that, so far as I can see, Gadamer does not regard as diverging from Heidegger's.) Gadamer says that "man's relation to the world is absolutely and fundamentally verbal in nature".[24] If a distinctively human relation to the world is in the space of linguistically expressible thought, it is pervasively conceptual. And Gadamer does not confine his thesis to our orientation towards features of the world other than those we respond to in our embodied coping. For Gadamer, our embodied coping is not exhausted by its similarity to the embodied coping of non-rational animals, as in Dreyfus's picture of a non-conceptual background. On the contrary, Gadamer argues that language introduces a "free, distanced orientation" towards what would otherwise have been merely features of an environment.[25] This is the thought I expressed by

24. *Truth and Method*, pp. 475–6.
25. *Truth and Method*, p. 445.

saying that once affordances are figuring for a subject as features of the world, they are no longer just inputs to a natural motivational makeup; they are available to the subject's rationality.

On this view, our relation to the world, including our perceptual relation to it, is pervasively shaped by our conceptual mindedness. An implication of this for perceptual content can be put like this: if a perceptual experience is world-disclosing, as opposed to belonging to the kind of coping with a mere environment that figures in the lives of creatures lacking orientation towards the world, any aspect of its content is present in a form in which it is suitable to constitute the content of a conceptual capacity.

Let me explain why I have put it like that.

I find it helpful to approach the idea in Kantian terms. If an experience is world-disclosing, any aspect of its content hangs together with other aspects of its content in a unity of the sort Kant identifies as categorial. And Kant connects the categorial unity that provides for world-disclosingness with the transcendental unity of apperception. Experiences in which the world is disclosed are apperceptive. Perception discloses the world only to a subject capable of the "I think" that expresses apperception.

To say that the content of a world-disclosing experience is categorially unified is not to imply that any aspect of that content is already, just as such, the content of a conceptual capacity possessed by the subject of the experience. Some aspects of the content of a world-disclosing experience are, in a typical case, already contents of conceptual capacities that the subject of the experience has, but on a perfectly natural understanding of what it is to have a conceptual capacity, some are not. The conception of conceptual capacities that makes this the right thing to say is the one Dreyfus cites Robert Brandom attributing to Sellars: "grasping a concept is mastering the use of a word".[26]

Now consider an aspect of the content of a world-disclosing experience that is not already the content of a conceptual capacity the subject possesses, in that sense. If it is to become the content of a conceptual capacity of hers, she needs to *determine* it to be the content of a conceptual capacity of hers. That requires her to carve it out from the categorially unified but as yet, in this respect, unarticulated experiential content of which it is an aspect, so that thought can focus on it by itself. It is overwhelmingly natural

---

26. *Articulating Reasons*, p. 6, cited at "Overcoming the Myth of the Mental", p. 55. I have left out Brandom's italics.

to cash out this image of carving out an aspect of content from a world-disclosing experience in terms of annexing a bit of language to it. (Not necessarily in an overt performance of naming; we can work with the idea of an inner analogue to such a performance.)[27]

This points to a picture on these lines. Some of what a perceptual experience discloses to us about the world is embraced by conceptual capacities, in Brandom's sense, that we already had before we enjoyed the experience; we already had words for those aspects of what is disclosed. We can equip ourselves with new conceptual capacities, in that sense, by isolating and focusing on—annexing bits of language to—other aspects of the categorially unified content of the experience, aspects that were hitherto not within the scope of our capacities for explicit thought. And surely some of the content of a typically rich world-disclosing experience never makes its way into constituting part of the content of our repertoire of conceptual capacities, in that sense.

This may make it seem urgent to ask: what is the point of insisting that the content of a world-disclosing experience is conceptual? There is an obvious sense in which content that never becomes the content of a conceptual capacity is not conceptual. So I am acknowledging that at least some of the content of a typical world-disclosing experience is not conceptual in that sense. And it is tempting to argue on these lines: surely *all* the content of an experience is present in it in the way in which I am acknowledging that some of its content is—that is, not conceptually in that sense.

But what is important is not whether an aspect of experiential content is, or becomes, the content of a conceptual capacity possessed by the subject of the experience, in the sense in which I have been talking about conceptual capacities. What is important is this: if an experience is world-disclosing, which implies that it is categorially unified, *all* its content is present in a *form* in which, as I put it before, it is suitable to constitute contents of conceptual capacities. All that would be needed for a bit of it to come to constitute the content of a conceptual capacity, if it is not already the content of a conceptual capacity, is for it to be focused on and made to be the meaning of a linguistic expression. As I acknowledged, that may not happen. But whether or not a bit of experiential content is focused on and brought within the reach of a vocabulary, either given a name for the first time or registered as fitting something already in the subject's linguistic repertoire,

27. Compare Sellars's "myth of Jones" in "Empiricism and the Philosophy of Mind".

it is anyway present in the content of a world-disclosing experience in a form in which it already either actually is, or has the potential to be simply appropriated as, the content of a conceptual capacity.[28] That the content of an experience has that form is part of what it is for the experience to be world-disclosing, categorially unified, apperceptive. And the content's being in the experience in that form is its being conceptually present in the experience, in a different sense from the one that figures in the objection.

This makes room for a different use of the idea of conceptual capacities (not competing with Brandom's use, just different). Using the idea in this different way, we can say that all the capacities that are operative in enjoying a world-disclosing experience, whether or not they are geared to aspects of the experience for which the subject has linguistic expressions, are conceptual, since they are capacities to enjoy content that is, in the sense I have introduced, conceptual in form.

The proposal of mine that Dreyfus takes issue with was that distinctively human perceptual experience is actualization of conceptual capacities in sensory consciousness. The proposal needs to be understood in terms of the interpretation of the idea of conceptual capacities that I have just introduced. This is clearly not the notion of conceptual capacities that Brandom credits to Sellars. We do not need to have words for all the content that is conceptually available to us, in the present sense: that is, available to us in the distinctive form that belongs with an experience's being such as to disclose the world. The Gadamerian thought is that language enables us to have experience that is categorially unified, apperceptive, and world-disclosing, and hence has content that is conceptual in the sense I have introduced; not, absurdly, that we are ready in advance with words for every aspect of the content of our experience, nor that we could equip ourselves with words for every aspect of the content of our experience. No aspect is unnameable, but that does not require us to pretend to make sense of an ideal position in which we have a name for every aspect, let alone to be in such a position.

To repeat, my claim is that when experience is world-disclosing, its content has a distinctive form. This does not imply anything about the *matter* of the

---

28. Because of the point about the form in which bits of content are present in experience, my talk of introducing conceptual capacities by annexing linguistic expressions to bits of such content does not fall foul of Wittgensteinian strictures against the Myth of the Private Ostensive Definition.

content that is present in that form—to bring in the other half of the metaphor that this talk of form involves. Materially identical content can show up
elsewhere in a different form. My experience might disclose to me that an
opening in a wall is big enough for me to go through. A cat might see that an
opening in a wall is big enough for it to go through. My experience would be
world-disclosing and so conceptual in form in the sense I have introduced.
The cat's perceptual intake would not be world-disclosing and so, in the relevant sense, not conceptual in form. It is irrelevant to this difference between
the cases that there is that match in what the cat and I would be getting to
know through the exercise of our perceptual capacities.[29]

5. I am all for the project of giving an insightful phenomenology of our embodied coping. But a phenomenology of embodiment should be conceived
not as a corrective to the thought that our orientation towards the world is
permeated with conceptual rationality, but as a supplementation, filling out
the details of something that needs to be presupposed by any acceptable
version of that thought. Phenomenological attention to embodied coping
should not be conceived as Dreyfus conceives it—as a way to answer the
question "how the non-conceptual given is converted into a given with
conceptual content".[30] That question should be rejected, not answered.

I have urged that the claim that conceptual rationality is everywhere in
our lives, in so far as our lives are distinctively human, cannot be unmasked
as a myth on the ground that it commits us to ignoring embodied coping
skills. The real myth in this neighbourhood is the thought that makes it look
as if affirming the pervasiveness of conceptual rationality will not cohere

29. In "Phenomenology and Nonconceptual Content", at p. 614, Christopher Peacocke
writes: "While being reluctant to attribute concepts to the lower animals, many of us
would also want to insist that the property of (say) representing a flat brown surface as
being at a certain distance from one can be common to the perceptions of humans and of
lower animals. . . . If the lower animals do not have states with conceptual content, but
some of their perceptual states have contents in common with human perceptions, it follows that some [human] perceptual representational content is nonconceptual." The com-
monality Peacocke appeals to is entirely at the level of what I am calling "matter". His argument is not responsive to what I have described as considerations about form. And the
argument is utterly unconvincing. A cat can see that a hole in a wall is big enough for it to
go through. On the principles of Peacocke's argument, this would imply that if I judge that
a hole in a wall is big enough for me to go through, the content of my judgment cannot be
conceptual in form.

30. "Overcoming the Myth of the Mental", p. 59.

with giving proper weight to the bodily character of our lives. This myth figures in Dreyfus's argument, in the shape of the idea that conceptual rationality is detached from bodily life, characterizable in abstraction from the specifics of the situations in which embodied coping is called for. This is—to give it a label—the Myth of the Disembodied Intellect.

The Myth of the Disembodied Intellect is familiar in philosophy. It is unlike the supposed Myth of the Mental in that almost everyone would agree that it is a myth, when it is set out explicitly in those terms. But it is surprisingly easy to lapse into it without realizing that one has done so, perhaps using impressionistic gestures to conceal from oneself that one is making oneself vulnerable to the familiar intractable questions that the Myth poses—questions that reflect the impossibility of bringing the intellect back into satisfactory connection with our embodied life, once we have expelled it from there.

I think Dreyfus falls into the Myth of the Disembodied Intellect, and so, at least occasionally, do his phenomenologist heroes. Let me stress that I am not suggesting this happens simply because Dreyfus and his heroes concern themselves with the phenomenology of embodiment. It happens because they tackle the phenomenology of embodiment in the context of the assumption I have attacked, that the phenomenology of embodiment must be kept free of involvement on the part of conceptual rationality.

I shall end with an instance of this in one of the phenomenologist heroes. In a passage Dreyfus quotes with approval, Merleau-Ponty writes:

> In perception we do not think the object and we do not think ourselves thinking it, we are given over to the object and we merge into this body which is better informed than we are about the world, and about the motives we have and the means at our disposal.[31]

Now I think talking of oneself as merging into something one could refer to as *this body* is one of those rhetorical gestures that serve to conceal a lapse into the Myth of the Disembodied Intellect. Once I have separated *me*—the thinking thing I am—from *this body*, it is too late to try to fix things by talking about the former merging into the latter. No one but a philosopher would take seriously the thought that in perception, or in action for that matter, I merge into my body. The fact is that there is nothing for me to

---

31. *Phenomenology of Perception*, p. 238, cited at "Overcoming the Myth of the Mental", pp. 56–7.

mean by "I", even though what I mean by "I" is correctly specified as *the thinking thing I am*, except the very thing I would be referring to (a bit strangely) if I said "this body"—at least if I said it in the sort of context in which Merleau-Ponty says it, with the thing in question said to be, for instance, informed about the world. (It might be different if the context were, say, medical, and I said something like "This body is beginning to fail me".) If I give "this body" the reference it must have in Merleau-Ponty's context, it is wrong to say I merge into that; I simply *am* that. This is mere sanity. To make it available, we need to reject the idea that the mindedness that marks me out as a thinking thing would have to be absent from an accurate phenomenology of embodiment.

Response to Dreyfus[1]

Dreyfus acknowledges that he was wrong to think practical intelligence, as I conceive it, is situation-independent. But he still thinks my view of mindedness can be characterized in terms of "detached conceptual intentionality". Now if you assume that mindedness is, as such, detached from immersion in activity, it is not surprising that mindedness should seem alien to the unreflective involvement that is characteristic of the exercise of skills. But the idea that mindedness is detached is just what I mean to oppose. The supposed Myth of the Mental is the result of reading me through the lens of what is by my lights a mythological conception of the mental.

In other work, I have invoked the image of stepping back, with a view to distinguishing rationality in a strong sense—responsiveness to reasons as such—from the kind of responding to reasons that is exemplified by, say, fleeing from danger, which is something non-rational animals can do. The idea was that in a subject with the ability to step back, the capacities that are operative in ordinary perceptual engagement with the world, and in ordinary bodily action, belong to the subject's rationality in that strong sense: they are conceptual in the sense in which I claim that our perceptual and active lives are conceptually shaped. When one is unreflectively immersed, one is exactly not exercising the ability to step back. But even so the capacities operative in one's perceiving or acting are conceptual, and their operations are conceptual.

Nothing is discursively explicit in these goings-on, so it might seem natural to say, as Dreyfus does, that my view is that they are *implicitly* conceptual. But it is easy to hear that as amounting to "*only* implicitly conceptual",

---

1. This is a response to Hubert L. Dreyfus, "Response to McDowell" (which is a response to Essay 18 above).

with an implication that conceptuality would be properly on the scene only after something had been made explicit in discourse or discursive thought—that is, only after the subject had exercised the ability to step back. And that is not my view at all. Making things explicit is not a theme of *my* thinking. I do not recognize a view of mine in the idea that exercises of rationality with the detachment characteristic of explicit *commentary* (on the passing scene or on what one is doing) constitute the proper or fundamental form of human activity.

This supposed connection of rationality with detachment is particularly damaging in the case of action. The involvement of rationality in human action, in my picture, is not a result of adding an "I think" to representations of one's actions. That would fit a detached, contemplative stance towards one's actions, but that is not my picture. Self-awareness in action is practical, not theoretical. It is a matter of an "I do" rather than an "I think". And the "I do" is not a representation added to representations, as Kant's "I think" is. Conceiving action in terms of the "I do" is a way of registering the essentially first-person character of the realization of practical rational capacities that acting is. The presence of the "I do" in a philosophical account of action marks the distinctive *form* of a kind of phenomenon, like the presence of the "I think", as at least able to accompany representations, in Kant's account of empirical consciousness.

The practical concepts realized in acting are concepts of things to do. Realizing such a concept is doing the thing in question, not thinking about doing it. In the most fundamental kind of case—the case of kinds of things to do that are basic actions for the agents in question, in one of the senses of that phrase—there is, by definition, no room for thought about how to do the thing in question. Such thought would need to traffic in concepts of other things to do, by doing which one would do the thing in question; and that would contradict the hypothesis that the thing in question is, in the relevant sense, a basic action for the agent in question. This means that the sad case of Chuck Knoblauch is no problem for me. Knoblauch had an ability to realize a certain practical concept (the concept of throwing efficiently to first base). But he lost his ability because he started thinking about "the mechanics", about how throwing efficiently to first base is done. The effect was that throwing efficiently to first base stopped being a basic action for him. The most this case could show is that when mindedness gets detached from immersion in activity, it can be the enemy of embodied coping (to echo Dreyfus's wording). It cannot show that mindedness is not in operation when one is immersed in embodied coping. When Knoblauch still had the bodily skill that he lost, his mindedness was in operation in exercises of his skill. His throwing efficiently to first base was his realizing a concept of a thing to do.

Knoblauch exemplifies a specific way in which practical intelligence can lose its grip on activity. That can happen when someone with a skill whose exercises belong to a basic action type tries to bring the limb movements that contribute to doing the thing in question within the scope of intention otherwise than under specifications like "whatever is needed to throw efficiently to first base". Before the loss of ability that takes that shape—the attempt to extend the scope of intentional control—the skill itself provided for the movements to be as they needed to be (the skill itself gave specificity to that "whatever is needed"), without the agent's means-end rationality being called on to intervene. This kind of loss of skill comes about when the agent's means-end rationality tries, so to speak, to take over control of the details of her bodily movements, and it cannot do as good a job at that as the skill itself used to do.

Dreyfus likes to put this point by saying, in a Merleau-Pontyesque vein, that the body knows what movements to make. That may be all right as a metaphorical way of noting that the person, the thinking thing, who is the agent does not need to determine the specific character of the limb movements involved in exercising a skill. She can leave that determination to her ingrained bodily habits. But the metaphor is dangerous in so far as it suggests that the body, in determining which movements are required for the thing in question to get done, exploits something that is like means-end rationality except that, since it belongs to the body as opposed to the person, it must be non-conceptual. And then when I claim that a rational agent's skilled bodily coping is permeated with her rationality, it looks to Dreyfus as if I must be claiming that the limb movements that figure in exercises of a skill are determined, not by a simulacrum of means-end rationality possessed by the body, but by the full-blown means-end rationality that belongs to the agent. An attempt on the part of means-end rationality to take control of limb movements is just what went wrong in the case of Knoblauch. So Dreyfus thinks I must be committed to the crazy idea that Knoblauch's case—in which a skill is actually lost—illustrates the general form of skilled bodily action.

But this is not my picture at all. The idea of a basic action, in the relevant sense, is the idea of a kind of thing one just does, not by doing something else in the relevant sense of that phrase. No doubt one does the thing in question—say, throwing efficiently to first base—by moving one's limbs appropriately. But that is not to say one makes the limb movements as a means to doing the thing in question. It is not to say one does the thing in question by doing something else in a sense that brings one's means-end rationality into operation.

So what difference does it make, according to me, for activity to be permeated with rationality—if it is not that it opens the way to a Knoblauch-like loss of unreflective skills? To answer this question, we need to think about skills that can be acquired by non-rational animals as well as rational animals; throwing efficiently to first base will not do as our example. So consider catching a flying object. When a rational agent catches a frisbee, she is realizing a concept of a thing to do. In the case of a skilled agent, she does not do that by realizing other concepts of things to do. She does not realize concepts of contributory things to do, in play for her as concepts of what she is to do by virtue of her means-end rationality in a context in which her overarching project is to catch the frisbee. But she does realize a concept of, say, catching *this*. (Think of a case in which, as one walks across a park, a frisbee flies towards one, and one catches it on the spur of the moment.) When a dog catches a frisbee, he is not realizing any practical concept; in the relevant sense, he has none. The point of saying that the rational agent, unlike the dog, is realizing a concept in doing what she does is that her doing, under a specification that captures the content of the practical concept that she is realizing, comes within the scope of her practical rationality—even if only in that, if asked why she caught the frisbee, she would answer "No particular reason; I just felt like it".

Dreyfus contrasts my Gadamerian conception of openness to the world with Heidegger's and Merleau-Ponty's. He thinks the world to which Gadamer and I provide for openness is a world of facts, in a sense that involves a separation from anything with practical significance. But I do not recognize this conception of the factual as mine. The point I want to make here is already implicit in the example I used in my essay. If someone is trying to get to the other side of a wall, the fact that a hole in the wall is of a certain size will be a solicitation. A subject to whom the world is disclosed is an agent. In that context the distinction Dreyfus insists on between affordances and solicitations does not amount to much. To an engaged agent an affordance can *be* a solicitation. And its being a solicitation does not conflict with its being a fact, something to which a rational animal can be open in operations of its conceptual capacities. Openness to the world is enjoyed by subjects who are essentially agents. What they are open to is not restricted to objects of disinterested contemplation. When Gadamer talks of a "free, distanced" orientation, he is not talking about an attitude that is contemplative as opposed to practically engaged.

Dreyfus objects to me from a standpoint at which he takes for granted that mindedness is detached from engagement in bodily life. This goes with a dualism of embodiment and mindedness that is reminiscent of Descartes. Of course this dualism is not exactly Cartesian; the body is not conceived as a machine. On the contrary, the body, as Merleau-Ponty and Dreyfus conceive it, is distinctly person-like. It is supposed to have practical knowledge. Now I could put what I urge at the end of "What Myth?" like this: *I* am the only person-like thing (person, actually) that is needed in a description of my bodily activity. If you distinguish me from my body, and give my body that person-like character, you have too many person-like things in the picture when you try to describe my bodily doings. And the need Dreyfus thinks there is for this awkward separation of me from my body reflects a conception of mindedness that I think we should discard. We should not start with the assumption that mindedness, the characteristic in virtue of which I am the thinking thing I am, is alien to unreflective immersion in bodily life. If we let our conception of mindedness be controlled by the thought that mindedness is operative even in our unreflective perceiving and acting, we can regain an integrated conception of ourselves, as animals, and—what comes with that—beings whose life is pervasively bodily, but of a distinctively rational kind.

BIBLIOGRAPHY

CREDITS

INDEX

Bibliography

Allan, D. J., "Aristotle's Account of the Origin of Moral Principles", *Proceedings of the XIth International Congress of Philosophy*, vol. 12 (Amsterdam: North-Holland, 1953).

———, "The Practical Syllogism", in *Autour d'Aristote* (Louvain: Presses Universitaires de Louvain, 1955).

Anscombe, G. E. M., "The First Person", in Samuel Guttenplan, ed., *Mind and Language* (Oxford: Clarendon Press, 1975).

———, "Thought and Action in Aristotle", in Renford Bambrough, ed., *New Essays on Plato and Aristotle* (London: Routledge and Kegan Paul, 1965).

Austin, J. L., *Sense and Sensibilia* (Oxford: Clarendon Press, 1962).

Baker, G. P., and P. M. S. Hacker, *An Analytic Commentary on Wittgenstein's Philosophical Investigations*, vol. 1 (Oxford: Blackwell, 1983).

Barwise, Jon, and John Perry, *Situations and Attitudes* (Cambridge, Mass.: MIT Press, 1983).

Bell, David, "How 'Russellian' was Frege?", *Mind* 99 (1990).

Bluck, R. S., *Plato's Sophist* (Manchester: Manchester University Press, 1975).

Brandom, Robert B., *Articulating Reasons* (Cambridge, Mass.: Harvard University Press, 2000).

———, "Knowledge and the Social Articulation of the Space of Reasons", *Philosophy and Phenomenological Research* 55 (1995).

———, *Making It Explicit: Reasoning, Representing, and Discursive Commitment* (Cambridge, Mass.: Harvard University Press, 1994).

———, "Perception and Rational Constraint", *Philosophy and Phenomenological Research* 58 (1998).

———, "Perception and Rational Constraint: McDowell's *Mind and World*", in Enrique Villanueva, ed., *Perception* (*Philosophical Issues* 7) (Atascadero, Calif.: Ridgeview, 1996).

———, "Replies", *Philosophy and Phenomenological Research* 57 (1997).

Broadie, Sarah, *Ethics with Aristotle* (New York: Oxford University Press, 1991).

Burnyeat, M. F., "Aristotle on Learning to be Good", in Amélie Oksenberg Rorty, ed., *Essays on Aristotle's Ethics* (Berkeley: University of California Press, 1980).

Carl, Wolfgang, *Frege's Theory of Sense and Reference: Its Origins and Scope* (Cambridge: Cambridge University Press, 1994).

Cooper, John M., *Reason and Human Good in Aristotle* (Cambridge, Mass.: Harvard University Press, 1975).

———, "Some Remarks on Aristotle's Moral Psychology", *Southern Journal of Philosophy* 27, Supplement.

Crombie, I. M., *An Examination of Plato's Doctrines*, vol. 2 (London: Routledge and Kegan Paul, 1963).

Davidson, Donald, "Actions, Reasons, and Causes", in Davidson, *Essays on Actions and Events* (Oxford: Clarendon Press, 1980).

———, "Afterthoughts" (a postscript to "A Coherence Theory of Truth and Knowledge"), in Alan Malachowski, ed., *Reading Rorty* (Oxford: Blackwell, 1990).

———, "A Coherence Theory of Truth and Knowledge", in Davidson, *Subjective, Intersubjective, Objective* (Oxford: Clarendon Press, 2001).

———, "Epistemology Externalized", *Dialectica* 45 (1991).

———, *Essays on Actions and Events* (Oxford: Clarendon Press, 1980).

———, "In Defence of Convention T", in Davidson, *Inquiries into Truth and Interpretation* (Oxford: Clarendon Press, 1984).

———, *Inquiries into Truth and Interpretation* (Oxford: Clarendon Press, 1984).

———, "Meaning, Truth and Evidence", in Robert B. Barrett and Roger F. Gibson, eds., *Perspectives on Quine* (Oxford: Basil Blackwell, 1990).

———, "Mental Events", in Davidson, *Essays on Actions and Events* (Oxford: Clarendon Press, 1980).

———, "The Myth of the Subjective", in Michael Krausz, ed., *Relativism: Interpretation and Confrontation* (Notre Dame, Ind.: Notre Dame University Press, 1989).

———, "A Nice Derangement of Epitaphs", in Ernest LePore, ed., *Truth and Interpretation: Perspectives on the Philosophy of Donald Davidson* (Oxford: Blackwell, 1986).

———, "On the Very Idea of a Conceptual Scheme", in Davidson, *Inquiries into Truth and Interpretation* (Oxford: Clarendon Press, 1984).

———, "The Social Aspect of Language", in B. McGuinness and G. Oliveri, eds., *The Philosophy of Michael Dummett* (Dordrecht: Kluwer, 1994).

———, "The Structure and Content of Truth", *Journal of Philosophy* 87 (1990).

———, *Subjective, Intersubjective, Objective* (Oxford: Oxford University Press, 2001).

———, "Three Varieties of Knowledge", in Davidson, *Subjective, Intersubjective, Objective* (Oxford: Oxford University Press, 2001).

———, "Truth and Meaning", in Davidson, *Inquiries into Truth and Interpretation* (Oxford: Clarendon Press, 1984).

Dennett, Daniel C., *Consciousness Explained* (Boston: Little, Brown, 1991).

———, *The Intentional Stance* (Cambridge, Mass.: MIT Press, 1987).

Dewey, John, *Experience and Nature* (New York: Dover, 1958).

Diamond, Cora, *The Realistic Spirit: Wittgenstein, Philosophy, and the Mind* (Cambridge, Mass.: MIT Press, 1991).

Dreyfus, Hubert L., "Overcoming the Myth of the Mental: How Philosophers Can Profit from the Phenomenology of Everyday Expertise" (APA Pacific Division

Presidential Address 2005), *Proceedings and Addresses of the American Philosophical Association* 79:2 (November 2005).

———, "Response to McDowell", in *Inquiry* 50 (2007).

Dummett, Michael, *Frege: Philosophy of Language* (Cambridge, Mass.: Harvard University Press, 1973).

———, "A Nice Derangement of Epitaphs: Some Comments on Davidson and Hacking", in Ernest LePore, ed., *Truth and Interpretation: Perspectives on the Philosophy of Donald Davidson* (Oxford: Blackwell, 1986).

Evans, Gareth, "Understanding Demonstratives", in Evans, *Collected Papers* (Oxford: Clarendon Press, 1985).

———, *The Varieties of Reference* (Oxford: Clarendon Press, 1982).

Frede, Michael, *Prädikation und Existenzaussage (Hypomnemata, Heft 18)* (Göttingen: Vandenhoeck & Ruprecht, 1967).

Frege, Gottlob, *Begriffsschrift: eine der arithmetischen nachgebildete Formelsprache des reinen Denkens* (Halle: Louis Nebert, 1879; reprinted Hildesheim: Georg Olms, 1964).

———, "Boole's Logical Calculus and the Concept-Script", in Hans Hermes, Friedrich Kambartel, and Friedrich Kaulbach, eds., *Posthumous Writings*, trans. Peter Long and Roger White (Oxford: Blackwell, 1979).

———, "On Sense and Reference", in Peter Geach and Max Black, *Translations from the Philosophical Writings of Gottlob Frege* (Oxford: Blackwell, 1960).

———, *Posthumous Writings*, ed. Hans Hermes, Friedrich Kambartel, and Friedrich Kaulbach, trans. Peter Long and Roger White (Oxford: Blackwell, 1979).

———, "The Thought: a Logical Inquiry", trans. A. M. and Marcelle Quinton, in P. F. Strawson, ed., *Philosophical Logic* (Oxford: Oxford University Press, 1967).

Friedman, Michael, "Exorcising the Philosophical Tradition: Comments on John McDowell's *Mind and World*", *The Philosophical Review* 105 (1996).

Furth, Montgomery, "Two Types of Designation", in Nicholas Rescher, ed., *Studies in Logical Theory* (American Philosophical Quarterly Monograph No. 2, 1968).

Gadamer, Hans-Georg, trans. Joel Weinsheimer and Donald Marshall, *Truth and Method* (New York: Crossroad, 1992).

Geach, P. T., *Mental Acts* (London: Routledge and Kegan Paul, 1957).

Goldfarb, Warren, "Wittgenstein on Understanding", in Peter A. French, Theodore E. Uehling, Jr., and Howard K. Wettstein, eds., *Midwest Studies in Philosophy, Vol. XVII: The Wittgenstein Legacy* (Notre Dame, Ind.: University of Notre Dame Press, 1992).

Heidegger, Martin, *Plato's Sophist* (Bloomington: Indiana University Press, 1997).

Herman, Barbara, "Making Room for Character", in Stephen Engstrom and Jennifer Whiting, eds., *Aristotle, Kant, and the Stoics* (Cambridge: Cambridge University Press, 1996).

Hinton, J. M., *Experiences* (Oxford: Clarendon Press, 1973).

Irwin, T. H., *Plato's Moral Theory* (Oxford: Clarendon Press, 1977).

———, "Some Rational Aspects of Incontinence", *Southern Journal of Philosophy* 27, Supplement (1988).

Kant, Immanuel, *Critique of Pure Reason*, trans. Norman Kemp Smith (London: Macmillan, 1929).

Kenny, Anthony, *Aristotle's Theory of the Will* (London: Duckworth,1979).

———, "The Practical Syllogism and Incontinence", *Phronesis* 11 (1966).

Kostman, James P., "False Logos and Not-Being in Plato's *Sophist*", in J. M. E. Moravcsik, ed., *Patterns in Plato's Thought* (Dordrecht: Reidel, 1973).

Kripke, Saul A., *Naming and Necessity* (Oxford: Blackwell, 1980).

———, *Wittgenstein on Rules and Private Language* (Oxford: Blackwell, 1982).

Lee, Edward N., "Plato on Negation and Not-Being in the *Sophist*", *Philosophical Review* 81 (1972).

Lewis, Frank A., "Plato on 'Not' ", *California Studies in Classical Antiquity* 9 (1976).

McDowell, John, "Criteria, Defeasibility, and Knowledge", in McDowell, *Meaning, Knowledge, and Reality* (Cambridge, Mass.: Harvard University Press, 1998).

———, "Having the World in View", *Journal of Philosophy* 95 (1998).

———, "Intentionality and Interiority in Wittgenstein", in McDowell, *Mind, Value, and Reality* (Cambridge, Mass.: Harvard University Press, 1998).

———, "Knowledge and the Internal", in McDowell, *Meaning, Knowledge, and Reality* (Cambridge, Mass.: Harvard University Press, 1998).

———, *Mind and World* (Cambridge, Mass.: Harvard University Press, 1994; second edition, 1996).

———, "One Strand in the Private Language Argument", in McDowell, *Mind, Value, and Reality* (Cambridge, Mass.: Harvard University Press, 1998).

———, "Putnam on Mind and Meaning", in McDowell, *Meaning, Knowledge, and Reality* (Cambridge, Mass.: Harvard University Press, 1998).

——— "The Role of *Eudaimonia* in Aristotle's Ethics", in McDowell, *Mind, Value, and Reality* (Cambridge, Mass.: Harvard University Press, 1998).

———, "Singular Thought and the Extent of Inner Space", in McDowell, *Meaning, Knowledge, and Reality* (Cambridge, Mass.: Harvard University Press, 1998).

———, "Some Issues in Aristotle's Moral Psychology", in McDowell, *Mind, Value, and Reality* (Cambridge, Mass.: Harvard University Press, 1998).

———, "Virtue and Reason", in McDowell, *Mind, Value, and Reality* (Cambridge, Mass.: Harvard University Press, 1998).

———, "Wittgenstein on Following a Rule", in McDowell, *Mind, Value, and Reality* (Cambridge, Mass.: Harvard University Press, 1998).

McGinn, Colin, "The Structure of Content", in Andrew Woodfield, ed., *Thought and Object* (Oxford: Clarendon Press, 1982).

Merleau-Ponty, Maurice, *Phenomenology of Perception* (London: Routledge and Kegan Paul, 1981).

Millikan, Ruth Garrett, "Perceptual Content and Fregean Myth", *Mind* 100 (1991).

———, "White Queen Psychology", in Millikan, *White Queen Psychology and Other Essays for Alice* (Cambridge, Mass.: MIT Press, 1993).

Nagel, Thomas, *The View from Nowhere* (New York: Oxford University Press, 1986).

Nussbaum, Martha C., *The Fragility of Goodness* (Cambridge: Cambridge University Press, 1986).

Owen, G. E. L., "Plato on Not-Being", in Gregory Vlastos, ed., *Plato, I: Metaphysics and Epistemology* (Garden City, N.Y.: Doubleday, 1971).

Peacocke, Christopher, "Phenomenology and Nonconceptual Content", *Philosophy and Phenomenological Research* 62 (2001).

Pears, David, "Aristotle's Analysis of Courage", *Midwest Studies in Philosophy* 3 (1978).

———, "Courage as a Mean", in Amélie Oksenberg Rorty, ed., *Essays on Aristotle's Ethics* (Berkeley: University of California Press, 1980).

———, *Ludwig Wittgenstein* (Cambridge, Mass.: Harvard University Press, 1986).

Perry, John, "Frege on Demonstratives", *Philosophical Review* 86 (1977).

Putnam, Hilary, *Meaning and the Moral Sciences* (London: Routledge and Kegan Paul, 1978).

Quine, W. V., "On the Very Idea of a Third Dogma", in Quine, *Theories and Things* (Cambridge, Mass.: Harvard University Press, 1981).

———, *Philosophy of Logic* (Englewood Cliffs, N. J.: Prentice-Hall, 1970).

———, "Two Dogmas of Empiricism", in Quine, *From a Logical Point of View* (Cambridge, Mass.: Harvard University Press, 1961).

———, *Word and Object* (Cambridge, Mass.: MIT Press, 1960).

Rorty, Richard, *Contingency, Irony, and Solidarity* (Cambridge: Cambridge University Press, 1989).

———, "Is Truth a Goal of Enquiry? Davidson vs. Wright", *Philosophical Quarterly* 45 (1995).

———, *Philosophy and the Mirror of Nature* (Princeton: Princeton University Press, 1979).

———, "Pragmatism, Davidson and Truth", in Rorty, *Objectivity, Relativism, and Truth* (Cambridge: Cambridge University Press, 1991).

———, "Putnam and the Relativist Menace", *Journal of Philosophy* 90 (1993).

———, "Response to Bernstein", in Herman J. Saatkamp, Jr., ed., *Rorty and Pragmatism: The Philosopher Responds to His Critics* (Nashville, Tenn.: Vanderbilt University Press, 1995).

———, "Solidarity or Objectivity?", in Rorty, *Objectivity, Relativism, and Truth* (Cambridge: Cambridge University Press, 1991).

Ross, Sir David, *The Nicomachean Ethics of Aristotle* (London: Oxford University Press, 1954).

Russell, Bertrand, "Knowledge by Acquaintance and Knowledge by Description", in Russell, *Mysticism and Logic* (London: George Allen and Unwin, 1917).

———, "On Denoting", in Russell, *Logic and Knowledge*, ed. R. C. Marsh (London: George Allen and Unwin, 1956).

———, *The Problems of Philosophy* (Oxford: Oxford University Press, 1912).

Ryle, Gilbert, *The Concept of Mind* (London: Hutchinson, 1949).

Sainsbury, Mark, "Russell on Names and Communication", in Sainsbury, *Departing from Frege* (London: Routledge, 2002).

———, "Names in Free Logical Truth Theory", in José Luis Bermúdez, ed., *Thought, Reference, and Experience: Themes from the Philosophy of Gareth Evans* (Oxford: Clarendon Press, 2005).

Salmon, Nathan, *Frege's Puzzle* (Cambridge, Mass.: MIT Press, 1986).

Searle, John R., *Intentionality: An Essay in the Philosophy of Mind* (Cambridge: Cambridge University Press, 1983).

——, "Proper Names", *Mind* 67 (1958).

Sellars, Wilfrid, "Empiricism and the Philosophy of Mind", in Herbert Feigl and Michael Scriven, eds., *Minnesota Studies in the Philosophy of Science*, vol. 1 (Minneapolis: University of Minnesota Press, 1956); reprinted (with some added footnotes) in Sellars, *Science, Perception, and Reality* (London: Routledge and Kegan Paul, 1963; reissued, Atascadero, Calif.: Ridgeview, 1991); reprinted as a monograph, with an Introduction by Richard Rorty and a Study Guide by Robert Brandom (Cambridge, Mass.: Harvard University Press, 1997).

——, "Inference and Meaning", in Jeffrey Sicha, ed., *Pure Pragmatics and Possible Worlds: The Early Essays of Wilfrid Sellars* (Reseda, Calif.: Ridgeview, 1980).

——, "Some Reflections on Language Games", in Sellars, *Science, Perception, and Reality* (London: Routledge and Kegan Paul, 1963; reissued, Atascadero, Calif.: Ridgeview, 1991).

Snowdon, Paul, "Perception, Vision, and Causation", *Proceedings of the Aristotelian Society* 81 (1980–1).

Stern, Robert, *Transcendental Arguments and Scepticism: Answering the Question of Justification* (Oxford: Clarendon Press, 2000).

Strawson, P. F., *The Bounds of Sense* (London: Methuen, 1966).

——, *Individuals* (London: Methuen, 1959).

——, *Skepticism and Naturalism: Some Varieties* (New York: Columbia University Press, 1985).

Stroud, Barry, "Epistemological Reflection on Knowledge of the External World", in Stroud, *Understanding Human Knowledge* (Oxford: Oxford University Press, 2000).

——, "Kantian Argument, Conceptual Capacities, and Invulnerability", in Stroud, *Understanding Human Knowledge* (Oxford: Oxford University Press, 2000).

——, "Mind, Meaning, and Practice", in Stroud, *Meaning, Understanding, and Practice* (Oxford: Oxford University Press, 2000).

——, "Reasonable Claims: Cavell and the Tradition", in Stroud, *Understanding Human Knowledge* (Oxford: Oxford University Press, 2000).

——, *The Significance of Philosophical Scepticism* (Oxford: Clarendon Press, 1984).

——, "Transcendental Arguments", in Stroud, *Understanding Human Knowledge* (Oxford: Oxford University Press, 2000).

——, "Wittgenstein on Meaning, Understanding, and Community", in Stroud, *Meaning, Understanding, and Practice* (Oxford: Oxford University Press, 2000).

Vlastos, Gregory, *Plato's Protagoras* (Indianapolis: Bobbs-Merrill, 1956).

Wiggins, David, "Deliberation and Practical Reason", in Wiggins, *Needs, Values, Truth* (Oxford: Blackwell, 1987).

——, "Sentence Meaning, Negation, and Plato's Problem of Non-Being", in Gregory Vlastos, ed., *Plato, I: Metaphysics and Epistemology* (Garden City, N.Y.: Doubleday, 1971).

——, "Weakness of Will, Commensurability, and the Objects of Deliberation and Desire", in Wiggins, *Needs, Values, Truth* (Oxford: Blackwell, 1987).

Williams, Bernard, *Ethics and the Limits of Philosophy* (London: Fontana/Collins, 1985).

Williams, Michael, "Exorcism and Enchantment", *Philosophical Quarterly* 46 (1996).

Wittgenstein, Ludwig, *The Blue and Brown Books* (Oxford: Blackwell, 1958).

———, *On Certainty* (Oxford: Blackwell, 1969).

———, *Philosophical Investigations* (Oxford: Blackwell, 1953).

———, *Remarks on the Foundations of Mathematics* (Oxford: Blackwell, 1978).

———, *Tractatus Logico-Philosophicus,* trans. D. F. Pears and B. F. McGuinness (London: Routledge and Kegan Paul, 1961).

———, *Zettel* (Oxford: Blackwell, 1967).

Wright, Crispin, "(Anti-)Sceptics Simple and Subtle: G. E. Moore and John McDowell", *Philosophy and Phenomenological Research* 65 (2002).

———, "Wittgenstein's Later Philosophy of Mind: Sensation, Privacy, and Intention", in Klaus Puhl, ed., *Meaning Scepticism* (Berlin: Walter de Gruyter, 1991).

Credits

Essay 1: Originally published in Malcolm Schofield and Martha Craven Nussbaum, eds., *Language and Logos: Studies in Ancient Greek Philosophy Presented to G. E. L. Owen* (Cambridge: Cambridge University Press, 1982), pp. 115–34. Reprinted with the permission of Cambridge University Press.

Essay 2: Originally published in Robert Heinaman, ed., *Aristotle and Moral Realism* (London: UCL Press, 1995), pp. 201–18. Reprinted by permission of Westview Press, a member of Perseus Books Group.

Essay 3: Originally published in Stephen Engstrom and Jennifer Whiting, eds., *Aristotle, Kant, and the Stoics* (Cambridge: Cambridge University Press, 1996), pp. 19–35. Reprinted with the permission of Cambridge University Press.

Essay 4: Originally published in Sabina Lovibond and Stephen Williams, eds., *Identity, Truth, and Value: Essays for David Wiggins* (Oxford: Blackwell, 1996), pp. 95–112.

Essay 5: Forthcoming in A. M. Ahmed, ed., *Essays on Wittgenstein* (Cambridge: Cambridge University Press).

Essay 6: Originally published in R. Haller and K. Puhl, eds., *Wittgenstein and the Future of Philosophy: A Reassessment after Fifty Years* (Vienna: öbvhpt, 2002), pp. 245–56.

Essay 7: Originally published in Lewis E. Hahn, ed., *The Philosophy of Donald Davidson* (Chicago: Open Court, 1999), pp. 87–104. Copyright © 1999 by The Library of Living Philosophers; reprinted by permission of Open Court Publishing Company, a division of Carus Publishing Company, Peru, Illinois.

Essay 8: Originally published in Jeff Malpas, Ulrich Arnswald, and Jens Kertscher, eds., *Gadamer's Century: Essays in Honor of Hans-George Gadamer* (Cambridge, Mass.: MIT Press, 2002).

Essay 9: Originally published in *Philosophy and Phenomenological Research* 67 (2003), pp. 675–81.

Essay 10: Originally published in José Luis Bermúdez, ed., *Thought, Reference, and Experience: Themes from the Philosophy of Gareth Evans* (Oxford: Clarendon Press, 2005), pp. 42–65. By permission of Oxford University Press.

Essay 11: Originally published in Lewis E. Hahn, ed., *The Philosophy of P. F. Strawson* (Chicago: Open Court, 1998), pp. 129–45. Copyright © 1998 by The Library of

339

Living Philosophers; reprinted by permission of Open Court Publishing Company, a division of Carus Publishing Company, Peru, Illinois.

Essay 12: Originally published in Robert B. Brandom, ed., *Rorty and His Critics* (Malden, Mass.: Blackwell, 2000), pp. 109–23.

Essay 13: Originally published in *Teorema* 25/1 (2006), pp. 19–33 (www.uniovi.es/Teorema).

Essay 14: Originally published in Marcus Willaschek, ed., *John McDowell, Reason and Nature: Lecture and Colloquium in Münster, 1999* (Münster: LIT Verlag, 2000), pp. 3–17.

Essay 15: Originally published in German in *Neue Rundschau* 100 (1999), pp. 48–69.

Essay 16: Originally published in *Philosophy and Phenomenological Research* 64 (2002), pp. 97–105.

Essay 17: Originally published in *Pragmatics and Cognition* 13 (2005), pp. 121–40. With kind permission by John Benjamins Publishing Company, Amsterdam/Philadelphia (www.benjamins.com).

Essay 18: Originally published in *Inquiry* 50 (2007), pp. 338–51. Reprinted by permission of the publisher, Taylor & Francis Ltd.

Essay 19: Originally published in *Inquiry* 50 (2007), pp. 366–70. Reprinted by permission of the publisher, Taylor & Francis Ltd.

Index

Action, 200–3, 308–9, 313–8, 321–3, 324–8
Agency. *See* Action
Akrasia, 24n, 33, 59–76
Allan, D. J., 43n, 44n
Anomalous monism, 254–6
Anscombe, G. E. M., 44n, 187–203
Aristotle, 18n, 23–40, 41–58, 59–76, 257–8, 309–13
Austin, J. L., 231n

Baker, G. P., 246n
Barwise, Jon, 176–8
Bell, David, 183n, 184n
Bermudez, José, 163n
Blackburn, Simon, 279n
Bluck, R. S., 13n
Boole, George, 299, 302
Brandom, Robert, 96–111, 148–51, 254–6, 267n, 279–87, 288–307, 318
Broadie, Sarah, 43n, 47–50
Burnyeat, M. F., 34n

Carl, Wolfgang, 177n, 182n, 184n
Cartesian philosophy of mind, 190–3, 255, 264–7, 273–5
Cooper, John M., 27n, 32n, 36n, 48n, 50n, 53n
Crombie, I. M., 20n

Davidson, Donald, 115–33, 134–51, 152–9, 169n, 184n, 209n, 216n, 217, 222–3, 246, 248, 254–6, 259, 260n, 263, 292n

Deliberation, 41–57, 59–74
Dennett, Daniel, 259, 263, 264, 269n, 271n, 274–5n, 303n
Descartes, René, 190–3, 194n, 199–200, 228, 232–3, 254–5, 265–7, 272–5, 287
Description theories of reference, 166–7, 171–2, 174. *See also* Russell's Theory of Descriptions
Dewey, John, 204–5, 206–7, 208–9, 222–3
Diamond, Cora, 93–4
Dretske, Fred, 239
Dreyfus, Hubert L., 308–23, 324–8
Dualism of scheme and content, 115–33
Dummett, Michael, 142n, 296, 298–9, 306

Empiricism, 118–9, 120–1, 124–33, 243–56
Ergon, 28–30
Ethical realism, 23–40
Eudaimonia, 23–40, 42, 43–57, 71–4
Eudaimonism, 30–3. See also *Eudaimonia*
Evans, Gareth, 163–85, 193n, 268n, 269n

Falsehood, 3–22
Fiction, 17n, 182–4
First-personal thought and speech. *See* "I"
Frede, Michael, 10n, 15n
Frege, Gottlob, 107–8, 111, 163–85, 188n, 267–72, 290, 298–303, 304n, 306
Freud, Sigmund, 205n, 223n
Friedman, Michael, 134–6, 138–41
Function. See *Ergon*
Furth, Montgomery, 174n

Gadamer, Hans-Georg, 134–51, 310–11, 317–18, 320, 327
Geach, P. T., 250
Goldfarb, Warren, 79, 80, 82n, 86

Habituation. *See* Upbringing
Hacker, P. M. S., 246n
Hegel, G. W. F., 291n
Heidegger, Martin, 150n, 309–11, 312–13, 314, 317, 327
Heinaman, Robert, 38n
Herman, Barbara, 57n
Hinton, J. M., 231n
Humboldt, Wilhelm von, 144–5, 146
Hume, David, 226

"I", 186–203
Incontinence. See *Akrasia*
Inferentialism, 282, 288–307
Intention, 88–92
Internalism and externalism in epistemology, 279–87
Irwin, T. H., 26n, 48n, 50n, 75n

James, William, 188, 223n

Kant, Immanuel, 41, 57–8, 96, 98–9, 108, 110–1, 115–6, 118, 124–5, 126n, 132, 158, 170n, 185, 191–2, 193–5, 202–3, 208–9, 225–7, 230, 233, 240, 243, 250–1, 261, 263n, 271, 290–2, 318–21, 325
Kenny, Anthony, 62n
Knoblauch, Chuck, 325–6
Kostman, James P., 4n
Kripke, Saul A., 171–2, 264n, 270n

Languages as shared, 141–51, 157
Lee, Edward N., 4n, 6n, 8n, 9n, 14n
Leibniz, G. W., 290
Lewis, Frank A., 6n, 7n, 8n
Locke, John, 170n, 263n

McGinn, Colin, 172n, 266n, 267n
Meaning as a mental state, 79–95
Merleau-Ponty, Maurice, 308, 322–3, 327, 328

Millikan, Ruth Garrett, 267–75
Moore, G. E., 233–7

Nagel, Thomas, 213
Naturalism, 131–3, 257–75
Negation, 3–22
Neurath, Otto, 34–5, 37
Nietzsche, Friedrich, 205, 208, 210
Normativity, 81–6, 96–111, 150–1, 214–22
Nussbaum, Martha C., 75n, 76n

Orwell, George, 211n
Owen, G. E. L., 3–22

Pagondiotis, Costas, 231n
Parmenides, 5–6, 8n, 22
Peacocke, Christopher, 321n
Pears, David, 68n, 92–5
Perceptual experience, 124–31, 134, 138–41, 157–9, 228–40, 243–56, 308–9, 314–17, 318–21
Perry, John, 176–8, 267n
Phronēsis, 24, 28, 39, 42–58, 66–74, 309–13
Plato, 3–22, 38n, 71–3, 75–6, 207, 210–12
Practical reason. *See* Deliberation
Practical wisdom. See *Phronēsis*
Psychologism, 107–8, 169–70, 271–2
Putnam, Hilary, 212–14, 219–20

"Quietism", 97–8, 104–6
Quine, W. V., 117, 118n, 119–21, 122–3, 126, 131, 216n, 244–5

Rationality, 45, 116–17, 124–33, 167–70, 178, 185, 259–60, 309–13, 324, 328
Reasons, space of, 135, 245, 246–8, 257–66, 280–7
Relativism, 135–41, 220n
Rödl, Sebastian, 231n
Rorty, Richard, 132n, 204–24, 244, 257n, 258, 260, 262–4, 265–6
Ross, Sir David, 62n
Rule-following, 80–6, 96–111
Russell, Bertrand, 163–7, 171–3, 179–80, 183–5

Russell's Theory of Descriptions, 163–7, 171–2, 173. *See also* Description theories of reference
Ryle, Gilbert, 265

Sainsbury, Mark, 166n, 167n, 170n, 174n, 179n, 179n, 181n, 183n, 185n
Salmon, Nathan, 178n
Scepticism, 120–4, 125–7, 129–30, 206–9, 225–40
Scheme-content dualism. *See* Dualism of scheme and content
Scholz, Heinrich, 180n
Schröder, Ernst, 299, 302
Scientism, 38–9, 86, 127–9, 275
Searle, John R., 166–7n, 174–5n, 274n
Self-consciousness, 186–203
Sellars, Wilfrid, 111n, 216n, 230–1, 240, 245, 246–8, 249, 252–4, 257–66, 271, 282–3, 284, 286, 297–8, 316–17, 318, 319n
Snowdon, Paul, 231n
Socrates, 59, 74–6
Spinoza, Baruch, 290
Stern, Robert, 227n

Strawson, P. F., 190–5, 199, 202–3, 225–7, 233
Stroud, Barry, 85n, 225–7, 228n, 235, 237, 239
Subjectivity, 122–3, 152–7, 254–6
Syntactic and semantic engines, 267–75

Tarski, Alfred, 216
Taylor, Charles, 310
Transcendental arguments, 225–40

Understanding as a mental state, 79–95
Upbringing, 28, 36–7, 39, 41, 46, 50–2, 53–7

Vlastos, Gregory, 76n

Weakness of will. See *Akrasia*
Wiggins, David, 8n, 14n, 15n, 17n, 20n, 43n, 59–76, 310
Williams, Bernard, 29n, 38n, 52n
Williams, Michael, 253–4
Wittgenstein, Ludwig, 21, 79–95, 96–111, 134, 146n, 157, 186–8, 214, 246, 272n, 283, 289–90, 320n
Wright, Crispin, 93n, 232n, 233–9

Milton Keynes UK
Ingram Content Group UK Ltd.
UKHW041258011224
451929UK00002B/63